International Taxation Law in Sports Events

This book is the first academic contribution that deals with international taxation of income sources from sports events.

Using an interdisciplinary approach, with in-depth analysis of both sports law and international tax law, it is notably the first academic work to conduct a thorough analysis in the fields of international taxation of eSports, sports betting as well as illegal/unlawful income sources that may be obtained in relation to a sporting event, such as kickback payments. After describing the general methodologies of income tax and VAT from an international standpoint, defining key terms such as 'eSports' and 'bidding procedure', the book examines in detail the taxation of the services that are rendered and the goods that are sold, thereby the income obtained, in relation to an international sports event from both income tax and VAT perspectives. Also analysed are government funding in the sports sector, along with its taxation modalities, as well as specific tax exemption regulations enacted for the purposes of mega sporting events. Highlighting the absence of an acceptable level of certainty in the field of taxation of international sports events, the work makes pertinent suggestions as to the future of international sporting event taxation law.

With international appeal, this comprehensive book constitutes essential reading for tax and sports law scholars.

Dr Alara Efsun Yazıcıoğlu is an assistant professor at Kadir Has University (Turkey), and holds the position of Head of the Financial Law Section. She is also an attorney at law.

International Taxation Law in Sports Events

Alara Efsun Yazıcıoğlu

Routledge
Taylor & Francis Group
LONDON AND NEW YORK

First published 2021
by Routledge
2 Park Square, Milton Park, Abingdon, Oxon OX14 4RN

and by Routledge
52 Vanderbilt Avenue, New York, NY 10017

Routledge is an imprint of the Taylor & Francis Group, an informa business

British Library Cataloguing-in-Publication Data
A catalogue record for this book is available from the British Library

Library of Congress Cataloging-in-Publication Data
Names: Yazıcıoğlu, Alara Efsun, author.
Title: International taxation law in sporting events : an income tax analysis / Alara Efsun Yazıcıoğlu.
Description: Abingdon, Oxon ; New York, NY : Routledge, 2020. |
Based on author's thesis (doctoral - Universitéde Genève, 2016). |
Includes bibliographical references and index.
Identifiers: LCCN 2020009834 (print) | LCCN 2020009835 (ebook) |
ISBN 9780367266257 (hardback) | ISBN 9780429328022 (ebook)
Subjects: LCSH: Sports--Taxation--Law and legislation. |
International business enterprises--Taxation--Law and legislation.
Classification: LCC K4487.S68 Y29 2020 (print) | LCC K4487.S68 (ebook) |
DDC 343.06/6--dc23
LC record available at https://lccn.loc.gov/2020009834
LC ebook record available at https://lccn.loc.gov/2020009835

ISBN: 978-0-367-26625-7 (hbk)
ISBN: 978-0-367-52154-7 (pbk)
ISBN: 978-0-429-32802-2 (ebk)

Typeset in Galliard
by Taylor & Francis Books

To Mustafa Kemal Atatürk

Contents

Acknowledgements

This book, partially based on my PhD thesis, is the result of 10 years of research and work. I would like to express my deepest gratitude to my family who have supported me continuously throughout this decade, namely Gülbin and Yusuf Yazıcıoğlu, Ülkü and Ahmet Somay, Püspüs and Bisou.

I would like to thank Dr Rijkele Betten, one of my PhD jury members, for his extremely valuable comments that I implemented while preparing the manuscript.

I would like to thank Nicola Sharpe, my editor, for all the patience she has shown and for all the encouragement and support she has provided me with during the finalisation process of the manuscript.

I would like to express my deepest gratitude to Professor Ian Blackshaw, one of my PhD jury members, for his encouragement, advice and support, all of which I could continuously count on over the years. I also would like to thank him for agreeing to write one of the forewords of this book.

I would like to thank Professor Xavier Oberson for all the guidance he has provided me with before (as my tax law professor), during (as my PhD supervisor) and after (as a constant mentor) the preparation of my PhD thesis and for agreeing to write one of the forewords of this book.

Last but not least, I would like to express my deepest gratitude to Mustafa Kemal Atatürk to whom I utterly owe each and every aspect of my life, including this book. He has been my greatest source of motivation and inspiration in every stage of my life. As an expression of my sincere gratefulness, this book is dedicated to him.

Forewords

The taxation of international sports organisations raises a number of delicate but fascinating issues. First, the complex structures of the sports business and activities have to be precisely described and understood. In other words, the facts patterns to which tax issues have to apply are based on specific and peculiar elements. Sports organisations exercise their activities beyond borders, in a global and multilateral framework that is difficult to ascertain. Second, the applicable rules rely on a juxtaposition of agreements, of multi and bilateral nature, recommendations, codes of conduct and domestic rules, constantly evolving and changing, which have to be properly analysed, coordinated and interpreted. Third, there are many potential streams of income, turnover and payments, which may be subject to multiple taxation (or no taxation), depending on their characterisation, localisation and source. Fourth, in order to attract international sports events into their jurisdiction, some states may enter into specific, sometimes disputable, derogations, or tax exemptions, which nowadays are subject to more and more scrutiny worldwide. Lastly, in parallel to the sports events as such, which may entail complex structures (federation, associations, foundations, corporations, etc), there are various sportsmen and sportswomen, employees and directors who are taking part in such events and who may also be subject to various taxes (notably income tax), sometimes giving rise to taxation conflicts.

Alara Efsun Yazıcıoğlu has successfully been able to grasp this delicate and complex field and to offer a broad, clear and convincing description and analysis of the main tax issues applicable to international sports organisations. This book is based on her PhD thesis and analyses in detail not only the existing structures of such events but also their peculiarities, including the specific tax exemptions applicable. The difficult characterisation and localisation of various streams of income are described (income from sports performances, royalties, TV rights, advertising, sponsoring, etc) along with the impact of double taxation treaties. The potential presence of a permanent establishment is also examined in detail. The evolution of the sports business model with the growing importance of TV rights and other types of income flowing from digital media and their specific streams of data forms a part of the analysis as well. Last but not least, the application of VAT rules, which are of crucial importance in this field, are also described.

We believe that this book will not only offer to the reader a global and very helpful understanding of international sports organisations and their tax treatment, but also propose adequate and helpful solutions to this challenging domain. Lastly, the book also encompasses a much broader perspective of the recent and new fundamental tax issues that the world is facing in line with the development of the digital economy, which will affect all major streams of income and turnover from such sporting events.

Professor Dr Xavier Oberson
Professor of Swiss and International Tax Law, and Director of the LLM Tax Program at the University of Geneva, attorney-at-law
Geneva, August 2019

I am very pleased to write the foreword to this book.

As the author indicates in her Introduction chapter, sport nowadays is big business and a product in its own right. In fact, it is worth some 3% of world trade. In other words, billions of US dollars. In the European Union, sport represents some 3.7% of the combined gross national product of the member states.

In view of these impressive financial statistics, the taxation of international sports events and sportspersons who participate in them, and the companies who sponsor them, raises a number of important considerations and issues which should not be overlooked. This book covers and explains all these matters.

The book also deals usefully with eSports, which have developed financially and also in terms of popularity at a phenomenal rate in recent years, as well as 'International Sports Events Tax Exemptions Acts', which are a common feature of and *sine qua non* for the hosting of major international sporting events, such as the Olympic Games and the FIFA World Cup.

The author is to be congratulated on the extent of her research and her comprehensive coverage of such a highly complex and technical subject.

The book is a welcome addition to the literature on sports law, which is developing with such alacrity, and will be very useful for all those involved in the commercialisation and business of sport, including their legal and tax advisors.

I have no hesitation whatsoever, therefore, in commending this book to such a wide readership, who will, I would venture to suggest, benefit greatly from it!

Professor Dr Ian Blackshaw
International sports lawyer, academic, author, and member of the Court of Arbitration for Sport
Cambridge, January 2020

List of Abbreviations and Acronyms

Amendment Act	South African Revenue Laws Amendment Act No 20, 2006.
ATP	Association of Tennis Professionals
AUD	Australian dollar
AVMSD	Directive 2010/13/EU of the European Parliament and of the Council of 10 March 2010 on the coordination of certain provisions laid down by law, regulation or administrative action in Member States concerning the provision of audiovisual media services (Audiovisual Media Services Directive)
B2B	Business-to-business
B2C	Business-to-consumer
BEPS	Base Erosion and Profit Shifting
BEPS Project	The OECD/G20 Base Erosion and Profit Shifting Project
CAD	Canadian dollar
CDPA	Copyright, Designs and Patents Act 1988, United Kingdom
CJEU	Court of Justice of the European Union
CopA	Swiss Federal Act on Copyright and Related Rights of 9 October 1992 [SC 231.1]
CS	Contracting State
DTT	Double Tax Treaty
EC	European Commission
EC State Aid Notice	Commission Notice on the notion of State aid as referred to in Article 107(1) of the Treaty on the Functioning of the European Union, 19.07.2016, [C 262/1]
ECHR	European Convention on Human Rights
ECTT	European Convention on Transfrontier Television, CETS No: 132.
EEA	European Economic Area
EU	European Union
EUR	Euro (currency)
EURO	UEFA European Football Championship
FA 2006	Finance Act 2006 (UK)
FA 2010	Finance Act 2010 (UK)

FA 2012	Finance Act 2012 (UK)
FDTL	Swiss Federal Direct Tax Law of 14 December 1990 [SC 642.11]
FE	Fixed establishment
FIA	Fédération Internationale de l'Automobile [in English: International Automobile Federation]
FIFA	Fédération Internationale de Football Association [in English: International Federation of Association Football]
FIFA RSTP	FIFA Regulations on the Status and Transfer of Players, June 2019 edition
FIFA Statutes	FIFA Statutes, Regulations Governing the Application of the Statutes, Standing Orders of the Congress, 2018 edition
FTHL	Swiss Federal Tax Harmonization Law of 14 December 1990 [SC 642.14]
FPS	First-person shooter
GB	Governing body
GBP	Pound sterling
HC	Host city
HCC	Host city contract
HMRC	HM Revenue & Customs (UK)
HS	Host State
IBC	International Broadcast Centre
ICC	International Chamber of Commerce
IF	International (sports) federation
IGB	International governing body
IMF SDR	International Monetary Fund special drawing rights
Implementing Regulation 282/2011/EU	Council Implementing Regulation (EU) No 282/2011 of 15 March 2011 laying down implementing measures for Directive 2006/112/EC on the common system of value added tax
IOC	International Olympic Committee
IPC	International Paralympic Committee
IRS	Internal Revenue Service (US)
IR signal	International radio signal
ISE	International sports event
ITV signal	International television signal
ITVR signal	International television and radio signal
KeSPA	Korea e-Sports Association
LOC	Local organising committee
LOCOG	London Organising Committee for the 2012 Olympic and Paralympic Games
LoL	League of Legends
Ltd	Limited
MC	Model Convention

MLI	Multilateral Convention to Implement Tax Treaty Related Measures to Prevent BEPS
MMO	Massively multiplayer online
MMORPG	Massively multiplayer online role-playing game
MS	Member State (European Union)
NBA	National Basketball Association, United States of America/ Canada
NGB	National Governing Body
NHL	National Hockey League, United States of America/Canada
NICs	National Insurance Contributions
NOC	National Olympic Committee
OAA 2010	Organising Association Agreement regarding 2010 FIFA World Cup™
OBS	Olympic Broadcasting Services S.A.
OCOG	Organising Committee for the Olympic Games
OECD	Organisation for Economic Co-operation and Development
OECD MC	OECD Model Tax Convention on Income and on Capital, 2017 edition
PAYE	Pay as you earn
PE	Permanent establishment
PoB	Place of business
PoE	Place of establishment
RS	Residence State
RTS	Real-time strategy
SAFA	South African Football Association
SC	Systematic Collection of Swiss Federal Laws
SCrC	Swiss Criminal Code of 21 December 1937 [SC 311.0]
SGB	Sports governing body
SOCOG	Sydney Organising Committee for the Olympic Games
South African Draft Guide	Draft Guide on the Taxation of Professional Sports Clubs and Players (South African Revenue Service)
SS	Source State
TFEU	The Treaty on the Functioning of the European Union, Official Journal of the European Union, 26.10.2012 [C 326/47]
The 2010 Regulations	London Olympic Games and Paralympic Games Tax Regulations 2010 (SI 2010/2913)
TOP Sponsorship Programme	The Olympic Partners Sponsorship Programme
UEFA	Union of European Football Associations
UEFA Champions League Regulations	Regulations of the UEFA Champions League 2018–21 Cycle, 2018/19 Season

UEFA Statutes	Rules of Procedure of the UEFA Congress, Regulations governing the Implementation of the UEFA Statutes, 2018 edition
UK	The United Kingdom
UN MC	United Nations Model Double Tax Convention between Developed and Developing Countries, 2017 edition
US	United States of America
USD	United States dollar
US MC	United States Model Income Tax Convention of 15 November 2006
VANOC	Vancouver Organising Committee for the 2010 Olympic and Paralympic Games
VAT	Value-added tax
VAT Directive	Council Directive 2006/112/EC of 28 November 2006 on the common system of value added tax
VCLT	Vienna Convention on the Law of Treaties of 23 May 1969
WIPO	World Intellectual Property Organization
WWE	World Wrestling Entertainment (formerly the World Wrestling Federation)

Table of Cases

Court of Justice of the European Union

Arnoud Gerritse v Finanzamt Neukölln-Nord, Case C-234/01 [2003] ECR I-5933 (cited as 'the Gerritse decision').

Berkholz v Finanzamt Hamburg-Mitte-Altstadt, Case C-168/84 [1985] ECR 2251 (cited as 'the Berkholz decision').

Card Protection Plan Ltd (CPP) v Commissioners of Customs & Excise, Case C-349/96 [1999] ECR I-00973 (cited as 'the CPP decision').

Diana Elisabeth Lindman, Reference for a preliminary ruling: Ålands förvaltningsdomstol – Finland, Case C-42/02 [2003] ECR I-13519 (cited as 'the Lindman decision').

Faaborg-Gelting Linien A/S v Finanzamt Flensburg, Case C-231/94 [1996] ECR I-02395 (cited as 'the Faaborg-Gelting Linien decision').

Field Fisher Waterhouse LLP v Commissioners for Her Majesty's Revenue and Customs, Case C-392/11, published in the electronic Reports of Cases (cited as 'the Field Fischer decision').

Finanzamt Köln-Altstadt v Roland Schumacker, Case C-279/93 [1995] ECR I-00225 (cited as 'the Schumacker decision').

FKP Scorpio Konzertproduktionen GmbH v Finanzamt Hamburg-Eimsbüttel, Case C-290/04 [2006] ECR I-9461 (cited as 'the Scorpio decision').

Football Association Premier League Ltd and Others v QC Leisure and Others, Karen Murphy v Media Protection Services Ltd, Joined cases C-403/08 and C-429/08 [2011] ECR I-9083.

Frans Gschwind v Finanzamt Aachen-Außenstadt, Case C-391/97 [1999] ECR I-05451 (cited as 'the Gschwind decision').

G.H.E.J. Wielockx v Inspecteur der directe belastingen, Case C-80/94 [1995] ECR I-02493 (cited as 'the Wielockx decision').

Jürgen Dudda v Finanzgericht Bergisch Gladbach, Case C-327/94 [1996] ECR I-04595 (cited as 'the Dudda decision').

Karlheinz Fischer v Finanzamt Donaueschingen, Case C-283/95 [1998] ECR I-03369 (cited as 'the Fischer decision').

Katja Ettwein v Finanzamt Konstanz, Case C-245/11, published in the electronic Reports of Cases (cited as 'the Ettwein decision').

Max Witzemann v Hauptzollamt München-Mitte, Case C-343/89 [1990] ECR I-04477 (cited as 'the Witzemann decision').

Město Žamberk v Finanční ředitelství v Hradci Králové, now Odvolací finanřní ředitelství, Case C-18/12, published in the electronic Reports of Cases (cited as 'the Žamberk decision').

Ministero dell'Economia e delle Finanze and Agenzia delle Entrate v FCE Bank plc, Case C-210/04, [2006] ECR I-02803 (cited as 'the FCE Bank decision').

Odvolací finanční ředitelství v Pavlína Baštová, Case C-432/15, published in the electronic Reports of Cases (cited as 'the Baštová decision').

Planzer Luxembourg Sàrl v Bundeszentralamt für Steuern, Case C-73/06 [2007] ECR I-05655 (cited as 'the Planzer Luxembourg decision').

Purple Parking Ltd and Airparks Services Ltd v The Commissioners for Her Majesty's Revenue & Customs, Case C-117/11, published in the electronic Reports of Cases (cited as 'the Purple Parking decision').

Svenska staten (Swedish State) v Stockholm Lindöpark AB and Stockholm Lindöpark AB v Svenska staten (Swedish State), Case C-150/99 [2001] ECR I-00493 (cited as 'the Lindöpark decision').

The English Bridge Union Limited v Commissioners for Her Majesty's Revenue & Customs, Case C-90/16, published in the electronic Reports of Cases (cited as 'the English Bridge Union decision').

Vereniging Happy Family Rustenburgerstraat v Inspecteur der Omzetbelasting, Case C-289/86 [1988] ECR 03655 (cited as 'the Happy Family decision').

Welmory sp. z o.o. v Dyrektor Izby Skarbowej w Gdańsku, Case C- 605/12 [2014] ECR 2298, published in the electronic Reports of Cases (cited as 'the Welmory decision').

Wilfried Lange v Finanzamt Fürstenfeldbruck, Case C-111/92 [1993] ECR I-04677 (cited as 'the Lange decision').

Australia

Seven Network Limited v Commissioner of Taxation [2014] FCA 1411 (cited as 'the Seven decision').

Canada

Cheek v The Queen, Tax Court of Canada [2002] Docket: 1999–1113(IT)G (cited as 'the Cheek decision').

Sumner v The Queen, Tax Court of Canada [1999] Docket: 1998-1222(IT)G; 1998–1410(IT)G (cited as 'the Sumner decision').

India

Commissioner of Income Tax v Delhi Race Club, High Court of Delhi, [1940] Ltd (ITA No.6/2014).
Formula One World Championship Ltd v Commissioner of Income Tax, International Taxation–3, Delhi & Anr., Supreme Court of India, Civil Appellate Jurisdiction, Civil Appeals No. 3850 and 3851 of 2017 (cited as 'the Formula 1 decision').

Italy

Luciano Pavarotti Judgment, Decision of the Tax Court of Second Instance of Bologna of 27 March 2000, published in *International Tax Law Reports*, 2001, p.72ff (cited as 'the Pavarotti decision').

Netherlands

Decision No 02/04607, The Court of Appeal of 's-Hertogenbosch, 5 November 2003.
Decision No 01/03822, The Court of Appeal of 's-Hertogenbosch, 10 June 2003.
Decision No 03/04112, The Court of Appeal of Amsterdam, 6 October 2004.

Switzerland

Swiss Federal Tribunal's decision of 06 October 1944, ATF 70 I 250.
Swiss Federal Tribunal's decision of 06 May 2008, No 2C_276/2007, published in RDAF 2008 II 374ff (cited as 'the Cyclist decision').

United Kingdom

BBC v TalkSport Ltd [2001] FSR 53 (cited as 'the TalkSport decision').
Proactive Sports Management Limited v Wayne Rooney, Coleen Rooney (formerly McLoughlin), Stoneygate 48 Limited and Speed 9849 Limited [2010] EWHC 1807 (QB) (cited as 'the Rooney decision').
Sports Club plc v Inspector of Taxes [2000] STC (SCD) 443.

United States of America

Hilliard v Black, United States District Court for the Northern District of Florida, Gainesville Division, [2000] 125 F.Supp.2d 1071.
Johansson v United States of America, United States Court of Appeals Fifth Circuit, [1964] 336 F.2d 809 (cited as 'the Johansson decision').
Ken Linseman v Commissioner of Internal Revenue, United States Tax Court, 82 T.C. 514 [1984] Docket No 23315-81.

Newman v Franchise Tax Bd., Court of Appeals of California, Second Appellate District, Division Four, [1989] 208 Cal.App.3d 972.

Retief Goosen v Commissioner of Internal Revenue, United States Tax Court, 136 T.C. No 27 [2011] Docket No 23323-09 (cited as 'the Goosen decision').

Sergio Garcia v Commissioner of Internal Revenue, United States Tax Court, 140 T.C. No 6 [2013] Docket No 13649-10 (cited as 'the Garcia decision').

Introduction

The frequency at which ISEs are held has increased in a dramatic manner during the 20th century. While the number of ISEs held throughout 1912 was limited to 20, in 2005 an average of three ISEs were being held per day.[1] Asserting that '[...] at any given time, there is at least one international sports event taking place somewhere on earth'[2] is not an overstatement. This popularity is clearly due to the outstanding level of entertainment offered by sporting competitions, with their gold medals, champions and world records.

Sport has thus become a highly valuable 'product'[3] in its own right, which is typically commercialised via sports events. This economic value translated, quite inevitably, into the creation of a prominent sector, where '[...] there is much to play for not only on but also off the field of play'.[4] As a matter of fact, behind the scenes of these spectacular events is a true legal spectacle: a wide web of contracts concluded between a myriad of different actors, such as broadcasters, sponsors and licensees and a highly complex set of tax rules.

A non-negligible number of individuals and companies active in various sectors derive their income from ISEs, and such income, along with the economic transactions, raise stimulating income tax and VAT issues. These issues constitute the subject of this book, which is divided into six chapters.

Chapter 1 describes the key concepts and the main actors of ISEs. To this end, it examines the concepts of 'sport' (and respectively 'eSports') and 'sports event', the bidding procedure and the main actors in charge of organising ISEs, as well as the unequal distribution of income within the sports sector. Chapter 2 describes the key tax law concepts and mechanisms that are frequently referred to throughout the analysis conducted in the book. Chapter 3 identifies income that may derive from ISEs and eSports tournaments, as well as examines the taxation modalities of the income sources (income tax) and transactions (VAT) concerned. Chapter 4 analyses the income tax (from an international perspective) and VAT modalities of different categories of government funding that may be provided in

1 ANDREFF, p.15.
2 CORNELIUS, *Media rights*, p.6.
3 More specifically a 'mixed good' (BOURG/GOUGUET, p.748).
4 BLACKSHAW, *Sports Marketing Agreements*, p.1.

relation to elite sport development and hosting of ISEs. The tax law analysis conducted in chapters 2, 3 and 4 is based mainly on the guidance provided by the OECD and the diverse documents published by the Organisation. The OECD's recommendations and observations are predominantly illustrated by means of common practices applied in Europe and examples from European jurisdictions. Chapter 5 briefly describes tax exemption regulations enacted for the purposes of one specific sports event.

Throughout the analysis made in chapters 1–5, it is observed that tax treatment of ISEs is far from being clear. Taxation modalities may vary to a great extent not only from HS to HS, but even within the same HS. The existing literature and the policy work conducted in this specific area indicate that an international solution would be extremely difficult to reach, at least in the near future. In the light of these observations, this book concludes, in chapter 6, with an effective and easy to implement solution with regard to taxation of ISEs: the adoption of 'International Sports Events Tax Exemptions Acts' and/or 'International Sports Events Taxation Acts' – both preferably accompanied by explanatory guidelines – at a domestic law level or the publication of a general explanatory report on the relevant domestic tax law provisions. This rather simple solution can successfully ease the current problems and restore legal certainty in this area where chaos reigns.

Nota bene: This book opts for the use of 'they' as a singular pronoun, in order to achieve sex neutrality.

1 Key concepts and main actors of international sports events

I. Introduction

This chapter describes the key concepts relating to ISEs and identifies the main actors in charge of organising such events. To this end, first the term 'sport' is defined and the fundamental characteristics of professional sports are established. The analysis of the concept of sport is completed by drawing a demarcation line between genuine sports activities and 'sportified activities' (such as eSports), as there is a terminological distinction between entertainment and sporting activities in international tax law. Second, the notion of 'sports event' is defined and different types of sports events (such as mega sporting events and hallmark sporting events) are elucidated, to the extent relevant for the purposes of the book. Third, bidding process and the main actors of ISEs (such as SGBs and LOCs) are briefly described. The chapter concludes by mentioning the unequal distribution of income within the sports sector.

II. Concept of 'sport'

> 'Sport cannot be reduced to physical superiority alone.' (Mustafa Kemal Atatürk)

A. Historical evolution and the linguistic scope of the term 'sport'

The term 'sport' finds its roots in the Latin word '*desporto*', which literally means 'to carry away'.[1] '*Desporto*' was subsequently transformed to '*desporter*' in Old French, which can be defined as 'to seek amusement'.[2] In the late 14th century, the Anglo-French word '*disporter*' signifying 'to divert, to amuse', was abbreviated to the verb '*disport*'.[3] The verb 'sport', meaning 'to take pleasure, to amuse oneself', derived from the verb '*disport*' at around 1400.[4] Finally, the word 'sport' as a noun was used for the first time in the mid-15th century.[5] Its meaning was 'game

1 GARDINER ET AL, p.13.
2 http://www.etymonline.com/index.php?term=disport&allowed_in_frame=0 (accessed on 26.06.2019).
3 Ibid.
4 Ibid.
5 https://www.etymonline.com/word/sport (accessed on 27.06.2019).

involving physical exercise'.[6] As evidenced by its very first definition, historically, 'sport' mostly signified an amusing activity necessitating physical effort.

Albeit being more elaborate, the contemporary definitions are congruent, to a great extent, with the very first definition of the term. The *Oxford Dictionary* defines sport as '[a]n activity involving physical exertion and skill in which an individual or team competes against another or others for entertainment'.[7] According to the *Cambridge Dictionary*, sport is 'a game, competition, or activity needing physical effort and skill that is played or done according to rules, for enjoyment and/or as a job'.[8] Lastly, as per the *Collins Dictionary*, sport is 'an individual or group activity pursued for exercise or pleasure, often involving the testing of physical capabilities and taking the form of a competitive game such as football, tennis, etc.'.[9]

Despite this historic compatibility, the exact scope of the term 'sport', from a linguistic point of view, seems to be unclear to a great extent. As underlined by the sports historian Tiedemann, 'sport' has developed into a colloquial, worldwide used concept that lacks a precise conceptual delimitation.[10] This is mainly due to the fact that in the everyday language, the term 'sport' is used as an umbrella term to describe four distinct types of activities: (i) professional sporting activities; (ii) amateur sporting activities; (iii) activities exercised for physical fitness; and (iv) entertainment activities that are 'sportified'. This statement can be illustrated by the following example: participating in professional kickboxing tournaments, participating in kickboxing tournaments for amateurs, practicing kick box (on an individual basis or with other people but without structured competition) exclusively for leisure purposes and taking part in shows ('spectacles') organised by the WWE are all considered to fall within the scope of the term 'sport'.

Prima facie, the lack of linguistic precision does not seem to result in any significant practical implications. To the extent necessary, the reference can be made to professional sport, amateur sport, physical exercise or sports-spectacles/entertainment. Even in cases where the term 'sport' is used on a stand-alone basis, the type of activity that is being referred to can easily be identified based on the context of the speech concerned. There exists one important caveat to this general observation: 'sport' being associated with many positive characteristics (such as mental and physical health, proficiency, fair play and commitment), labelling a non-sporting activity as a 'sport' may be extremely beneficial for the development of the activity concerned (especially in terms of gaining popularity, having a 'healthy' image and, thereby, obtaining funding from sponsors). This process of labelling is referred to as 'sportification'. Lopez-Gonzalez and Griffiths define sportification as '[...] the process of incorporating the logics of sport to

6 Ibid.
7 https://www.lexico.com/en/definition/sport (accessed on 27.06.2019).
8 https://dictionary.cambridge.org/dictionary/english/sport (accessed on 27.06.2019).
9 https://www.collinsdictionary.com/dictionary/english/sport (accessed on 27.06.2019).
10 TIEDEMANN, p.2.

non-sporting contexts'.[11] It is clear that sportification plays a role in distinguishing sports-spectacles/entertainment activities from genuine sporting activities.

Although not resulting in any major obstacles in practice, the existing linguistic imprecision is not deemed to be suitable for scientific purposes. A number of scientists have made suggestions to clarify the exact scope of the concept of sport. These suggestions mainly aim to distinguish between sports activities exercised for leisure and sports activities exercised in a more organised (professional and/or amateur) manner. According to Caillat, the term 'desport' or 'disport' should be used in order to describe daily sporting activities, such as fitness activities or team sports exercised only for leisure purposes.[12] Stone argues that sport is generally composed of two distinct sorts of behaviour: 'play' and 'dis-play'.[13] In cases where the participant's motivations mostly relate to that individual's relationship with the given activity, i.e. when the main aim is to practice the sporting activity concerned, the participant needs to be considered as 'playing'.[14] On the other hand, if the participant is essentially concerned with spectators, i.e. when the notion of spectacle becomes more important than the sport itself, they should be considered as 'dis-playing'.[15] Lastly, Tiedemann suggests to distinguish between 'culture of human motion' and 'sport'. The author defines the former concept as follows: '[...] a field of activity, in which people come to terms with their nature and environment and consciously develop, form and represent their particularly physical abilities and accomplishments for to experience a meaningful individual or also common benefit and pleasure'[16] and the latter concept as follows: 'a cultural field of activity, in which human beings voluntarily go into a real or only imagined relation to other people with the conscious intention to develop their abilities and accomplishments particularly in the area of skilled motion and to compare themselves with these other people according to rules put self or adopted without intending to damage them or themselves deliberately'.[17] Tiedemann completes his definition by enumerating the *sine qua non* characteristics of sports activities, which are voluntariness, relation with other people, intention to compare with each other (i.e. competition), skilled (as opposed to 'everyday') motion (not exclusively limited to the motion of the body but the motion of a human being as a whole – body, mind, soul and spirit), rules that are adopted or agreed to belong to the cultural field of activity called sport and absence of intention to damage other persons (or the participants themselves).[18]

To recapitulate, in the light of its historical evolution, the observations made by the scientists working in the field and the everyday use of the term, the

11 LOPEZ-GONZALEZ/GRIFFITHS, p.8.
12 CAILLAT, p.12.
13 STONE G., American Sports: Play and Dis-play, in *Chicago Review*, Volume 9, 1965, p.83, cited by GARDINER ET AL, p.7.
14 Ibid.
15 Ibid.
16 TIEDEMANN, p.3.
17 Ibid.
18 Ibid, pp.4–5.

different activities encompassed by the term 'sport' can be grouped into four distinct categories:

1 professional sport;
2 structured amateur sport;
3 physical fitness activities for leisure purposes (as a group or on an individual basis);
4 entertainment activities that are 'sportified'.

Professional and structured amateur sport are highly similar, except for, as their names quite clearly indicate, the level of professionalism involved. The main differences between the professional/structured amateur sport and the physical fitness for leisure purposes are competition and observation of strict rules. Physical fitness activities for leisure purposes do not generally involve any competition, and in cases where the participants wish to compete against each other they do not do so in a highly structured environment governed by strict rules. The most challenging demarcation is the one between entertainment activities that are 'sportified' and professional/amateur sport. Sportified entertainment activities tend to involve a significant level of professionalism, to have a strict set of rules and to be organised in a meticulous manner. These three characteristics combined with the intentional sportification of such activities may cause the general public to mistake this formal similarity to sporting activities for equality. Once the public opinion is formed, the debate is necessarily taken to a scientific and legal level.

The main purpose of this book is to concentrate on professional sport. This being stated, both the sports law and the tax law analysis also apply, *mutatis mutandis*, to structured amateur sport, to the extent where an international amateur sports event gives rise to the same income sources (from a legal standpoint) as an international professional sports event. The analysis made is also pertinent for the sportified entertainment activities, as well as for regular entertainment activities, due to the similarity of the contracts concluded for the purposes of a sports event and an entertainment event as well as the identical tax treatment of entertainers and sportspersons[19] adopted by the relevant international organisations and the majority of countries. Physical fitness activities for leisure purposes fall out of the scope of this book.

B. Legal scope of the term 'sport'

A precise legal definition of the term 'sport' is lacking both on an international and on a national level (for most jurisdictions). This absence, undesirable not only for scientific purposes but also in practice due to the uncertainty it creates, may be justified to a certain extent by the cultural nature of the concept of sport. Due to its predominant cultural component, what is being understood by 'sport' tends to vary from country to country (local) and from century to century (temporal).

19 The terms 'sportsperson' and 'athlete' are used as equivalents in this book, except in cases where a distinction is expressly drawn.

The local cultural differences were more emphasised in the past. Leisure activities and playful competitions, as well as the words used to describe them, showed a remarkable cultural diversity.[20] While the Roman Empire had '*ludi*'[21] and '*munera*',[22] the Sumerians had '*lirùm*'[23] and the Greeks had '*agônes*'[24] and '*aethla*'.[25, 26] Although cultural divergences still exist (e.g. popularity of sports activities may vary from country to country), their extent is quite limited. The local singularities of sporting activities have been significantly reduced to create, as coined by EICHBERG, a 'sports monoculture'.[27] This monoculture is mainly the result of detailed sets of rules determined and applied worldwide by SGBs.

The cultural transformation of sport through time is mainly emphasised by sports historians. What was once seen as a sport, such as the *gladiatura* in ancient Rome, may not be currently considered as such. This being stated, the cultural evolution of sport is not pertinent merely for the past, but also for the future of sport. For instance, Wagner asserts that while in the industrial age physical fitness constituted one of the most dominant values in society, competencies in the use of information and communication technologies (the so-called 'cyberfitness') form the current prevailing asset.[28] For Wagner, it is natural for such a cultural shift to be reflected in sports activities: traditional sports disciplines aim to measure the physical fitness of the contestants, whereas sports activities invented by today's societies, such as eSports, can aim to assess the cyberfitness.[29]

Regardless of the ever-evolving nature of the concept, from a legal standpoint, a precise definition of sport can be, and must be, given by means of cumulative criteria. Qualification of an activity as a sport gives rise to a number of legal consequences, ranging from visa procedures to applicable tax rules. The ability of all interested parties to assess, on the basis of pre-determined criteria, which activities are to be granted the legal status of sport should be guaranteed for the sake of respecting the principle of legal certainty, which is one of the main requirements of a state of law. Needless to say, should the need arise, due to a cultural shift and/or technological developments, the criteria used to define sport may be altered.

However, it seems that, instead of moving forward, the relevant organisations are taking a step back in the provision of a precise definition of sport. In 2016, when the author last accessed SportAccord's[30] website, it contained a set of

20 SCANLON, p.3.
21 The term can be translated as 'games'.
22 The term can be translated as 'shows'.
23 The term can be translated as 'athletics'.
24 The term can be translated as 'contest'.
25 The term can be translated as 'contest'.
26 SCANLON, p.3.
27 The term is used by EICHBERG in EICHBERG HENNING, *Body cultures: Essays on sport, space and identity*, Routledge, 1997.
28 WAGNER, pp.2–3.
29 Ibid.
30 SportAccord, the umbrella organisation for both Olympic and non-Olympic international sports federations as well as organisers of international sporting events, was renamed Global Association of International Sports Federations (GAISF) in 2017.

criteria that could be used to determine whether a certain activity could be considered as sport. The criteria concerned were: element of competition, absence of harm to living creatures, not being dependent on equipment provided by a single supplier, not being dependent on any luck element specifically designed into the activity.[31] It was specifically underlined that SportAccord did not intend to provide a 'general and scientifically sound' definition, but rather to make a clear and pragmatic description of activities that may be categorised as sport. The criteria have since been removed from the website of the organisation,[32] which does not currently provide for any relevant criteria or definition of the term. Similarly, the Australian Sports Foundation's website, which used to define sport as 'a human activity capable of achieving a result requiring physical exertion and/or physical skill, which, by its nature and organization, is competitive and is generally accepted as being a sport',[33] does not currently[34] contain any information on the definition of the concept of sport.

This being stated, some organisations do opt for rather explicit definitions. For instance, in the European Sports Charter, the Council of Europe defines sport as '[a]ll forms of physical activity, which, through casual or organised participation, aim at expressing or improving physical fitness and mental well-being, forming social relationships or obtaining results in competition at all levels'.[35] The European White Paper on Sport opts for the exact same definition.[36] The most precise definition that the author has come across is the one provided by the German Olympic Sports Confederation.[37] In article 3 of its *Aufnahmeordnung*,[38] the Confederation enumerates the following cumulative requirements for an activity to be considered as sport: (i) the activity must pursue the practice of a sporting motor activity (such an activity is not deemed to exist in brain games, handicraft and model-building activities, dressage that does not involve human motion and technical equipment use that does not involve human motion); (ii) the motor activity concerned should be the sole purpose of the activity under examination (work-related activities, everyday activities and mere physiological state changes are excluded); and (iii) the activity concerned should respect ethical values, safeguard equality of opportunity and have rules and/or a system regulating the competition (this condition is deemed not to be fulfilled in cases where the activity contains an actual or simulated bodily harm in accordance with its set of rules).

31 The definition provided by SportAccord may be found at the following link: http://web.archive.org/web/20111028112912/http://www.sportaccord.com/en/members/index.php?idIndex=32&idContent=14881 (accessed on 29.06.2019).
32 https://gaisf.sport/ (accessed on 29.06.2019).
33 http://asf.org.au/who/definition_of_sport (accessed on 14.07.2013).
34 June 2019.
35 Article 2, paragraph 1 of the European Sports Charter adopted on 24 September 1992.
36 Commission of the European Communities, *White Paper on Sport*, 11.07.2007, COM/2007/0391, p.2.
37 Deutscher Olympischer Sportbund (DOSB).
38 *Aufnahmeordnung des DOSB* (December 2018).

C. Fundamental characteristics of professional sport

Even though a precise legal definition of the term 'sport' is lacking, it can be observed that all existing definitions of 'sport', whether provided by academicians such as Tiedemann or enacted by sports organisations such as the German Olympic Sports Confederation, seem to underline similar characteristics. In the light of these pre-established features, it can be concluded that for an activity to constitute a sport exercised on a professional level, the following 10 requirements should be fulfilled in a cumulative manner: (1) human exertion; (2) absence of any luck element specifically designed into the activity; (3) absence of unethical or illegal behaviour (including absence of intentional harm to living creatures); (4) improvement of physical fitness and mental well-being; (5) entertainment; (6) competition; (7) uncertainty of the outcome and competitive balance; (8) recognisable organisational structure; (9) set of rules; and (10) level playing field.

1. Human exertion

One of the most recurrent descriptive features of the term sport is 'physical exertion'. As per most definitions, '[…] sport needs some notion of being a physical activity, in that there is "the use of physical skill, physical prowess or physical exertion"'.[39]

Nonetheless, physical exertion is not a *sine qua non* characteristic of sport. The IOC's grant of Recognised International Sports Federations status to bridge and chess organisations in, respectively, 1995 and 1999,[40] demonstrates that even activities that require a minimal physical effort can be categorised as sport. Accordingly, while it is undisputable that sport necessitates a certain effort, the exertion provided by participants may be either predominantly physical or predominantly mental.

Requirement of exertion translates into the necessity of regular training in order to cultivate the relevant skills and to gain expertise in the activity concerned. It is important to underline that exertion must involve a considerable level of human effort; it cannot derive from an animal or a technical equipment on a quasi-exclusive basis.

2. Absence of any luck element specifically designed into the activity

In line with the requirement of an effort, a sports activity should not rely on any element of luck specifically integrated in it. This implies that the result obtained in a sports activity should have a causal link with the skills and abilities of its participants and not be determined by pure (or predominant) chance. It is clear that chance is a factor that always plays a part in all sorts of activities. A very skilled sportsperson may fail to effectuate a certain motion or miss an opportunity that they would have normally taken advantage of for no apparent reason. While it

39 GARDINER ET AL, p.6.
40 Should Chess Be an Olympic Sport? by Meaghan Haire, article in *Time* published on 5 August 2008, http://www.time.com/time/world/article/0,8599,1827716,00.html (accessed on 14.07.2013).

would be unreasonable to argue that sports activities should completely eliminate all potential influence of chance, it is legitimate to require the exclusion of any elements exclusively (or predominantly) reliant on chance. Needless to say, the reference is not made to some minor decisions taken by means of coin flipping (or similar methods) for the sake of fair play, but to the element of luck determining at least one of the activity's main components (such as randomly dealt cards) that may exert an influence on the success level of the participants.

3. Absence of unethical or illegal behaviour

Sporting activities cannot incorporate any unethical or illegal components. For example, hunting is not a recognised sport as it contains violence against animals, which is unethical and, in some cases, illegal. Similarly, dwarf-throwing does not constitute a sporting activity, since it is largely considered to be unethical.

Absence of unethical or illegal behaviour should be interpreted as encompassing the prohibition of intentional (either on a factual or on a virtual basis) physical damage to other living creatures.

In this regard, boxing is problematic, since it involves physical damage to a certain extent. Certainly, physical damage inflicted to opponents may not exceed a threshold meticulously determined by the SGBs' regulations and the consent given by participants renders such physical damage legal.[41]

4. Improvement of physical fitness and mental well-being

Sport is associated with good health, both on a physical level and on a mental level. This is due to the fact that sporting activities, such as playing tennis and running, tend to improve both physical fitness and mental well-being. Undoubtedly, most sports activities are not free from any risk of injury. Moreover, sports activities may provoke health problems when exercised at a professional level in the form of either physical injuries or mental disorders such as panic attacks. Nevertheless, the essence of a sporting activity itself reveals to be overall beneficial to health.

5. Entertainment

Although, *prima facie*, entertainment seems to be a more predominant component in amateur sport, it is, in fact, a key characteristic of sport on both amateur and professional levels. The sole difference is the category of persons who are being entertained: at an amateur level, the participants, whereas at a professional level, the audience. Without an entertained audience, which also translates into a fan base, the professional sports industry would certainly not have reached its current proportions.

41 For an interesting analysis of this matter, see CORNELIUS STEVE, The expendables: do sports people really assume the risk of injury, Part one [1], and Part two [2] in *Global Sports Law and Taxation Reports (GSLTR)*, December 2015, Volume 6, No 4 and March 2016, Volume 7, No 1.

6. Competition

'Sports leagues are in the business of selling competition on the playing field [...]'.[42] Without the comparison of the participants' performances (individuals or teams) with each other, professional sport would simply not have existed. As designated by the renowned Olympic motto '*Citius, Altius, Fortius*', professional sport is about being 'faster, higher, stronger' than others.

For professional sport to be genuinely competitive (as well as fair, equitable and entertaining), two other components must necessarily be present: uncertainty of the outcome and competitive balance.

7. Uncertainty of the outcome and competitive balance

A. UNCERTAINTY OF THE OUTCOME

Uncertainty of the outcome can be defined as the unpredictability of the outcome of a sports competition before it actually takes place. In other words, '[u]ncertainty of the outcome concerns the ability to predict (or more specifically, not to predict) the outcome of a match before the event begins or to predict the league champion before the season is played'.[43]

Uncertainty of the outcome is the key that unlocks the emotional process linked to sports events.[44] It must exist on five different levels: (i) match; (ii) championship; (iii) seasonal; (iv) promotion and relegation;[45] and (v) long run (i.e. whether a team/an individual is dominating over a period of several years or not).[46] Its deficiency will cause the affected sports field's appeal to decline, which will, in turn, translate into an economic loss. The most basic example illustrating this phenomenon is the decrease in the broadcasting rights' value once the match is played and the result is broadly known.

The only way to achieve an appropriate level of uncertainty of the outcome is to maintain a certain level of competition, which is solely possible by safeguarding competitive balance.

B. COMPETITIVE BALANCE

Participants of a sports competition collectively create a product.[47] In order to be appealing and popular, the product concerned must contain a number of features such as excitement and display of physical prowess and skill.[48] The more its participants are equally matched, the more interesting the sports competition becomes.[49]

42 FORT/QUIRK, p.1265.
43 MCKEOWN, p.521.
44 SCHOENY, p.20.
45 To the extent where the league concerned has a promotion and relegation system.
46 GRATTON/SOLBERG, p.152; GROOT, p.33.
47 MCKEOWN, p.521.
48 Ibid.
49 Ibid, pp.522–523.

Competitive balance affects not only the on-field performance and income from ticket sales, but also outside-the-stadium revenues such as broadcasting income and advertising deals.[50] Consequently, in order to be able to compete with other sports competitions and similar entertainment products, in more straightforward terms 'to survive', a sports event must maintain its competitive balance.

The three most problematic issues that produce a negative impact on competitive balance are: (i) the significant superiority of one of the competitors; (ii) corruption; and (iii) doping. Despite the fact that SBGs are taking all reasonable measures to combat these and other potential problems, the perfect competitive balance is an unattainable aim. Therefore, what sports authorities aim to establish by means of technical rules and other relevant regulations is '[...] a degree of competitive balance on the field that is acceptable to fans'.[51] A very illustrative example of this effort is the modification of ATP tournaments structure and rules[52] in order to make the sporting events more competitive, and thereby more appealing for the audience.[53]

8. *Recognisable organisational structure*

Professional sport needs to have a well-established organisational structure, which generally consists of a hierarchical pyramid (see Figure 1.1).[54] A typical hierarchical pyramid has the following form: sportspersons, constituting the base of

50 Ibid, p.524.
51 FORT/QUIRK, p.1265.
52 To fulfil sports fans' desire to see the 'top' sportspersons compete against each other, the ranking system of the ATP tournaments was modified and the format was simplified. To this end, the status of some events was downgraded, the point values were adjusted and it was decided that 'top' sportspersons would participate in all Tier I events.
53 MCKEOWN, p.523.
54 The reference is made to the most commonly used European model of sports organisation. Models of sports organisation may diverge in accordance with geographical areas. For instance, in opposition to the European sports model, the organisational structure of the North American Sport may be described as 'closed', i.e. sharply distinguishing between professional and amateur sports, each with its own unintegrated structure (for more information on this point, see NAFZIGER A.R. JAMES, European and North American Models of Sports Organization in NAFZIGER A.R. JAMES/ROSS F. STEPHEN (eds), *Handbook on International Sports Law*, Research Handbooks in International Law, Edward Elgar Publishing Limited, 2011, p.88ff). It must be noted that even in Europe, some sports are not organised as a hierarchical pyramid. The most typical example is Formula 1 that has three stakeholders, namely FIA, Formula One Group and the competing teams, which are independent from each other. The rather complex business relations between these three parties are organised by means of the agreements put in place in this respect. Nonetheless, it can safely be stated that the hierarchical pyramid constitutes the most commonly used sports organisation model in Europe. It should also be underlined that most IFs prefer to organise their sports via a hierarchical pyramid, despite the fact that the model of sports organisation within some geographical areas may differ. A classic example of this way of doing can be observed in football.

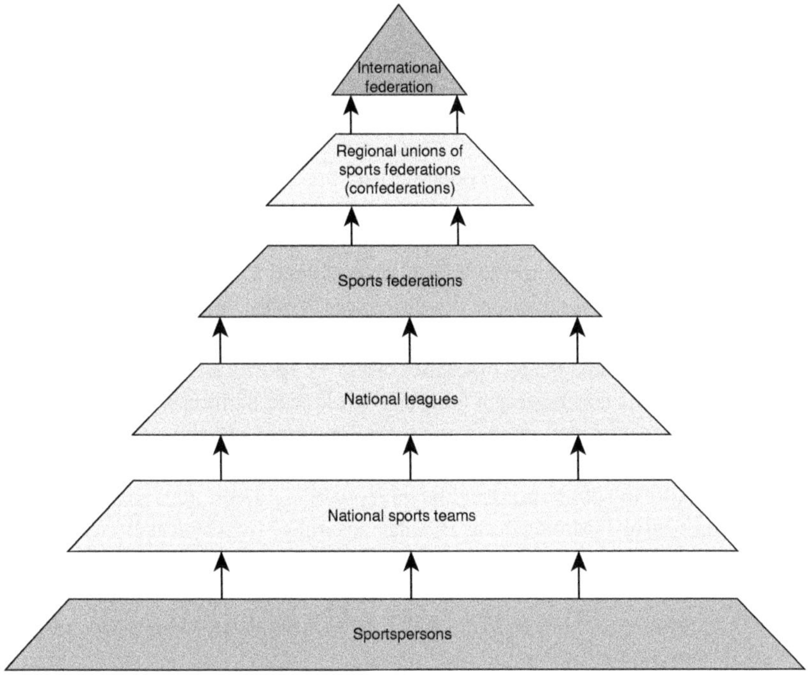

Figure 1.1

the pyramid, are affiliated to sports teams;[55] sports teams are regrouped into national leagues in accordance with their sporting level (such as Premier League and Second Division); national leagues are attached to a national sports federation; national sports federations of different countries are members of a regional union, commonly referred to as a 'confederation' and confederations of different regions are affiliated to the IF that is situated at the top of the pyramid.

9. Set of rules

Professional sport is regulated in a comprehensive manner. The IF of a given sport is generally the ultimate source of laws of the game and has a regulatory function in policing them. While enacting sets of rules, IFs take into consideration a number of important aspects such as safety issues, the need to ensure uncertainty of the outcome, preserving a competitive balance between participants and the need for internationally harmonised rules.

55 Teams of different sports branches are often regrouped under the aegis of a sports club. For the purposes of this book, the terms 'sports team' and 'sports club' are used as equivalents, unless otherwise specified. It must also be underlined that in some sports, such as golf and tennis, affiliation to a team may not be necessary.

It is clear that the rules enacted by sporting federations and confederations, respectively, are only binding on sportspersons and sporting organisations occupying a place in the hierarchical structure of the sport concerned. In other words, rules put in place by sporting federations cannot be imposed on third parties, such as governments and commercial partners, per se, unless a specific agreement is concluded with the third party concerned to this end. It should be emphasised that even when such an agreement does exist, its scope will be limited to certain rules and regulations enacted by the sporting federation, such as regulations related to sponsoring, and not to the whole set of rules.

There exist three main categories of written sports rules, namely: (i) technical rules; (ii) rules of sporting conduct; and (iii) rules affecting sport as an economic activity. Technical rules determine the technicalities of a given sport, such as the measurements of a ball and the acts constituting a foul. The worldwide harmonisation of these rules allows the unanimous functioning of the sport concerned and the creation of a sports monoculture. Rules of sporting conduct aim to achieve competitive balance (e.g. transfer windows) and/or to preserve the integrity of competition (typically by seeking to prevent participants from securing an unfair advantage over their opponents and/or undermining the traditional values of the given sport, e.g. anti-doping rules). Rules affecting sport as an economic activity focus on the economic aspects of the sporting activity (e.g. articles 13ff of the FIFA RSTP, which regulates employment contracts concluded between footballers and their clubs).

A sporting activity may also have unwritten rules that derive from the playing culture without being imposed by the SGBs. The participants are expected to act in compliance with such rules in the spirit of the game. For instance, in football, it is customary to kick the ball into touch when a player is injured on the field.

10. Level playing field

In a nutshell, level playing field signifies that 'sporting competition should not be based on a participant having an unfair advantage over another [...]'.[56] The 'unfair advantage' concerned does not relate to the equal chances of winning, which is associated with competitive balance, but to the fact that all participants are subject to the same set of rules and setting. This being stated, application of the same set of rules and setting to all participants also has a considerable equalising effect on chances of winning. For instance, the fact that teams change ends at half-time during a football game (i.e. each team occupies both goalposts during one-half of the game) constitutes a typical example of a rule intended to guarantee level playing field.

D. 'Sportified' entertainment activities

In the same manner as entertainment features are integrated into professional sport to keep the public interest alive and attract audiences, sporting components are incorporated into certain entertainment activities to allow the industries

56 GARDINER ET AL, p.9.

concerned to capitalise on the positive attributes of sport (such as popularity, engagement and health references), to increase their association with joy and excitement[57] and to benefit from the legal status of 'sport'. Such sportification is achieved by adding sports-world elements, such as stadium-like facilities, cheering stands, sponsors, high level of competition, instant replays, jumbotrons[58] and referees, to the chosen entertainment activity.[59] Regardless of their sportification, these activities should be categorised in accordance with their true nature (i.e. entertainment), so long as they do not fulfil the conditions that need to be met by sporting activities.

The events organised by the WWE constitute a typical example of sportified entertainment activities. Despite being labelled as 'championships', the artificially created 'battles' that have pre-determined results are pure spectacles rather than sports competitions.[60] As a matter of fact, since the outcome of the battle is fixed beforehand, uncertainty of the outcome and genuine competition, which are both fundamental characteristics of professional sport, are missing.

Situated in the grey zone are monster truck shows and tractor pulling contests. Despite their predominant entertainment characteristic, these activities should not be considered as 'sportified' entertainment activities but as 'sporting' activities, since they seem to bear all the fundamental characteristics of sport. Both activities are organised in accordance with a set of rules enacted by associations, namely the Monster Truck Racing Association and, for example, the National Tractor Pullers Association; they involve a competition that safeguards the uncertainty of the outcome and they do not contain any unethical or illegal behaviour.

Another highly debated example is professional poker, the analysis of which is, in fact, rather straightforward. Poker incorporates an element of luck in its very design. In other words, the participants may obtain success by pure chance. Thereupon, poker is more akin to a 'game of chance' than 'sport'.

The most recent, and controversial, debate concerns the characterisation of eSports ('electronic sports'), which means competitive video gaming.[61] The games that are used in competitive gaming can be regrouped into five main categories on the basis of their contents: (i) games depicting and mimicking traditional sports activities (such as football); (ii) FPS games (e.g. Counter-Strike); (iii) RTS games (e.g. Starcraft); (iv) MMO games or MMORPGs (e.g. World of Warcraft); and (v) battle royale games (e.g. Fortnite). Scholz argues that these different categories should be considered as distinct sports disciplines (such as basketball and volleyball), which are to be regrouped under the umbrella term 'eSports' (which is, therefore, akin to the term 'sport').[62] The most quoted definition of eSports belongs to Wagner, who defined the concept as '[…] an area of *sport activities* in

57 LOPEZ-GONZALEZ/GRIFFITHS, p.8.
58 A very large video display screen, typically used in venues such as sports stadiums.
59 LOPEZ-GONZALEZ/GRIFFITHS, p.8.
60 See also GARDINER ET AL, p.8.
61 'Competitive video gaming' designates the competitive practice (not the inherent competitive nature) of video games.
62 SCHOLZ, p.8.

which people develop and train mental or physical abilities in the use of information and communication technologies'.[63]

Although eSports professionals do employ a considerable physical and mental effort during competitions,[64] eSports should not be categorised as a sports activity, since it fails to meet three prerequisites to be characterised as 'sport', namely: absence of unethical or illegal behaviour, recognisable organisational structure and improvement of physical fitness and mental well-being.

The main purpose of most frequently used eSports titles, such as Counter-Strike and LoL, is to kill and/or to cause physical damage to, on a virtual and yet – in some cases – violent manner, members of the other team. Albeit being a mere simulation, such violence should not be deemed appropriate in the context of a sporting activity. This point was also underlined in the Communiqué of the 7th Olympic Summit, which indicates that 'some egames are not compatible with the Olympic values [...]'.[65] A more straightforward reference to the violence contained in eSports titles was made by the President of the IOC, Thomas Bach, who reportedly stated that '[i]f you have egames where it's about killing somebody, this cannot be brought into line with our Olympic values [...] [o]f course every combat sport has its origins in a real fight among people[,] [b]ut sport is the civilized expression about this'.[66]

To date, eSports remain largely industry-driven. The titles are created, designed and curated by video game developers, who also act as gatekeepers of their games.[67] Game developers may unilaterally decide to change the rules of their games and in most cases, i.e. unless they signed a deal with a tournament organiser, they determine the organisational details relating to the tournaments, such as how they are played and how teams are formed. Simply put, they self-regulate to a great extent. That is not to indicate that eSports do not have any GBs. National GBs (the most preeminent example being KeSPA), the International e-Sports Federation, the World Esports Association and the Esports Integrity Coalition are some examples of the existing GBs in the eSports arena. Nevertheless, a top–down governance structure that is currently present in traditional sports activities does not exist in the area of eSports, given the fact that no GB is powerful enough to enforce such regulations to the entire sector.[68] This issue was also put forward in the Communiqué of the 7th Olympic Summit, which underlines that the eSports industry is commercially driven and fragmented in nature due to tough competition between commercial

63 WAGNER, p.3 (emphasis added by the author).

64 For more information on this point, see for example, Science shows that eSports professionals are real athletes by Martin Schütz, article on *DW* published on 12 March 2016, https://www.dw.com/en/science-shows-that-esports-professionals-are-real-athletes/a-19084993 (accessed on 30.06.2019).

65 *Communiqué of the 7th Olympic Summit*, 8 December 2018, available at the following link: https://www.olympic.org/news/communique-of-the-7th-olympic-summit (accessed on 01.07.2019).

66 https://www.bbc.com/news/newsbeat-45407667 (accessed on 01.07.2019).

67 SCHOLZ, p.5.

68 See SCHOLZ, pp.73–77.

operators.[69] Recognisable organisational structure is one of the key components of professional sport, and the argument that '[c]ompanies like McDonald's, Mastercard, Mercedes-Benz, or DHL show that they are committed to the eSports industry and that legitimizes its self-governance'[70] is simply not pertinent from a legal perspective.

It is not possible to objectively state that playing video games with violent content improves physical health and mental well-being. It is clear that when exercised at a professional level such activities may require a considerable physical effort and may have a beneficial effect on hand–eye coordination as well as strategic decision making. Nevertheless, the act of playing violent video games, per se, is likely to have a negative effect both on physical fitness and on mental well-being. Studies conducted by a number of scientists have demonstrated that playing violent video games increases aggressive emotions, provokes desensitisation to violence, increases physiological arousal, decreases prosocial behaviour and, last but not least, may cause addiction.[71]

For these reasons, while it cannot be denied that eSports is a rapidly growing industry, from a legal standpoint, it should be classified as a sportified entertainment activity and not as a sports activity. Obviously, this observation does not prevent governments from applying similar (or the same) legal rules to both sports activities and to eSports in certain areas, to the extent where it is deemed appropriate. For example, as a result of Riot Games' efforts,[72] the United States Citizenship and Immigration Services recognised LoL players as athletes for visa purposes.[73] Also, in the eventuality of the competent authorities (such as the IOC and governments) formally deciding that eSports should be categorised as 'sport', this discussion, albeit being intriguing from a conceptual perspective, would be rendered largely inconsequential.

Despite being similar to a certain extent, sportified entertainment activities and sports activities are not 'equals', i.e. they constitute different types of activities. This divergence echoes on the participants of the activities concerned. The professionals of sportified entertainment activities are 'entertainers', whereas the professionals of sports activities are 'sportspersons'. The terminology adopted in this book distinguishes eSports professionals from other entertainers, by adopting the term 'pro-gamers' (the

69 *Communiqué of the 7th Olympic Summit*, op. cit. n.65.
70 SCHOLZ, p.76.
71 See, for example, ANDERSON CRAIG A./BUSHMAN BRAD J., Effects of violent games on aggressive behavior, aggressive cognition, aggressive affect, physiological arousal, and prosocial behavior: A meta-analytic review of the scientific literature in *Psychological Science*, Volume 12, Number 5, 2001, p.353ff; GENTILE DOUGLAS A. ET AL, The effects of violent video game habits on adolescent hostility, aggressive behaviors, and school performance in *Journal of Adolescence*, Volume 27, 2004, p.5ff and BROCKMYER FUNK JEANNE, Playing violent video games and desensitization to violence in *Child and Adolescent Psychiatric Clinics of North America*, Volume 24, Issue 1, 2015, p.65ff.
72 A video game developer based in the US.
73 This recognition does not, however, extend to all eSports titles (the relevant decisions are taken by the competent authorities on the basis of a case-by-case analysis) and a formal rule on this issue (currently) does not exist.

short form of 'professional gamers'). The term 'player' is deliberately avoided in this context, since participants of a number of traditional sports events, such as football, basketball and tennis, are often referred to as 'players'.

III. Concept of 'sports event'

A. Definition of sports event

Deriving from the Latin word '*eventus*', the past participle of '*evenire*' that signifies to come out, to happen and to result;[74] the term 'event' is used to describe an occasion.[75] It may be loosely defined as 'a significant gathering of people for cultural, educational, charitable, sporting, business, political or recreational purposes'.[76]

'Event' refers to an occasion that has a specified date and location.[77] The occasion concerned must be distinguishable from other occasions by its importance and originality.[78] Events usually have an objective, a theme and an element of formality.[79] They are prepared by a group of people for another group of people that is more numerous.[80]

Sports events can be described as events organised for sporting purposes. They have two main features that distinguish them from other events: competition[81] and uncertainty of the outcome.[82]

B. Different categories of sports events

1. Overview

There are a large variety of sports events in existence (see Figure 1.2). They may be organised at a national or an international level, on a short-term or a long-term basis, at a specific location every time or different locations each time. They may also be distinguished by the number of spectators, the significance of the media attention, the value of their broadcasting rights and other similar criteria.

Other parameters such as the nature of the organising body (e.g. international organisations and business organisations),[83] variety of sports comprising the event (i.e. multisport events or single sport events) and a common characteristic of participants (such as youth events, events for people with disabilities and events

74 https://www.etymonline.com/word/event (accessed on 30.06.2019).
75 BECKER, p.2.
76 Ibid.
77 SCHOENY, p.20.
78 Ibid.
79 BECKER, p.2.
80 SCHOENY, p.20.
81 GREENWELL ET AL, p.7.
82 SCHOENY, p.21.
83 On this point, see SCHOENY, p.22.

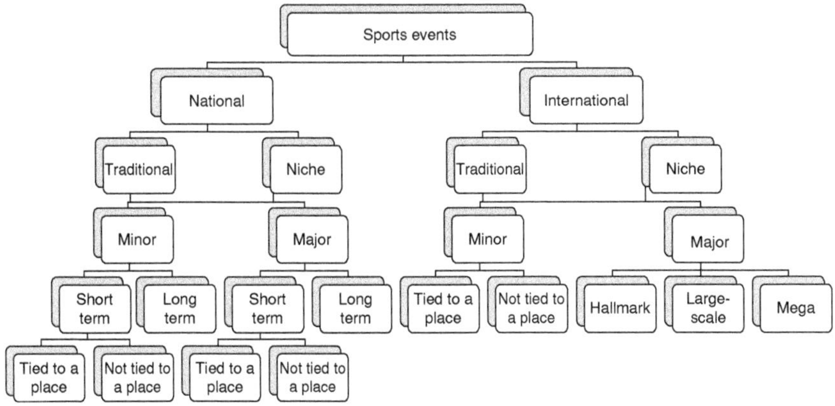

Figure 1.2

specifically organised for a certain cultural or religious group)[84] may also be used. However, the classification adopted for the purposes of this book has the merit of illustrating a general overview of all types of sports events. In other words, all sports events belong to one of the categories illustrated in Figure 1.2 regardless of other characteristics (such as multisport or youth) they may have.

The specificities of each sports event category are shortly described by means of differentiating the contrasting categories, i.e. national versus international, traditional versus niche, minor versus major, short-term versus long-term, events tied to a place versus events not tied to a place, and three distinct categories of international major sports events: hallmark, large-scale and mega.

2. National versus International

Sports events may be distinguished depending on their national or international status. The criterion of distinction between these two categories is the country of residence[85] of the participants. National sports events reunite competitors domiciled in the same country as the event. For example, the Premier League is a national sports event that takes place in the UK, i.e. all of the participating teams are UK teams and the tournaments take place in the same country. On the other hand, competitors of ISEs are from – at least two – different countries. For instance, The Championships, Wimbledon is an ISE that takes place in the UK, i.e. the event itself is held in the UK, but the participating sportspersons come from all over the world.

The ever-growing international sportsperson flow does not have any effect on the national or international status of a given sports event. Even if foreign sportspersons who take part in a national championship as members of local teams add

84 On this point, see GREENWELL ET AL, p.11ff.

85 In this chapter, the terms 'residence', 'domiciled' and 'domicile' are used in their everyday meaning. They do not refer to the national law of a given country.

an international component to national sports events, the events concerned cannot be characterised as ISEs. As a matter of fact, foreign sportspersons who become members of local teams begin to reside in the country where the sports event takes place. For example, while playing for Real Madrid, David Beckham was domiciled in Spain. It is clear that La Liga[86] was not categorised as an ISE during that time frame.

It should be noted that professional leagues comprising teams from different countries constitute ISEs. There are numerous examples of these 'multinational' leagues, such as the NHL (Canada and the US), the ABA League (Bosnia and Herzegovina, Croatia, Macedonia, Montenegro, Serbia and Slovenia) and the Nordic Golf League (Denmark, Finland, Norway and Sweden).

3. Traditional versus Niche

A. TRADITIONAL SPORTS EVENTS

Traditional events have two main characteristics: (i) standards and regulations followed during the event, e.g. number of participants and acceptable actions, are established by a GB; and (ii) the activity exercised at the event is a recognisable and time-honoured sport.[87] For example, the FIFA World Cup™,[88] the Olympic Games and the Arctic Winter Games are traditional sports events, since the sporting activities – such as football, swimming and ice hockey – taking place at those events are standardised by SGBs.

Undoubtedly, regulations of traditional events are not immutable. Exceptions may occur, especially in order to adapt to a certain culture (such as sumo wrestling in Japan and box lacrosse in Canada) or to a new technology.[89] However, change is limited. Usually, the event is conducted repeatedly in the same manner and in accordance with the universally implemented rules and regulations.[90]

B. NICHE SPORTS EVENTS

Niche events have two main attributes: (i) there does not have to be a traditional GB regulating niche events, but an organising committee providing rules and regulations always exists; and (ii) although they may exhibit recognisable traditional event components, niche events are forged through innovations that alter or renew traditional events.[91]

86 The premier football league of Spain.
87 MALLEN/ADAMS, p.2.
88 For the purposes of this book, the term 'FIFA World Cup' refers to the quadrennial competition of the senior men's national (A) teams of the FIFA member associations. The trademark designation is not used throughout the book in order to facilitate reading.
89 MALLEN/ADAMS, p.2.
90 Ibid.
91 Ibid, p.3.

Niche events may be created by: (i) altering some components of a traditional event, e.g. playing basketball on a series of trampolines instead of a traditional basketball court;[92] (ii) combining different traditional events and forming a new event, such as triathlon;[93] (iii) adapting traditional events to a specific category of person, for example the World Dwarf Games; or (iv) inventing a completely new event. This latter possibility will rarely, if ever, be effectively put to use in the sports sector.

4. *Minor versus Major*

Not all sports events are of the same scale, some are 'minor' whereas some are 'major'. Giving precise definitions of 'minor' and 'major', sports events would be impractical, as the two concepts are not delineated by immutable boundaries. These two categories of sports events may, however, be distinguished by means of several criteria such as: the number and the degree of professionalism of the participating sportspersons, the geographic reach of the event (community level, nationwide or international), attendance at the event and whether or not the event is broadcasted. While these criteria are usually linked to each other, i.e. the realisation of one will mean the concretisation of others, they should not be considered as cumulative.

As a general rule, the degree of professionalism of the participating sportspersons or teams to a given competition, and thereby the general sporting level of the event, has a significant role in the qualification of the event concerned as 'major'. The more successful the event from a sporting point of view, the more it is likely to attract an audience, to be broadcasted, to be lucrative and thereby to be deemed as 'major'. National premier leagues and international competitions such as the FIFA World Cup are illustrations of major sports events, whilst amateur leagues are typical examples of minor sports events.

Some sports events may attract considerable public interest, and thereby be categorised as 'major', despite the fact that their participants do not demonstrate any exceptional sporting skills. A typical example is the New York City Marathon. Even if most of its participants are not professional sportspersons, the New York City Marathon is one of the largest marathons in the world and is widely mediatised.

5. *Short-term versus Long-term*

Sports events may also be distinguished by their duration. It is possible to categorise them as 'short-term' and 'long-term'. Short-term events take approximately two months or less. The US Open Tennis Championship is a short-term sports event, which lasts approximately 15 days. Le Tour de France is another example of short-term sports event, with an approximate duration of 20 days. Long-term sports events seem to go on for an approximate period of nine months. National leagues form the most typical example of long-term sports events.

92 Ibid, p.4.

93 Ibid, p.5. It is important to underline that the triathlon has now evolved into a traditional event. However, it is still continuing to develop in several aspects as a niche event.

6. Tied to a place versus Not tied to a place

Sports events may be held in the same country in a recurring manner (events 'tied to a place'). For example, The Championships, Wimbledon has been held in the All England Club, in London, since its inception in 1877.

Sports events may also be held at different locations, or in different countries, each time (events 'not tied to a place'). It is not excluded that the event is held in the same country or at the same location for two or more editions, but this will generally not be the case for two consecutive editions. The Commonwealth Games, the Pan American Games and the Olympic Games constitute typical examples of sports events not tied to a place.

7. Special categories of international major sports events

International major sports events can be subdivided into three categories: (a) hallmark sporting events; (b) large-scale sporting events; and (c) mega sporting events. The demarcation between these three categories is rather ambiguous. Nonetheless, each category has some distinct characteristics that may be used to distinguish it from the other two.

A. HALLMARK SPORTING EVENTS

A hallmark event can be defined as: '[…] a recurring event that possesses such significance, in terms of tradition, attractiveness, image or publicity, that the event provides the host venue, community or destination with a competitive advantage. Over time the event and destination can become inseparable'.[94] As can be deduced from the definition, hallmark sports events are recurring major sports events that are tied to a place.

A typical example of a hallmark event is The Championships, Wimbledon, which is: (i) a major sports event; (ii) of a recurring character (i.e. takes place each year); and (iii) tied to a place (i.e. the All England Club in London). Another classical example is the Boston Marathon.

B. LARGE-SCALE SPORTING EVENTS

Large-scale sporting events provide similar types of legacies and benefits with hallmark sporting events and mega sporting events.[95] They can be distinguished from hallmark sporting events by the fact that they are not tied to a place, i.e. their HC/HS varies from edition to edition. They diverge from mega sporting events by their scale: large-scale events are less significant than mega sporting events. However, demarcation between large-scale sporting events and mega sporting events is far from being clear. Apart from some typical examples of mega sporting

94 GETZ DONALD, *Event Management and Event Tourism*, 2nd edition, Cognizant, 2005, p.5 cited in GETZ ET AL, p.50.
95 PARENT/SMITH-SWAN, p.4.

events, which are detailed in the following paragraph, no clear line can be traced between mega and large-scale sporting events. Therefore, the distinction remains somewhat subjective. Commonly accepted examples of large-scale sporting events are the Commonwealth Games and the Pan American Games.[96]

C. MEGA SPORTING EVENTS

As indicated by its name, a 'mega' sporting event is a large or great sporting event.[97] The main problem resides in determining when a sporting event becomes 'mega'. For Roberts, what renders certain sports events 'mega' is their discontinuous character and their out of the ordinary composition.[98] According to Roberts, in order to be considered as 'mega', the sporting event must have the ability to transmit promotional messages to billions of people via television and other means of telecommunications.[99] Similar criteria are also used by Roche, who defines mega events as 'large-scale cultural (including commercial and sporting) events, which have a dramatic character, mass popular appeal and international significance'.[100]

As per the literature, mega sporting events may be distinguished from other sporting events by means of the following criteria: (i) number of participating athletes; (ii) attendance at the event; (iii) television viewership of the event; (iv) the international significance of the event; and (v) the long-term consequences for the cities and countries, respectively, that stage the short-term event.[101]

The criteria must be applied in a cumulative manner. Applied solely, each criterion may be misleading. For example, large-scale sporting events can attract an equal, or even greater, number of participants than mega sporting events.[102] This was the case with the 2009 Sydney World Masters Games that attracted 30,000 participants, while the 2008 Beijing Olympic Games attracted 10,942 athletes.[103] Television viewership of the event might also fluctuate depending on several factors, such as the individuals or teams that are competing and the location where the event takes place.[104] In the same vein, if only ratings or attendance were to be considered in determining whether an event is 'mega', it could be concluded that a golfing event with Tiger Woods was a mega event, whereas the same tournament without him was not.[105]

However, even when all the criteria are reviewed in relation to a given event, a precise conclusion cannot be drawn effortlessly. This is due to the fact that the criteria used may be affected by further issues, such as other sports events taking

96 Ibid.
97 MAENNIG/ZIMBALIST, *Mega Sporting Event*, p.9.
98 ROBERTS KEN, *The Leisure Industries*, Palgrave, 2004, p.108 cited in HORNE, p.82.
99 Ibid.
100 ROCHE MAURICE, *Mega-Events and Modernity*, Routledge, 2000, p.1 cited in HORNE, p.81.
101 MAENNIG/ZIMBALIST, *Mega Sporting Event*, pp.9–12.
102 PARENT/ SMITH-SWAN, p.4.
103 Ibid.
104 MAENNIG/ZIMBALIST, *Mega Sporting Event*, p.10.
105 Ibid.

place at the same time. Thereupon, demarcation of a 'mega' sporting event from other sports events necessarily involves a rather subjective aspect.

Nevertheless, some sports events appear to be considered as 'mega' in the literature in a quasi-unanimous manner. These are the Olympic Games (summer and winter), the FIFA World Cup and the final game of the UEFA Champions League. Even if the rationale of this classification seems clear at first sight, whether the grandeur and the economic impact of these events are significantly different from other events remains debatable. For example, research has shown that the Winter Olympic Games does not have an equal impact to the Summer Olympic Games.[106] In fact, the Winter Olympic Games is approximately one-quarter the size of the Summer Olympics in terms of athletes and events.[107] Also, when compared to the Commonwealth Games, which is considered to be a large-scale sports event in the literature, the Winter Olympics does not seem to be dramatically distinct.[108] This observation can be illustrated by the following example: the 2010 Vancouver Winter Olympics lasted for 17 days, with the participation of 2,556 athletes from 82 countries, whereas the 2010 Delhi Commonwealth Games lasted 12 days, with the participation of 7,000 athletes from 71 countries.[109] While the Vancouver Winter Olympics was viewed by three billion television spectators, the opening ceremonies of the Delhi Commonwealth Games were watched by over a billion people.[110]

It is possible to conclude that the distinction between large-scale and mega sporting events is not straightforward. This being stated, three events, namely the Olympic Games (summer and winter), the FIFA World Cup and the final game of the UEFA Champions League, are considered to be 'mega' events by the majority of authors. Accordingly, for the purposes of this book, only these three events are considered as mega sporting events.

IV. Bidding procedure and key actors of an ISE

The majority of large-scale and mega sporting events can be hosted only after undergoing a bidding procedure, during which the interested cities or countries bid to the rights-holder of the event, which is most commonly the SGB. While bidding processes diverge from sports event to sports event, their general outlines are similar to a great extent.

The bidding procedure is conducted by bidding committees, with the participation of various levels of governments.[111] Bidding is both a lengthy and a financially burdensome process. It typically takes one to three years once it is started.[112] This duration is much longer in reality, as the interested bidding committees should begin their preparations long before the official starting date of the bidding procedure.

106 COATES, p.407.
107 HORNE, endnote 2.
108 COATES, p.403.
109 Ibid.
110 Ibid.
111 PARENT/SMITH-SWAN, p.14.
112 Ibid.

By putting in place a bidding system, SGBs aim to ensure a series of commodities, such as facilities that are up to a certain standard and ready on time for the event, comfortable lodgings at the disposal of both spectators and participants, undisturbed travelling to the venues, modern and high-quality coverage of the event via broadcast and print media facilities,[113] protection of the intellectual property linked to the event and tax exemptions.

Those requirements form the subject matter of HCCs,[114] which contain specific and detailed clauses for various obligations of HSs[115]. HCCs may be defined as non-negotiable contracts that are signed between the SGB and the HS, alternatively, during or at the end of bidding procedures. Since they determine the obligations of the HS, they may be considered as 'the core contract' of a given ISE.

The clauses contained in an HCC may be illustrated by means of the three following examples:

- The HCC signed by Rio de Janeiro for the 2016 Olympic Games contains the following clause on security:

  [t]he appropriate authorities of the Host Country shall be responsible for all aspects of security in relation to the Games, including the financial, planning and operational aspects related thereto. The City and the Government, the NOC, the OCOG and the aforementioned authorities shall ensure that all appropriate and necessary measures shall be taken in order to guarantee the safe and peaceful celebration of the Games [...].[116]

- The HCC concluded between South Africa and FIFA for the 2010 FIFA World Cup[117] contains, among others, the following clauses on broadcasting rights:

  FIFA is the sole owner of all the Broadcast Rights to the Championship. FIFA shall be entitled to retain all revenues generated from the exploitation of the Broadcast Rights, save as expressly outlined in this Agreement'[118] and 'FIFA is entitled, at its sole and absolute discretion, to determine the manner in which the Broadcast Rights are to be exploited.[119]

113 COATES, p.416.
114 It is important to note that 'Host City Contract' is the term used by the IOC for the hosting of the Olympic Games. The denomination of the contract may differ from event to event. This book uses the term 'Host City Contract' as a generic term, covering all contracts of the same type.
115 HCCs may be signed by and may impose obligations upon HCs and/or HSs. The details of this issue fall out of the scope of this book. For the sake of simplicity, the reference is exclusively made to HSs in this section.
116 Article 23 of the HCC.
117 The exact title of the contract is, *Organising Association Agreement between FIFA and South African Football Association, 2010 FIFA World Cup*[TM].
118 Article 28.1.1 of the HCC.
119 Article 28.2.1 of the HCC.

- The HCC signed by London for the 2012 Olympic Games includes the following clause on taxation of sportspersons:

> [t]he City and the OCOG shall ensure that either (i) there shall not be any taxes imposed in the Host Country upon the competitors in relation to any financial or other rewards received by the competitors as a result of their performance at the Games, or (ii) should any such taxes be imposed in the Host Country, the financial or other rewards shall be increased and paid by the OCOG so that the competitors, after the applicable taxes, receive an amount that equals the amount they would have received had there been no such taxes.[120]

Upon the completion of the bidding process, the successful bidding committee is transformed into the LOC, ideally in six to eight months.[121] The LOC undertakes all relevant organisational steps in the HS, namely planning the event, raising the necessary funds, implementing the plans and wrapping up the event (i.e. writing the final report and managing the event's legacy).[122] An LOC remains active for approximately nine years[123] and then ceases to exist. It co-operates with the government to fulfil the rights-holder's requirements enumerated in different documents, such as the HCC and the regulations of the event. It remains under close supervision of SGBs during its existence. For example, the IOC supervises the general preparation of each edition of the Olympic Games through its coordination commissions, which regularly visit the HS to oversee the Games' preparations.

V. Unequal distribution of income within the sports sector

While this book analyses a wide array of income sources that may be derived from an ISE, it must be borne in mind that a non-negligible number of sports events may not give rise to the majority of income sources that are being examined. Sport is, indeed, an extremely competitive market, dominated by a handful of actors.

For sportspersons, the struggle with opponents begins at a very early stage: the entry to the market. For example, in China, only 5 percent of the young sportspersons trained to become Olympic athletes can actually take part in the Olympic Games.[124] The remaining 95 percent leave their sports schools with no formal primary and secondary education qualifications and certainly not as professional athletes.[125]

The small group of survivors of this initial combat find themselves in an even greater battle: sports business. Sports competitions are akin to television series with a limited number of 'sports stars' appearing on a regular-basis,[126] a small number of new faces joining the show every season and one or two 'main characters' leaving the

120 Article 49(c) of the HCC.
121 PARENT/SMITH-SWAN, p.10.
122 Ibid, p.11 and 270ff.
123 Ibid, p.11, Figure 1.3.
124 HONG, p.53.
125 Ibid.
126 SOBRY, p.35.

show from time to time. Distribution of the earnings occurs accordingly: main characters get the lion's share; smaller roles get a significantly lower share; and, lastly, walk-ons end up with almost nothing.

This situation is mainly due to the organisation scheme of sports competitions. As a matter of fact, rights-holders tend to opt for a highly competitive pattern of prize money distribution. Therefore, a minor difference between two sporting performances usually translates into a large discrepancy between the sums obtained by the sportspersons concerned. For example, at the 2015 Tour de France, the prize money attributed to the winner amounted to 450,000 EUR, while the sum assigned for the second place was 200,000 EUR.[127] Consequently, Nairo Quintana, who completed the competition merely one minute and twelve seconds[128] after the 2015 champion Christopher Froome, earned 250,000 EUR less than his competitor. Similarly, during the 2012–2015 cycle, the winners of the UEFA Champions League were expected to obtain 15 million EUR, whereas the runners-up, which usually have an identical performance level, were looking at 10.5 million EUR.[129]

This remarkable difference also reflects on the sports market in general. In fact, sport consists of a winner-take-all-market, where only the highest performers are turned into stars with the relentless assistance of media.[130] As a result, while the privileged small group of stars earn tremendous amounts of money, the rest of the sportspersons obtain very modest sums. To proceed with the example of Christopher Froome, on top of his Tour de France prize money, the cyclist was also entitled to a salary of approximately 3 million GBP in 2015.[131] On the other hand, a cyclist who participated in the Tour de France had a great chance of leaving the competition with prize money amounting to 400 EUR,[132] while earning an annual salary of 29,370 EUR.[133] Moreover, while sports stars benefit from a myriad of contracts relating to the exploitation of their image, the grand majority of sportspersons '[...] would scarcely prompt a second glance off the field of play'.[134] Undoubtedly, not all tennis players can derive 86 million USD from the exploitation of their image, as Roger Federer does.[135]

127 Le Tour de France, 102nd edition, *Race Regulations*, pp.20–21; available online at the following link: http://www.letour.com/le-tour/2015/docs/TDF15_Reglement-BD.pdf (accessed on 14.08.2015).
128 Final standings of the cyclists are available online at the following link: http://www.letour.com/le-tour/2015/us/overall-route.html (accessed on 14.08.2015).
129 http://www.uefa.com/uefachampionsleague/news/newsid=1858497.html (accessed on 11.08.2015).
130 SOBRY, p.40.
131 Just how much do Chris Froome and the rest of the peloton earn? by Lia Hervey, article on *SkySports* published on 15 July 2015, http://www.skysports.com/cycling/news/21683/9914043/just-how-much-do-chris-froome-and-the-rest-of-the-peloton-earn (accessed on 15.08.2015).
132 Le Tour de France, 102nd edition, *Race Regulations*, op. cit. n. 127, pp.20–21.
133 Minimum wage of a new professional as determined by the Union Cycliste Internationale in *UCI Cycling Regulations*, June 2015 Version, Part 2 Road Races, §2.15.139.
134 HIGGINS ET AL, p.1156.
135 *The 2019 Forbes World's Highest-Paid Athletes List*, available at the following link: https://www.forbes.com/athletes/#58b38f3e55ae (accessed on 01.08.2019) (referred to as '*The 2019 Forbes List*' throughout this book).

Sex also seems to play part in the distribution of the income within the sports sector. For example, only three sportswomen, namely Maria Sharapova (34th rank), Li Na (41st rank) and Serena Williams (55th rank), figured on The 2014 Forbes World's Highest-Paid Athletes List[136] comprising 100 sportspersons. In 2019, this number was reduced to one, namely Serena Williams (63rd rank).[137]

The situation is identical for sports events. Only a limited number of sports events that regroup sports stars can benefit from broadcasting, sponsoring and other similar contracts amounting to several billion dollars. The majority of sports events are small-scale events that are not transmitted on any broadcast mediums and that have one or two commercial partners, which usually consist of local enterprises.

136 *The 2014 Forbes World's Highest-Paid Athletes List*, available online at the following link: http://www.forbes.com/pictures/mli45eimdj/1-floyd-mayweather/#b6b62cc44bad (accessed on 01.08.2019).

137 *The 2019 Forbes List.*

2 Main tax law concepts and mechanisms

I. Introduction

This book examines taxation of ISEs from income tax and VAT perspectives. Despite their similarities on certain points, these two types of taxes have entirely distinct systems and, thereby, must be analysed separately. This chapter describes the principal concepts of both taxes, especially with regard to cross-border economic activities that are likely to occur in relation to an ISE. The analysis begins with the main concepts of income tax (II) and proceeds with the principal concepts of VAT (III). Given the specificities of the taxation modalities of illegal/unlawful activities, the final section of this chapter is dedicated to the examination of such activities both from an income tax point of view and from a VAT point of view (IV).

II. Income tax

A. Introduction

This section makes some general international tax observations in relation to ISEs (B) and examines the key distributive rules that are applied in chapters 3 and 4 for the purposes of the analysis of taxation modalities of income sources deriving from ISEs (C).

B. General international tax observations regarding ISEs

1. SS and RS

A country's jurisdiction to tax is determined by means of connecting factors, commonly referred to as 'nexus'. A nexus may be established by means of income producing activities conducted in a country (objective nexus, economic attachment) or of persons earning a taxable income (personal nexus).

An objective nexus is deemed to exist in cases where non-resident individuals and/or legal entities are deriving income from activities that have an identifiable and tangible connection with a country.[1] Such income is considered to have its

1 HOLMES, *International Tax Policy*, p.20.

'source' in that country and the country concerned is commonly referred to as the SS. From an ISE perspective, the SS is the country in which the event takes place, commonly known as the HS.

A personal nexus implies a connection between a country and the person earning the income. It is incumbent upon the countries' domestic laws to establish the pertinent criteria that fiscally connect a person to their territories. A country constitutes the RS of the persons having a personal nexus with it. Regarding an ISE, RSs are all countries of which individuals and legal entities deriving an income in relation to the event are residents.

2. Chosen MC for the purposes of the analysis

As is common knowledge, currently most of the DTTs concluded between States, even those that are entered into by non-OECD Member countries, are based on the OECD MC.[2] The role of the UN MC has gradually declined, with its residual role confined mostly to some specific clauses of DTTs.[3] The relevance of the OECD MC in the current tax environment is described as follows by Pistone '[…] [there is] a growing trend to use the OECD Model as a vehicle to aggregate the rules of all tax treaties around some consolidated and homogeneous legal standards, thus facilitating the voluntary building-up of internationally accepted standards'.[4]

On these grounds, the OECD MC has been chosen as the basis of the analysis conducted in this book. Where relevant, reference is also made to the UN as well as to the US MCs. It is also important to underline that for the purposes of this book, the MLI, i.e. the end-result of the BEPS Project, is rarely taken into consideration since the issues under examination remain largely unaffected by the Multilateral Instrument.

3. General methodology

Is typically applied for the purposes of the income tax analysis of cross-border economic activities a four-step methodology, which consists of: (a) the analysis under the applicable domestic laws; (b) the existence and the scope of application of a DTT; (c) the application of the distributive rules; and (d) the elimination of the residual double taxation. This sub-subsection explains the assumptions that have been made for the purposes of this book in relation to each of the relevant steps.

A. ANALYSIS UNDER THE APPLICABLE DOMESTIC LAWS

Income sources examined in this book may not be submitted to tax by each State. As a general rule, in the absence of a domestic tax, the relevant disposition of the DTT, which aims to limit the taxation power of the CSs, does not need to be applied. For

2 RASMUSSEN, p.3.
3 PISTONE, p.2
4 Ibid, p.6.

the sake of simplicity, throughout this book it is assumed that both the HS' and the RS' domestic laws are submitting the income source under examination to tax, except in cases where the HS enacted specific exemption provisions in relation to the ISE.

B. EXISTENCE AND THE SCOPE OF APPLICATION OF A DTT

Albeit there is a large network of DTTs, it is clear that not all countries have concluded a DTT with each other. In the absence of a DTT, the provisions of the domestic laws of the countries are applied without any international limitations. Needless to say, if there is a DTT concluded by the countries, it must also be verified as to whether the case in hand falls within its personal, material, temporal and territorial scopes of application.

For the purposes of this book, it is assumed that all relevant countries concluded DTTs with each other, which are applicable to all income sources deriving from ISEs (i.e. issues that may arise with regard to a DTT's scope of application are not examined). The problems that may be caused by the absence of a DTT are mentioned where relevant.

C. APPLICATION OF THE DISTRIBUTIVE RULES

In the presence of an applicable DTT, one must categorise the income source to determine the appropriate distributive rule. Depending on the specificities of the case in hand, certain income sources may fall under more than one category, and thereby more than one article. This situation is problematic given the schedular nature of the OECD MC's distributive rules, which provide different taxation modalities for different income sources. The remedy is to establish a certain hierarchy among the rules concerned, in order to be able to determine which provision takes precedence in case of a conflict. While a precise hierarchy is lacking, it is generally accepted that categories referring to passive income take priority over those related to active income.[5] Also, some articles contain a specific conflict rule that determines which provision is to be applied in case of conflict (e.g. article 7(4) of the OECD MC).

The general modalities of the key distributive rules used for the purposes of the analysis are briefly examined in subsection C.

D. ELIMINATION OF THE RESIDUAL DOUBLE TAXATION

In certain cases, distributive rules may not completely eliminate but merely alleviate the double taxation, giving, thereby, rise to a 'residual double taxation'. The residual double taxation may be relieved by means of the methods offered by articles 23A and 23B of the OECD MC, namely the exemption method and the credit method. The modalities of these two articles fall beyond the scope of this book, and therefore no further developments are made in this regard.

5 HOLMES, *International Tax Policy*, p.98.

C. *Key distributive rules*

This subsection examines the basic modalities of the most-commonly-applied distributive rules throughout the analysis conducted within this book, namely: (1) business profits; (2) independent personal services; (3) income from employment; (4) royalties; (5) technical services fees; (6) income derived as an entertainer or a sportsperson; and (7) income from immovable property.

1. Business profits

A. GENERAL ASPECTS

As per the general rule contained in article 7(1) of the OECD MC, business profits are taxable exclusively in the RS,[6] except in cases where the enterprise concerned carries on business in the other CS, i.e. the SS, through a PE situated therein.[7] If there is a PE in the SS, the profits that are attributable to it may be taxed by this State,[8] in conformity with the allocation rules elucidated by the OECD Commentary and the modalities provided by the national law. The existence of a PE is determined in accordance with article 5 of the OECD MC, which provides for two different types of PE; namely 'fixed place PE'[9] and 'dependent agent PE'[10] (see Figure 2.1 for the general structure of article 5). Some DTTs contain an additional type of PE, namely 'service PE'.

i. Fixed place PE This subparagraph succinctly describes the three cumulative conditions that need to be fulfilled for a fixed place PE to be formed, namely: (i.a) a PoB at the disposal of the enterprise residing in the other CS; (i.b) the 'fixed' nature of the PoB concerned; and (i.c.) the exercise of 'the core functions' of the enterprise through that particular PoB.

i.a. PoB at the disposal of the enterprise A PoB may be defined as any premises, facilities or installations used for carrying on the business of the non-resident enterprise, regardless of whether such place of business is exclusively used for that purpose or not[11] and whether the enterprise concerned has a formal legal right to use the place or not.[12] It follows that PoB is a concept that is interpreted broadly, varying from a factory[13] to 'a certain amount of space'.[14] For example, the following were considered as PoBs: a desk

6 Article 7(1) of the OECD MC uses the term 'shall be taxable only'.
7 Ibid, article 7(1), first sentence.
8 Ibid, article 7(1), second sentence.
9 Ibid, article 5(1).
10 Ibid, article 5(5).
11 *OECD Commentary* on article 5, §10.
12 Ibid, §11.
13 As mentioned in (d) of the non-exhaustive list of examples provided by article 5(2) of the OECD MC.
14 *OECD Commentary* on article 5, §10.

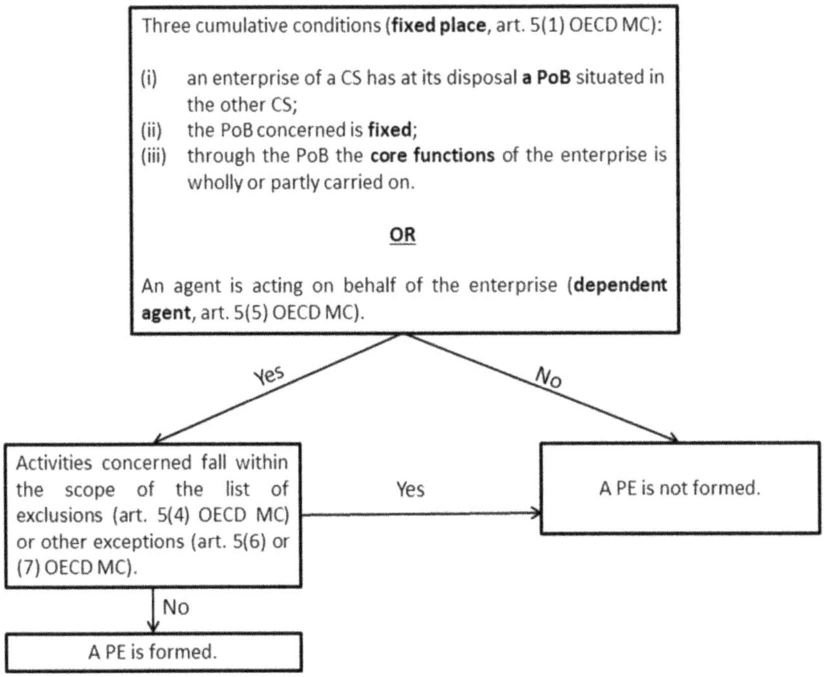

Figure 2.1

and a filing cabinet in a corner of a private residence, an open-air place in a forest where logging equipment is demonstrated and the wharf of a shipping enterprise.[15]

i.b. 'Fixed nature' of the PoB To be considered as 'fixed', a PoB needs to be located at a specific geographical nexus[16] and it must not be of a purely temporary nature.[17] The requirement of being geographically 'fixed' does not imply that the PoB should be literally fixed to the soil.[18] Underground facilities[19] and movable place of businesses[20] may also constitute 'fixed' places. To constitute a PE, a movable PoB should move around within a geographically coherent area and perform a systematic commercial activity, such as a market-place.[21]

Regarding the relevant time threshold, although most countries consider a place as fixed only if it is maintained for at least six months,[22] a PE may also be deemed

15 SASSEVILLE/SKAAR, p.24.
16 Ibid, p.25.
17 *OECD Commentary* on article 5, §6.
18 SASSEVILLE/SKAAR, p.26.
19 Such as pipelines and mines.
20 Such as a transportable newsstand, a tent or a van equipped for selling products (SASSEVILLE/SKAAR, p.26).
21 SASSEVILLE/SKAAR, p.27.
22 *OECD Commentary* on article 5, §28; SASSEVILLE/SKAAR, pp.29–30.

to exist in cases where the PoB is kept for a very short period of time because the nature of the business is such that it will only be carried on for that short period of time.[23] This may typically be the case for recurrent activities and for activities exclusively carried on in the State concerned.[24]

i.c. Core functions The business conducted through the PoB must relate to the main ('core') functions of the enterprise. What constitutes the core functions of the enterprise depends on the nature of business carried on by that enterprise.[25] For instance, providing legal services falls within the core functions of a law firm. Similarly, organising sports tournaments constitutes one of the core functions of an SGB. A PE is not deemed to exist if the activities exercised through the PoB fall within the exclusion list provided in paragraph 4,[26] i.e. if they are of a purely preparatory or auxiliary character.

ii. Dependent agent PE In cases where a fixed place PE is not formed, it must be verified whether a dependent agent PE exists. For this latter form of PE to be constituted, the following cumulative conditions must be met: there must be a person who: (i) acts in one CS on behalf of an enterprise of the other CS; (ii) must not constitute an 'independent agent' under article 5(6); (iii) must have the authority to conclude contracts in the name of the enterprise or play the principal role leading to the conclusion of contracts that are routinely concluded without material modification by the enterprise; (iv) must exercise this authority in an habitual manner; and (v) must not exercise merely auxiliary and preparatory activities[27] on behalf of the enterprise.[28]

An independent agent signifies an agent that is acting in the ordinary course of their/its own business and that is legally[29] and economically[30] independent of the non-resident enterprise.[31] An agent will typically be considered as being 'dependent', in cases where their/its commercial activities are subject to detailed

23 *OECD Commentary* on article 5, §28.
24 Ibid.
25 Ibid, §130.
26 Article 5(4) of the OECD MC.
27 Ibid.
28 Article 12 of the MLI, entitled 'Artificial Avoidance of Permanent Establishment Status through Commissionaire Arrangements and Similar Strategies' aims to prevent a purely artificial avoidance of the formation of a dependent agent PE. It can, however, be observed that most RSs of multinational enterprises did not 'opt-in' for the application of the article concerned, which leaves its applicability extremely limited.
29 Legal independence signifies that the principle has no control over, or power to interfere with, the day-to-day business of the agent (HOLMES, *International Tax Policy*, p.164).
30 Economic independence means that the agent conducts its own business and bears the entrepreneurial risk of the business in its entirety or to a great extent (HOLMES, *International Tax Policy*, p.164).
31 Article 5(6) of the OECD MC.

instructions or comprehensive control of the enterprise, they/it is acting for only one principal and/or they/it does not take any significant entrepreneurial risks.[32]

iii. Service PE Some service providers may carry on a substantial level of business in an SS without necessitating any fixed PoB. A number of countries consider that the profits deriving from such services should be submitted to tax in the SS even when a fixed place or a dependent agent PE is not deemed to be constituted in the territory of that State.[33] To enable a certain uniformity on the matter, the OECD inserted an optional service PE provision in its Commentary on article 5 in 2008. The optional clause provides for the establishment of a PE due to the mere provision of services meeting certain conditions and exceeding a temporal threshold (183 days in any 12-month period).[34] A fixed PoB or a dependent agent is not required for the service PE to be formed. A similar clause is found in article 5(3)(b) of the UN MC.

B. SPECIFIC CASE OF 'E-COMMERCE'

i. Concept of 'e-commerce' The concept 'e-commerce' can be defined as '[…] commercial transactions involving the production, distribution, sale and delivery of goods and services that are carried out over open networks like the Internet'.[35] There exists two categories of e-commerce, namely 'online' (or 'direct') and 'off-line' (or 'indirect').[36] The former category refers to a transaction that is wholly completed on the internet and the latter category refers to cases where the order is registered on the online sales system but the delivery is made in a physical manner.[37] In offline e-commerce the payment may either be effectuated online or against invoice upon the receipt of the product.

E-commerce activities are usually conducted through a website, which can be described as a location (site) situated on the World Wide Web.[38] Websites are combinations of software and electronic data[39] that reside on computers, commonly referred to as servers, which are in turn connected to the internet. Any computer can be turned into a web server by being installed with server software and by being connected to the internet.[40] The accessibility of a website is not limited to the country where the server is located. The servers are commonly maintained by internet service providers, but they may also be owned, operated and maintained directly by other enterprises.[41]

32 See also HOLMES, *International Tax Policy*, pp.162 and 164.
33 *OECD Commentary* on article 5, §§136–137.
34 Ibid, §144.
35 PINTO, p.2.
36 Ibid, p.4.
37 Ibid, p.5.
38 http://www.webopedia.com/TERM/W/web_site.html (accessed on 08.09.2015).
39 *OECD Commentary* on article 5, §42.2.
40 http://www.webopedia.com/TERM/W/Web_server.html (accessed on 08.09.2015).
41 PINTO, p.3.

ii. Server as a 'fixed PoB' Enterprises active in a number of different sectors may reach their clients by means of a website that can accomplish a significant part of the (or the entire) sales process. As expressly indicated in the OECD Commentary, a website cannot constitute a PoB, since it is not a tangible property consisting of facilities such as premises, machinery or equipment.[42] On the other hand, a server on which the website concerned is stored and through which it is accessible is a piece of equipment having a physical location that is susceptible to constitute a fixed PoB of the enterprise operating that server.[43] While servers are actually computers, which can easily be moved, the criterion of being 'fixed' does not refer to the possibility of moving the equipment, but to the fact that it is actually moved.[44]

It can, therefore, be stated that, as a general rule, a server is susceptible to constitute a fixed place PE, to the extent where the other relevant requirements are met, while a website is not. When applying this general rule to a specific case two main points should be taken into consideration: (ii.a) the nature of the activities conducted through the server; and (ii.b) the enterprise operating the server.

ii.a. Nature of the activities conducted through the server To constitute a fixed place PE, the server needs to be used in the accomplishment of the enterprise's core functions, and not only for the purposes of preparatory or auxiliary activities. For instance, if the enterprise is active in selling intangible goods, the typical functions related to a sale, such as the conclusion of the contract with the customer, the processing of the payment and the delivery of the intangible products, should be performed through the server.[45] If, for example, the customers may only see the products and make reservations to pick up the goods from the nearest store, the activities fulfilled through the server should be considered as preparatory and auxiliary.[46]

ii.b. Enterprise operating the server Servers are usually maintained by internet service providers. The enterprise owning the website pays a fee to the service provider in exchange for the hosting of the website on a server at the disposal of the service provider. These agreements do not generally result in the server and its location being at the disposal of the enterprise commercialising online products.[47] This holds true even in cases where the enterprise is able to determine the particular server on which the website should be hosted.[48] Consequently, the enterprise does not have a physical presence at the location of the server and, therefore,

42 *OECD Commentary* on article 5, §123.
43 Ibid.
44 Ibid, §125.
45 Ibid, §130.
46 Ibid, §128.
47 Ibid, §124.
48 Ibid.

it cannot be considered as having acquired a PoB in the country where the server is located, i.e. a fixed place PE is not formed.[49]

In cases where the enterprise is carrying on business through a website and is not operating its website through an internet service provider but on its own, by means of a server at its own disposal (e.g. when it owns – or leases – and operates the server on which the website is stored and used), the server is susceptible to constitute a fixed place PE.[50] This being stated, an enterprise maintaining and operating its own server would be quite rare in practice, at least in the sports sector.

In theory, even if a server operated by an internet service provider may not constitute a fixed place PE of the enterprise owning the website, a PE may still be created in the country where the server is located to the extent where the internet service provider may be considered as a dependent agent of the enterprise concerned. Nonetheless, this will usually not be the case in practice, as internet service providers are generally neither legally nor economically dependent on the website owners. Moreover, in principle, they do not have the authority to interfere with the business contracts concluded by the enterprise owning the website.[51] They are merely commercial partners of the website owners, acting in the ordinary course of their business, i.e. to host and maintain websites of different enterprises.[52]

iii. Towards a new PE nexus? It is undisputed that PE is one of the key concepts of international tax law. Almost all DTTs include the PE concept and use it as a key element to determine the allocation of taxing rights on cross-border business income.[53] For a significant period of time, the current PE concept was indeed the best possible proxy to determine the existence of a sufficient nexus in the SS.[54] It cannot be denied that e-commerce disrupted the system, which is mostly fit for brick and mortar businesses. Websites allow enterprises to reach a global customer base without the need to create any fixed place or dependent agent PE in respective SSs. In the future, websites could be replaced, or accompanied, by other technologies, such as blockchain, but the taxation problem would remain the same. In the absence of a PE, SSs cannot tax the profits deriving from the activities conducted by means of digital technology.

Given the substantiality of the tax revenue foregone because of this problem, not only international but also national efforts have been concentrated on finding a solution. At an international level, the most notable effort is, unsurprisingly, assumed by the OECD, which aimed to address the issues arising from the digital economy in Action 1 of the BEPS Project. Neither a viable international solution nor an adequate level of guidance could, however, be provided as a result of the work conducted within the BEPS Project. The OECD's work on the matter is expected to

49 Ibid.
50 Ibid.
51 Ibid, §131.
52 Independent agents under article 5(6) of the OECD MC.
53 HONGLER PETER/PISTONE PASQUALE, *Blueprints for a New PE Nexus to Tax Business Income in the Era of the Digital Economy, IBFD Working Paper*, 2015, p.15.
54 Ibid.

be finalised by the end of 2020. While an international consensus could not be reached at the time of writing, a new PE nexus linked on ('significant') digital presence has been intensively discussed. The latest document published by the OECD[55] implies that a standalone rule, on top of the existing PE rules, may be preferred to limit any unintended spill-over effect on the current allocation system of business profits.[56] The new rule is to have a nexus based on 'sustained and significant involvement in the economy of a market jurisdiction', which is likely to be defined by a revenue threshold adapted to the size of the market.[57] The new nexus is to be accompanied with its own specific allocation rules.[58]

Due to the lack of a swiftly available solution, some countries consider to implement unilateral measures, whereas some already have.[59] Such unilateral measures, which may reveal to be temporary when an international consensus is found, as well the new potential nexus on digital presence fall beyond the scope of this book, mainly due to their uncertain contours. The developments in the area remain to be seen.

2. *Independent personal services*

A. GENERAL ASPECTS

Taxation of independent personal services was regulated by a specific article of the OECD MC, namely article 14, until its removal in 2000.[60] Although deleted from the MC, article 14 is still present not only in a great number of DTTs but also in the UN MC.[61] Since the abrogation of article 14 of the OECD MC, independent personal services fall within the scope of article 7.[62] Even if these two distributive rules are similar to some extent,[63] their application may reach diverging results in practice. In cases where a service PE provision, as suggested by the OECD Commentary,[64] is present in a DTT, independent personal services that do not create a PE under article 5 as provided by the OECD MC, may be deemed to constitute a

55 Public consultation document, *Secretariat Proposal for a 'Unified Approach' under Pillar One*, 9 October 2019–12 November 2019.
56 Ibid, §22.
57 Ibid.
58 Ibid, §27.
59 For more information on unilateral measures, see, for example, SARFO NANA AMA, Finding Middle Ground over Unilateral Digital Taxation in *Bulletin for International Taxation*, Volume 72, Number 4a, 2018, published online.
60 Article 14 was removed by *The 2000 Update to the Model Tax Convention* adopted by the OECD Committee on Fiscal Affairs on 29 April 2000.
61 Article 14 of the UN MC.
62 On this point, see also article 3(1)(h) of the OECD MC, which states that 'the term "business" includes the performance of professional services and of other activities of an independent character'.
63 They were similar to a greater extent until the modification of article 7 by the *2010 Update to the OECD MC.*
64 *OECD Commentary* on article 5, §144. See also article 5(3)(b) of the UN MC.

PE and submitted to tax in the SS accordingly. Concepts of PE and business profits are examined in the previous sub-subsection (1). This sub-subsection concentrates on 'independent personal services' as regulated by article 14.

Under article 14 of the OECD MC, the income derived in respect of professional services or other activities of an independent character is taxable only in the RS of the service provider, unless a 'fixed base' situated in the SS is 'regularly available' to the provider concerned. Should such a 'fixed base' exist, the income attributable to that 'base' may be submitted to tax by the SS.[65] The principles laid down in article 7 – especially those relating to allocation of profits and treatment of expenses incurred – also apply in the context of article 14.[66] A list of examples[67] aiming to describe activities constituting professional services is to be found in paragraph 2 of the article. The list includes independent artistic or educational activities, as well as the independent activities of physicians, lawyers, engineers, architects, dentists and accountants.[68]

While it is generally admitted that the personal scope of application of article 14 is limited to individuals, some countries consider that the distributive rule also covers legal persons. It is not possible to indicate with precision whether legal persons fall within the scope of the article, since the OECD Commentary did not deal with this particular issue.[69] Although the UN Commentary clearly refers to individuals, this reference cannot be applied by analogy to the OECD MC, since the UN MC contains an additional clause based on the duration of the stay in its article 14(b).[70] This book opts for following the dominant view on the matter, i.e. it considers that the personal scope of application of article 14 is limited to individuals.

B. CONCEPT OF 'FIXED BASE'

The concept of 'fixed base' has never been defined by the OECD MC or the OECD Commentary. Quite the contrary, the authors of the Commentary indicated that 'it has not been thought appropriate' to attempt to define the term 'fixed base'.[71] This voluntary lack of definition was not compensated by means of a straightforward analogy with another similar concept (namely PE) either. In fact, while the OECD Commentary stated that the provisions of article 7 and the Commentary thereon could be used as guidance for interpreting and applying article 14,[72] such a parallel was not expressly drawn with article 5.[73] The

65 Deleted article 14(1) of the OECD MC.
66 *OECD Commentary* on article 14, §3 (deleted on 29 April 2000).
67 Ibid, §2.
68 Deleted article 14(2) of the OECD MC.
69 OECD, *Issues related to article 14*, §13.
70 *UN Commentary* on article 14, §9. See paragraph c of this sub-subsection for more details on the additional clause concerned.
71 HUSTON, p.283.
72 *OECD Commentary* on article 14, §3 (deleted on 29 April 2000).
73 On this point see also HUSTON, p.284.

Commentary merely contained an authoritative statement relating to the concept of fixed base ('centre of activity of a fixed or a permanent character'[74]) and gave three examples that constitute fixed bases, namely a physician's consulting room, the office of an architect and the office of a lawyer.[75]

It was argued in the literature that albeit being similar to a great extent to PE, fixed base was 'more relaxed'. This conclusion was drawn from two theoretical assumptions: (i) for a fixed base to be formed, it is not necessary for the service provider to conduct its business activities through the place concerned on 'a regular basis' (as it is the case for the purposes of PE); it suffices that the activities are undertaken at that base 'at certain intervals';[76] and (ii) a PE needs to be equipped for the business activities, whereas a fixed base does not (for instance, a hotel room may constitute a fixed base, but it cannot form a PE).[77] Despite these theoretical distinctions, concepts of PE and fixed base seem to be indistinguishable. As stated by the OECD, examples of fixed bases that do not constitute PEs, and vice versa, simply cannot be found in practice.[78] This can be illustrated by the fact that the 'fixed base' examples enumerated in the Commentary are also constitutive of PEs.[79] As a natural result of the quasi-identical character of the two concepts, most countries determine whether or not a fixed base is constituted by means of employing, *mutatis mutandis*, the principles used for the purpose of determining whether a PE exists.[80] It would, thus, seem that, as Huston put it, 'fixed base' does not constitute a distinct concept but merely a substitute for the term 'PE' in the context of independent personal services.[81]

The OECD's removal of article 14, without confirming or refuting that fixed base is indeed 'more relaxed' than PE, left the correct meaning of the term in doubt.[82] The UN Commentary, which mainly reproduces the former OECD Commentary on article 14, does not provide any further guidance either.[83] This lack of precision inevitably translated into room for interpretation.[84] Developing countries may opt for a more extensive interpretation of the term 'fixed base' in order to safeguard their ability to tax, while developed countries are likely to prefer a narrow approach, assimilating 'fixed base' to PE.[85] Given the blurry contours of the difference (if any) between fixed base and PE, this book opts for assimilating the concept of fixed base to the one of PE.

74 *OECD Commentary* on article 14, §3 (deleted on 29 April 2000).
75 Ibid, §2.
76 This argument is based on the French text of the *OECD Commentary*.
77 MICHAUX ERIC, An Analysis of the notion 'fixed base' and its relation to the notion 'permanent establishment' in the OECD model in *Intertax*, 1987/3, p.71.
78 OECD, *Issues related to article 14*, §28.
79 See also ibid; HUSTON, pp.283–284.
80 COULOMBE, p.54.
81 HUSTON, p.283.
82 See also HAN, p.204.
83 See *UN Commentary* on article 14.
84 See also HAN, p.204.
85 Ibid.

C. 183-DAY RULE

In addition to the fixed base rule,[86] the UN MC also provides for a 183-day rule.[87] As per this rule, even in the absence of a fixed base, the income derived by a person providing independent personal services from their activities exercised in the SS may still be taxed in that State, in cases where their stay in the SS amounts to a period, or periods, of 183 days in any 12-month period commencing or ending in the fiscal year concerned.[88] Such a clause is often contained in DTTs concluded by developing countries, which do not find it appropriate to restrict their taxing rights as much as it is suggested by the OECD MC.[89]

3. *Income from employment*

As per the general rule contained in article 15(1) of the OECD MC, the income of employees may be taxed in the State where the employment is exercised, i.e. the SS.[90] Paragraph 2 of article 15 provides for an exception – commonly referred to as the 183-day rule[91] – to this general rule. Accordingly, an employee shall be taxable only in their RS if the three following conditions are met: (i) the recipient, i.e. the employee, is present in the SS for a period or periods not exceeding in the aggregate 183 days in any 12-month period commencing or ending in the fiscal year concerned; (ii) the remuneration is paid by, or on behalf of, an employer that is not a resident of the SS; and (iii) the remuneration is not borne by a PE that the employer has in the SS.[92]

The 183-day period is determined in conformity with the 'days of physical presence' method.[93] As its name indicates, this method consists of establishing whether or not the individual is present in the SS.[94] Included in the calculation of the 183-day period are: part of a day, day of arrival, day of departure and all other days spent inside the State of activity (such as Saturdays and Sundays, national holidays, holidays before, during and after the activity, short breaks, days of sickness and death or sickness in the family).[95]

4. *Royalties*

A. CONCEPT OF 'ROYALTIES'

'Royalties' can be defined as rental payments received in consideration of the use or the right to use certain intellectual property and information. Article 12(2) of

86 Article 14(1)(a) of the UN MC.
87 Ibid, Article 14(1)(b).
88 Ibid.
89 See also COULOMBE, p.52.
90 Article 15(1) *in fine* of the OECD MC.
91 '*Clause du monteur*' in French.
92 Article 15(2) of the OECD MC.
93 *OECD Commentary* on article 15, §5.
94 Ibid.
95 Ibid. See also AUMAYR, pp.113–122.

the OECD MC delimits the contours of the term by providing a list, which is intended to be exhaustive, of the relevant intellectual properties and information types.[96] Before their deletion in 1992,[97] the definition given by the article also contained the words 'or for the use of, or the right to use, industrial, commercial or scientific equipment', which are still included in the UN MC.[98]

Income generated by the use of rights that are not mentioned in article 12 cannot be considered as royalties, regardless of their similarity to the rights that are enumerated in the article and their legal treatment under the domestic laws of the CSs.[99] It is, however, clear that the CSs may modify or expand the definition of royalties when they enter into a DTT. This is, in fact, often the case.[100] For example, some OECD countries extend the definition of royalties to include payments for transmissions by satellite, cable, optic fibre or similar technology.[101]

It must be underlined that whether the rights covered by the definition have been, or are required to be, registered in a public register is irrelevant for the purposes of article 12 of the OECD MC.[102] In the same vein, the fact that a trademark is or is not internationally protected is not pertinent for the application of the article concerned.[103]

While the term 'royalties' is not to be interpreted by means of the national laws of the CSs (since it is specifically defined in the OECD MC), the other terms contained in the definition of royalties, such as 'the use of', 'trademark' and 'design', should be interpreted in the light of the CSs' domestic laws.[104]

The payments, which are effectuated for the transfer of the full ownership of an element of property referred to in the royalties definition, cannot be considered as being effectuated in consideration 'for the use of, or the right to use' that property and cannot, therefore, represent a royalty.[105] In fact, where the ownership of rights has been alienated, the consideration cannot be for 'the use of the rights'.[106] Such payments are likely to constitute business profits under article 7 or capital gains within article 13.[107]

96 MALHERBE ET AL, §54.
97 By the report entitled *The Revision of the Model Convention adopted by the OECD Council on 23 July 1992.*
98 Article 12(3) of the UN MC.
99 MALHERBE ET AL, §54.
100 HOLMES, *International Tax Policy*, p.274. A number of countries made reservations on this point (*OECD Commentary* on article 12, §§38–47).
101 This is, for example, the case of the Hungary-India DTT (HOLMES, *International Tax Policy*, p.274).
102 *OECD Commentary* on article 12, §8.
103 MALHERBE ET AL, §53.
104 Article 3(2) of the OECD MC.
105 *OECD Commentary* on article 12, §8.2.
106 Ibid.
107 Ibid.

B. ALLOCATION OF THE TAXING RIGHTS

Article 12(1) of the OECD MC grants the exclusive right[108] to tax the royalties to the RS of the beneficial owner. A number of countries reserved the right to depart from this general rule and tax royalties at source.[109] Such a practice is, in fact, more in line with the UN MC. Article 12(2) of the UN MC allows the SS to impose a tax on the gross income of royalties up to a certain percentage, which is to be determined by the CSs. The main purpose of this variation is to favour the capital-importing SSs, particularly developing countries, for the economic development of which the importation of technology and other intangible property is vital.[110] It is interesting to note, however, that most of the OECD countries that made a reservation to the principle of exclusive taxation in the RS cannot be regarded as developing countries.[111]

SSs imposing a tax on royalties generally do so by a final non-resident withholding tax on the gross amount of the royalty obtained by the non-resident provider.[112] It is usually incumbent upon the user of the intangible property right, which is a resident of the SS, to withhold and pay the tax concerned to competent tax authorities.

In cases where the beneficial owner of the royalties carries on business in the SS by means of a PE, or a fixed base, and the right or property in respect of which the royalties are paid is effectively connected with the PE, or the fixed base, concerned, article 7 or article 14, respectively, takes precedence over the provisions of article 12.[113]

5. *Technical services fees*

A. CONCEPT OF 'TECHNICAL SERVICES FEES'

A non-negligible number of DTTs concluded by developing countries contain an additional income source, namely 'technical services fees', which is mentioned neither in the OECD MC nor in the OECD Commentary.[114] Despite the rather wide use of the concept, an international consensus on its definition was lacking for a long period of time.[115] Some countries considered that provision of 'brainwork' and technical services was already covered by the concept of 'royalties',[116] while some countries opted for a brief definition or, at least, an explicit mention of 'technical services fees' in their DTTs.[117]

108 The clause uses the term 'shall be taxable only'.
109 *OECD Commentary* on article 12, §§32–37.
110 HOLMES, *International Tax Policy*, pp.270–271.
111 Ibid, p.272.
112 Ibid, p.269.
113 Article 12(3) of the OECD MC.
114 The *OECD Commentary* does, however, refer to 'provision of services' and 'technical assistance' (*OECD Commentary* on article 12, §§11.1–11.6).
115 See VAN DER BRUGGEN, pp.42–43.
116 *UN Commentary* on article 12A, §5.
117 See VAN DER BRUGGEN, pp.42–43.

Regardless of the fact that most countries used the same term, its scope varied to a great extent from country to country.[118] In some countries, technical services referred to services that involve the application of specialist knowledge such as know-how and engineering expertise;[119] in some others they referred to services connected with the transfer of knowledge or expertise;[120] and, lastly, some countries opted for a wide approach and took the view that almost all of the services provided to the country's residents by non-resident providers could be categorised as technical services.[121] Such significant differences in interpretation inevitably gave rise to uncertainty.

To eliminate this ambiguity, at least to a certain extent, article 12A, entitled 'fees for technical services', was added to the UN MC in 2017.[122] Article 12A(3) defines the concept, in an exhaustive manner,[123] as '[...] any payment in consideration for any service of a managerial, technical or consultancy nature [...]'.[124] Excluded from the scope of the term are payments made: to an employee of the person making the payment; for teaching in/by an educational institution and by an individual for services for the personal use of an individual.[125]

The UN Commentary contributes in a significant manner to determining the contours of technical services covered by the article 12A. The Commentary indicates that the services must involve the application by the service provider of specialised knowledge, skill or expertise on behalf of a client or the transfer of knowledge, skill or expertise to the client[126] (other than a transfer of information covered by the definition of 'royalties'[127]).[128] This implies that services of a routine nature that do not involve the application of such specialised knowledge, skill or expertise cannot be considered as 'technical services'.[129] This interpretation seems to be in line with the view adopted by Indian courts, which indicated in a number of different decisions that a mere collection of a fee for use of a standard facility or equipment (which may have been developed by the enterprise commercialising its use), without any human intervention, does not amount to provision of technical services.[130] The UN

118 PICKERING, p.33.
119 Ibid.
120 Ibid.
121 This is, for example, the case in Brazil (ROCHA, p.158).
122 *UN Commentary* on article 12A, §1.
123 Ibid, §61.
124 It is interesting to note that an almost identical definition was already contained in bilateral treaties of India, Pakistan and Malaysia (VAN DER BRUGGEN, pp.42–43).
125 Article 12A(3) of the UN MC.
126 In the same vein, the *OECD Commentary* defines contracts for 'provision of services' in this context as contracts in which one of the parties undertakes the use of the customary skills of their calling to execute the work themself for the other party (*OECD Commentary* on article 12, §11.2).
127 For the difference between transfer of 'know-how' and 'technical services fees', see VAN DER BRUGGEN, pp.50–52 and *UN Commentary* on article 12A, §§85 and 100–103.
128 *UN Commentary* on article 12A, §62.
129 Ibid.
130 See MEHTA AMAR, Importance of Human Involvement for Income Characterization as Fees for Technical Services in *Asia-Pacific Tax Bulletin*, 2016, Volume 22, Number 2, published online.

Commentary completes its definition by describing the terms 'management', 'technical' and 'consultancy' and underlining that these three terms, which do not have precise meanings, may overlap.[131]

While the UN MC and its Commentary filled in a crucial gap and provided for the necessary international framework in the area of 'technical services fees', it remains to be seen whether the distinct approaches adopted and applied for a rather long period of time by some developing countries will remain intact or fade away and slowly merge into the mould offered by the UN.

B. ALLOCATION OF THE TAXING RIGHTS

Fees for technical services have traditionally been treated as passive income and given the same tax treatment as royalties.[132] This approach has been taken for allowing developing countries, which are disproportionately importing technical services, to submit to tax the income earned by non-resident enterprises providing substantial services to their residents, without constituting a PE or a fixed base. Although service PE and the UN Model's 'other income' article[133] provide for alternative ways to capture that income, not all treaties contain the clauses concerned and even when they do the income can still escape source taxation.

Instead of extending the definition of royalties to cover technical services fees or inserting a separate paragraph dedicated to such services in its article 12 governing royalties, the UN MC opted for adding a separate article.[134] This being stated, article 12A provides for an allocation of taxing rights that is similar to taxation of royalties, by granting the right to tax to both the RS and the SS and imposing a certain maximum percentage (to be determined by the CSs) to the tax that may be imposed by the SS.[135] Applying the same rate of withholding tax both to royalties and to technical services fees may be beneficial for the tax treatment of mixed contracts combining royalties and technical services fees as well as for ease of administration.[136] This approach is followed in practice by several countries, such as Brazil[137] and India.[138]

In cases where the beneficial owner of the fees for technical services carries on business in the SS by means of a PE, or a fixed base, and the fees are effectively connected with the PE, or the fixed base, concerned, article 7 or article 14, respectively, takes precedence over the provisions of article 12A.[139]

131 *UN Commentary* on article 12A, §§63–67.
132 PICKERING, p.47.
133 Article 21(3) of the UN MC.
134 In the author's opinion such a differentiation is justified for policy reasons. Also, article 12A contains additional clauses that are relevant for the purposes of taxation of technical services fees.
135 Article 12A(1) and (2) of the UN MC.
136 *UN Commentary* on article 12A, §§4 and 45.
137 ROCHA, p.159.
138 BHATTACHARYA SAURAV/SANGHAVI DHAVAL, Enterprise Services, India in *IFA Cahiers*, 2012, Volume 97a, p.355.
139 Article 12A(4) of the UN MC.

6. Income derived as an entertainer or a sportsperson

A. GENERAL ASPECTS

The OECD MC contains a specific distributive rule on income derived by 'entertainers and sportspersons' in its article 17. This sub-subsection analyses the personal (b) and the material (c) scopes of application of this allocation rule.

Before beginning the analysis, it must be underlined that article 17 has been severely criticised by many authors, especially for its lack of clarity, for causing an excessive tax burden and, in some cases, for resulting in a double taxation that cannot be eliminated by the application of DTTs.[140] All types of measures, from its abrogation[141] to an amendment of both its personal and material scopes of application,[142] have been suggested over the years. As various and as interesting as the suggestions made by the authors may be, the wording of article 17 remained largely unchanged. In 2010, the OECD launched a Discussion Draft on the application of article 17 in order to clarify some problematic issues by amending the OECD Commentary. The modifications were incorporated in the 2014 version of the Commentary. It must be noted that none of the drastic changes suggested in the literature has been implemented. Nevertheless, the new version of the Commentary clarified a number of controversial matters regarding the application of article 17.

Although a future amendment or the abrogation of article 17 cannot be excluded altogether, it is possible to argue that a substantial modification is not likely to materialise in the near future, as demonstrated by the outcome reached by the Discussion Draft. For this reason, this book does not examine the arguments made in favour of amending, replacing or deleting article 17. This being stated, some of the major problems caused by this allocation rule are briefly mentioned where relevant.

B. PERSONAL SCOPE OF APPLICATION

i. General aspects Albeit having some distinct features, the concepts of 'sportsperson' and 'entertainer' also have common characteristics, namely requirement of public performance, inclusion of amateurs and application to both independent and employed entertainers/sportspersons.

The scope of article 17 of the OECD MC is exclusively limited to entertainers and sportspersons who effectuate a public performance. This key requirement, which is not explicitly mentioned in the article, finds its roots in the English text[143] of the 1963 OECD MC, which referred to 'public entertainers'.[144] The word 'public' was omitted in the 1977 OECD MC on the grounds of being

140 See notably NITIKMAN, MOLENAAR,*Taxation of Artistes* and SANDLER, *Artistes and Sportsmen* on this point.
141 See for example NITIKMAN, p.247.
142 See for example SANDLER, *Artistes and Sportsmen*, pp.239–243.
143 The French text referred to '*professionnels du spectacle*'.
144 ZOUBEK, p.50.

unnecessary.[145] The deletion of the word implies that there was a general understanding on the application of the article to 'public performers' only. The terms 'athlete', 'sportsman' and 'sportsperson' have never been accompanied with the word 'public'. Nonetheless, it has been commonly understood that the requirement of 'public performance' extended to this second category of taxpayers as well.[146]

The term 'public performance' should be understood as including 'direct public performances', which implies performing physically in front of an audience as well as 'indirect public performances', which means appearing to the public through technical means, i.e. media.[147] Accordingly, sportspersons participating to sporting activities to which spectators are allowed and/or to sporting activities that are transmitted via media channels fall within the scope of article 17. On the other hand, sportspersons taking part in activities that do not involve a public performance, e.g. mountaineering with a private group, are outside the scope of the article concerned. In the same vein, 'creating artistes', such as sculptors and painters, are not covered by this distributive rule, unless they combine their artistic activity with a public performance and derive income from it.[148] For instance, revenue generated by a painter from the sale of one of their paintings does not fall within the scope of article 17, whereas, if the painter concerned carries out the act of painting itself in public and sells the painting at the end of the 'show', the income derived by the sale is covered by the article. Lastly, 'behind-the-scene individuals', such as cameramen, choreographers and technical staff, do not fall within the scope of article 17 of the OECD MC.[149]

To be categorised as an 'entertainer' or a 'sportsperson' under article 17 of the OECD MC, an individual does not necessarily have to act in a professional manner. As explicitly stated by the OECD Commentary since 2014,[150] '[t]he reference to an "entertainer or sportsperson" includes anyone who acts as such, even for a single event'.[151] For instance, within the scope of application of article 17 falls a person who takes part in sporting activities solely for leisure purposes and wins (a) monetary sports prize(s) and a person who gets remunerated for a 'once-in-a-lifetime' appearance in a television commercial.[152]

Article 17 covers both persons performing on an individual basis (e.g. tennis players) and those performing as a member of a group (e.g. football players and members of an orchestra). Before 2014, article 17 explicitly stated that it applied '[n]otwithstanding the provisions of Articles 7 and 15'.[153] In cases where the

145 Ibid.
146 SANDLER, *Problems taxing sportsmen*, p.203.
147 KREISL, p.142.
148 See also ibid, pp.144–146.
149 *OECD Commentary* on article 17, §3.
150 The scope of article 17 was not limited to professionals before 2014 either. For more information on this point, see ZOUBEK, p.45 and OBERSON, §90.
151 *OECD Commentary* on article 17, §9.1 (added to the Commentary in 2014).
152 Ibid.
153 Article 17(1) and (2) of the OECD MC.

applicable DTT contained a specific article on independent personal services (article 14), article 17 also superseded that provision. In 2014, the wording of article 17 was modified to expressly mention only the derogation to article 15.[154] Nonetheless, article 17 continues to constitute an exception to article 7 as well, as per the general rule contained in article 7(4)[155] and to the specific article on independent personal services (article 14).

This being stated, some countries may choose to exclude entertainers/sportspersons employed by a group from the scope of application of article 17. To this end, the words '[n]otwithstanding the provisions of Article 15' may be replaced with 'subject to the provisions of Article 15'.[156] Regarding sportspersons, this exclusion may also be limited to those employed by a team that participates in a multinational league. This is for example the case of the US-Canada DTT,[157] article XVI(3) of which reads as follows: '[t]he provisions of this Article shall not apply to the income of an athlete in respect of an employment with a team which participates in a league with regularly schedule games in both Contracting States'.[158]

In the absence of the specific distributive rule provided in article 17, entertainers/sportspersons performing on an individual basis would fall within the scope of either article 7 or article 14 depending on the applicable DTT, while entertainers/sportspersons competing as a group member would fall under article 15.

ii. Concept of 'sportsperson' To the extent known, the earliest version of a provision similar to article 17 was article XI(d) of the 1939 US-Sweden DTT, which referred to 'professional athletes'.[159] The first version of the OECD MC, which was published in 1963, opted for 'athletes', omitting thereby the term 'professional' employed in the US-Sweden DTT. In 1992, the term 'athlete' used in the OECD MC was replaced with 'sportsman'[160] in order to clarify the exact personal scope of application of article 17.[161] As a matter of fact, despite the relatively restricted meaning that the term 'athlete' may have,[162] the intention has always

154 Ibid, article 17(1) begins with the following words: '[n]otwithstanding the provisions of Article 15 [...]'.
155 *OECD Commentary* on article 17, §1.
156 Ibid, §2.
157 The Convention between the United States of America and Canada with respect to taxes on income and on capital, signed on 26 September 1980, as amended by the Protocol signed on 14 June 1983 and the Protocol signed on 28 March 1984.
158 Article XVI(3) of the DTT concerned. On this point, see also the provision suggested in the *OECD Commentary* on article 17, §14.1.
159 NITIKMAN, p.269.
160 The amendment was made by *The Revision of the Model Convention*, adopted by the OECD Council on 23 July 1992.
161 See also ZOUBEK, p.40.
162 Etymologically, the word '*athlêtês*', finding its roots in the Ancient Greece, means one who competes for a prize (JONES, p.114). Accordingly, it does not cover some sporting activities by excluding others. However, the current meaning of the word 'athlete' seems to be more limited. It is commonly understood that 'athletes' are persons who participate in 'athletics'.

been to cover 'sportsman' in the broad sense of the word.[163] Finally, in 2014, the term 'sportsman' was replaced by the term 'sportsperson' to attain sex neutrality.

The term 'sportsperson' is not defined in article 17. It is not defined in the OECD Commentary either, which provides, however, an explanation by asserting that the term is not restricted to participants in traditional athletic events (such as running, jumping and swimming) and that it also covers participants in other sports, such as football, golf, equestrianism, cricket, tennis and auto racing.[164] In the light of the observations contained in the OECD Commentary, the term 'sportsperson' can simply be defined as a person effectuating a public performance while taking part in a sporting activity.

Since sporting activity has not been defined in details by the OECD, the term should be given its ordinary meaning, which is described in chapter 1, section II. An individual 'taking part' in a sporting activity should be understood as a person effectively 'playing the game itself', i.e. a competitor. Other individuals playing a part in the course of the competition – such as coaches, referees and technical staff – cannot be considered as sportspersons. To effectuate a public performance, the person concerned must participate in a sporting activity that is specifically conducted in front of spectators (and not merely observed by passers-by) and/or that is transmitted via media channels. In the light of these explanations, it can be stated that competitors taking part in ISEs can clearly be categorised as 'sportspersons' for the purposes of article 17.

As per the OECD Commentary, article 17 is also applicable to '[...] income from other activities which are usually regarded as of an *entertainment character*, such as those deriving from billiards and snooker, chess and bridge tournaments'.[165] This statement encompasses two distinct types of activities: predominantly mental sporting activities and 'sportified' entertainment activities (such as eSports). Albeit the income derived by the participants of both types of activities is covered by article 17, the individuals concerned are not categorised as 'sportspersons' but as 'entertainers'. This distinct qualification does not, however, engender any legal and/or practical consequences.

It is important to note that sportspersons may also be categorised as 'entertainers' for the purposes article 17 in some cases.[166] The OECD Commentary gives the example of a former sportsperson who appears in a television commercial.[167] Another example would be an active sportsperson who did not qualify for the event, but who still takes part in it as a play-by-play commentator, i.e. a person who is in charge of narrating the actions of sportspersons throughout the encounter. Sportspersons who are considered as entertainers for the purposes of article 17 of the OECD MC are also taxed in accordance with this distributive rule.

163 *The 1987 Report*, §70. It is interesting to note that the OECD Committee on Fiscal Affairs used the terms 'athletes' and 'sportsmen' almost interchangeably, which would indicate that the borderline between these two terms is rather thin, and thereby they inherently overlap one another (ZOUBEK, p.39).

164 *OECD Commentary* on article 17, §5.

165 Ibid, §6 (emphasis added by the author).

166 Ibid, §3.

167 Ibid.

iii. Concept of 'entertainer' Prior to its modification in 2014, the title of article 17 of the OECD MC referred to 'artistes', whereas its text contained the term 'entertainers'. Given the fact that neither the OECD Commentary nor article 17 defined either of these terms,[168] the scopes of 'artiste' and 'entertainer' have been subject to controversy. Since 2014, the term 'artiste' has been removed from the title as well as from the Commentary of article 17. Accordingly, reference is exclusively made to 'entertainers' in the current[169] wording of the distributive rule concerned.

Although they were used as quasi-synonyms in the previous versions of the OECD MC and its Commentary, the terms 'entertainer' and 'artiste' must be distinguished. The word 'artiste' seems to refer to the term '*Hochkunst*' in German, which comprises more serious expressions of performing arts, such as classical dance, music, theatre and opera.[170] On the other hand, the word 'entertainer' seems to cover three different types of activities: (i) '*Hochkunst*'; (ii) activities that are referred to as '*Unterhaltungskunst*' in German, i.e. the lighter versions of performing arts;[171] and (iii) activities that are performed merely for providing someone with amusement or enjoyment,[172] i.e. without any artistic component. It is therefore possible to state that the scope of the term 'entertainer' is significantly larger than the scope of the term 'artiste'. As utterly clarified by the deletion of the term 'artiste' from both the OECD MC and the OECD Commentary, article 17 is intended to cover income earned by 'entertainers'.

For the purposes of the distributive rule concerned, the term 'entertainer' may be defined in the light of the following cumulative criteria: (i) the individual concerned makes a performance; (ii) the performance is public; (iii) the performance has as its primary aim to provide the audience with amusement or enjoyment;[173] and (iv) the individual themself is the direct or indirect reason for which the audience is listening or watching the performance.[174] To fulfil the fourth criterion,

168 Ibid, §3. Before 2014, the Commentary referred to 'artiste' instead of 'entertainer'.
169 2019.
170 MOLENAAR, *Taxation of Artistes*, p.69.
171 Ibid. MOLENAAR states that the term 'entertainer' seems to cover '*Unterhaltungskunst*'. The two other types of activities have been added by the author.
172 *The Oxford Dictionary* defines the term 'entertainment' as '[t]he action of providing or being provided with amusement or enjoyment' and alternatively as '[a]n event, performance or activity designed to entertain others' (https://www.lexico.com/en/definition/entertainment, accessed on 07.07.2019). The verb 'to entertain' is defined as '[p]rovide (someone) with amusement or enjoyment' (https://www.lexico.com/en/definition/entertain, accessed on 07.07.2019).
173 The first three criteria have been inspired by the definition of the term 'artiste' given by MOLENAAR, which reads as follows: '[…] there must be a performance; the performance is in public, i.e. directly before an audience or recorded and later reproduced for an audience; and the predominant element of the performance must be artistic and entertaining, but the level is irrelevant' (MOLENAAR, *Taxation of Artistes*, p.91).
174 This last criterion was suggested by MATIJEVIC following the Cheek decision (MATIJEVIC MILAN, The Notion of Artistes in Article 17 of the OECD Model Tax Convention in LOUKOTA WALTER/STEFANER MARKUS (eds), *Taxation of Artistes and Sportsmen in International Tax Law*, Linde Verlag, 2007, pp.30–33).

the individual must perform the entertaining activity themself. For example, in a dance performance, the individual should be one of the dancers. Clearly, a sportsperson who does not effectuate a sporting performance but who fulfils these criteria for the purposes of an activity will also be categorised as an 'entertainer'.

The suggested criteria seem to be in line with the reasoning of the OECD.[175] This can be illustrated by the application of the criteria concerned to play-by-play commentators.

Since 2014, the OECD Commentary expressly states that play-by-play commentators cannot be considered as entertainers under article 17, to the extent where they do not themselves participate to the public performance as an entertainer or a sportsperson.[176] A play-by-play commentator is: (i) an individual who makes a performance; (ii) the performance concerned is made in 'public' – indirectly via the media; and (iii) the performance has as its primary aim to provide the audience concerned with amusement or enjoyment. Nonetheless, the commentator themself is not the direct or indirect reason for which the audience is listening or watching the performance. As also stated in the Cheek decision, fans purchase tickets and attend the performance concerned to see the entertainers or the sportspersons perform.[177] They watch the performance on television or listen to it on the radio for the same reason.[178] A commentator as such is generally not the reason for which a sports fan turns on their television or radio,[179] whereas the entertainer or the sportsperson is.[180] Consequently, the fourth criterion is not fulfilled and, thereby, play-by-play commentators should not be considered as entertainers under article 17. The application of the four cumulative criteria thus reaches a characterisation that is in line with the OECD Commentary.

C. MATERIAL SCOPE OF APPLICATION OF ARTICLE 17

The income falling within the scope of application of article 17 has been described as: (i) having a 'close connection' with the public performance;[181] and (ii) being 'derived directly or indirectly' from a performance by an individual entertainer or sportsperson[182] by the OECD Commentary.

Some DTTs may limit the material scope of application of article 17. A frequently used limitation, which had already been contained in the US MC and was

175 The reasoning followed by the OECD on this matter cannot be precisely determined, as it is not explicitly stated in the *OECD Commentary* or in any other similar document.
176 *OECD Commentary* on article 17, §9.1.
177 The Cheek decision, §29.
178 Ibid.
179 Ibid, §39.
180 On the other hand, a talk show host fulfils the fourth criterion, along with the three others, since the host is the direct reason for which the audience is watching, or listening to, the performance.
181 *OECD Commentary* on article 17, §9.
182 Ibid, §8.

added to the OECD Commentary in 2014, is the *de minimis* exemption[183] (iii). An even more frequently used limitation is the exclusion of the income derived from events forming part of an official cultural exchange, charitable events or State-sponsored events from the scope of application of article 17 ('article 17(3)'[184]) (iv).[185]

i. Close connection According to the OECD Commentary, the income that has a 'close connection' with the public performance is covered by article 17.[186] Such a connection is deemed to exist where it cannot be reasonably considered that the income would have been derived in the absence of the public performance concerned.[187] The connection may be related to the timing of the income-generating event (e.g. a payment received for an interview given during the sports event) or to the nature of the service provided in consideration of the payment (e.g. a payment made to a tennis player for the use of their picture on posters advertising a tournament in which they will participate).[188]

Although royalties obtained in exchange for the use of – or the right to use – intellectual property rights will normally be covered by article 12, rather than article 17, the latter distributive rule applies to advertising and sponsorship income that has a close connection with the public performance provided by the entertainer/sportsperson.[189] This exception made for advertising and sponsorship income finds its roots in the 1987 Report. While it was recognised in the Report that application of article 17 to a contract concluded with a firm in one country for the exercise of activities throughout the world – which is generally the case of advertising and sponsoring contracts – would give rise to substantial administrative difficulties and risk of double taxation, income derived from advertising and sponsoring contracts was deemed to fall within the material scope of application of article 17.[190] This choice of policy was motivated by the fact that article 12 was 'rather restrictive' and a number of countries would not consider advertising and sponsoring fees as royalties.[191] The approach followed by the OECD has been subject to controversy in the tax law literature.[192]

183 Ibid, §10.1.
184 An additional paragraph that may be added to the DTT concluded between the CSs to that end is provided in *OECD Commentary* on article 17, §14.
185 Article 17(3) seems to be the most commonly used limitation (SANDLER, *Non-resident entertainers and athletes*, p.16).
186 *OECD Commentary* on article 17, §9. Before 2014, the *OECD Commentary* used the term 'direct link' instead of 'close connection'.
187 Ibid.
188 Ibid.
189 Ibid.
190 *The 1987 Report*, §§81–83
191 Ibid.
192 Before its modification in 2014, the *OECD Commentary* indicated that '[i]n general, other Articles would apply whenever there was no *direct* link between the income and a public exhibition by the performer in the country concerned' but 'Article 17 will apply to advertising or sponsorship income, etc. which is related *directly or indirectly* to performances or appearances in a given State' (emphasis added by the author)

ii. Derived directly or indirectly from a performance

ii.a. General aspects By income derived 'directly or indirectly' from a performance, the reference is made to the payment method. As stated by the OECD Commentary, in some cases the income will not be paid to the individual, or their impresario or agent, directly with respect to a specific performance.[193] For example, a sportsperson who is employed by a team is entitled to a salary that comprises remuneration paid for participation in a number of sports events. In such cases, where the income is derived in an 'indirect manner', the SS may tax an 'appropriate proportion' of it.[194]

Similarly, in cases where the payment related to performances accrues to a one-person company, or other similar devices, the SS may tax an appropriate proportion of any remuneration paid to the entertainer/sportsperson by that company.[195] To the extent where the domestic law of the SS allows to 'look-through' such entities and, thereby, to attribute the income directly to the entertainer/sportsperson, the SS may also tax the entirety of the income accruing to the company concerned from performances taking place in its territory under article 17(1) of the OECD MC.[196] These entities, commonly referred to as 'rent-a-star' companies, form the subject matter of article 17(2) and thereby necessitate a more detailed examination.

ii.b. Rent-a-star companies

ii.b.i. General aspects Taxation of income accruing to one-person companies has been the subject of controversy since the beginning of the 1970s due to cases of abuse. In fact, in the 1970s, some countries had reported to the OECD that top-earning entertainers and sportspersons had frequent recourse to the so-called 'rent-a-star' companies[197] to circumvent the application of article 17, which was – at that time – only comprised of the general rule provided in article 17(1) in its current wording.[198]

A 'rent-a-star' company can be defined as a service company personally owned by the entertainer or the sportsperson, usually with an aim to reduce the tax burden.[199] The mechanism put in place may be summarised as follows: (i) the entertainer/sportsperson sets up a company in a low-tax jurisdiction; (ii) the

(*OECD Commentary* on article 17, §9). The *OECD Commentary* was criticised for lack of coherence on this point (see, for example, OBERSON, §§114–115).

193 *OECD Commentary* on article 17, §8.

194 Ibid.

195 Ibid.

196 Ibid.

197 MOLENAAR/GRAMS, *Rent-A-Star*, p.501.

198 In the 1963 version of the OECD MC, article 17 read as follows: '[n]otwithstanding the provisions of Articles 14 and 15, income derived by public entertainers, such as theatre, motion picture, radio or television artistes, and musicians, and by athletes, from their personal activities as such may be taxed in the Contracting State in which these activities are exercised'.

199 JAU MARTIN, Star Companies in International Tax Law in LOUKOTA WALTER/STEFANER MARKUS (eds), *Taxation of Artistes and Sportsmen in International Tax Law*, Linde Verlag, 2007, p.249.

entertainer/sportsperson enters into an employment contract with the company concerned; (iii) contracts concluded in relation with the public performances are entered into between third parties and the company; (iv) the company receives the income deriving from public performances and attributes only a considerably small proportion of it to the entertainer/sportsperson; and (v) the company distributes its profits to the entertainer/sportsperson in the form of dividends.[200]

As stated by the Tax Court of Canada in its Sumner decision,[201] it is somewhat improbable that a company, the sole function of which is to handle an individual's public performances and which is committed to pay to the person concerned a large share – in the Sumner's case, 95 percent – of its profits, would be at arm's length with the individual concerned. Subsequently, the proportion of the income paid to the entertainer/sportsperson by the company usually does not correspond to the remuneration that the performer would normally be entitled to. As a result, by having recourse to a rent-a-star company, the entertainer/sportsperson significantly reduces their tax liability in the SS, thereby circumventing the application of article 17(1).

ii.b.ii. Article 17(2) of the OECD MC Under certain circumstances, it was possible to counteract abusive devices by means of the applicable DTT without a specific rule for rent-a-star companies.[202] In addition, some countries' domestic laws allowed to 'look-through' abusive structures, attributing thereby the income concerned to the person 'behind' the structure, i.e. the entertainer/sportsperson.[203] However, the legislation of many other countries was not as flexible as necessary to fight the tax avoidance schemes concerned.[204] To provide these countries with a viable international solution, article 17(2) was incorporated into the 1977 version of the OECD MC.[205]

The purpose of the newly-added provision was to counteract the tax avoidance schemes put in place by an entertainer/sportsperson.[206] Interestingly, however, its

200 Dividends can be defined as the formal distribution of retained earnings of a company to its shareholders (IBFD, *International Tax Glossary*, p.137).
201 The Sumner decision, §16.
202 See, for instance, the Johansson decision, in which employment of the article on the residence of the DTT (i.e. the equivalent of article 4 of the OECD MC) was sufficient to counteract the abusive scheme put in place by the taxpayer. The Johansson case, where a rent-a-star company was used, constitutes a typical example of treaty shopping by recourse to a nominee.
203 The 'look-through' approach is not developed in detail in this book. For more information on the approach concerned and its implications, see JUÁREZ ANGEL J., Limitations to the Cross-Border Taxation of Artistes and Sportsmen under the Look-Through Approach in Article 17(1) of the OECD Model Convention (Part I) in *European Taxation*, Volume 43, Number 11, 2003, p.409ff and Part II of the article in *European Taxation*, Volume 43, Number 12, 2003, p.457ff.
204 MOLENAAR/GRAMS, *Rent-A-Star*, p.501.
205 Which was adopted by the OECD Council on 11 April 1977.
206 *The 1987 Report*, §88.

wording[207] was much broader than necessary for this purpose.[208] In the 1987 Report, it was agreed that the broad wording of article 17(2) would be put in use by applying the provision not only to tax avoidance devices but also to all other cases, i.e. including non-abusive ones, where the income was received by a third party. To that end, it was decided that the provisions of article 17 would enable SSs to levy tax on: (i) amounts paid to entertainers and sportspersons through a separate entity, but accruing to them; as well as (ii) amounts allocated to an entity, but not paid to the entertainer/sportsperson.[209]

The 1987 Report was implemented in the 1992 OECD Commentary on article 17. Since that date, the OECD Commentary provides that not only rent-a-star companies[210] are subject to tax in the SS, in accordance with the provisions of article 17, but also management companies that receive income for the appearance of a group of entertainers/sportspersons – which are not constituted as legal entities themselves – and employers of entertainers/sportspersons (such as teams, troupes and orchestras), which are constituted as legal entities.[211]

The approach originally followed by the OECD, i.e. counteracting tax avoidance schemes, is commonly referred to as the 'limited approach', whereas the 'enlarged' approach adopted with the 1987 Report, is referred to as 'unlimited approach'. Canada, Switzerland and the US registered their observation on the unlimited approach,[212] by stating that they reserve the right to apply article 17(2) to abusive tax schemes only.[213]

It is important to underline that article 17(2) does not comprise third parties that do not derive income from personal activities of entertainers and sportspersons. For example, the prize money that the owner of a horse (or the team to which a racing car belongs) obtains from the results of the horse (or the racing car) during a race is not covered by article 17(2).[214] In fact, in such cases, the prize money is paid in consideration of the activities related to the ownership and training of the horse (or the design, construction, ownership and maintenance of the car) and not in consideration of personal activities of the jockey (or the

207 Article 17(2) read as follows in the 1977 OECD MC: '[w]here income in respect of personal activities exercised by an entertainer or an athlete in his capacity as such accrues not to the entertainer or athlete himself but to another person, that income may, notwithstanding the provisions of Articles 7, 14 and 15, be taxed in the Contracting State in which the activities of the entertainer or athlete are exercised'.

208 MOLENAAR/GRAMS, *Rent-A-Star*, p.501.

209 *The 1987 Report*, §89.

210 *OECD Commentary* on article 17, §11(c).

211 Ibid, §11(a) and (b).

212 Ibid, §16. 86 percent of the US DTTs, 54 percent of the Canadian DTTs and 45 percent of the Swiss DTTs contain an article 17(2) with a limited approach (MOLENAAR, *Taxation of Artistes*, p.123).

213 The unlimited approach has also been criticised by several authors. See for example MOLENAAR/GRAMS, *Rent-A-Star*, pp.507–509; SANDLER, *Problems taxing sportsmen*, pp.211–213.

214 *OECD Commentary* on article 17, §11.2.

driver).[215] In the same vein, article 17(2) does not cover the income of all enterprises that are involved in the production of entertainment or sports events.[216]

Last but not least, application of article 17(2) is not limited to cases where both the entertainer/sportsperson and the other person to whom/which the income accrues are residents of the same CS.[217] Subsequently, the fact that the third party receiving the payment is a resident of a third State (the so-called 'triangular situations') does not prevent the income from being taxed in the SS.[218]

ii.b.iii. Overview of the mechanism of article 17 of the OECD MC In the light of the developments made in this subparagraph, the mechanism of article 17 can be summarised as follows:

- Article 17 grants to the SS the right to tax at source the income derived by a non-resident entertainer/sportsperson from a public performance taking place in its territory.
- Article 17(1) enables the SS to tax the income in the hands of the entertainer/sportsperson in cases where: (i) the income accrues directly to the individual concerned; and (ii) the income accrues to a third party and the domestic law of the SS provides for a look-through approach.
- Article 17(2) enables the SS to tax the income in the hands of the third party, in cases where the income derived from the personal activities of the entertainer or the sportsperson accrues to the third party concerned.

The SS may either use one of the paragraphs or combine them to tax at source the income derived by the performer. This being stated, the income should not be taxed twice through the simultaneous application of the two paragraphs.[219] Such a situation may typically occur in cases where the performer's rent-a-star company is taxed in accordance with paragraph 2 on the payment it received with respect to activities performed by the entertainer/sportsperson in the SS and the remuneration paid by that company to the performer themself in relation to the activities concerned is taxed under paragraph 1.[220]

215 Ibid.
216 Ibid, §11.4.
217 Ibid, §11.1. This paragraph was added to the *OECD Commentary* in 2000. Before that date, whether article 17(2) was applicable in cases where the performer and the entity concerned were resident of different States was subject to controversy. For more information on this matter, see BETTEN RIJKELE/LOMBARDI MARCO, Article 17 (2) of the OECD Model in Triangular Situations, Does Article 17 (2) Apply if the Artiste or Sportsman is Resident in a Third State? in *Bulletin for International Fiscal Documentation*, Volume 51, Number 12, 1997, p.560ff.
218 *OECD Commentary* on article 17, §11.1.
219 Ibid, §11.5.
220 Ibid.

To avoid double taxation[221] of the income concerned, the SS should follow one of the following three approaches: (i) taxing exclusively the company in accordance with article 17(2); (ii) taxing only the performer in accordance with article 17(1); and (iii) taxing both persons exclusively on part of the income they receive, i.e. by taxing the income received by the company but allowing a deduction for the relevant part of the remuneration paid to the performer and taxing that part in the hands of the performer and vice versa.[222]

iii. De minimis exemption It has long been argued that a monetary threshold (a so-called '*de minimis* exemption') should be included in article 17 of the OECD MC,[223] which essentially targets a few 'top' entertainers and sportspersons who earn substantial sums of money in a very short period of time. Since the distribution of income is highly unequal in the entertainment and sports sectors and the greater proportion of entertainers/sportspersons earn modest amounts from their performances, the general opinion on the matter is that by including the income earned by all entertainers and sportspersons within the scope of article 17, 'the net is cast wider than it need be'.[224] This point of view was also expressed during Seminar E[225] of the 2010 IFA Congress,[226] where four panellists[227] out of seven claimed to be in favour of the inclusion of a *de minimis* clause in article 17.

The suggestion made by the scholars had, in fact, long been concretised by the US MC, which provides a *de minimis* clause since 1977.[228] The rationale of the clause is explained as follows in the Technical Explanation of the US MC:

> '[...] to distinguish between two groups of entertainers and athletes – those who are paid relatively large sums of money for very short periods of service, and who would, therefore, normally be exempt from host country tax under

221 The double taxation concerned is an 'economic double taxation', as different taxpayers, i.e. the company and the performer, are being imposed in two or more States in respect of the same subject matter for identical periods.
222 *OECD Commentary* on article 17, §11.5.
223 See for example, SANDLER, *Artistes and Sportsmen*, pp.239–243 and MOLENAAR, *Discussion of Daniel Sandler's Paper*, pp.249–250.
224 SANDLER, *Non-resident entertainers and athletes*, p.19.
225 The Seminar concerned was entitled '*Red Card 17?*'.
226 64th IFA Congress, Rome.
227 Namely: Andrew Dawson, Chair of WP1, UK; Marry Bennett and Jacques Sasseville OECD; and Xavier Oberson, University of Geneva, Switzerland.
228 The 1977 US MC included a 15,000 USD threshold in its article 17. The 1981 US MC would have increased the threshold to 20,000 USD, if it had been adopted. However, the Model was withdrawn in 1992 and a new US MC was introduced in 1996, with a 20,000 USD threshold. The amount of the threshold remained unchanged in the 2006 (current) version of the US MC (SANDLER, *Artistes and Sportsmen*, p.240, n.62).

> the standard personal services income rules, and those who earn relatively modest amounts and are, therefore, not easily distinguishable from those who earn other types of personal service income.'[229]

The OECD decided to following suit as of 2014. Since its 2014 version, the Commentary provides for an optional *de minimis* clause that suggests to exclude from the scope of article 17 all income inferior to 15,000 IMF SDR.[230] The amount refers to the gross amount earned during a taxation year.[231]

The OECD Commentary does not provide for a detailed explanation of the optional *de minimis* clause. However, it is possible to presume that the clause was intended to be similar to the one contained in the US MC. Since the text of the OECD provision indicates that the monetary threshold applies to the 'gross amount' of the income derived by the entertainer or the sportsperson,[232] it can be assumed that, like the *de minimis* clause of the US MC, the 15,000 IMF SDR includes expenses reimbursed by the individual or borne on their behalf.[233] Similarly, in cases where the gross amount of the income exceeds 15,000 IMF SDR, the full amount, not just the excess, may be taxed in the SS.[234]

Since it is often unclear until the end of the year whether the income of the entertainer/sportsperson derived in the SS will exceed the threshold or not, the SS may collect the tax at the time the relevant income is earned and refund it after the end of the year once it is established that the minimum amount has not been exceeded.[235] To counteract the splitting of the amount over several years with an aim to escape taxation in the SS, payments made in years prior or subsequent to the year in which the services are performed should be included when computing the threshold amount during the year concerned.[236]

To avoid administrative burdens that may result from an annual threshold, CSs may opt for per-day or per-event thresholds.[237] A per-day limitation is included in a number of US DTTs, either in addition to or in substitution of the

229 *Technical Explanation of the US MC*, pp.50–51.
230 *OECD Commentary* on article 17, §10.1. The *OECD Commentary* underlines that the amount referred to in the provision is purely illustrative (*OECD Commentary* on article 17, §10.2).
231 Ibid, §10.1.
232 *OECD Commentary* on article 17, §10.1.
233 *Technical Explanation of the US MC*, p.50. MOLENAAR argues that the clause 'expenses borne on behalf of the performer' is ambiguous. See MOLENAAR, *Taxation of Artistes*, pp.47–49 and BRINKMANN, p.358 on that point.
234 *Technical Explanation of the US MC*, p.50.
235 *OECD Commentary* on article 17, §10.3; *Technical Explanation of the US MC*, p.51.
236 BRINKMANN, pp.359–360. See also *Technical Explanation of the US MC*, p.52.
237 These two types of threshold are not mentioned in the *OECD Commentary*.

annual threshold.[238] For example, the Egypt[239] and Israel[240] DTTs both provide for a 400 USD daily threshold[241] and the Barbados DTT[242] provides for a limitation of 250 USD per day or 4,000 USD per year.[243] The per-event threshold has been suggested by Brinkmann.[244] Although such a limitation has not yet been used in practice as far as the author is aware, it has the merit of providing for a straightforward solution.

It must be noted that the *de minimis* rule is not applicable to the paragraph 2 of article 17.[245] If income accrued to a third party was also subject to a monetary threshold, a fragmentation of contracts among several entities in order to avoid taxation in the SS would have been encouraged.[246] For the purposes of this book, it is assumed that the income derived by entertainers/sportspersons taking part in an ISE exceeds the monetary threshold, if any, provided by the applicable DTT. *De minimis* clauses are, thereupon, not analysed further.

iv. Events sponsored by public means This limitation is examined in this paragraph since the OECD Commentary refers to 'events supported from public funds'.[247] Nevertheless, the limitation concerns not only the material but also the personal scope of application of article 17.

Public support constitutes an important method of financing both in the sports and in the entertainment industries. While policies put in place to that end vary to a great extent from country to country, it can be observed that the majority of countries subsidise, either entirely or to a certain extent, a number of entertainers/sportspersons.

As a general rule, article 17 of the OECD MC applies to entertainers and sportspersons who are employed by a government and who derive income from the government concerned.[248] Article 17 thus constitutes an exception to the general rule provided in article 19 on this point.[249] Article 17 covers entertainers/

238 BETTEN RIJKELE (ed), United States in *The International Guide to the Taxation of Sportsmen and Sportswomen*, NOLOT BV, 2004, p.51.
239 Convention between the Government of the United States of America and the Government of the Arab Republic of Egypt for the avoidance of double taxation and the prevention of fiscal evasion with respect to taxes on income, signed on 24 August 1980.
240 Convention between the Government of the United States of America and the Government of the State of Israel with respect to taxes on income, signed on 20 November 1975.
241 Article 17 of the US-Egypt DTT, op. cit. n.239 and article 18 of the US-Israel DTT, op. cit. n.240.
242 Convention between the United States of America and Barbados for the avoidance of double taxation and the prevention of fiscal evasion with respect to taxes on income, signed on 31 December 1984.
243 Ibid, article 17(1).
244 BRINKMANN, pp.362–363.
245 *OECD Commentary* on article 17, §10.4.
246 Ibid.
247 Ibid, §14.
248 Ibid, §13.
249 Article 19(3) of the OECD MC.

sportspersons who are subsidised by their governments as well. It cannot be stated that article 17 supersedes article 19 on this matter, since the personal scope of application of the latter article is limited to State employees and persons deriving income from past employment by a State[250] – which is not the case of a sportsperson/entertainer entitled to subsidies.

For States preferring to exclude events sponsored by public funds from the scope of application of article 17, the OECD Commentary suggests an additional paragraph, commonly referred to as article 17(3), which reads as follows:

> [t]he provisions of paragraphs 1 and 2 shall not apply to income derived from activities performed in a Contracting State by entertainers or sportspersons if the visit to that State is *wholly or mainly supported by public funds* of one or both of the Contracting States or political subdivisions or local authorities thereof. In such a case, the income is taxable only in the Contracting State in which the entertainer or the sportsperson is a resident.[251]

This exception aims to avoid the cutback of the subsidy granted by the RS, and thereby the need to increase the amount of the subsidy concerned, due to the taxes levied by the SS. Article 17(3) is probably the most frequently used limitation on the application of article 17 of the OECD MC.[252] It is in fact included in the majority (approximately 66 percent) of DTTs.[253] Article 17(3) also constitutes a standard addition to the Nordic Multilateral Income Tax Treaty, the Intra-ASEAN Model Double Taxation Agreement[254] and the CARICOM Agreement.[255,256]

The wording and the scope of article 17(3) may differ from DTT to DTT on several points. First, while some DTTs explicitly grant an exclusive taxing right to the RS, other DTTs provide that paragraphs 1 and 2 of article 17 do not apply.[257] The outcome of both dispositions are, however, the same in most cases, since articles 7 and 15, which become applicable when article 17 does not apply, usually allocate the taxing right to the RS as well.[258] Second, while some DTTs use the words 'wholly or mainly' supported by public funds, other DTTs refer to 'substantially' financed by public funds.[259] It is unfortunately not possible to indicate a

250 *OECD Commentary* on article 19, §2.1.
251 *OECD Commentary* on article 17, §14 (emphasis added by the author).
252 SANDLER, *Non-resident entertainers and athletes*, p.16.
253 MOLENAAR/GRAMS, *Article 17(3)*, p.272.
254 The 1987 Intra-ASEAN Model Double Tax Convention for members of the Association of South East Asian Nations.
255 Agreement among the Governments of the Member States of the Caribbean Community for the avoidance of double taxation and the prevention of fiscal evasion with respect to taxes on income, profits or gains and capital gains and for the encouragement of regional trade and investment.
256 Article 18(3) of the CARICOM Agreement contains a provision that is more detailed than article 17(3) of the OECD MC.
257 PRACHT, p.344.
258 Ibid, p.345.
259 MOLENAAR/GRAMS, *Article 17(3)*, p.274.

generally accepted percentage of funding for the provision to apply. The practices of countries vary to a great extent on this point. For example, Belgium and Netherlands agreed in a commentary to their 2001 DTT that the word 'mainly' should be interpreted as 30 percent of total earnings.[260] On the other hand, Germany considers that the subsidy provided by the RS should amount to at least one-third of the costs for the provision to apply.[261] Third, some DTTs may determine the scope of application of the provision with different terms such as 'cultural exchange', 'cultural cooperation' and 'cultural and sports exchange'.[262] These terms should be avoided as much as possible, since they may easily result in obscurity as to which activities are exactly covered by the provision.[263] Fourth, some DTTs do not refer to 'the visit' to the SS but to the public funding of 'the stay' or of 'the performance/activity' in the SS.[264] Nevertheless, the divergence between the terms concerned does not seem to have a practical implication, as the visit/stay is usually made for providing a performance/activity in the SS.[265] Fifth, although in the majority of DTTs the exemption applies exclusively in cases of subsidies granted by the RS or political subdivisions or local authorities thereof, some DTTs also include funding provided by charitable organisations recognised as such in the RS.[266, 267]

Even if the wording of article 17(3) seems to imply a direct link between the visit and the public funding, subsidies having an indirect link with the performance concerned should also be included within the scope of the provision.[268] This would for example be the case of a government-subsidised theatre troupe, which makes a performance in a State other than its RS.[269]

It can be concluded that entertainers/sportspersons subsidised by their governments may benefit from the exemption provided by article 17(3). The modalities of the exemption, and whether such an exemption exists at all, depend largely on the applicable DTT and the practices of the CSs on the matter. For the purposes of the analysis conducted in this book, it is assumed that entertainers/sportspersons deriving income from ISEs do not benefit from a provision similar to article 17(3). It is, however, important to underline that sportspersons participating in ISEs may benefit from the exemption concerned, whereas entertainers performing during ISEs, such as singers and dancers, are not likely to be subsidised by their government(s), and thereby to benefit from the exemption.

260 Ibid.
261 Ibid.
262 Ibid.
263 *The 1987 Report*, §98.
264 PRACHT, p.345.
265 Ibid.
266 Extending the exemptions to sportspersons financially supported by charitable organisations is especially important for countries such as the US where direct funding to promote athletes' careers is not provided by the government or other State authorities but by charitable organisations. On this point, see also chapter 4.
267 PRACHT, p.346.
268 HAHN-JOECKS GABRIELE, *Zur Problematik der Besteuerung ausländischer Künstler und Sportler*, Nomos Verlag, 1999, p.168.
269 Ibid, p.169.

7. Income from immovable property

As per the general rule contained in article 6(1) of the OECD MC, the income derived from immovable property may be submitted to tax in the country where the property concerned is situated, i.e. the *situs* of the property. Article 6 exclusively applies to income that a resident of a CS derives from immovable property situated in the other CS.[270] Not encompassed by this distributive rule is property situated in the CS of which the recipient is a resident or in a third State.[271] It is also to be noted that the provision does not limit the taxing right of the recipient's RS.

The scope of the term 'immovable property' is to be defined in accordance with the domestic law of the SS.[272] Nonetheless, article 6(2) of the OECD MC provides a list of assets and rights that always need to be considered as immovable property, such as rights to which the provisions of a general law relating to landed property apply. Although the interpretation of the term may cause some issues in practice,[273] the properties examined in this book, such as a sports venue, do generally not cause any specific qualification problems.

For article 6 to be applicable, the recipient does not need to be the owner of the property. A legal right to use the immovable property suffice. Also, the article covers not only income derived from direct use (e.g. renting the venue) but also from 'use in any other form of immovable property'.[274] Furthermore, the scope of the distributive rule is not limited to privately held immovable rights and assets; it extends to income from immovable property of industrial, commercial and other enterprises.[275] Regarding this last point, it is important to underline that the *situs* of the immovable property principle – article 6 – takes precedence over the PE principle – article 7.[276] However, in cases where a business entrepreneur derives income from immovable property under article 6(1), they/it will still have to observe the rules of article 7 with regard to the same items of income where the latter article contains a rule but the former article remains silent.[277]

III. VAT

A. Introduction

VAT is 'a modern tax phenomenon' that became common only since the 1970s.[278] It has, however, spread rapidly across the globe and is now imposed by all OECD countries (with the notable exception of the US) as well as by a

270 *OECD Commentary* on article 6, §1.
271 Ibid.
272 Article 6(2) of the OECD MC.
273 See FALTIN, §§53–54 on this point.
274 Article 6(3) of the OECD MC.
275 Ibid, article 6(4); *OECD Commentary* on article 6, §3.
276 Articles 6(4) and 7(4) of the OECD MC. See also, REIMER, p.3.
277 REIMER, p.4; article 6(4) of the OECD MC.
278 THURONYI/BROOKS/KOLOZS, p.275.

majority of developing countries.[279] A number of terms are used to refer to the tax concerned by various countries, the most common of such denominations being 'Goods and Services Tax' (GST). Throughout the book the reference is made to 'VAT', since that is the term used in Europe.

This section indicates the chosen VAT Model for the purposes of the analysis and clarifies the rationale behind this choice (B), explains the general methodology that needs to be applied for the purposes of a VAT analysis (C), describes the concept of 'sport' from a VAT perspective (D), examines the modalities of place-of-supply rules, which form the core matter of the VAT analysis conducted in chapters 3 and 4 (E) and, finally, elucidates VAT registration of non-resident suppliers and reverse-charge mechanism (F).

B. Chosen VAT model for the purposes of the analysis

There does not exist a model treaty as precise and widespread as the OECD MC in the area of indirect taxes. This being stated, the OECD published a document entitled 'The International VAT/GST Guidelines' that describes the internationally agreed principles and standards for the VAT treatment of the most common types of international transactions. The main purpose of the Guidelines is to minimise inconsistencies in the application of VAT in a cross-border context.[280] Since the Guidelines are not formulated as a model legislation, they cannot constitute the sole legal basis of a detailed VAT analysis. For this reason, a VAT legislation needed to be chosen to serve as a model for the purposes of the analysis conducted in this book.

Albeit containing some differences, VAT laws are remarkably similar, especially when compared to income tax laws.[281] The EU legislation plays a key role in this similarity. Although each MS has its own VAT law, the main features of VAT are harmonised by means of the VAT Directive that provides a uniform legal framework, while allowing variations from MS to MS. The impact of the EU VAT legislation has not been limited to MSs, it also served as a basis for the VAT laws of a great majority of the OECD countries.[282] Given both its broader geographical reach when compared to other VAT laws and its significant international impact, the VAT Directive was chosen as the main model to be used throughout the book. Specificities relating to intra-community transactions are left out for the ease of analysis.

C. General methodology

A four-step methodology is traditionally followed for VAT purposes. The four sequential steps are: (i) determining whether there is a taxable transaction; (ii) establishing whether the transaction is localised within the jurisdiction of the

279 Ibid.
280 *International VAT/GST Guidelines*, Foreword.
281 THURONYI/BROOKS/KOLOZS, p.281.
282 Ibid, p.282.

relevant country; (iii) checking whether the transaction is tax-exempt; and (iv) verifying that the taxable transaction is made by a taxable person acting as such.

Taxable transaction: VAT is a tax levied on, and by means of, transactions. Taxable transactions for VAT purposes are supply of goods and services. Supply of goods is typically defined as the transfer of the ownership of tangible properties. Supply of services is generally defined in a broader manner, like 'any transaction which does not constitute a supply of goods'.[283]

While each transaction should normally be regarded as distinct and independent, transactions comprising a bundle of features and acts may form, under certain circumstances, a 'complex single supply' (or a 'single composite transaction').[284] To determine whether such a complex supply exists, the essential features of the transaction must be ascertained in order to establish whether the taxable person is supplying the customers[285] with several distinct principal services or with a single service.[286] Where two or more elements or acts supplied by the taxable person to the customers are so closely linked that they form, objectively, a single, indivisible economic supply, which can only be artificially split, the existence of a single composite transaction needs to be admitted.[287] The fact that, in other circumstances, the elements concerned can be supplied separately is inherent to the concept of a 'single composite transaction', and thereby irrelevant.[288]

A complex single supply consists of a bundle of principal and ancillary supplies. The latter type of supply can be defined as a supply that does not constitute an aim in itself for customers but a means of better enjoying the principal supply.[289] The tax treatment of the single composite transaction is determined by its principal supplies. In other words, ancillary supplies share the tax treatment of the principal supplies.[290]

Location of taxable supplies: VAT is imposed on taxable supplies made in the taxing country.[291] Thus, determination of the place where the supply occurs (location) is crucial for taxation purposes. Such place is identified by means of the 'place-of-supply rules', which aim to establish a single place of supply for each transaction in an unambiguous manner. Regarding cross-border transactions, place-of-supply rules are comparable to the distributive rules of the OECD MC. They allow to effectuate the allocation of the taxing rights between jurisdictions.

283 Article 24 of the VAT Directive.
284 The Field Fischer decision, §14; the CPP decision, §§28–29.
285 It is important to remind that the term 'customer' should be differentiated from the term 'consumer'. While 'consumer' is used to refer to persons who acquire goods and/or services for personal consumption (i.e. not for the purposes of a professional activity), 'customer' includes all recipients of a good or service (i.e. businesses and end-users).
286 The CPP decision, §29.
287 The Purple Parking decision, §29.
288 Ibid, §31.
289 The CPP decision, §30.
290 Ibid.
291 Under the territorial VAT system, which is the predominant system used throughout the world, including Europe. A few countries opt for a 'worldwide VAT system', which uses the criterion of residence of the supplier as an initial nexus.

Since the place-of-supply rules are domestic rules, they do not seek to eliminate international double taxation per se. In case of conflict between the relevant countries' rules and/or their interpretation, a double taxation may arise. This being stated, since the VAT legislations are similar to a certain extent, there is rather limited room for international double taxation to occur.

Exemptions: It must be checked whether the transaction under analysis is tax-exempt under the applicable VAT legislation.

Taxable person acting as such: To be taxable, the transaction must be effectuated by a taxable person acting as such. A taxable person may be defined as any person who, independently, carries out an economic activity, regardless of the purpose or the effective outcome of the activity concerned.[292] As also clarified in the definition, both natural persons and legal persons may be considered as taxable persons to the extent where they carry out an economic activity on an independent basis, i.e. employees are not taxable persons. Some small enterprises with an annual turnover not exceeding a certain threshold, commonly referred to as 'registration threshold', may be tax-exempt.[293] It is important to note that taxable persons are registered for VAT purposes.

For the transaction to be submitted to VAT, the taxable person must act 'as such', which implies that the transaction must be linked to their/its economic activity. While a consideration will typically exist in such cases, it is not mandatory. For instance, withdrawing items from a company for personal use (most typically by the majority shareholder) and providing some benefits to employees for free also constitute taxable transactions. Transactions effectuated by taxable persons for private purposes (like sale of personal belongings) are, on the other hand, not subject to tax.

Given the fact that the collection of the VAT is ensured by businesses at each stage of production and distribution, taxable persons pay VAT in respect of goods and services acquired for the purpose of their businesses. The VAT paid by taxable persons under such circumstances, referred to as 'input VAT', can, however, be deducted fully or to a certain extent depending on the specificities of the transactions concerned. Generally, the input VAT is credited against the output VAT charged on the sales effectuated by the taxable person and the outstanding amount is remitted to the tax authorities.

For the purposes of the VAT analysis conducted in this book, it is assumed that all persons deriving an income from ISEs are taxable persons (with the notable exception of employees, which cannot be considered as such). Exemptions are only developed to the extent relevant due to the characteristics of the transactions under examination. Since the book exclusively concentrates on cross-border transactions, the main focus is on the place-of-supply rules.

D. Concept of 'sport'

This subsection describes the concept of sport in a VAT context, to identify which activities may be considered as such. Neither the VAT Directive nor its drafting

292 Article 9 of the VAT Directive.
293 See, for example, article 287 of the VAT Directive.

history provides for a definition of the term 'sport'.[294] There does not exist an EU-wide all-encompassing definition of the term which would apply throughout the Union for every act of primary and secondary law either.[295] What should be understood by the term 'sport' for VAT purposes has been elucidated by the CJEU to a great extent. The key decisions rendered by the Court in this area relate to the exemption provided for the supply of services closely linked to sport or physical education by non-profit making organisations provided in article 132 (1)(m) of the Directive. Thus, the principal characteristics of 'sport' mentioned by the Court also take into consideration the rationale behind the exemption concerned, which is to promote participation in sporting and physical education activities, as well as the need for a strict interpretation of exemptions. Nonetheless, the approach followed by the Court in the decisions concerned shed some light to the concept of sport that is to be adopted for VAT purposes.

Exemptions provided in article 132 of the VAT Directive are autonomous concepts of EU law, which should be interpreted in a harmonious manner throughout the Union, i.e. without any reference to domestic laws of the MSs.[296] This being stated, the term 'sport' does not have a universally accepted meaning across EU law.[297] The meaning and the scope of the terms for which EU Law provides no definition must be determined by reference to their usual meaning in everyday language and in the light of the context they are used and the purposes of the rules which they are part.[298] It is important to note that while Advocate General Szpunar underlined that SGBs' interpretation of 'sport' should be relevant in delineating the contours of the term,[299] the CJEU has not, so far, made reference to the SGBs' approach while defining the concept.

In everyday language, the term 'sport' is used to refer to an activity characterised by a not negligible physical element.[300] The CJEU uses this criterion as the key requirement for an activity to be categorised as 'sport'. This implies that the activities that involve a predominant mental effort, such as bridge and chess, do not fall within the concept of 'sport' for VAT purposes, since they lack a significant physical effort.

The CJEU underlined a few other points in relation to the term 'sport' contained in article 132 of the VAT Directive. First, while sporting activities are beneficial for the mental and the physical health of regular participants; activities of pure rest and relaxation do not constitute sporting activities solely on the basis that they are beneficial for mental and physical health.[301] Second, non-organised and unsystematic sporting activities which are not aimed at participation in sports competitions, i.e. which do not involve any competition, may also be characterised as taking part in 'sport'.[302]

294 The English Bridge Union decision, Opinion of Advocate General Szpunar, §29.
295 Ibid, §22.
296 The English Bridge Union decision, §17; the Žamberk decision, §17.
297 The English Bridge Union decision, Opinion of Advocate General Szpunar, §35.
298 The English Bridge Union decision, §18.
299 The English Bridge Union decision, Opinion of Advocate General Szpunar, §39.
300 The English Bridge Union decision, §§19, 22 and 27.
301 The English Bridge Union decision, §24; the Žamberk decision, §22.
302 The English Bridge Union decision, §25; the Žamberk decision, §22.

It can be concluded that activities involving a significant physical effort that are beneficial for the mental and physical health of regular participants can be categorised as sporting activities for VAT purposes, regardless of their competitiveness and level of professionalism.

It must, however, be born in mind that this definition was given for the purposes of the interpretation of the scope of an exemption. To be taxable, a transaction needs to be effectuated by a taxable person acting as such, which implies the existence of a sustainable economic activity.

E. Place-of-supply rules

1. Generalities

Place-of-supply rules are enacted in accordance with the destination principle or the origin principle. Under the destination principle, tax is levied only on the final consumption in the jurisdiction of consumption. Under the origin principle, on the other hand, tax is levied in the various jurisdictions where the value was added.[303] The OECD underlines that VAT being a tax on consumption, it would be more appropriate for the tax revenue to accrue to the jurisdiction where the final consumption occurs.[304] There also exists a widespread consensus on the general assumption that the destination principle is preferable to the origin principle from both a theoretical and a practical standpoint.[305] Accordingly, most of the rules in force are intended to tax supplies of goods and services within the jurisdiction where the consumption takes place.[306]

Taxable VAT transactions consist of two general categories, namely supply of goods and supply of services (including intangibles). It is important to emphasise that delivery of digitised products may be considered as supply of goods or services depending on the method of delivery. Supply of digitised products delivered over the internet or an electronic network is usually considered as forming a supply of service (more precisely 'e-services' or 'electronically supplied services'), while supply of digitised products by means of tangibles (such as CD-ROMs and DVDs) is deemed to constitute a supply of goods. Due to their intrinsic characteristics, the place-of-supply rules relating to supply of goods and those applicable to supply of services are examined separately.

2. Supply of goods

Existence of border controls and fiscal frontiers allow the destination principle to be implemented rather effortlessly with respect to supply of goods.[307] Three

303 *International VAT/GST Guidelines*, §1.8.
304 Ibid, §1.10.
305 Ibid, §1.11.
306 Ibid, §1.12.
307 Ibid, §1.13.

general place-of-supply rules exist in relation to goods: (i) the goods are submitted to tax at the place where they are located at the time of their delivery; (ii) the exported goods are free of VAT in the supplier's jurisdiction; and (iii) the imported goods are subject to the same VAT as equivalent domestic goods in the purchaser's jurisdiction.[308]

3. Supply of services and intangibles

Place-of-supply rules regarding supply of services and intangibles allocate the taxing right on the basis of two main factors: customer status and customer location.

A. CUSTOMER STATUS

VAT rules typically establish a distinction between B2B and B2C transactions, hence the necessity to properly qualify the customer status, i.e. 'business' or 'not a business'. Such qualification may derive from rules specifically enacted for VAT purposes or from other provisions of the national law, notably in jurisdictions that have not implemented a VAT.[309] Countries generally set specific rules and provide clear guidance to enable the suppliers to correctly establish the status of their customer. VAT registration numbers and business tax identification numbers are examples of indicia demonstrating the 'business' status of the customer.[310] Under the European system, the predominant decisive criterion is the VAT identification number.[311]

B. CUSTOMER LOCATION

The destination principle also applies for the purposes of supply of services, despite its rather complex implementation given the impossibility of effectuating a border control similar to the supply of goods.[312] To ensure a taxation according to the rules of the jurisdiction of consumption, VAT rules typically aim to identify the actual place of business use for B2B transactions and the actual place of final consumption for B2C transactions.[313] Albeit being ideal, such identification may not be feasible due to the fact that the VAT is charged before the actual business use or consumption.[314] For this reason, VAT laws generally opt for using proxies in view of determining the place of taxation of supplies of services and intangibles for both B2B and B2C transactions.[315]

308 Ibid.
309 Ibid, §3.7.
310 Ibid, §3.8.
311 See article 18 of the Implementing Regulation 282/2011/EU.
312 *International VAT/GST Guidelines*, §3.3.
313 Ibid, §3.6.
314 Ibid.
315 Ibid.

i. B2B transactions Place-of-supply rules of B2B transactions usually consist of one general rule and a detailed set of specific exceptions. For instance, under the European system, the general rule is provided by article 44 of the VAT Directive, while the exceptions are enumerated in articles 46–59a of the Directive.

i.a. General rule The jurisdiction of the customer's (services' recipient) location is considered to stand as the appropriate proxy to establish the actual place of business use.[316]

Under the European system, the customer's location is primarily determined by means of its business' PoE.[317] The PoE is defined as the place where the functions of the business' central administration are carried out.[318] Are relevant to determine the PoE, the location where the essential decisions concerning the general management of the business are taken, the place where the registered office of the business is located and the place where management meets.[319]

In cases where the services are provided to an FE of the customer located in a place other than its business' PoE, the place of supply is considered to be the place where the FE is located.[320] Albeit appearing to have similar traits to, and giving rise to similar discussions with, the concept of PE,[321] FE is a separate term that needs to be defined and interpreted independently. In fact, as it has already been underlined by the CJEU, the OECD MC, as well as the OECD Commentary, are irrelevant for the purposes of FE's interpretation, since they concern direct taxes whereas VAT is an indirect tax.[322]

FE is defined in the Implementing Regulation as any establishment, other than the PoE, characterised by a sufficient degree of permanence and a suitable structure in terms of human and technical resources to enable it to receive and use the services supplied to it for its own needs or to provide the services which it supplies.[323] This definition leaves the MSs room for their own interpretation, especially with regards to the 'suitability' of the structure in terms of human and technical resources and the 'sufficient' degree of permanence.[324] Since the Implementing Regulation's FE definition has been directly inspired by the CJEU's case-law,[325] the Court's interpretation of the term needs to be taken into consideration when delineating its contours.[326]

316 Ibid, guideline 3.2.
317 Article 44 of the VAT Directive.
318 Article 10(1) of the Implementing Regulation 282/2011/EU.
319 Ibid, article 10(2).
320 Article 44 of the VAT Directive.
321 In the French language, the term '*établissement stable*' is used to cover both FE and PE.
322 The FCE Bank decision, §39.
323 Article 11 of the Implementing Regulation 282/2011/EU.
324 KERN, p.221.
325 The Welmory decision, §58.
326 On this point, see, most notably, the Berkholz decision, the Faaborg-Gelting Linien decision, the Planzer Luxembourg decision and the Welmory decision.

The exact scope of the concept of FE is far from being clear for the moment being. Only a small percentage of national court cases are referred to the CJEU, which renders its decisions on the basis of the factual circumstances of each case, taking also into consideration other relevant issues such as competition law and abusive practices.[327] In the absence of clearly established guidelines, MSs may also opt for diverging interpretations of the term. Accordingly, it is extremely difficult to establish with a reasonable level of certainty whether enterprises deriving income from an ISE may constitute an FE in the HS, or in another State, without examining the exact factual circumstances under which the enterprises concerned are rendering their services.

It is important to emphasise that the short duration of an ISE is not sufficient to exclude the formation of an FE in the HS per se. For instance, the Austrian Federal Ministry of Finance held that a foreign company, which serves foods and beverages on the occasion of a festival lasting only for a few days, constitutes an FE in Austria.[328] In fact, 'degree of permanence' is yet to be interpreted by the CJEU. In the absence of a guidance on the matter, the time threshold necessary for an FE to be formed cannot be established with certainty.[329] The relevant degree of temporal permanence is, therefore, to be determined on a case-by-case basis in the light of the particular circumstances under examination.[330]

For these reasons and according to CJEU's well-established jurisprudence stating that only to the extent where the PoE of the business does not lead to a rational result or creates conflict with another MS that another establishment, such as FE, may come into consideration as a proxy,[331] this book uses the PoE as the only proxy and does not examine the issue of FE any further.

In the absence of both a PoE and an FE, the EU legislation uses the permanent address or the place of usual residence to designate the customer's location.[332] These secondary proxies are not examined any further either.

i.b. Examples of exceptions The general place-of-supply rule is applicable only to the extent where the supply of service is not covered by one of the specific place-of-supply rules. Some of the most common exceptions that are pertinent for the purposes of this book are as follows: the place of supply of services connected with immovable property is the place where the immovable property is located;[333] the place of supply of services in respect of admission to cultural, artistic, sporting, entertainment and similar events is the place where such events actually take place;[334] and the place of supply of restaurant and catering services is the place where the services are physically carried out.[335]

327 TSIELEPIS, p.6.
328 KERN, p.221.
329 TSIELEPIS, p.4.
330 Ibid.
331 The Welmory decision, §53.
332 Article 44 of the VAT Directive.
333 Ibid, article 47.
334 Ibid, article 53.
335 Ibid, article 55.

ii. B2C transactions In the B2C context, the objective is simply to tax the final consumption in the jurisdiction where it occurs, with the tax burden resting on the final consumer (end-user).[336] To achieve that purpose, countries tend to apply two separate rules: one for on-the-spot supplies and one for all other supplies.

ii.a. On-the-spot supplies On-the-spot supplies have three main (cumulative) characteristics, they: (i) are physically performed at a readily identifiable place; (ii) are ordinarily consumed at the same time and at the same place where they are physically performed; and (iii) ordinarily require the physical presence of the person performing the supply and the person consuming the service or intangible at the same time and place where the supply of such a service or intangible is physically performed.[337] For instance, accommodation, restaurant and catering services as well as attendance at sports competitions constitute on-the-spot supplies.[338] To ensure a taxation in the jurisdiction where the final consumption occurs, on-the-spot supplies are generally submitted to tax in the jurisdiction in which the supply is physically performed.[339]

On-the-spot supplies can be acquired not only by consumers but also by businesses. Jurisdictions can adopt the same place-of-supply rule for the purposes of both B2C and B2B on-the-spot supply transactions, in order to relieve the suppliers of the compliance burden of having to distinguish between final consumers and businesses when making their taxing decision.[340] In fact, imposing on such suppliers, which provide services or intangibles to a large number of customers for relatively small amounts in a short period of time, an obligation to identify and provide evidence of their customers' status and location would translate into not only a significant compliance burden but also a considerable risk of having to bear the under-declared tax to the extent where the customer status and/or location cannot be properly identified.[341]

The European system tends to apply the same place-of-supply rules for the purposes of both B2C and B2B transactions with regards to on-the-spot supplies. For example, the place-of-supply rule in respect of admission to cultural, artistic, sporting, entertainment and similar events[342] and the place-of-supply rule concerning restaurant and catering services[343] do not make any distinctions in relation to the customer status.

ii.b. Other supplies Other supplies can be defined as all supplies that are not 'on-the-spot' supplies. Fall within this category, among others, supplies of services

336 *International VAT/GST Guidelines*, §3.110.
337 Ibid, guideline 3.5.
338 Ibid, §3.117.
339 Ibid, guideline 3.5.
340 Ibid, §3.119.
341 Ibid, §3.166.
342 Article 53 of the VAT Directive.
343 Ibid, article 55.

and intangibles that are likely to be consumed at some time other than the time of performance and services and intangibles that can easily be provided and consumed remotely (including e-commerce supplies).[344] Consultancy, telecommunication and broadcasting services, online supplies of software and software maintenance, online supplies of digital content and online gaming are typical examples of 'other supplies'.[345]

Since it can be assumed that such supplies are ordinarily consumed where the consumer has their usual residence, the taxing right tends to be allocated to the jurisdiction in which the consumer regularly lives or has established a home.[346] Consumers are not considered as having their usual residence in a jurisdiction where they are only temporary/transitory visitors (such as tourists).[347] To determine a consumer's usual residence, suppliers should be allowed to rely, as much as possible, on information they routinely collect from their customers in the ordinary course of their business activity.[348] The admissible *indicia* may vary from jurisdiction to jurisdiction and in accordance with the type of business or product involved. The following examples can be deemed to constitute reliable information: bank details, credit card information, address provided by the consumer, contact telephone number and the internet protocol address of the device used to download digital content.[349]

For instance, under the European system, B2C supplies of telecommunications, broadcasting and electronic services are taxable at the place where the consumer is established, has their permanent address or usually resides.[350] *Indicia* that can be used to determine the consumer's location include the location of a wi-fi hot spot, the place of installation of the fixed landline, the mobile country code of the SIM card used when receiving the services and the location of a decoder.[351]

F. VAT registration of non-resident suppliers and reverse-charge mechanism

The correct charging, collection and remittance of VAT, along with the associated reporting obligations, are, as a general rule, the responsibility of suppliers.[352] In accordance with this general rule, a non-resident supplier is required to register for VAT purposes in the jurisdiction of taxation in order to fulfil its obligations. Such a requirement is complex and burdensome both for the non-resident suppliers, which may conduct business activities in a number of different countries – in some cases – without any physical presence, and for the tax administrations that need to ensure the enforcement and administration of the relevant rules and regulations in respect of suppliers that may not have any presence in their countries.[353]

344 *International VAT/GST Guidelines*, §3.120.
345 Ibid, §3.122.
346 Ibid, guideline 3.6 and §3.123.
347 Ibid, §3.123.
348 Ibid, §3.126.
349 Ibid, §3.127.
350 Articles 58 and 59 of the VAT Directive.
351 Articles 24a and 24b of the Implementing Regulation 282/2011/EU.
352 *International VAT/GST Guidelines*, §3.128.
353 Ibid.

To relieve the suppliers as well as the tax administrations from this non-negligible burden, countries may opt for the application of the 'reverse-charge mechanism' to certain transactions. In a nutshell, reverse-charge mechanism (also referred to as 'self-assessment') shifts the liability to declare and pay the tax from the supplier to the customer. Under this mechanism, customers typically account for VAT on the received supply by means of their periodic VAT return or any other forms specifically designated by the tax administration to this end. If the customer is entitled to a full input tax deduction, the net payable balance will generally be zero, since the tax due under the reverse-charge mechanism is usually deductible as input VAT on the same return.[354] In such cases, the local VAT legislations may opt for not requiring the reverse-charge to be made.[355] Application of the reverse-charge mechanism relieves the non-resident supplier of the requirement to register for VAT purposes and to account for tax in the jurisdiction of taxation.[356]

The reverse-charge mechanism can be applied both for supply of goods and for supply of services and intangibles, even though its use is more common for the latter category of supplies.

IV. Taxation modalities of illegal and unlawful activities

A. General observations

Since this book examines the taxation modalities of the most frequently conducted activities in relation to ISEs, it inevitably includes some income sources, and thereby transactions, that are linked to illegal and/or unlawful activities.[357] It is important to emphasise that the scope of the term 'unlawful activity' is much wider than it appears to be. The term does not refer exclusively to behaviour that is wholly unrelated to any legitimate enterprise, such as murder-for-hire.[358] It may also refer to economic benefits from peripheral misconduct in a business that is entirely lawful (such as an officer who exercises an influence on the decision of an enterprise in consideration of a 'kickback'[359]) or from an unlawful enterprise that could be conducted – though perhaps less profitably – in total conformity with the law (such as items sold on the black market).[360] Unlawful transactions conducted in relation to ISEs are usually not generated from an activity that is wholly unrelated to any legitimate enterprise. They oftentimes derive from an unlawful enterprise that may have been conducted in conformity with the law or a misconduct in a business that is entirely lawful.

354 IBFD, *International Tax Glossary*, p.364.
355 *International VAT/GST Guidelines*, §3.129.
356 Ibid.
357 For the sake of simplicity, the term 'unlawful activities/income sources' is intended to cover both illegal and unlawful activities/income sources throughout this book.
358 BITTKER, p.138.
359 'A kickback is a form of bribe paid to a person of influence within an organisation, in return for them securing some kind of benefit from their organisation for the person paying the bribe' (*Bribery and Corruption Awareness Handbook*, p.11).
360 BITTKER, p.138.

This section provides some general information on taxation modalities of unlawful activities from an income tax (B) and a VAT (C) point of view.

B. Income tax

1. Introduction

Taxation of unlawful activities generally occurs in accordance with – and highly depend on – the domestic law of the RS of the person deriving the income. International taxation issues typically arise in cases where the conductor of the unlawful activity is sentenced to effectuate a compensatory payment to the aggrieved party residing in another State. Accordingly, some explanations regarding the domestic laws are in order.

Whether profits generated from unlawful activities should be submitted to tax or not was a subject of controversy in the 1970s. Currently, however, the approach followed by most governments seems to be rather straightforward: income deriving from unlawful activities is submitted to tax just as income generated by the exercise of lawful activities.[361] In other words, if the taxpayer incurs an income, they/it is subject to income tax regardless of the 'legal nature' of the activity that gave rise to the income concerned. On this point, the Swiss Federal Tribunal states that '*[e]s ist auch kein Grund ersichtlich, der es rechtfertigen würde, unrechtmässigen Gewinn vor einer Belastung auszunehmen, der die rechtmässigen Gewinne geschäftlicher Unternehmungen unterworfen werden*'.[362]

Despite being common practice, taxation of this particular category of income gives rise to several non-negligible problems at a domestic law level. The most commonly encountered ones are: obligation to repay the amount (2), burden caused by the investigations that need to be conducted by the tax authorities (3), qualification of the income (4) and deductions allowed (5). Although no specific examination of these issues is made in relation to unlawful income sources examined in this book, a brief explanation of the most relevant problems is given in this subsection to provide a general overview.

2. Obligation to repay the amount

Should the unlawful activity be detected, the taxpayer will usually be under the obligation to repay the amount concerned either to the government or to the person harmed. In the event that an obligation to reimburse the amount arises, either as a result of a criminal prosecution or a civil law procedure, no taxable

361 See, for example, the statement made by the IRS, https://www.irs.gov/compliance/criminal-investigation/narcotics-related-financial-investigations-criminal-investigation-ci (accessed on 25.09.2015) and AULT/ARNOLD, p.229.

362 The Swiss Federal Tribunal's decision of 6 October 1944, ATF 70 I 250, §1. The sentence can be translated as 'there is no plausible justification to not to submit income generated from unlawful activities to the same tax as income obtained by enterprises in a lawful manner' (translated by the author).

income should be deemed to exist. As a matter of fact, all of the income derived from the unlawful activity, usually accompanied with penalties, will either be forfeited or be repaid to the rightful owner. Accordingly, the person exercising the unlawful activity will not be able to make use of the money or the benefit that is convertible to money that they/it received in consideration of the activity concerned. As a result, they/it cannot be considered as having 'received' an income, since the amount concerned does not 'come in'[363] to accrue their/its profits/wealth.

A compensation payment must be distinguished from an obligation to repay. A compensation payment may be defined as an amount fixed by the competent court in view of repairing the damage caused to the aggrieved party. Therefore, such payments do not technically amount to a repayment of the income generated from the unlawful activity, although they may consist of an amount that is equal to – or in most cases more substantial than – the income derived by the activity concerned. A compensation payment may also be imposed on the conductor as an additional payment, on top of the obligation to repay.

A compensation payment, either of a purely compensatory nature or of a punitive nature, should be treated as an expense linked to the professional activity. Whether the amount of the compensation exceeds the overall income generated by the unlawful activity or not is not relevant. Consequently, this sort of payment should be taken into consideration not during the assessment of the taxable income but during the calculation of admissible deductions. The admissibility of such a payment as a deduction depends on the modalities of the applicable national law.

3. Burden caused by the investigations that need to be conducted by the tax authorities

Without a doubt, income derived from unlawful activities is usually not accurately reported by its recipients.[364] All records of the assets concerned tend to be either concealed or destroyed.[365] While tax examiners and auditors are in a very strong position to identify indicators of possible unlawful activities and may notice traces of unlawful payments in the regular course of their business,[366] pinpointing the scheme put in place by the taxpayer and/or unlawful transactions inevitably requires supplementary research and inquiries. Additional information requested by tax administrations is most likely to remain unanswered as a result of the right to silence and the privilege against self-incrimination.[367] Consequently, it may be

363 On this point, see HOLMES, *Concept of Income*, p.158ff.
364 BITTKER, p.139.
365 Ibid.
366 *Bribery and Corruption Awareness Handbook*, p.13.
367 The right to silence and the privilege against self-incrimination constitute both constitutional rights and human rights within article 6 of the ECHR, even if they are not expressly mentioned in this latter article. For more information on this point, see GOSS, p.89ff.

argued that, in most cases, tax administrations will have to engage in costly investigations in an effort to enforce the applicable tax law, with no assurance that the taxes actually collected will exceed the expenses.[368]

4. *Qualification of the income*

In the event that an income deriving from an unlawful activity may effectively be subject to tax, an additional problem arises: fitting the income in one of the taxable income categories determined by the applicable domestic law.[369] This qualification issue mostly concerns tax systems using a schedular definitional structure of income and not the systems that opted for employing a global definitional structure.

Qualification of income derived from unlawful activities varies from country to country and, in some countries, in accordance with the main modalities of the activity concerned. For instance, in Germany, unlawful income is often considered to fall into the category of income from trade or business, but may be characterised as 'other income' in some cases where the performance of the service concerned is effectuated on an occasional basis, for example espionage.[370] It is interesting to note that New Zealand took a revolutionary step on this matter and included 'stolen property' as a specific income type in its Income Tax Act.[371]

5. *Deductions allowed*

Issues caused by deductions in relation to unlawful activities may be regrouped into three distinct categories: deduction of expenses incurred in the course of an unlawful activity (a), deduction of unlawful expenses incurred in the course of a lawful business, more specifically bribe as a deductible expense (b) and deduction of expenses incurred as a result of an unlawful activity conducted in the course of a lawful business, more specifically deductibility of penalties, fines and associated procedural costs (c).

A. DEDUCTION OF EXPENSES INCURRED IN THE COURSE OF AN UNLAWFUL ACTIVITY

Since the legal nature of the activity giving rise to the income concerned is not pertinent for taxation purposes, deduction of expenses incurred in the course of an unlawful activity should be allowed within the same limits as a lawful activity. This follows from the fact that income tax is not levied on income deriving from unlawful activities with an aim of penalising the taxpayer. That latter purpose is achieved by the relevant dispositions of the laws applicable to the unlawful activity concerned.

368 BITTKER, p.139.
369 AULT/ARNOLD, p.229.
370 Ibid.
371 CB 32 'Property obtained by theft' of the New Zealand Income Tax Act 2007, Public Act 2007, No 97. See also GUPTA, pp.118–119.

As per this line of reasoning, which is shared by the author, deduction of 'legal expenses' of an unlawful business, such as salaries and rent, should be allowed, while deduction of 'unlawful expenses', such as bribes, may be disallowed, if their deduction is also prohibited for lawful activities.[372] This being stated, admissible deductions are determined by national laws and some countries may simply refuse to allow any deductions in relation to unlawful activities.

B. BRIBE AS A DEDUCTIBLE EXPENSE

A bribe can be defined as a payment made to a public official, or to a decision-maker of another enterprise, in order to secure an advantage. Traditionally, bribes were categorised as commercially justified expenses under many jurisdictions. In the last 20 years, the OECD made significant efforts to raise an awareness of damages caused by bribery and corruption. In 1996, the Recommendation on the Tax Deductibility of Bribes to Foreign Public Officials in International Business Transactions was adopted, in order to send a clear message indicating that bribery would no longer be treated as a business expense and that it is a criminal offense subject to serious penalties.[373] In 2009, the Recommendation on Tax Measures for Further Combatting Bribery of Foreign Public Officials in International Business Transactions was adopted. This second Recommendation requires the OECD Member countries and other parties to the OECD Anti-Bribery Convention[374] to explicitly disallow the tax deductibility of bribes paid to foreign public officials.[375]

Consequently, bribes paid to foreign public officials cannot be deducted in the jurisdictions concerned. This exclusion typically extends to bribes paid to national public officials as well.

C. DEDUCTIBILITY OF PENALTIES, FINES AND ASSOCIATED PROCEDURAL COSTS

Some activities conducted in the course of a lawful business may give rise to compensatory or punitive damages (penalties). Deductibility of compensatory and punitive damages depends on the applicable national law. For example, the UK Upper Tribunal (Tax and Chancery Chamber)[376] denied the deductibility of a 32 million GBP penalty that McLaren Racing Ltd had to pay to the FIA as a result of an unlawful flow of information obtained by an employee of the company concerned

372 BITTKER, pp.145–146.
373 *Bribery and Corruption Awareness Handbook*, p.3.
374 The Convention on Combating Bribery of Foreign Public Officials in International Business Transactions was adopted on 21 November 1997. It has been ratified by all OECD countries and eight non-OECD countries (status as of May 2018, ratification status is available at the following link: http://www.oecd.org/daf/anti-bribery/WGBRatificationStatus.pdf (accessed on 28.10.2019)).
375 *Bribery and Corruption Awareness Handbook*, p.7.
376 Appeal No FTC/93/2012.

from one of the employees of Ferrari.[377] A national law may also distinguish between these two types of damages and allow one of them as a deductible expense, most likely compensatory damages, and to reject the deduction of the other.

In the same vein, deductibility of fines and similar financial sanctions as well as procedural costs relating to them depends on the applicable domestic law. For instance, while the US and Germany allow the deduction of procedural costs,[378] the draft bill presented by the Swiss Federal Council suggests disallowing them.[379]

C. VAT

While the VAT treatment of unlawful transactions may vary from jurisdiction to jurisdiction, it can be stated that, as a general rule, the principle of fiscal neutrality precludes a strict distinction from being drawn between lawful and unlawful transactions.[380] Accordingly, unlawful transactions that may compete with lawful transactions should be treated in the same manner as their lawful counterpart.[381]

Such a competition occurs in cases where the activity giving rise to the unlawful transaction is not forbidden per se, but the supplier failed to obtain the relevant authorisation(s) and/or to respect the limits provided by the applicable law. For instance, in a country where games of chance are not forbidden but subject to authorisation, a person who provides betting services without an adequate authorisation is providing unlawful supplies that are in competition with lawful supplies.[382]

Since unlawful and lawful transactions are to be treated in the same manner for VAT purposes, if a lawful transaction is exempt or submitted to a reduced rate, its unlawful counterpart must also be treated as being exempt or submitted to a reduced rate. To continue with the example of games of chance, if the lawful games of chance are exempt, unlawful games of chance must be considered as being exempt as well.[383]

Supplies whose release into the economic and commercial channels are, by definition, absolutely precluded due to their special characteristics and which could give rise only to penalties under the criminal law do not fall within the scope of the VAT.[384] For example, commercialisation of narcotic drugs[385] and circulation of counterfeit currency,[386] which constitute activities that are forbidden per se, do

377 For more information on this point, see HEDLEY JULIAN, McLaren Racing Ltd: tax deduction for penalties, in *Global Sports Law and Taxation Reports (GSLTR)*, Volume 5, Number 3, September 2014, p.17ff.

378 *Explanatory report on financial sanctions*, §§1.5.1–1.5.2.

379 The draft bill entitled Federal Law on tax treatment of financial sanctions (*'Loi fédérale sur le traitement fiscal des sanctions financières'*).

380 The Field Fischer decision, §21.

381 Ibid, §§22 and 28; the Lange decision, §19.

382 See the Field Fischer decision.

383 Ibid, §28.

384 The Lange decision, §§12–13.

385 See the Happy Family decision.

386 See the Witzemann decision.

not give rise to a VAT liability. Since all competition with a lawful sector is excluded in such cases, the fact that the transactions concerned are considered to be out of the scope of VAT cannot affect the principle of fiscal neutrality.[387] The same reasoning holds true for customs duties.[388]

387 The Happy Family decision, §20.
388 The Witzemann decision, §§11–16.

3 Taxation of commercial income sources deriving from international sports events

I. Introduction

ISEs, especially the ones illustrating high sportive skills, form an important economic sector. There is a wide web of contracts concluded in relation to a sports event between different service providers, participants, sponsors, merchandisers, event organisers and other interested parties. In addition to those, there exist several other agreements entered into in a more general context (such as employment and endorsement contracts of a sportsperson) that provide their effects during a number of sports events.

This chapter identifies the main income sources deriving from this variety of contractual arrangements and examines their taxation modalities. Needless to say, while the contracts examined are usually concluded for the purposes of major sporting events, some of them may not be necessary during events of a smaller scale due to the lack of any financial interests. It is also important to underline that income accruing to entities, and thereby the modalities of taxation, vary from sports event to sports event. As it is not possible to examine the taxation of ISEs under all possible organisation schemes, this chapter conducts a general analysis on the basis of the most frequently used organisational patterns.

To this end, the chapter examines: contractual clauses regarding taxes that may exist in all the contracts concluded in relation to an ISE (II), tax treatment of organising sports bodies (III), general observations relating to PE, which are relevant for the analysis of all commercial income sources (IV) and, last but not least, taxation of commercial income sources deriving from an ISE (V).

Prior to begin the analysis, some general observations relating to the structure and the use of words opted for throughout this chapter need to be made.

'Major sports events' is used as an umbrella term, covering all ISEs having attained a certain magnitude. Reference is made to specific types of sports events, such as large-scale and mega, where necessary.

Albeit not being a traditional sport, eSports tournaments are akin to sports events, due to the voluntary 'sportification' of competitive gaming. For the sake of simplicity, the analysis mainly refers to genuine sports events, and specificities related to eSports tournaments are mentioned where and to the extent relevant.

The terms 'event owner', 'rights-holder' and 'rights owner' are used as synonyms and they refer both to the ultimate rights owner (most commonly an SGB and a game developer) and to other rights-holders authorised by the former. In fact, during most major sporting events, not only the ultimate rights holders, i.e. the international sports federation or confederation concerned, but also the LOCs (authorised rights-holders) are entitled to commercialise the event. In the same vein, in the eSports sector, game developers (ultimate rights holders) may license the rights to host a tournament in a given geographic region to their regional affiliates.

The analysis conducted is mainly limited to cross-border activities. In cases where the provider and the purchaser of a given service/good are both residents of the same State and a cross-border taxation issue does not arise due to any other specificities of the case at hand, the taxation occurs in accordance with the provisions of the domestic law of the country concerned. While such cases are outside the scope of this book, reference is made to applicable national laws where necessary in order to provide a thorough analysis.

All articles refer to the articles of the OECD MC, unless otherwise specified.

II. Contractual clauses regarding taxes

Some enterprises may opt for including in contracts they conclude with their commercial partners a clause requiring the remuneration agreed upon by the parties to be free of any taxes that are imposed by the SS. Such a clause translates into the obligation of the commercial partner to increase the amount of the payment in such a manner that the enterprise concerned receives a net amount – after the taxes concerned are paid – equal to the amount otherwise due as per the contract. The responsibility of the commercial partner may be limited to a certain percentage of tax, for example, taxes equal to or lower than 10 percent. Contractual clauses regarding taxes are frequently employed by rights-holders.

The effect of this type of clauses can be demonstrated by the following example: if the contract provides for a 10 million USD consideration for the right to use a number of intellectual properties of the rights-holder and the SS levies a 10 percent withholding tax on the income concerned, the commercial partner's payment will amount to circa 11,111,111 USD. The tax levied by the SS will equal to approximately 1,111,111 USD and the rights-holder will receive 10 million USD as set out in the contract.

As demonstrated by this example, the existence of such a clause does not alter in any manner the taxation mechanism. In fact, the tax concerned is still collected by the SS[1] on the income earned by the rights-holder. The only difference is the fact that the commercial partner agrees to pay a more substantial amount.

1 The tax is generally collected and transmitted to the competent tax authority of the SS by the commercial partner. This aspect is regulated by the applicable domestic law.

III. Tax treatment of organising sports bodies

A. Taxation modalities in the RS

1. Organising committees/national sports organisations

A. INCOME TAX

With regard to the taxation of the income derived by an LOC, or a similar national sports organisation, from an ISE, three observations need to be made.

First, LOCs not only organise but also fund the sports events. As the operational costs are generally as substantial as – or even more substantial than – the income derived from the sports event, LOCs do not usually make any profit. As a matter of fact, most LOCs break even.[2] For example, the VANOC obtained 74.4 million CAD from the Canadian Government,[3] 269.5 million CAD from ticket sales,[4] 54.6 million CAD from licensing and merchandising,[5] 173.5 million CAD from the TOP Sponsorship Programme,[6] 730.2 million CAD from domestic sponsorship[7] as well as 479.7 million CAD from broadcasting rights – granted by the IOC.[8] And yet, at the end of the 2010 Olympic Games, the balance of the VANOC's revenues and the operating costs of the event 'amounted to' zero.[9]

Second, LOCs collaborate with governments to host ISEs in the States concerned. In this respect, it is possible to argue that they are non-profit organisations pursuing a 'public service goal' or acting 'in the public interest'.[10] Most States exempt these sort of entities from corporate income tax. If, exceptionally, that is not the case in a given HS, it is also possible to exempt the LOC of the sports event via a specific law or circular enacted to this end.

Third, even in cases where the LOC manages to make a profit and is not tax-exempt, most of its income is derived from domestic sources, with the notable exception of the amount[11] granted by the SGB.[12] Thereupon, LOCs are mainly taxed in accordance with the domestic law of the HS. Is only subject to international tax law rules, the income granted by the rights-holder to the LOC,

2 As any outstanding amount will be reimbursed by HSs' governments, they should not incur an effective loss.
3 PARENT/SMITH-SWAN, p.61.
4 Ibid, p.56.
5 Ibid, p.57.
6 Ibid.
7 Ibid.
8 Ibid.
9 Ibid.
10 These two terms are used in article 56(g) of the FDTL (Switzerland). Other terms may be used by other States to refer to the same concept.
11 It is customary for the SGB to allocate a part of the income it derives from the sports event to the LOC, national sports organisations and/or participant teams.
12 In most cases the rights-holder and the LOC are not residents of the same State.

which will, however, also be submitted to tax exclusively in the HS since it constitutes business profits.[13]

B. VAT

Whether organising committees/national sports organisations can be considered as taxable persons for VAT purposes depends on the applicable national legislation. This being stated, in most cases, such entities constitute (subject to the registration threshold) taxable persons. The same conclusion is likely to hold true for entities formed only for the purposes of one sports event and dissolved upon the wrap-up of that particular event.

2. *Rights-holders*

The rights-holder of an ISE is usually either an international federation or a confederation. With a significant number of international sports federations and organisations residing in its territory,[14] Switzerland is the RS of more SGBs than any other country in the world.[15] More importantly for the purposes of this book, all three of the SGBs organising the mega sporting events – namely FIFA, the IOC and UEFA – are situated in Switzerland. Based on these facts, it is assumed throughout this book that the rights-holder is a Swiss resident.

Corporate income tax is due both at a federal and a cantonal level in Switzerland. Collection of the tax is effectuated by cantonal authorities, which reimburse the share of the Confederation. The tax is assessed on net worldwide income generated by Swiss resident joint-stock companies, cooperatives, associations, foundations and Swiss investment funds directly owning immovable property with the exception of income attributable to foreign enterprises, PEs or real estate (articles 49(1) and (2) and 52 of the FDTL, article 20(1) of the FTHL). Accordingly, international sports federations and confederations, which are usually organised as associations, are, in principle, subject to corporate income tax in Switzerland.

Nonetheless, in practice, some cantonal tax authorities had been granting tax exemptions to international sports organisations on the grounds that such entities were pursuing a 'public service goal' (article 56(g) of the FDTL, article 23(f) of the FTHL). After EURO 2008, which was co-hosted by Austria and Switzerland, it was debated whether such a tax exemption was justified considering the substantial profits made by

13 Article 7(1). Clearly no PE will be constituted in this specific case.

14 The approximate number of international sports federations and organisations residing in Switzerland is 65 (https://www.swissinfo.ch/eng/new-rules_swiss-set-to-get-tough-over-sports-corruption/40801520 (accessed on 29.10.2019)). For a list of the international sports organisations concerned, see *The Economic Impact of International Sports Organisations in Switzerland 2008–2013*, by International Academy of Sports Science and Technology, April 2015, pp.21–22.

15 Switzerland's closest rival on this matter, Monaco, has only five international sports organisations established in its territory (http://www.swissinfo.ch/eng/how-switzerland-champions-champions/8149794 (accessed on 29.10.2019)).

some international sports organisations every year. In its decision of 5 December 2008, the Swiss Federal Council decided to confirm the practice initiated by some of the cantons. Following this decision, a Circular Letter[16] was published by the Swiss Federal Tax Administration on 12 December 2008. As per the Circular Letter, international sports federations as well as confederations that reside in Switzerland and that are affiliated to the IOC may be deemed to be tax-exempt by the cantonal authorities in accordance with article 56(g) of the FDTL.

The Circular Letter regulates the modalities of this exemption by enumerating the following principles that should be applied on a nationwide basis, i.e. by all cantonal authorities: the exemption applies exclusively: (i) to corporate income tax and not to other taxes levied by the Confederation, such as VAT; and (ii) to international sports organisations themselves and not to their employees, board members, officials and other similar individuals.

Most international sports organisations benefit from the exemption provided by the Circular Letter. This being stated, there are some noteworthy counter-examples. For instance, FIFA is subject to corporate income tax at a federal and a cantonal level, in accordance with the taxation rules for associations. As per the FIFA Financial Report 2018, the organisation paid 28.96 million USD in taxes and duties during the 2018 fiscal year.[17]

It is possible to conclude that most rights-holders are either exempt from corporate income tax or subject to corporate income tax at a low rate due to their association status in their RS, i.e. Switzerland. Consequently, income derived by rights-holders from ISEs is rarely exposed to a double taxation risk.

It must be noted that a tax exemption granted by the RS does not signify that rights-holders cannot benefit from the DTTs concluded by their RS. As a matter of fact, Switzerland takes the view that entities benefitting from a tax exemption based on domestic tax regulations, in particular due to the pursuit of a goal of public interest, are 'residents' within the meaning of article 4.[18] Accordingly, the relevant dispositions of the DTTs may be invoked by international sports organisations with regard to the taxes due in the SS(s).

As with national sports organisations, rights-holders are generally considered as taxable persons for VAT purposes in accordance with the Swiss law and other applicable national legislations (subject to the registration threshold and other criteria determined by the relevant legislation).

B. Taxation modalities of unlawful income

1. General considerations

Some sports organisation officials may be inclined to accept unlawful payments and/or benefits-in-kind in exchange for voting in favour of a certain HS or

16 Swiss Federal Tax Administration's Circular Letter of 12 December 2008, '*Exonération des fédérations internationales sportives*'.
17 *FIFA Financial Report 2018*, p.98.
18 It is important to note that this view is not shared by all countries.

influencing the sports organisation's vote or decision in other issues. Such benefits may be categorised as 'kickbacks', which is a form of a bribe paid to a person of influence within an organisation that is not aware of the payment made to its official.[19]

2. *Income tax*

A. RELEVANT DOMESTIC LAW ASPECTS

The official receiving a kickback will usually be considered to have committed a criminal offence (most commonly in the form of 'criminal mismanagement' and/or 'misappropriation') in accordance with the applicable domestic law and, thereby, the amount concerned will be forfeited. As a result, a taxable income will not arise. Although a kickback, or a similar payment, is not likely to constitute a mere infringement of civil law, should that effectively be the case, the compensation paid by the official to the sports organisation concerned should be taken into consideration during the calculation of admissible deductions.

B. INTERNATIONAL TAX LAW ASPECTS

To the extent where the amount obtained as a kickback is not forfeited and the official and the person paying the amount are residents of different States, the income concerned should be categorised as 'other income' within article 21[20] and be submitted to tax exclusively in the official's RS.[21]

The official may be sentenced to pay compensation to the sports body concerned. If the official and the sports body are residents of the same State, which will usually be the case, taxation of the compensation will occur in accordance with the domestic law of that State. If the official and the sports body are residents of different States, the income concerned will be taxed in accordance with the DTT concluded between the two RSs. Such income should be categorised as 'business profits' within article 7, since unlawful actions of its officials are most likely to cause a significant profit loss for the sports organisation concerned. Accordingly, the compensation payment will be effectuated predominantly to reimburse the profit loss. As per article 7, the income will be taxed exclusively in the RS of the sports body.[22]

Should the payment concerned be categorised as 'other income' within article 21 due to the specificities of the case at hand, the taxation will still occur exclusively in the RS of the sports body.[23]

19 *Bribery and Corruption Awareness Handbook*, p.11.
20 The applicable DTT is the one concluded between the RS of the official and the RS of the person effectuating the payment.
21 Article 21(1).
22 Article 7(1).
23 Article 21(1).

3. VAT

The payment of kickbacks is an activity subject to a total prohibition, which cannot enter into competition with any lawful transactions.[24] Accordingly, such payments are not likely to constitute a taxable VAT transaction.

IV. Observations relating to PE

A. General remarks

General observations regarding the concept of PE and taxation of business profits can be found in chapter 2.[25] While a great number of entities examined in this chapter may make use of one or several PE(s) situated in one or several SS(s) for the purposes of rendering their services related to an ISE, a detailed PE analysis is not conducted for each entity for the sake of avoiding unnecessary repetition. The chapter mentions only the main issues that may be relevant for the purposes of determining whether a PE effectively exists. An exception is made for rights-holders, given the relevance of the formation of a PE in the HS for the taxation of the entity concerned as well as the particularly interesting tax law issues that arise during that analysis.

B. Rights-holder's PE

As a general remark, it is important to mention that the income sources of the right-s-holder that are not specifically dealt with by other distributive rules of the OECD MC fall within the scope of its article 7. This is due to the fact that a rights-holder is an enterprise under article 3(1)(c).[26] Accordingly, the income derived by it constitutes a business profit in any case. For this reason, article 21, which applies to income that are not dealt with by any specific distributive rules of the OECD MC, is, in principle, not applicable to the income sources obtained by a rights-holder from an ISE.

While determining whether a PE of the rights-holder is susceptible to be constituted in the HS or not, a distinction needs to be drawn between sports events that are organised with the collaboration of an LOC and the ones that are organised without such collaboration.

1. Events organised without the collaboration of an LOC

A. FIXED PLACE PE

i. Existence of a PoB To have a PoB in the HS, the rights-holder should have a 'certain amount of space' at its disposal.[27] This requirement is systematically

24 The Happy Family decision, §20.
25 See chapter 2, II, C, 1.
26 Article 3(1)(c) defines the term 'enterprise' as '[...] carrying on of any business'.
27 *OECD Commentary* on article 5, §10.

fulfilled, since, for all sports events, the rights-holder necessitates at least one competitive venue and, in some cases, (a) non-competitive venue(s). The existence of a PoB is not affected by the 'fixed nature' of the venue (e.g. the venue may be a short-term facility constructed only for the duration of the event) or by the modalities of the legal arrangement that grants the rights-holder the right to use the venue (e.g. the venue may be rented by the rights-holder or put at its disposal by another entity, such as a sponsor or the HS' government).

For a PoB to be formed, the rights-holder should have the effective power to use the location and a certain level of presence at that particular location.[28] This requirement is systematically fulfilled as well, since it is typical for the rights-holder and its affiliates to have the exclusive (or almost exclusive) physical control of the venue(s) during, and (in most cases) a certain time before and after the event.

Under these circumstances, it can be safely stated that the rights-holder has at its disposal a PoB in the HS.

ii. Exercise of the core business through the PoB Through the PoB (the venue), the core business (organisation of a sports event) of the enterprise (the rights-holder) is carried on. As already mentioned, the rights-holder is generally an international sports federation or a confederation, the main objectives of which are to ensure the proper and homogenous organisation of the sport concerned at an international level and to promote it via different means, including ISEs. Consequently, the organisation of an ISE falls within the scope of the rights-holder's 'core business'.

iii. The 'fixed' character of the PoB This third condition is more controversial than the first two. To be considered as 'fixed', a PoB needs to display some stability both location-wise and duration-wise.

With regard to the necessary level of geographical link, 'immovable' sports venues, such as stadiums, do not cause any specific interpretation problems, since they are literally 'fixed' to the soil. On the other hand, the categorisation of 'movable' sports venues, such as short-term constructions built during endurance events, is more delicate. To be considered as PEs, movable PoBs must form a geographical and commercial whole.[29] This does not seem to be the case for short-term sports events constructions, which are only used for the duration of a one-off sports event and then dismantled. In this respect, such venues are similar to travelling circuses and funfairs that do not meet the geographical link test in most States.[30]

The relevant time threshold is generally considered to be six months.[31] While the maximum duration of a short-term sports event is two months, a typical short-term sports event takes two to three weeks. The venue(s) is/are at the

28 Ibid, §12.
29 SASSEVILLE/SKAAR, p.27.
30 Ibid.
31 *OECD Commentary* on article 5, §28.

disposal of the rights-holder during the event, and, in some cases, a short period after and before the event. Accordingly, the rights-holder's presence in the HS does not usually exceed the six-month threshold[32] and, thereby, the PoB cannot be considered as 'fixed' duration-wise.

As per the OECD Commentary, a PE is also deemed to exist in cases where the PoB is kept for a very short period of time because the nature of the business is such that it will only be carried for that short period of time.[33] Undoubtedly, a short-term sports event fits into this definition. Nonetheless, in practice, most countries do not support the view that one-off projects that are of a short duration due to their nature are 'permanent' enough to create a PE.[34] Examples considered as not being sufficiently long-lasting are a rock star's concerts, teaching classes for a few days, a trade fair of a week and, last but not least, a sporting event of one week.[35]

Another exception to the six-month threshold has been made for the purposes of the cases where the activities under examination constitute a business that is exclusively carried on in the SS.[36] In these situations, the business may have a short duration because of its nature but since it is wholly carried on in the SS, its connection with that State is stronger.[37] Even if international short-term sports and cultural events appear to be the cases specifically targeted by this exception at a first glance,[38] this assumption does not hold true in most cases given the fact that the exception exclusively covers temporary entrepreneurs, i.e. enterprises that are set up specifically for the purposes of rendering their services during that particular activity and that are terminated right after.[39] It is clearly not possible to categorise a rights-holder as a 'temporary entrepreneur' that organises only one isolated sports event. Consequently, it can be stated that the exception to the six-month threshold does not apply to rights-holders of ISEs.[40]

Last but not least, the recurrent nature of an activity may render the PoB 'fixed' enough for a PE to be formed.[41] In cases where the sports event is held at the same place in a repeated manner, such as a Formula 1 race held on the same circuit on several occasions, a fixed PoB, and thereby a PE, may be created. For instance, the Supreme Court of India held that the Buddh International Circuit, which was used six weeks per year (three days for the event itself and the

32 That is unless the rights-holder has at its disposal another fixed PoB in the HS, such as an office, used for the purposes of the ISE concerned for at least six months.
33 *OECD Commentary* on article 5, §28.
34 SASSEVILLE/SKAAR, p.31; BENARD ET AL, §§43–44.
35 SASSEVILLE/SKAAR, p.31.
36 *OECD Commentary* on article 5, §6.
37 Ibid.
38 PERDELWITZ, p.44.
39 *OECD Commentary* on article 5, §30.
40 It does not apply for the activities exercised by other enterprises examined in this book either. As a matter of fact, none of the enterprises described in this contribution can be qualified as 'temporary entrepreneurs'. However, if exceptionally the services described are rendered by temporary entrepreneurs, this exception shall become applicable.
41 *OECD Commentary* on article 5, §§23 and 28.

remaining period for preparations and wrap-up), where Formula 1 races were held constituted a PE, given the fact that the venue was put at the disposal of the rights-holder in a recurrent manner, i.e. for five editions of the event.[42]

As a result, it can be argued that a fixed place PE is usually not deemed to be formed, due to the temporary nature of sports events and the general practice on the matter, with the notable exception of events of a recurrent nature held at the same place for several editions (such as Formula 1).

B. DEPENDENT AGENT PE

In the absence of an LOC, the rights-holder may prefer to organise the event with the collaboration of an event manager or (a) commercial sales agent(s), which will proceed with the necessary organisational steps (including entering into contracts with commercial partners on behalf of the rights-holder) both in the HS and in other States – to the extent relevant. Both event managers and commercial sales agents being agents of independent status acting in the ordinary course of their business,[43] their activities cannot be constitutive of a PE in an SS per se.

C. CONCLUSION

It is therefore possible to conclude that a PE is generally not created during a sports event organised without the collaboration of an LOC, with the notable exception of a fixed place PE that may be formed for the purposes of an event of a recurrent nature held at the same place for several editions (such as Formula 1).

2. Events organised with the collaboration of an LOC

Most large-scale and mega sporting events are organised with the collaboration of an LOC. This sub-subsection analyses whether or not a PE may be constituted in the HS as a result of this co-operation.

A. RELATION BETWEEN THE LOC AND THE RIGHTS-HOLDER

The LOC's funding sources generally include ticketing income, domestic sponsorship, food and merchandise sales at the venue as well as government and SGB grants. The LOC enters into contract with third parties under its name and on its behalf and, thereby, it is entitled to the income deriving from the contracts concerned. The rights-holder usually does not get a share of the domestic income, including ticketing. It commercialises the sports event at an international level, i.e. via international sponsors, broadcasting and international licensing and supplying programmes.

42 The contract also provided for an additional extension of five years. See the Formula 1 decision, §§68 and 70.

43 Article 5(6).

In the light of this information, the collaboration between the rights-holder and the LOC can be summarised as follows:

- the LOC organises the event following the guidelines provided by the rights-holder, bears the financial risk linked to the event with the government of the HS and collects the income deriving from domestic sources;
- the rights-holder supervises the preparations, contributes to the expenses related to the event to a certain extent without bearing any financial risks, commercialises the event on an international scale and grants a share of this international revenue to the LOC.

B. FIXED PLACE PE

There are two main differences between a sports event organised without an LOC and the one that is organised by means of an LOC. In the latter case, the rights-holder does not enter into a venue hire contract and the LOC is entitled to – a part or the entirety of – the income deriving from domestic sources.

The absence of a venue hire contract concluded by the rights-holder is not pertinent for taxation purposes. As a matter of fact, the rights-holder has a legal right to use the venue in accordance with its contractual relationship with the LOC and the government of the HS. Accordingly, it is possible to state that the rights-holder has a PoB in the HS.

Although the event is organised by the LOC and the income deriving from domestic sources mostly belongs to it, the rights-holder also participates in both the organisation – by granting the right to host and by supervising the preparations – and the commercialisation – by selling its broadcasting rights, by allowing its sponsors to be associated with the event and by other similar commercial activities – of the event. Consequently, the rights-holder derives a profit from the exercise of its core activity, i.e. organisation of sports events, in the HS.

However, the PoB – the venue – through which the business – the organisation of sports events – of an enterprise – the rights-holder – is partly carried on cannot be considered as being 'fixed' due to the temporary nature of an ISE. Thereupon, a fixed place PE will not be deemed to exist.

C. DEPENDENT AGENT PE

The LOC has neither the authority to enter into agreements on behalf of the rights-holder nor any legal or economic dependence towards this latter entity. The main function of the LOC is to ensure that all necessary preparations for the HS to be able to host the event are completed in due time. While achieving this purpose, the LOC enjoys a significant level of autonomy with regard to the organisation and the management of the event.[44]

44 See on this point BENARD ET AL, §§132–134.

The fact that the LOC is under an obligation to respect the guidelines provided by the rights-holder, and is constantly supervised by this latter, cannot be interpreted as legal dependence since the rights-holder does not control – or directly participate in – the decision-making process of the LOC. It is therefore possible to deduce that the LOC collaborates with the rights-holder as an independent partner and not as a subordinate.

From an economic standpoint, it is common for the rights-holder to allocate a certain percentage of the overall net income obtained by the event to the LOC. Nonetheless, this does not amount to an economic dependence. In fact, LOCs co-operate with governments to cover the necessary costs of the preparations. The sum distributed at the end of the event by the rights-holder allows for the reimbursing of costs incurred by the LOC and the government concerned only to a certain extent.

As a result, it may be concluded that a dependent agent PE is not likely to be formed either.

D. CONCLUSION

The fact that a sports event is organised with the collaboration of an LOC does not have any impact on the constitution of a PE in the HS.

3. Taxation of the rights-holder's PE in the HS

As demonstrated by the analysis conducted in this subsection, a PE is usually not deemed to be formed in the HS during an ISE, due to the temporary nature of this latter. Accordingly, the taxation of the rights-holder in the HS does generally not differ from its taxation in other SSs. This being stated, the possibility of the creation of a PE in the HS cannot be excluded altogether. As a matter of fact, a fixed place PE will be formed in cases where: (i) the event has a recurrent nature (such as Formula 1); or (ii) the HS considers that the PoB of the sports event – i.e. the venue – is sufficiently 'fixed'.

The existence of a PE in the HS entails that the profits of the rights-holder that are attributable to the PE may be taxed in the State concerned.[45] This attribution concerns only the business profits under article 7, i.e. excluding all sources of income that are dealt with separately in other dispositions of the applicable DTT.[46] With regard to the income earned by a rights-holder of a sports event, fees paid by some commercial partners (such as merchandisees and broadcasters) should be categorised as royalties[47] and not as business profits. The income sources that may be taken into consideration for the taxation of the PE are mainly the following: ticketing income, a percentage of the hospitality packages sales allocated to the rights-holder by the hospitality provider, fees paid by suppliers, fees paid by

45 Article 7(1).
46 Article 7(4).
47 Article 12.

sponsors in relation to the event, fees paid by advertisers, fees paid by broadcasters to transmit the event live and to access to some areas and facilities at the event's venue.

The term 'profits' is interpreted in accordance with each State's domestic law, as it has not been defined in the OECD MC. Consequently, the exact extent of the profits attributable to the PE is determined in the light of the HS' domestic law. Countries generally tend to adopt a broad interpretation, which includes all profits derived from the exploitation of the enterprise concerned.[48] The RS must eliminate the double taxation on the profits 'properly' attributable to the PE, in accordance with articles 23A and 23B.[49] In other words, a double taxation may occur if the RS considers that the profits, or a part of them, taxed in the HS were not attributable to the PE.[50] This residual double taxation may be eliminated with the mechanism provided in article 7(3), which is similar to the system used in transfer pricing.[51]

Concerning the rights-holder of a sports event, the attribution of a part of its income to a PE may be especially problematic for two main reasons. First, as an ISE is commercialised in an international manner, another PE may be deemed to be created in another SS with respect to the same income source or an income source attributed to the PE by the HS may simply be taxed in another SS (source-source conflict[52]). For example, the HS may attribute the ticketing income to the venue and thereby to the PE situated in its territory, whereas the SS in which the server[53] is situated may also consider the same ticketing profits as being attributable to the PE in its territory. Source-source conflicts are particularly complex, since they are not regulated by any of the DTTs concluded between the States concerned.[54] Thereupon, they mostly result in a double taxation that cannot be eliminated.

Second, most fees are not obtained for the purpose of only the sports event but for a more long-lasting collaboration. For instance, the TOP Sponsorship Programme operates on a four-year term and includes global marketing rights with regard to the IOC, all active NOCs and their Olympic teams, the two OCOGs, one Summer Games and one Winter Games.[55] Accordingly, if the HS considers sponsoring fees as being attributable to the PE, it has to proceed to an allocation

48 *OECD Commentary* on article 7, §71.
49 Article 7(2); *OECD Commentary* on article 7, §18.
50 *OECD Commentary* on article 7, §18.
51 Article 9.
52 A source-source conflict occurs when two countries each assert, in terms of their respective domestic tax laws, that it is the source of the taxpayer's income (HOLMES, *International Tax Policy*, p.23).
53 In cases where the tickets are commercialised online.
54 As a matter of fact, in a source-source conflict regarding the income of the rights-holder, both the HS and the SS consider that a PE is formed in their respective territories. The DTTs concluded between RS-HS and RS-SS do not offer a solution, since they do not contain any dispositions regarding the taxation effectuated by a third State. The DTT concluded between HS-SS does not apply at all, as the rights-holder is not a resident of either of the States concerned (article 1).
55 *Olympic Marketing Fact File*, p.15.

of the fees. The allocation key applied will depend on the interpretation and the domestic law of the HS and may result in a potential double taxation, depending on the allocation key(s) adopted by other SSs and the RS.

V. Taxation of commercial income sources

A. Generalities

This section examines the taxation modalities of the income deriving from: organisation of the event (B), venue hire and construction (C), ticketing (D), hospitality (E), supplies of goods and services (F), merchandising (G), broadcasting (H), sponsoring (I), endorsement (J), advertisement (K), sporting or gaming performance (L), image rights (M), provision of services by the workforce (N), sports betting (O), commercialisation of digital compendiums in relation to eSports tournaments (P) and sports agency (Q).

For each income source, first the main characteristics of the contracts concluded between the commercial partners, along with the most typical remuneration methods, are briefly laid out. Then, the income tax modalities are examined. The analysis concludes with the relevant VAT aspects.

B. Organisation of the event

1. Specificities of the contracts

The rights-holder may appoint an agency specialised in sports marketing and/or management for the exploitation of the commercial rights and/or management of the event. Similarly, in eSports, game developers tend to cooperate with tournament organisers. This is especially the case for the purposes of 'mixed' tournaments having several game titles from various developers, which cannot be organised by a sole game developer, since one developer does not hold the rights to commercially exploit the games of other developers.

Two distinct types of contracts are typically concluded in relation to the organisation of an ISE, namely commercial rights sales agency contracts and event management contracts. It is not uncommon for commercial rights sales agents to also act as the event managers. In those cases, both types of activities may be regulated by means of one contract.

A. COMMERCIAL RIGHTS SALES AGENCY CONTRACTS

A commercial rights sales agent is appointed by the rights-holder to find potential buyers, to negotiate and ultimately to sell a bundle of commercial sports rights to the chosen commercial partner on this latter's behalf.[56] A number of different commercial sports rights exist, such as audio-visual rights, sponsorship rights and merchandising rights. The rights-owner may appoint a unique agent for the entire

56 VEROW, p.1329.

event or designate several agents for different sets of rights and distinct stages of the process.[57] Commercial exploitation of major sports events is generally conducted by several agencies combined with in-house operations.

The remuneration of the agent may consist of a fixed percentage of the commercial value of the rights packages sold, a fixed fee, an hourly rate or a combination of these different types of payments.

B. EVENT MANAGEMENT CONTRACTS

Rather than managing the sporting event itself, the rights-holder generally opts for appointing an event manager (most commonly on an exclusive basis and in a defined geographical territory) to carry out, under its close supervision and direction, the actual management and staging of the event.[58] There is a wide range of services that can be provided by the event manager. These services may include, among others, venue preparation and management, hospitality and catering in relation to the event, ticket printing and distribution as well as promotion/marketing of the event.[59]

In exchange for their services, event managers are entitled to a fee that may be paid up-front in one lump sum or in several instalments.[60] Event managers may enter into agreements with third parties, i.e. subcontractors, to fulfil some of their contractual obligations. Should that effectively be the case, the subcontractors concerned are usually remunerated by the event manager itself.

For the purposes of this book, it is assumed that the rights-holder hired an event manager that also acts as a commercial rights sales agent. In the negative, all commercial contracts that are described in this chapter will, in principle, be concluded directly by the rights-holder with its commercial partners. The fact that event managers may subcontract some of their obligations is also taken into consideration in the analysis conducted.

2. *Taxation modalities*

A. INCOME TAX

The applicable DTT is the one concluded between the RS of the rights-holder and the RS of the agent/manager. The former is the SS and the latter is the RS for the purposes of the economic activity under examination.

The income derived by the agent/manager may be categorised as 'business profits' or 'technical services fees'. While the services provided by an event manager or a commercial sales agent seem to involve the application of specialised knowledge and expertise on behalf of the rights-holder, whether or not the income derived by these entities can effectively be categorised as 'technical services fees', depends on the domestic law interpretation of the term opted by the SS.

57 Ibid, p.1330.
58 BLACKSHAW, *Sports Marketing Agreements*, p.73.
59 Ibid.
60 BECKER, p.193.

Should the income be categorised as 'business profits', the SS should abstain from taxing the profits of the entities concerned, which would be exclusively submitted to tax in the RS in accordance with article 7(1). It is, in fact, evident that no PE is constituted in this specific case in the RS of the rights-holder or in another State. To the extent where the income may be characterised as 'technical services fees', both the RS of the agent/manager and the SS may tax the profits.[61] This latter State's taxing right is generally limited to a certain percentage provided in the DTT.

B. VAT

Commercial rights sales agency contracts and event management contracts give rise to supply of services in a B2B context. Both the service provider(s), i.e. the agent/manager, and the customer, i.e. the rights-holder, constitute businesses. Accordingly, the services concerned should be submitted to tax in the jurisdiction of the services' recipient's location, i.e. rights-holder's business' PoE.[62]

C. Venue hire and construction

1. Securing a venue for the purposes of an ISE

ISEs take place in one or several venues that need to be secured beforehand. Sports events may have more than one 'competitive' and 'non-competitive' venues.[63] Competitive venues are places where sportspersons compete,[64] such as stadiums. Non-competitive venues are places where all other activities related to the event take place, such as athletes' villages and training sites.[65] In most cases, the rights-holder of an ISE does not own or occupy a venue in the HS. Venues are either: (a) rented from venue owners; or (b) provided by the HS' government, or another public entity, on a free of charge basis.

The situation is rather similar in eSports tournaments, which may be held in a variety of venues, from stadiums to hotel conference rooms. They do not generally benefit, at least for the moment, from a free of charge provision of venues by HSs. This being stated, game developers, or their regional affiliates, may own an 'eSports arena', a stadium-like place specifically built to host eSports tournaments.

A. HIRING VENUES FROM PRIVATE PARTIES

Hiring venues from private parties gives rise to 'venue hire contracts', which can be defined as contracts concluded by rights-holders with venue owners to secure the right to use the venues for a certain limited period of time for the purposes

61 Article 12A(1) and (2) of the UN MC.
62 Article 44 of the VAT Directive.
63 PARENT/SMITH-SWAN, p.150.
64 Ibid.
65 Ibid.

of staging an event.[66] Some of the key obligations of venue owners are to allow access to the venues, to grant the use of certain areas and to provide electricity, heating, refrigeration, water and a certain number of staff (such as security guards and cleaning personnel). With regard to ISEs, venue owners may also be under the obligation of providing a 'clean venue', i.e. a venue devoid of all commercial, political, religious and ethical influence as well as any kind of publicity. Securing a venue may be more complex for endurance events such as road race cycling and triathlons,[67] during which short-term facilities need to be constructed on a series of sites generally owned by different persons.[68] Thereupon, organisers of endurance events need to enter into contracts with a number of venue owners.[69]

In exchange for providing the venues and complying with other relevant obligations, venue owners may obtain from the rights-holder a rental fee and/or a share of the ticketing income of the event. Venue owners may also rent stands (or similar installations) to suppliers that would like to provide their services to the audience at the venue during the event, such as caterers. Suppliers may remunerate venue owners by means of a flat rental fee and/or a certain percentage of the proceeds of sale.

B. VENUES PROVIDED BY PUBLIC ENTITIES

For the purposes of endurance events, and other ISEs as the case may be, during which races usually take place on public roads and/or in national waters, the use of the public places is subject to authorisations of the competent authorities. Such authorisations may be subject to fees that are payable to the relevant authorities when a request is made, but (as a general rule) they do not give rise to the payment of a rental, or a similar, consideration for the use of the places concerned.

With regard to some ISEs, most commonly large-scale and mega sports events, HSs may provide competitive and/or non-competitive venues on a free of charge basis. In fact, since construction of new venues forms a strong argument during the bidding process, most HSs not only put the existing venues at the rights-holder's disposal, but also build brand new ones.[70] For example, Qatar, the host of the 2022 FIFA World Cup, has proposed to construct nine new stadia and to renovate three stadia during its bidding procedure.[71] HCCs generally contain a specific clause which provides that the venues mentioned in the course of the

66 BECKER, p.43.
67 O'DOWD, p.1141.
68 Ibid.
69 Ibid.
70 The inevitable outcome of the relentless, and not necessarily indispensable, construction of new venues for major sports events is the creation of the so-called 'white elephants', i.e. structures that require a considerable maintenance, while being either unused or significantly underutilised (for more information, see MAENNIG/ZIMBALIST, *Future Challenges*, pp.572–573 and HORNE, endnote 8).
71 PARENT/SMITH-SWAN, p.139.

bidding procedure should be made available during the event.[72] Architects and construction companies working on the constructions undertaken for the purposes of an ISE are generally chosen from local companies.

It is also possible for the HS to put at the disposal of the rights-holder venues belonging to private parties, such as a stadium owned by a sports club. In such cases, the rental fee will be reimbursed by the HS' government, to the extent where the venue owner(s) do(es) not agree to grant the right to use the venue(s) to the government, and thereby to the rights-holder, on a free of charge basis.

Taxation modalities of any income that may derive from provision of venues by public entities are determined in accordance with the applicable domestic law. Even if some international components, such as a non-resident architecture firm providing its services, may be present and therefore international tax law rules may apply, these aspects, which do not give rise to any legal developments linked to sporting activities, fall beyond the scope of this book.

2. *Taxation modalities of the income obtained by the owners of the existent venues*

A. INCOME TAX

Traditional sports venues constitute immovable properties, without a shadow of a doubt. This may also hold true for constructions used during endurance events, especially in cases where the rights-holder obtains a right to use the land(s) or stopover port(s) belonging to different landowners.

The rental fees obtained from the rights-holder and suppliers (if any) clearly constitute rental fees deriving from immovable property. The same categorisation also applies to the percentage of the suppliers' proceeds of sale and the share of the ticketing income, to the extent where the venue owner is not providing an additional ticketing service. Accordingly, the taxation modalities of these different remuneration types are examined together. For the sake of simplicity, reference is only made to 'rights-holders', which implies 'rights-holders and/or suppliers'.

In cases where the government puts a privately-owned venue at the disposal of the rights-holder, it will remunerate the venue owner itself. This income will be submitted to tax in accordance with the domestic law of the country concerned.

In cases where the venue is hired by the rights-holder, the rental fee paid to the venue owner may be subject to international tax law rules depending on the specificities of the case. If the rights-holder and the venue owner are residents of the same State and the venue is situated in that particular State as well, no international taxation case will arise. The venue owner will be submitted to tax in accordance with the domestic law of the State concerned. In all other cases, which are examined below, the relevant DTTs should be applied.

72 See, for example, annex 5(i) and (ii) of the Bidding Agreement regarding the submission of bids for the right to host and stage the 2018 FIFA World Cup™ and 2022 FIFA World Cup™ and article 35 of the Host City Contract for the Games of the XXXI Olympiad in the year 2016 – RIO DE JANEIRO.

i. The rights-holder is not a resident of the HS, whereas the venue owner is a resident of the HS In this first scenario, the applicable DTT is the one concluded between the RS of the rights-holder and the HS. Article 6 is not applicable even if the income is derived from an immovable property. In fact, to fall within the scope of application of article 6, the income must be derived by a resident of a CS from an immovable property situated in the other CS.[73] Yet, if the venue owner is a resident of the HS, it derives an income from an immovable property situated in their/its RS.

Such income should be taxed in accordance with article 21(1),[74] which states that items of income of a resident of a CS, wherever arising, not dealt with in other articles of the OECD MC shall be taxable only in that State, i.e. the RS of the venue owner, which is the HS.

Consequently, it is possible to conclude that in this first case, the income derived by the venue owner shall exclusively be submitted to tax in the HS.

ii. The rights-holder is a resident of the HS, whereas the venue owner is not a resident of the HS In this second scenario, the applicable DTT is the one concluded between the HS and the RS of the venue owner. This situation falls within the scope of application of article 6, as the venue owner derives an income from an immovable property situated in a State other than their/its RS, that is the HS. Accordingly, the income derived by the venue owner may be subject to tax in the *situs* of the venue, i.e. the HS.[75]

iii. The rights-holder is a resident of RS1, the venue owner is a resident of RS2 In this third scenario, the rights-holder is a resident of one State (RS1); the venue owner is a resident of another State (RS2) and neither of them is a resident of the HS.

The applicable DTT is the one concluded between the RS2 and the HS. In fact, the venue owner, a resident of the RS2, derives an income from an immovable property situated in the HS. Consequently, the situation falls within the scope of article 6 of the DTT RS2-HS. The RS of the payer, *in casu* RS1, is not relevant for the application of this distributive rule.[76] Therefore, in accordance with article 6(1),[77] the income of the venue owner may be taxed in the HS.

iv. The rights-holder and the venue owner are residents of the same State, which is not the HS In this fourth and last scenario, the rights-holder and the venue owner are residents of the same State, whereas the event is hosted in another

73 Article 6(1).
74 *OECD Commentary* on article 6, §1. It is important to note that it is highly debated whether article 7 or article 21 should apply in those circumstances (to the extent where the income is obtained by an enterprise).
75 Article 6(1) and (4).
76 FALTIN, §7.
77 And article 6(4), in cases where it is relevant.

State. As only two States are concerned, the DTT concluded between them will be applied to the case at hand.

The venue owner derives its income from an immovable property situated in the HS. Subsequently, the income concerned may be taxed by the HS, the *situs* of the property.[78]

B. VAT

When the venue(s) is (are) supplied by public entities, the transaction is likely to be outside the scope of VAT, given the fact that government authorities and bodies governed by public law are usually not regarded as taxable persons in respect of activities or transactions in which they engage as public authorities.[79]

Regarding the cases where the venue is provided by a private party, the key issue that needs to be underlined is the fact that rights-holders generally obtain the exclusive right to use the venue in its entirety and gains complete control of the premises during the ISE as well as a certain period before and after such event. Consequently, the venue owner's supply consists of 'the passive activity of making the venue available'.[80] In cases where the venue owner provides services that may be considered as having a close link to sporting activities or as amounting to use of sporting facilities, it must be verified whether there exists an exemption, or a reduced rate, relating to sports activities that becomes applicable.[81]

The letting of a venue constitutes a supply of service connected with immovable property, due to the fact that the immovable property (i.e. the venue) makes up a constituent element of the service and is essential for the service to be supplied.[82] Such services are usually submitted to tax in the jurisdiction where the immovable property is located, i.e. the HS, regardless of whether the recipient of the service is a business or a consumer.[83] Most countries opt for exempting the leasing or letting of immovable property.[84]

D. Ticketing

1. General observations

A ticket is, essentially, a licence to occupy a pre-defined place in the sports event's venue for a limited period of time.[85] In addition to forming a considerable source of revenue, ticketing also constitutes a mechanism that protects both the integrity

78 As per article 6(1) and (4).
79 See, for instance, article 13 of the VAT Directive.
80 The Lindöpark decision, §26.
81 Subject to fulfilment of other relevant conditions. See, for instance, article 132(1)(m) and annex III(14) of the VAT Directive. See the Lindöpark decision for more information.
82 Article 31a(1)(a) of the Implementing Regulation 282/2011/EU.
83 Article 47 of the VAT Directive, *Explanatory notes on immovable property*, §137.
84 See, for example, article 135(1)(l) of the VAT Directive.
85 BELOFF ET AL, p.183.

of the event and the value of the commercial rights arising from it.[86] As a matter of fact, well-drafted ticket terms and conditions allow rights-holders to contractually control the activities of purchasers and to prevent, at least to a certain degree, a number of ambushing activities, such as ticket touting, transmittal of unauthorised recordings of the event and ambush marketing. For this reason, most SGBs take due care in drafting solid terms and conditions for the tickets of their sports events. In cases where the event's tickets are commercialised not by the SGB itself but by third parties, such as participating teams, the governing body may impose minimum provisions that should be contained in the ticket terms and conditions.[87]

This subsection concentrates on ticketing as a source of income. To this end, it examines, along with their taxation modalities, lawful commercialisation of tickets (2) and ticket touting (3).

2. *Lawful commercialisation of tickets*

A. GENERAL ASPECTS

Ticketing constitutes one of the most significant revenue streams of minor sports events. For instance, at the major university level of collegiate sport in the US, ticket sales amount to almost 30 percent of the overall income.[88] Albeit being 'overshadowed' by other commercial contracts, such as broadcasting and sponsoring, ticket sales also form a non-negligible source of income for major sports events. For example, the income derived from ticketing by the OCOGs in the 2013–2016 Olympiad amounted to 527 million USD.[89]

As a general rule, the majority of revenue generated through the sale of tickets is retained by sports bodies.[90] Regarding mega sporting events, the allocation of ticketing income between sports organisations can be presented as follows:

- The Olympic Games ticketing program is managed by the OCOG, with the support of the IOC.[91] The income derived by ticket sales is used to cover, to a certain extent, the expenses deriving from the staging of the Games.[92]
- FIFA's net revenue from the World Cup ticket sales is passed on to the LOC, in order to cover, as far as possible, the operational expenses of the latter.[93]
- Each club retains the receipts from the sale of the match tickets and bears all the expenses during play-offs and the UEFA Champions League.[94] Concerning the

86 BECKER, p.73.
87 See, for example, article 67.15 of the UEFA Champions League Regulations.
88 CROMPTON, p.1368.
89 *Olympic Marketing Fact File*, p.9.
90 O'DOWD, p.1143.
91 *Olympic Marketing Fact File*, p.32.
92 Ibid.
93 See, for example, *FIFA Financial Report 2010*, p.38.
94 Article 60.01 of the UEFA Champions League Regulations.

final's ticketing income, the UEFA Executive Committee decides on the financial distribution model in favour of: the two finalists, the host association (in accordance with the staging agreement) and UEFA.[95]

Although it is possible for the tickets to be exclusively commercialised by the rights-holder, in general one or more business partners of the rights-holder intervene(s) in ticket sales. The three most commonly employed commercialisation schemes are the following: (i) the rights-holder enters into a profit share agreement with the venue owner in return for the provision of ticketing services by the latter; the venue owner may also be entitled to a fixed fee for the services it renders; (ii) the rights-holder appoints a ticket agency to manage the sales; even though the financial provisions of such arrangements may vary, ticket agencies are usually remunerated by means of commissions on the effectuated sales; and (iii) the rights-holder enters into agreement with a hospitality provider, which sells packages including the tickets to the event. Ticketing income related to hospitality contracts is examined in the following subsection (E). This subsection analyses income obtained via commercialisation of the tickets by the rights-holder, by the venue owner and lastly by ticket agencies.

B. INCOME TAX ANALYSIS OF TICKETS COMMERCIALISED BY THE RIGHTS-HOLDER

i. General observations The revenue generated from ticket sales constitutes business profits under article 7. Accordingly, ticketing income is taxable in the RS of the entity commercialising the tickets unless a PE is constituted in the territory of one of the SSs.[96] In this latter eventuality the profits that are attributable to the PE may be submitted to tax in the SS.[97]

Due to the discrepancies with regard to the constitution of a PE, examined separately are the taxation modalities of tickets sold online by the rights-holder itself, tickets sold via vending points by the rights-holder itself, tickets sold via the combination of both methods by the rights-holder itself and tickets sold by the commercial partners of the rights-holder.

ii. E-commercialisation of tickets by the rights-holder

ii.a. Server as a fixed place PE It is reasonable to assume that online sale of tickets will usually be conducted via a website that is accessible in several countries and that is hosted by a server situated in one country. The ability of the seller to commercialise the tickets in a number of countries merely by means of a website, i.e. without maintaining any physical presence, renders the taxation of this type of income particularly problematic. While the countries concerned may admit the creation of a PE in their territories – and thereby tax a part of the income –

95 Ibid, article 61.02.
96 Article 7(1).
97 Ibid.

under their domestics laws on the basis of different criteria such as location of the payer, place of delivery of goods, place of contract, place where the telecommunications infrastructure is used and place where the website or the server is situated,[98] under the current version of the OECD MC only the server is susceptible to constitute a fixed PoB.

Clearly, for a server to constitute a fixed place PE all the requirements enumerated in article 5(1) must be met. A server hosting a website by means of which tickets to a sports event are commercialised forms a fixed PoB through which the core business of the rights-holder is exercised. As a matter of fact, since organising sports events forms an important component of a rights-holder's core business, selling tickets for the purposes of such events should also be regarded as a part of the business concerned.

A potential obstacle to the creation of a PE may be the preparatory or auxiliary nature of the activities conducted by the server. The activities are not to be considered as merely preparatory or auxiliary if the typical functions related to a sale, such as the conclusion of the contract with the customer, the processing of the payment and the delivery of the intangible products, are performed at the location where the server is situated.[99]

Online ticket sales constitute an e-tailing service that may be effectuated on a direct (via an e-delivery of the ticket) or an indirect (via a physical delivery of the ticket at a later stage) basis. Under both methods, as a general rule, the conclusion of the sales contract and the payment are effectuated online. In other words, typical functions related to a sale are conducted through the website, regardless of the fact that the ticket is delivered electronically or physically. It is, therefore, possible to state that, in most cases, the activities cannot be considered as merely preparatory or auxiliary in nature.

On the other hand, the activity should be categorised as having a preparatory nature if the website allows only to make a reservation of the ticket. As a matter of fact, in such a case none of the typical functions of a sale are performed: a contract is not concluded between the seller and the buyer – as the reservation may be cancelled at a later stage, the payment is not made and the ticket is not delivered.

A more prevailing obstacle, which usually results in the non-creation of a PE in the SS, is the entity maintaining and operating the server. To constitute a PE, the fixed PoB must be operated by the enterprise obtaining the income, i.e. in the case at hand the rights-holder, at its own predominant discretion. Accordingly, a PE may only be created in cases where the enterprise commercialising the tickets by means of a website is operating the server on its own, i.e. without the intermediation of an internet service provider. Servers, however, are traditionally maintained and operated by internet service providers and not by enterprises using websites for their commercial activities. For this reason, a server is not likely to constitute a fixed place PE of the rights-holder.

98 PINTO, pp.91–100; SPRAGUE/BOYLE, pp.29–40.
99 *OECD Commentary* on article 5, §130.

ii.b. Internet service provider as a dependent agent In the absence of a fixed place PE, it must be verified whether a dependent agent PE may be created. For the purposes of online ticket sales, the only person that may qualify as a 'dependent agent' is the internet service provider operating the server. Nevertheless, it is clear that internet service providers cannot constitute dependent agents, due to the simple fact that they are merely commercial partners of rights-holders, acting in the ordinary course of their business, i.e. to host and maintain websites of different enterprises.

ii.c. Allocation of the taxing rights In most cases, the relevant server will not be operated by the rights-holder and thereby no PE will be formed in any of the SSs (including the HS) and the income deriving from the online ticket sales will be taxable exclusively in the rights-holder's RS.[100]

Should the rights-holder operate the server itself, the allocation of the taxing rights will depend on the country where the server concerned is situated. If the server is located in the RS of the rights-holder, the ticketing income will be submitted to tax in the RS in its entirety. If, however, the server is located in another State, the State concerned may submit to tax the income attributable to the PE situated in its territory.

iii. Tickets sold via vending points by the rights-holder Tickets may also be commercialised via selling spots, such as box offices. If all the vending points are situated in the RS of the rights-holder, income deriving from the ticket sales will usually be taxed exclusively by the RS in accordance with the applicable domestic law.[101]

In cases where some of the vending points are situated abroad, in one or several other States, it must be determined whether a PE may be formed in the States concerned or not. A vending point clearly constitutes a fixed PoB through which the core business of the rights-holder is partly carried on.[102]Thereupon, (a) PE(s) may be formed in all the States where the rights-holder operates vending points. The SSs concerned may tax the profits they deem to be attributable to the PE situated in their territory in accordance with article 7(1). Depending on the allocation key used by the SSs for calculating the income attributable to the PE situated in their territory, source-source conflicts may arise.[103]

iv. Tickets sold by the rights-holder via the combination of both methods The combination of methods by the rights-holder does not alter the legal reasoning applicable to the commercialising methods concerned.

100 Article 7(1).
101 With the notable exception of a PE situated in the HS.
102 Article 5(1).
103 For more information on source-source conflicts, see n.52 and n.54.

v. Tickets sold by the commercial partners of the rights-holder This subparagraph examines the income derived by the rights-holder from the ticket commercialisation effectuated by its business partners. As a matter of fact, while the business partners may be entitled to a fixed fee and/or a certain percentage of the proceeds of sale, the majority of the income obtained by the ticket sales accrues to the rights-holder.

In cases where the venue owner and/or the ticket agency are residents of the same State as the rights-holder and they are not commercialising the tickets in any other State – which would be extremely rare for an ISE – no specific international taxation problems arise. The revenue generated by the tickets will be submitted to tax in the RS in accordance with the applicable domestic law.

The situation is more complex in cases where the commercial partners are residents of other States and/or they commercialise the tickets in other States. In accordance with article 7(1), the rights-holder may be subject to tax in these different States to the extent that it has a PE in the States concerned. As the rights-holder is not commercialising the tickets itself, it will not have a PoB at its disposal and, thereby, it will not have a fixed place PE in any of the States concerned.[104] Accordingly, the main question is whether the activities of the commercial partners give rise to the existence of (a) dependent agent PE(s) of the rights-holder in these States.

It seems clear that both the venue owner and the ticket agency are independent third parties acting in the ordinary course of their business under article 5(6). They are generally not controlled by the rights-holder in any manner. Consequently, a PE will not usually be formed in any of the States where the tickets are commercialised; and the income obtained by the rights-holder from the tickets sold by its commercial partners will exclusively be taxed in its RS. Needless to state, in cases where the venue owner or the ticket agency can be categorised as a dependent agent of the rights-holder,[105] a PE (s) of the rights-holder is(are) likely to be formed in the SS(s) concerned and the profits deemed to be attributable to the PE(s) may be taxed by the SS(s).[106]

C. INCOME TAX ANALYSIS OF TICKETS COMMERCIALISED BY THE VENUE OWNER

This paragraph first addresses: (i) the issue of the categorisation of the income; and then separately analyses the two following situations: (ii) the venue owner is a resident of the HS; and (iii) the venue owner is not a resident of the HS.

i. Categorisation of the income Since the rights-holder agrees to allocate a fixed fee and/or a certain percentage of the revenue raised by the ticket sales to the venue owner in consideration of the ticketing services that the latter provides, it is possible to argue that the income derived by the venue owner constitutes business profits within article 7. On the other hand, the venue owner clearly obtains the

104 Article 5(1).
105 Article 5(5).
106 Article 7(1).

income concerned by means of its immovable property, i.e. the venue. Although, the income does not derive from the direct use of the property itself, for example, renting the venue, it can still be categorised as income from immovable property, as article 6 also applies to 'use in any other form of immovable property'[107] including the income generated in course of a business.[108]

Article 6 does not apply when the venue owner is a resident of the State where the venue is situated, i.e. the HS.[109] It is highly debated whether article 7 or article 21 should apply in these cases. For the purposes of the case at hand, it seems more appropriate to categorise the income obtained by the venue owner as business profits within article 7; since a ticketing service, which can potentially create PEs in different States, is being rendered by the owner. The categorisation becomes even more delicate when the venue owner is not a resident of the State where the venue is situated, as in that case the income may potentially fall within the scope of application of both article 6 and article 7.

It is possible to conclude that, depending on the specific circumstances of the case at hand, the share of the ticketing income obtained by the venue owner may be categorised as income from immovable property or business profits by the State applying the DTT and taxed accordingly.

ii. The venue owner is a resident of the HS The income concerned should be categorised as 'business profits' and should, therefore, be submitted to tax exclusively in the RS of the venue owner, unless a PE is constituted in the RS of the rights-holder or in another State.[110] The creation of a PE with respect to ticket sales is examined in the previous paragraph b and is not further developed here.

iii. The venue owner is not a resident of the HS In this subparagraph, for the sake of simplicity, RSV refers to the RS of the venue owner and RSR refers to the RS of the rights-holder.

Article 6 is applicable to this specific case, as a resident of a CS, the RSV, derives an income from an immovable property situated in the other CS, the HS. Whether or not the rights-holder is a resident of one of these two States is insignificant for the application of article 6 of the DTT concluded between the RSV and the HS.[111]

This being stated, the RSR may have an influence on the applicability of article 7. On this point, two situations need to be distinguished: (a) the rights-holder is a resident of the HS or the same State as the venue owner and (b) the rights-holder is a resident of a third State.

107 Article 6(3).
108 REIMER, p.3; FALTIN, §§116–120.
109 Article 6(1).
110 If a PE is created in another State than the RS of the rights-holder, the applicable DTT is the one concluded between the RS of the venue owner and the State where the PE is created.
111 FALTIN, §7.

iii.a. The rights-holder is a resident of the HS or the same State as the venue owner In this first scenario, both article 6 and article 7 of the DTT concluded between the RSV and the HS are applicable. In accordance with article 6(1), the income may be taxed in the HS.[112] As per article 7(1), the income shall be taxed exclusively in the RSV, unless a PE is formed in the HS. In this latter case, the profits that are attributable to the PE may be taxed by the HS.[113]

Consequently, if a PE is considered to be formed in the HS, both article 6 and article 7 provide for a source-taxation, i.e. taxation in the HS. Article 7 offers a more comprehensive regulation on this point, as it allows taking into consideration the expenses of the enterprise[114] and provides both for an adjustment mechanism and a consultation between the two CSs with a view of determining the benefits attributable to the PE in case of a conflict.[115, 116] Thereupon, it is possible to argue that in cases where a PE is formed in the HS, the taxation should occur in accordance with article 7.

If a PE is not formed in the HS, article 6 provides for a source-taxation, whereas article 7 attributes the exclusive right to tax to the RSV. As examined in chapter 2,[117] in case of a conflict between the two distributive rules, article 6 should take precedence. Subsequently, it is possible to conclude that the income may be subject to tax in the *situs* of the immovable property, i.e. the HS.

iii.b. The rights-holder is a resident of a third State This triangular scenario is illustrated in Figure 3.1. The taxation in accordance with the RSV-HS DTT is

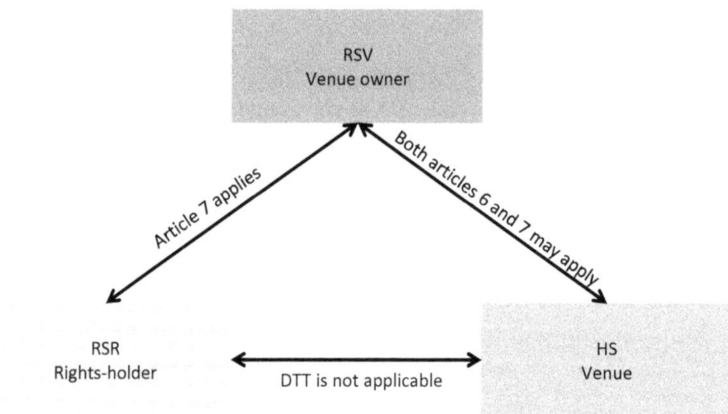

Figure 3.1

112 Article 6(1).
113 Article 7(1).
114 Article 7(2). The PE is considered as 'a separate and independent enterprise'.
115 Article 7(3).
116 FALTIN, §127.
117 Chapter 2, II, C, 7.

examined in the previous sub-subparagraph and is not further developed here. As per the RSV-RSR DTT, its article 7 will grant the exclusive right to tax to the RSV to the extent where no PE is formed in the RSR. The applicable taxation modalities can be summarised as follows in this case: no tax will be levied by the RSR, the HS will be entitled to tax the income deriving from the venue and the RSV will either exempt such income[118] or credit[119] the tax paid in the HS by the venue owner.

If a PE is formed in the RSR due to the ticketing services, the RSV-RSR DTT will grant to the RSR the right to tax the profits attributable to the PE.[120] Depending on the income considered to be attributable to the PE situated in its territory by the RSR and the HS, respectively, this situation may amount to a source-source conflict.[121] This conflict cannot be resolved via the RSR-HS DTT, since the venue owner is not a resident of either of the States concerned.[122] As a result, the double taxation will most probably subsist in this specific case.

D. INCOME TAX ANALYSIS OF TICKETS COMMERCIALISED BY TICKET AGENCIES

Ticket agencies may be entitled to receive a commission on the tickets sold or a fixed fee paid by the rights-holder. Both types of income should be categorised as 'business profits' within article 7. As per the first paragraph of this distributive rule, ticket agencies shall exclusively be taxable in their RS, unless they have a PE in another SS. In this latter case, the SS where the PE is situated may tax the profits attributable to that PE, as per the DTT concluded between the RS of the ticket agency and the SS concerned.[123] The constitution of a PE is subject to the same observations made with regard to tickets commercialised by the rights-holder.[124] The fact that the ticket agency is remunerated by the rights-holder is clearly not sufficient to constitute a PE in the RS of the rights-holder per se.

E. VAT MODALITIES

Admission to sports events constitutes a typical example of on-the-spot supply of services taxable at the location where the event concerned actually takes place, i.e. the HS, regardless of whether the tickets are purchased by businesses or by consumers.[125] This observation holds true for the purposes of entertainment activities, such as eSports, as well. Tickets of some sports events may include ancillary services, such as parking and catering. Such services also form on-the-spot supply of services that are taxable at the location where the event takes place, to the extent where they are physically carried out. The fact that the tickets are commercialised

118 Article 23A.
119 Article 23B.
120 Article 7(1).
121 Defined in n.52.
122 Article 1.
123 Article 7(1).
124 See paragraph b of this sub-subsection.
125 See, for example, articles 53 and 54 of the VAT Directive.

by the rights-holder or by other authorised parties does not, as a general rule, give rise to a change of the applicable place-of-supply rule.[126]

Most States opt for exempting or applying a reduced rate to sports events tickets (entertainment activities may not benefit from this special treatment).[127] In cases where the ticket grants the right to obtain additional services that attract VAT at a higher rate than the admission to the event (respectively that are not exempt), it would be advisable for such services to be distinctly indicated on the ticket (or on the invoice) along with the portion of the ticket price paid for them. In fact, if the services concerned cannot be considered as ancillary to admission to the sporting event,[128] they will attract VAT at their usual rate.

It is important to note that some countries may opt for exempting the tickets of sports events, and other similar activities, from VAT in favour of another consumption tax, such as an 'entertainment tax'.

3. Ticket touting

A. GENERAL CONSIDERATIONS

Ticket touting can be defined as the act of obtaining tickets to events in order to sell them at an inflated price without being duly authorised to do so by the rights-holder. Needless to say, the fact that an official of the rights-holder is cooperating with the ticket tout in view of obtaining a personal gain does not amount to an authorisation. Ticket touting thus refers to a 'black market' or a 'secondary ticket market'[129] formed by unauthorised re-sellers. This unlawful activity, the practice of which has become even more facilitated with the expansion of e-commerce,[130] constitutes a non-negligible problem for the sports industry.

B. INCOME TAX ANALYSIS

i. Relevant domestic law aspects Taxation of the income derived by a ticket tout occurs in accordance with the domestic law of their/its RS. Ticket touting forms an unlawful activity that may be considered as a criminal offence, as it is the case in a number of European countries,[131] or as amounting to a violation of civil law. In countries where ticket touting is classified as a criminal offence, the income deriving from such an activity will usually either be forfeited or be passed on to the harmed person for the purpose of restoring the prior lawful position, to the extent where the unlawful activity can be identified and prosecuted – which may be significantly difficult due to its predominantly 'online' nature. In countries where

126 See, for example, article 33a of the Implementing Regulation 282/2011/EU.
127 See, for example, annex III(13) and annex X, part B(1) of the VAT Directive.
128 The scope of this categorisation depends on the applicable domestic law.
129 See PARENT/SMITH-SWAN, p.255.
130 See, for example, TORKILDSEN, p.18.
131 Ibid.

ticket touting is not categorised as a criminal offence, an obligation to repay may still arise under the civil law, provided that the harmed party makes an enforceable claim. Undoubtedly, if the officials of the SGB themselves are involved in ticket touting activities, the chances for such a claim to be made are slim.

Clearly, to the extent not detected by the authorities, the income obtained from unauthorised sale of second-hand tickets will not, usually, be declared for taxation purposes by the ticket touts. The detection of the activities concerned by the authorities will, on the other hand, translate into an obligation to repay in most cases. An obligation to repay entails that no taxable income exists. It is, therefore, possible to conclude that the profits made by a ticket tout are not likely to be submitted to income tax in their/its RS.

ii. International tax law aspects In cases where the ticket touting activity is effectively identified and prosecuted, the rights-holder may be entitled to an amount paid by the ticket tout.[132] The amount concerned may be formed by: (i) repayment of the income generated from the unlawful activity; (ii) a compensation payment in view of repairing the damage caused to the rights-holder (both in terms of business profits and reputational or similar damage); or (iii) a combination of both.

The payment made for compensating the profit loss constitutes ‘business profits’ within article 7. All payments going beyond the profit loss, most typically payments effectuated for repairing the reputational damage, should be categorised as ‘other income’ under article 21. Since ticket touting generally consists of buying the tickets at their regular price and then selling them in the second-hand market at a mark-up, the income that would otherwise have been obtained by the rights-holder from ticket sales is usually not reduced. Thereupon, the amount paid by the ticket tout to the rights-holder falls, in most cases, within the scope of article 21.

On the other hand, in cases where the ticket tout is collaborating with an official of the rights-holder and manages to obtain the tickets at a reduced price – incurring thereby a loss to the rights-holder – the part of the payment made by the ticket tout relating to the profit loss should be categorised as ‘business profits’ under article 7. The payment effectuated by the ticket tout will generally not be exclusively composed of the reimbursement of the profit loss. It will also include a compensation for reputational and other similar damage. In that event an apportionment may be necessary for categorisation purposes, since the latter income is not covered by article 7 but by article 21.

This being stated, this apportionment will only have a theoretical significance, as both distributive rules grant the right to tax the income to the RS of the rights-holder.[133] Consequently, it is possible to state that the rights-holder will be submitted to tax exclusively in its RS on the income concerned.[134]

132 The applicable DTT is the one concluded between the RS of the rights-holder and the RS of the ticket tout.
133 Articles 7(1) and 21(1). On this point, it is important to underline that activities conducted by ticket touts will not generally form a PE of the rights-holder.
134 Both distributive rules use the term ‘shall be taxable only’.

To the extent that an unlawful payment was made to an individual[135] in order to conduct the ticket touting activities, most probably an official of the right-s-holder, such payment should also be categorised as 'other income' under article 21. Thereupon, the income concerned will be subject to tax exclusively in the RS of the individual,[136] in accordance with the domestic law of that State.

C. VAT ANALYSIS

VAT treatment of tickets sold in the black market may vary from jurisdiction to jurisdiction. Under the European system, such transactions fall within the scope of VAT. Ticket touts effectuate an activity that is not absolutely prohibited per se (i.e. commercialising tickets), without having obtained the relevant authorisations from the rights-holder (i.e. in an unlawful manner).[137] Unlawfully commercialised tickets by ticket touts are clearly in competition with lawfully marketed tickets. Accordingly, the VAT treatment of unauthorised sale of second-hand tickets should not diverge from the treatment of authorised sale of tickets,[138] which implies that if a reduced rate (or exemption) is applicable to sports events tickets commercialised in a lawful manner, the same rate (or exemption) should also be applied to tickets sold in the black market.

Payments made (if any) by ticket touts to rights-holders to compensate the loss and/or the reputational damage suffered by the latter are usually considered to fall outside the scope of VAT, since a supply for consideration does not exist in such cases.

E. Hospitality

1. General observations

Hospitality is a global industry worth around 15 billion USD annually[139] that constitutes an important source of revenue for venue owners, rights-holders and hospitality providers (for a typical hospitality structure, see Figure 3.2). Hospitality commonly refers to a package of event-related benefits sold to third parties. The main components of a hospitality package are tickets to the event, entertainment, food and beverage. Packages may also include transport, management and administration services, booking facilities and company care.

Rights-holders tend to enter into hospitality agreements with hospitality providers in view of the commercialisation of their events' hospitality packages. The hospitality provider(s) that concluded a contract with the rights-holder of the event, is/are referred to as the 'official hospitality provider(s)' of the event concerned. Appointing an official provider constitutes a highly beneficial practice for

135 The applicable DTT is the one concluded between the RS of the individual concerned and the RS of the ticket tout.
136 Article 21(1).
137 The Lange decision, §§12–13; the Fischer decision, §§19–20.
138 The Lange decision, §19; the Fischer decision, §§22 and 28.
139 BLACKSHAW, *Sports Marketing Agreements*, p.89.

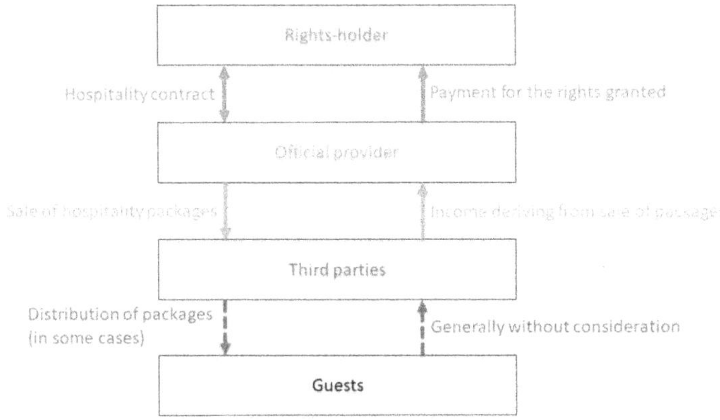

Figure 3.2

event owners, mainly for the following three reasons: (i) the remuneration obtained from the official hospitality provider(s) constitutes an additional revenue stream for the rights-holder; (ii) the prevalence of unofficial activities is reduced; and (iii) the provision and the quality of the hospitality packages are secured.[140]

Official providers derive their income from the sale of hospitality packages to third parties, i.e. their clients. Since hospitality forms a lucrative business, unofficial hospitality providers are relentlessly trying to get a piece of the pie. Unofficial providers acquire tickets to the event and try to secure access rights to the venue from unauthorised sources.[141] Given the manner in which they are formed, the unofficial packages are far from being reliable. It is even possible for the purchasers of such packages to find out that their tickets do not provide a legitimate entrance to the event.[142]

Purchasers of hospitality packages may use them for 'corporate hospitality' purposes, such as entertaining their clients and rewarding their employees.[143] Such use implies that the packages are distributed on a free of charge basis. Regarding the employees, the obtained packages will form a benefit-in-kind remuneration.[144]

2. *Taxation of official hospitality providers*

A. INCOME TAX

Official hospitality providers derive their income from the sales of hospitality packages, which may – like tickets – be commercialised online or via vending points. Given the

140 BECKER, p.124.
141 Ibid, pp.123–124.
142 Ibid, p.69.
143 BLACKSHAW, *Sports Marketing Agreements*, p.89.
144 For taxation modalities of these benefit-in-kind remunerations, see paragraphs N, 2, b and c of this section.

similarity of the commercialisation methods, the income tax modalities of the income obtained by the official hospitality providers are identical to ticket agencies.[145]

B. VAT ANALYSIS

Hospitality packages consist of a bundle of different services, which necessarily include tickets to the event and catering services, and which may include other services such as transport and accommodation. Regardless of being commercialised as 'one package', the services concerned are, in fact, independent of each other, i.e. none of them can be considered as being ancillary to one principal service. Thereupon, each service supplied needs to be considered as a separate service and submitted to tax in accordance with the relevant place-of-supply rule. Since the hospitality provider acts as an intermediary in the provision of all the services concerned, it is important to verify whether a specific place-of-supply rule is provided in the applicable VAT legislation for the services rendered by intermediaries.[146]

Admission to the event and catering services form typical examples of on-the-spot supplies that are taxable at the location where they are physically carried out, i.e. in the HS, regardless of whether they are provided to businesses or consumers.[147] As per the predominant practice, both supplies are likely to benefit from a reduced rate.[148] Accommodation provided in the hotels and similar establishments is usually submitted to tax at the place where the immovable property is located, i.e. the HS.[149] Such services tend to be subject to a reduced rate as well.[150] Other services that may be provided are to be analysed in accordance with the domestic VAT legislation.

It is important to note that the national legislation may provide for an exemption (with a right to deduct the input tax) of hospitality services provided on a free-of-charge basis to government and/or rights-holder officials attending the event.[151]

3. Taxation of unofficial hospitality providers

A. GENERAL CONSIDERATIONS

Unofficial hospitality providers commercialise travel packages that include second-hand, i.e. unauthorised, tickets to the event. There are two main unlawful components of such an activity: (i) incorporation of second-hand tickets in the hospitality packages; and (ii) use of the name and/or logo of the event and/or the

145 See paragraph D, 2, d of this section.
146 Such as article 46 of the VAT Directive.
147 See, for example, ibid, articles 53, 54 and 55.
148 See, for instance, ibid, annex III(12a) and (13).
149 See, for example, ibid, article 47.
150 See, for instance, ibid, annex III(12).
151 This is, for example, the case in Switzerland. See *Info TVA*, §10.6.

rights-holder in an unauthorised manner. The rest of the services provided, i.e. tickets secured for travelling, accommodation and other similar touristic attractions, are not unlawful.

B. DOMESTIC TAX LAW ASPECTS

The tax treatment of ticket touting is described in the previous subsection.[152] Unauthorised use of the event's and/or the right-holder's name and/or logo will usually violate the intellectual property laws or a special law or statute protecting the intellectual property of the event concerned.[153] This violation may give rise to an injunction to use the intellectual property in question, payment of damages to the rights-holder and/or other legal remedies.

In cases where the unofficial hospitality provider is required to reimburse the amount derived from ticket sales to the rights-holder, the repaid amount should not be taken into consideration as a part of the hospitality provider's taxable income. Subsequently, the income of the taxpayer must be assessed with regard to sums generated by the commercialisation of the remaining components of the packages.

The benefit obtained by the unofficial hospitality provider from the unauthorised use of intellectual property should be distinguished from the income generated via the sale of second-hand tickets. Ticket touting is an unlawful activity that directly gives rise to an income, i.e. a ticket is sold in consideration of a certain amount. On the other hand, the unauthorised use of the event's and/or the rights-holder's name and/or logo does not generate an income as such, since what is being commercialised is a hospitality package and not the intellectual property concerned. Such unauthorised use merely associates the hospitality provider with the event and/or the rights-holder with an aim to increase the sales.

Accordingly, the unauthorised use of the event's and/or the rights-holder's logo will usually not give rise to an obligation to repay the amount earned by the unlawful activity. In other words, the unofficial hospitality provider will not generally have an obligation to reimburse the income earned by their/its activity to the rights-holder purely on this basis.[154] It will, however, have an obligation to pay a certain amount determined by the competent court to compensate the damages incurred as a result of the unlawful conduct. Depending on the applicable national law, the damages may have a purely 'compensatory' or 'punitive' character or a combination of both. This payment should be taken into consideration not during the assessment of the taxable income but during the calculation of admissible deductions. Whether such a payment is an admissible deduction or not will depend on the modalities of the applicable national law.

152 Sub-subsection D, 3 of this section.
153 Enactment of a specific law or statute protecting the intellectual property of the event may be required by the SGB for awarding an HS the right to stage the sports event. This is for example the case for the FIFA World Cup. For the example of South Africa, see BLACKSHAW, *Ambush Marketing*, p.5ff.
154 The assets will not be forfeited either, since violating an intellectual property right does not generally amount to a criminal offence.

C. INTERNATIONAL TAX LAW ASPECTS

International tax law aspects of payments that can be made by unofficial hospitality providers to rights-holders, to the extent where the unlawful activities can be effectively detected and prosecuted, are highly similar to international tax law aspects of ticket touting examined in the previous subsection.[155] It is, however, important to underline that compensatory payments made for repairing the damage caused by the unauthorised use of the name and/or the logo of the event and/or of the rights-holder should be categorised as 'other income' within article 21 and taxed accordingly.[156]

D. VAT MODALITIES

While the VAT modalities of unofficial hospitality packages may vary from jurisdiction to jurisdiction, they are likely to be the same as the official hospitality packages, given the facts that the majority of the components of the packages concerned are not unlawful; and the unlawful services provided by unofficial hospitality providers consist of activities that can compete with their lawful counterparts.[157]

Compensatory payments made (if any) by unofficial hospitality providers to rights-holders are usually considered to fall outside the scope of VAT, due to the lack of a supply for consideration.

4. *Taxation of the rights-holder*

A. GENERAL OBSERVATIONS

The rights granted by the rights-holder to an official hospitality provider under a hospitality contract may be grouped under three main categories: (i) the right to use the name, the logo and other similar intellectual properties of the event and the rights-holder; (ii) the right to commercialise the event's hospitality packages (which typically includes the right to buy tickets at a certain price); and (iii) the rights to have access to and to make use of certain areas of the venue.

In consideration of the concessions made by the rights-holder, the official provider is under the obligation to pay a fee. The rights-holder's remuneration usually occurs by means of the three following methods (alternatively or cumulatively): (i) a fixed fee, which may be reimbursed in the form of a licence fee paid (generally) prior to the beginning of the event (in one or several instalments) – for use of the event's name, logo and photographs – or as a minimum guaranteed amount of the hospitality sales revenues; (ii) a percentage of revenues or profits deriving from the hospitality sales; and (iii) the cost of tickets.[158]

155 See paragraph D, 3, b of this section.
156 The applicable DTT is the one concluded between the RS of the rights-holder and the RS of the unofficial hospitality provider.
157 See the Lange decision, §19; the Fischer decision, §§22 and 28.
158 BECKER, p.129.

Taxation modalities of each set of rights granted by the rights-holder differ to a great extent. Hence, a separate analysis is necessary. Distinct tax treatment translates into the necessity to establish the amount obtained for each group of rights. Should the contract concluded between the parties already specify the remuneration for each set, the apportionment may be more effortless.[159] If the contract provides for an overall fee, the apportionment may be made by the competent authorities. The modalities of such apportionment depend on the specificities of the contract at hand as well as on the practice and the domestic law(s) of the State(s) concerned.

B. INCOME TAX

To the extent where the official hospitality provider is a resident of the rights-holder's RS, taxation occurs in accordance with the domestic law of the State concerned and an international tax problem does not arise.[160] In cases where the hospitality provider is a resident of another State, an international tax law analysis needs to be conducted to determine whether this latter State may submit the income concerned to tax. Accordingly, for the purposes of the following analysis, it is assumed that the official hospitality provider is a resident of a State other than the rights-holder's RS.

i. Right to use the name, logo and other similar intellectual properties of the rights-holder The name, the logo[161] and other similar intellectual properties related to a sports event usually constitute copyrights, trademarks or both. Consequently, granting the right to use them is akin to a licence agreement and the consideration obtained in exchange of the rights concerned should be categorised as royalties. In accordance with article 12(1), the income derived by the rights-holder shall be taxable exclusively in its RS. In other words, the RS of the official hospitality provider, and thereby the SS of the royalties, is not entitled to impose a tax on the revenue concerned. This being stated, DTTs often provide for a source-taxation as well. Consequently, the rights-holder may be subject to tax both in the RS – corporate income tax – and in the SS – a final withholding tax up to a certain percentage determined by the DTT.

ii. Right to commercialise the event's hospitality packages In exchange for granting the right to commercialise the event's hospitality packages, the rights-holder usually receives from the official hospitality provider either a minimum guaranteed amount of the hospitality sales or a percentage of the profits deriving from the

159 It is important to remind that the competent authorities are not bound by the apportionment made by the parties.

160 With the notable exception of a PE situated in the HS, as described in subsection IV, B of this chapter. It should, however, be noted that not all profits deriving from hospitality agreements are business profits, as is developed further in this sub-subsection.

161 Whether protected by a copyright, a trademark or both.

package sales. In both cases, the profits obtained by the rights-holder should be categorised as business profits under article 7.

Accordingly, the profits concerned are taxable in the rights-holder's RS.[162] In fact, the activities of the official hospitality provider are not susceptible to constitute a PE of the rights-holder, as the former is an independent commercial partner acting in the ordinary course of its business.[163]

iii. Rights to have access to and to make use of certain areas of the venue The rights-holder may also grant to the official hospitality provider an access to and the right to use certain areas of the venue. Consideration obtained for this right to access to and use of the venue is akin to a rental income. In fact, the rights-holder, which is the tenant of the venue for a certain period of time, sublets the right to use a certain part of it to a third party, i.e. the hospitality provider.

Since a typical sports venue clearly constitutes an immovable property, taxation of this rental income falls, in principle, within the scope of application of article 6. The fact that the rights-holder does not own the venue is not relevant for the application of the distributive rule concerned.

In cases where the official hospitality provider is not a resident of either the rights-holder's RS or the HS, a triangular situation, along with the necessity of determining the applicable DTT, will arise. The RS of the legal person paying the fee, *in casu* the official hospitality provider, is not relevant for the purposes of the allocation rule concerned.[164] Only the RS of the legal person entitled to the income and the State where the immovable property is situated are determinant. As the sports venue is situated in the HS, the applicable DTT is the one concluded between the HS and the RS of the rights-holder.

It can, therefore, be stated that the income obtained by the rights-holder in exchange for the right to use the venue is submitted to tax[165] in the HS where the venue is situated.[166]

The most notable exception to this general observation may occur in the specific case of endurance events, during which no conventional venue exists. Hospitality areas of such events generally consist of short-term constructions, such as tents and stalls. These short-term constructions are rather unlikely to be categorised as an immovable property by the HS. In that eventuality, the income concerned should be characterised as business profits under article 7 and taxed accordingly.

C. VAT

Granting the right to use the name, logo and/or similar intellectual properties as well as the right to commercialise the event's hospitality packages constitute

162 Article 7(1).
163 Article 5(6).
164 FALTIN, §7.
165 The provision contains the term 'may be taxed'.
166 Article 6(1).

supplies of services effectuated by the rights-holder for the benefit of the official hospitality provider (B2B transactions). Accordingly, these transactions are to be submitted to tax in the jurisdiction of the hospitality provider's location (i.e. its business' PoE).

On the other hand, the rights to have access to and use certain areas of the venue constitute a supply of service (effectuated by the rights-holder for the hospitality provider) that has a sufficiently direct connection with an immovable property.[167] It is, in fact, clear that the venue makes up a constituent element of the service and is central to, and essential for, the service being supplied.[168] Consequently, the taxing right belongs to the jurisdiction in which the immovable property is located, i.e. the HS. The location of the recipient of the service (official hospitality provider) is not pertinent for the VAT treatment.[169]

In cases where the official hospitality provider has its business' PoE in the HS, no specific problems arise, since the entirety of the supply of services becomes taxable in the State concerned. In cases where the official hospitality provider's location is not situated in the HS, however, the applicable place-of-supply rules allocate the right to tax to different States. In such circumstances, the rule applicable to the characteristic features of the service concerned (i.e. the principal supply) is usually applied to the entirety of the service. It can be argued that hospitality services being prominently linked to the venue, the principal supply of service is the grant of the rights to have access to and to make use of the venue to the official hospitality provider and, therefore, the right to tax should be granted to the HS.

F. Supplies of goods and services

1. General aspects

Several goods and services, such as transportation, custodial services, waste management, security, lighting, event timing (also called on-venue result management) and catering, are provided by different suppliers during an ISE. Suppliers are generally entitled to a fee in exchange for their activity. Some suppliers, such as caterers, may operate via a stand or a concession situated at the venue. Such suppliers derive their income from the sales made. They usually pay the rights-holder a certain percentage of the income generated at the event.[170] The percentage may be based on gross or net revenues, depending on the arrangement between the parties.[171]

A supplier may agree to provide its goods or services either free of charge or at a lower price, in order to secure some benefits-in-kind, usually a set of rights related to the event.[172] For example, the supplier might obtain the right to be designated

167 Article 31a(1) of the Implementing Regulation 282/2011/EU.
168 Ibid, article 31a(1)(a). For more information, see *Explanatory notes on immovable property*, §139.
169 *Explanatory notes on immovable property*, §138.
170 BECKER, p.110.
171 Ibid.
172 Ibid, pp.100–101.

as the 'official supplier', the right to use the event's trademarks, advertising rights or hospitality rights to a certain extent.[173] In most cases, the official supplier arrangement is in fact a sponsorship deal. The sponsor becomes the official supplier in order to associate its product(s) and/or its service(s) with the event.[174] This status is examined in detail under the subsection relating to sponsorship contracts.[175]

Suppliers may need to deploy a certain number of their employees and some equipment to the venue in order to render their services. They may also have to obtain some permits and licences (e.g. an alcohol licence) where the responsibility to obtain such authorisations is not borne by the event manager. It is also important to underline that suppliers may enter into contracts with subcontractors in order to fulfil their obligations, to the extent where subcontracting is not expressly excluded in the relevant supplier contract. Subcontractors are generally remunerated by the suppliers.

2. *Taxation modalities*

A. INCOME TAX

Suppliers may: (i) be remunerated by the rights-holder for the services and/or the goods they provide; (ii) derive an income from their concessions/stands at the venue; or (iii) generate revenue from a combination of both. Taxation of the suppliers falling within the third category is not examined separately, given the fact that a combination of the profit-making methods does not alter the taxation modalities.

Prior to beginning the analysis, it is important to underline that in all cases, the revenue derived by suppliers from a sports event should be categorised as business profits under article 7 and taxed accordingly.

i. Remuneration obtained from the rights-holder To the extent where the rights-holder and the supplier are both residents of the State where the event takes place, the income of the supplier will be taxed in accordance with the HS' domestic law. In other cases, the rules of the relevant DTT will apply.

If the supplier is a resident of the HS, the remuneration paid by the rights-holder shall be exclusively subject to tax in the HS in accordance with article 7(1).[176] The supplier will usually not have a PE in the RS of the rights-holder, or in any other States, as the services will be rendered directly at the sports venue, which is situated in the HS.

If the supplier is a resident of a State other than the HS, article 7 of the DTT concluded between the RS of the rights-holder and the RS of the supplier will grant the right to tax exclusively to the latter State, in the absence of a PE in the

173 Ibid.
174 MACLEAN/MOORHOUSE, p.1244.
175 See subsection I of this section.
176 The applicable DTT is the one concluded between the rights-holder's RS and the HS.

former State.[177] It must, however, also be verified whether the HS may be entitled to tax a part of the income in accordance with the DTT concluded between the HS and the RS of the supplier, which would be the case if the supplier has a PE in the HS.

As a matter of fact, the supplier will generally have at its disposal the relevant parts of the sports venue or another structure, which may be considered as a PoB. The business of the supplier will usually be carried on through that particular PoB. In cases where the supplier takes at least six months to provide the services concerned, the 'fixed' criterion will also be satisfied and a fixed place PE may be formed in the HS.[178] While the creation of a fixed place PE is more likely than the other types of PE, the existence of a dependent agent or a service PE cannot be excluded altogether. A detailed PE analysis needs to be effectuated on a case-by-case basis and in the light of all relevant circumstances.

ii. Income generated from the stands at the venue If the supplier is a resident of the HS, the income generated from the stands at the venue will be taxed in accordance with the HS' domestic law. If the supplier is a resident of another State, the relevant distributive rules of the DTT concluded between the HS and the RS of the supplier will apply.

Business profits are exclusively taxable in the RS of the supplier, except in cases where a PE is formed in the HS.[179] With regard to activities conducted by means of stands at the venue, the type of PE that risks being constituted is a fixed place PE. A stand is undisputedly a PoB. In cases where it is effectively used to commercialise the products, for example, sale of food and beverage, the core business of the enterprise will be carried on through that PoB. If the stand is held only for promotional purposes, this condition will not be fulfilled and a PE will not be formed in the HS.[180]This being stated, the 'fixed' criterion will generally not be fulfilled in any case as the stands at the sports venue will be used for a period significantly shorter than six months. Therefore, it is possible to argue that the probability of a PE being formed in the HS is extremely low, and that the suppliers are taxable only in their RS.[181]

B. VAT

The VAT treatment of the transactions effectuated by the suppliers heavily depends on the type and specificities of the activities undertaken by the suppliers concerned. Accordingly, it is not possible to make a generalised VAT analysis that holds true for all supplier transactions taking place during an ISE. A number of observations may, however, be made.

177 Article 7(1).
178 Article 5(1).
179 Article 7(1).
180 Fixed places of business held exclusively for advertising purposes fall within the scope of article 5(4)(e). See also *OECD Commentary* on article 5, §71 on this point.
181 Article 7(1).

The services provided by suppliers to the rights-holder constitute B2B services, taxable, as a general rule, at the place where this latter established its business.[182] To the extent where the applicable legislation considers the services provided by a given supplier as being a 'prerequisite' for the performance of the sporting activity, the services concerned may be deemed to be ancillary to the sporting activity and be submitted to tax at the location where the event actually takes place, i.e. the HS.[183] The application of this place-of-supply rule will, usually, not be dependent upon the sporting level of the service concerned or the identity of the person providing it.[184] For instance, on-venue result management services may be considered as being a prerequisite for the performance of an ISE by the HS.

If suppliers are selling goods to the rights-holder, the exported goods will be free of VAT in the supplier's jurisdiction and the imported goods will be submitted to tax at the place where they are located at the time of their delivery, most likely the HS, at the same rate as the domestic goods of the jurisdiction concerned. Goods may also be subject to customs duties, unless they fall within the scope of a low-value threshold or qualify for a temporary importation procedure.

The services provided by suppliers directly to consumers by means of the stands situated at the venue are likely to form typical on-the-spot supplies taxable at the place where they are physically carried out, i.e. the HS.

G. Merchandising

1. General aspects

A merchandising contract is an agreement whereby a person ('merchandisor') grants to a third party ('merchandisee') the right to affix a trademark to products or services that are notably different in nature from the products or services for which the trademark has originally been created and registered, in order to allow the merchandisee to commercially exploit the trademark's reputation.[185] Albeit the existence of several categories of merchandising, such as 'logo merchandising',[186] 'personality merchandising'[187] and 'character merchandising',[188, 189] the main characteristics of merchandising agreements remain largely the same. The most common merchandising arrangements that have a link with an ISE are the ones entered into by rights-holders, sports teams and sportspersons.

182 Article 44 of the VAT Directive.
183 See, for example, article 54 of the VAT Directive and the Dudda decision, §27.
184 The Dudda decision, §§25 and 28.
185 TERCIER PIERRE/FAVRE PASCAL G., *Les contrats spéciaux*, 4th edition, Schulthess, 2009, §7968.
186 Merchandising of the logo(s) and/or the emblem(s) of the event or the team concerned.
187 Merchandising related to individuals, e.g. sportspersons.
188 Merchandising by the use of a fictional character, i.e. the mascot of the event or the team (e.g. Fuleco the Armadillo of the 2014 FIFA World Cup).
189 BLACKSHAW, *Sports Marketing Agreements*, p.223.

ISE merchandising involves the sale of merchandise by reference to the event itself.[190] The exploitation of the event's merchandising rights is most typically effectuated by the rights-holder. This type of merchandising implies that a manufacturer produces a range of products, such as T-shirts, caps and key chains, carrying the logo or trademarks of the event concerned.[191] These products, allowing fans to commemorate their attendance at the event, can be sold directly at the venue, at retail stores and/or online. Personality merchandising is a process whereby one or several of the essential attributes – such as name, nickname, image, voice and signature – of a sportsperson is affixed on a product or a service. As the person whose attributes are 'commercialised' is usually well-known to the public at large, this form of merchandising is also referred to as 'reputation merchandising'.[192] Numerous examples of personality merchandising may be observed among sportspersons, not exclusively for sporting products but also for everyday items. Puma's running shoes bearing Usain Bolt's signature and perfume bottles labelled with David Beckham's name are typical examples of personality merchandising. Sports team merchandising is akin to personality merchandising. It forms a way of commercially exploiting the team's reputation.

The main obligation of the merchandisor is to grant the right to use the relevant intellectual property to the merchandisee(s). Most typically, rights relating to different product categories (such as soft goods, hard goods, electronic games and memorabilia)[193] are licensed to different merchandisees. At their end, the merchandisees are required to manufacture, promote, distribute and sell the merchandised items as well as to pay royalties to the merchandisor in exchange for the rights granted.

In sports merchandising contracts, royalties are generally structured to have three components: periodic payments, advance and minimum-guarantee.[194] Periodic payments are usually calculated as a percentage of the income derived by the sales of the licensed products.[195] An advance can be defined as an upfront payment to be credited against the periodic payments to be made in the future.[196] The amount of the advance is subject to negotiation between the contracting parties; however, it usually represents a considerable percentage of the periodic payments expected to be made over the merchandising term.[197] The minimum-guarantee indicates a sum that the merchandisee should pay, regardless of whether or not it actually succeeds in selling a sufficient volume of licensed products to generate the amount concerned.[198] In other words, the minimum-guarantee constitutes a non-refundable minimum payment. In addition to royalties, the parties may also agree on a licence

190 BECKER, p.163.
191 Ibid.
192 WIPO, *Report on Character Merchandising*, WO/INF/108, December 1994, p.9.
193 WISE/MEYER, p.1901.
194 Ibid, p.1907.
195 BECKER, p.167.
196 WISE/MEYER, p.1907.
197 Ibid.
198 Ibid

fee, which is a lump-sum paid upon the signature of the merchandising contract. The licence fee is usually neither refundable nor recoupable.[199] It is considered to be a one-off payment to obtain the relevant rights.[200]

It is common for merchandisors to require an additional payment from merchandisees, which will generally correspond to a certain percentage of product sales, in order to constitute an advertising and promotion fund.[201] As the fund will be used to promote the merchandised articles, it benefits both the merchandisor and the merchandisee. Accordingly, the payments made for the fund should not be considered as royalties.[202] Business expenses would be a more appropriate categorisation.

Should the merchandisee have recourse to subcontractors, the remuneration method of this particular contractual relation will be different, given the fact that subcontractors are suppliers and not licensees. For this reason, their remuneration is akin to the remuneration methods of supplier agreements, i.e. a fee paid for the provision of goods and/or services and not royalties. Certainly, if the merchandisee makes use of sublicensees instead of subcontractors, the remuneration methods described in this subsection apply to the contractual relations concerned.

It is important to underline that some teams or rights-holders may prefer to effectively produce their own lines of merchandise and branded goods, or to engage manufacturers to fabricate these items in accordance with their specifications, without concluding any merchandising agreements.[203] In those cases, the contracts concluded can be categorised as commercial manufacturing and supplier arrangements.

2. Taxation modalities

A. INCOME TAX

i. Income obtained by the rights-holder and sports teams In cases where the merchandisee and the rights-holder/sports team are residents of the same State, the taxation will be effectuated in accordance with the domestic law of that State. In other cases, the DTT concluded between the RS of the merchandisee and the RS of the rights-holder/sports team will apply.

The categorisation of the merchandising income as royalties within article 12 (2) does not cause any specific problems. Consequently, the fees obtained by the rights-holder/sports team from its merchandisees, either as periodic payments or as a lump-sum amount, should exclusively be taxed in the RS of the rights-holder/sports team in accordance with article 12(1). In cases where the applicable DTT also provides for a source taxation of royalties, the rights-holder/sports team may be subject to tax both in its RS – corporate income

199 BECKER, p.168.
200 Ibid.
201 WISE/MEYER, p.1902.
202 Ibid.
203 LAWRENCE, p.1279.

tax – and in the RS of its merchandisee (i.e. the SS) – a final withholding tax up to a certain percentage determined by the DTT.

ii. Income obtained by sportspersons As provided clearly by the OECD Commentary since 2014, to the extent where the merchandising income obtained by a sportsperson can be categorised as royalties, the income concerned should be taxed in accordance with article 12.[204] The categorisation of the merchandising income as royalties depends on the modalities of national legislations. An important number of countries allow sportspersons' essential attributes to be protected by means of trademark registration. Many sportspersons have opted to make use of this possibility. For instance, Usain Bolt registered his 'Lightning Bolt' pose as well as his 'to di world' slogan.[205]

To the extent where the HS' domestic law considers sportspersons' attributes as intellectual property, the country will have to refrain from taxing the merchandising income under article 17. This would imply that the HS will not be entitled to tax the income concerned at all, unless it is also the RS of the merchandisee, i.e. the SS of the royalties concerned. The income would thus become solely taxable under the DTT concluded between the RSs of the sportsperson and the merchandisee. If the RSs concerned categorise the merchandising income as royalties, the income obtained by the sportsperson will be taxable only in their RS in accordance with article 12 of the relevant DTT. Should the DTT follow the UN MC on this point, the SS[206] will also have a right to tax royalties at source up to a certain percentage.[207]

In cases where the relevant domestic laws do not categorise merchandising income as royalties, the HS may either consider that the income is closely connected with the public performance taking place in its territory, and thereby taxable under article 17, or that the income is not closely connected with the public performance concerned, and thereupon taxable under article 7 (respectively article 14 of the UN MC) or article 15, depending on the circumstances of the case at hand.

On this point, the main issue resides in determining the extent of the term 'closely connected' with regard to merchandising. Undoubtedly, income deriving from products bearing the trademark, the logo or a similar designation of the sports event along with the personal attributes of the sportsperson is closely connected to the sports event concerned, to the extent where the products are commercialised before or during the sports event, regardless of whether directly at the venue or in the territory of the HS. Products commercialised after the event should not fall within the scope of article 17 for the sake of avoiding a disproportionate burden – both administrative and tax – as well as an increased risk of double taxation[208] placed on sportspersons. Products that do not bear any

204 *OECD Commentary* on article 17, §9.
205 http://www.wipo.int/ip-sport/en/branding.html (accessed on 23.06.2015).
206 The RS of the merchandisee.
207 As provided in article 12(2) of the UN MC.
208 In the eventuality where the income is considered as closely connected to a public performance, an apportionment problem will arise.

designation relating to the event should not be considered as having a close connection with the event concerned either, even if the sportsperson whose personal attributes are being used takes part in the event. As a matter of fact, merchandised items may be sold in the HS throughout the year, for a shorter period or for a longer period. To consider that all products, sporting or not, on which one of the personal attributes of the sportsperson is affixed are 'closely connected' to a public performance rendered in the HS widens the scope of article 17 excessively.[209]

To conclude, it can be stated that depending on the approach followed by the RS of the merchandisee and/or the HS, income derived by merchandising may be taxed at source, in accordance with article 17 or article 12(2) of the UN MC, or not, under articles 7, 12, 14 of the UN MC or 15.

B. VAT

Merchandising constitutes a B2B supply of service taxable at the PoE of the merchandisee's business.[210] It is important to underline that sportspersons acting in a self-employed manner in a given business transaction should also be considered as taxable persons for the purposes of VAT. Rent-a-star companies that may enter into contracts directly with the business partners of sportspersons constitute separate VAT subjects.

H. Broadcasting

1. General observations on lawful broadcasting activities

A. INTRODUCTION

The sale and exploitation of sports broadcasting rights are generally considered to be the most important and lucrative component ('the oxygen') of the sports marketing mix.[211] Without a doubt, sports broadcasting contributes tremendous amounts to many sports and sports events, including the Summer and Winter Olympic Games and the FIFA World Cup.[212] For example, between the years 2011 and 2014, the sale of the FIFA World Cup's television broadcasting rights generated 2.418 million USD for FIFA out of the total of 4.149 million USD derived from the commercialisation of the event.[213]

209 It is important to underline that for article 17 to apply, the sportsperson does not need to commercialise the items themself. As a matter of fact, article 17 applies regardless of who pays the income to the sportsperson (*OECD Commentary* on article 17, §8.1). Accordingly, payments made by merchandisees in relation to items sold before or during the event are also covered by this distributive rule.

210 In terms of the general B2B services place-of-supply rule of the applicable legislation, such as article 44 of the VAT Directive.

211 BLACKSHAW,*Sports Marketing Agreements*, p.285.

212 Ibid.

213 *Statement on the Report on the Inquiry into the 2018/2022 FIFA World Cup Bidding Process*, p.6.

Clearly, not all sports events benefit from substantially lucrative broadcasting deals. In fact, most sports can expect very little, if any, income from selling the broadcasting rights to their competitions.[214] This situation, however, has begun to change in the last decade. As new methods of television broadcasting have increased the programme capacity that may be offered by broadcasters, minority sports, such as darts and snooker, began to become part of the sports broadcasting calendar.[215] Recent broadcasting methods – commonly referred to as the 'new media'[216] – also broadened the mediatisation of rather small-scale sporting events. For instance, minor competitions that are not broadcast on television may nevertheless reach their public via online video-streaming.

To establish the taxable income that may derive from the web of broadcasting contracts, this sub-subsection first determines the owner of the sports event's broadcasting rights (b). Then the traditionally marketed broadcast packages are briefly described (c). The analysis proceeds with the production process (d) and the owner of the feed (e), before the succinct examination of sports broadcast contracts (f).

B. OWNERSHIP OF BROADCASTING RIGHTS

Sportspersons, teams and SGBs all contribute to the creation of the final 'product', i.e. the event, which is eligible for broadcasting. Should all these different parties be entitled to commercialise this joint product, not only legal but also commercial chaos would certainly arise. The broadcasting rights of an event are traditionally commercialised only by their ultimate owner: the SGB, which may not be the 'natural' ultimate owner of all copyrights linked to an event. To eliminate all legal entanglement, sportspersons and/or sports clubs assign their rights to SGBs by contractual means.

i. Sports sector[217] It may be argued that the logical extension of the right of publicity is that sportspersons may also control the broadcasting of their sporting performances.[218] The legal basis of this 'control' does not, however, need to be examined in detail as sportspersons systematically grant their broadcasting rights either to the rights-holder of the event by means of a participation contract (sportspersons who compete on an individual basis) or to their sports clubs by means of an employment contract (sportspersons who compete as a member of a team).

Sports clubs are, thus, the owners of the broadcasting rights of their team(s). Nonetheless, it is common ground for leagues and SGBs to require sports clubs to transfer their broadcasting rights to them. This aspect, along with the exploitation of other commercial rights related to relevant sports events, is generally regulated

214 GRATTON/SOLBERG, p.79.
215 BURAIMO, p.100; BOLOTNY/BOURG, p.116.
216 Mainly the internet and mobile phones (smartphones).
217 See Figure 3.3 for a typical rights assignment scheme in the sports sector.
218 BLAIS, p.533.

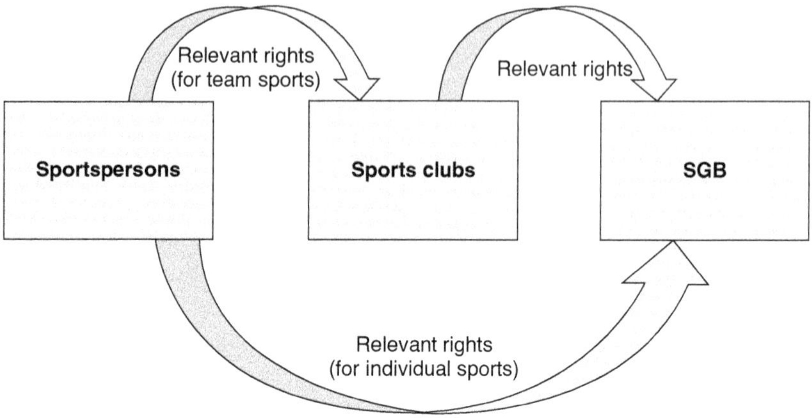

Figure 3.3

in the statutes and/or regulations of the respective league and/or the SGB.[219] Sports clubs may be allowed to continue to exploit their broadcasting rights to a certain – and extremely limited – extent, as determined by SGBs in the relevant statutes and/or regulations. For instance, sports clubs may exploit live audio-visual media rights in an EU/EEA country, but only in cases where UEFA notifies the clubs of the fact that such rights have not been acquired by a UEFA media partner in that particular country.[220]

The SGB, which obtains the broadcasting rights from all participants, 'bundles' them and commercialises them as one product. This practice, commonly referred to as 'collective selling', implies that SGBs are the exclusive owners of sports events' broadcasting rights. Since the collective selling mechanism prevents a participant-basis commercialisation of the broadcasting rights, a hindrance of the competition within the sports broadcasting market might occur. The competition law issues are beyond the scope of this book and are not further developed. It is important to highlight that participants do take their fair share of the commercialisation of the event's broadcasting rights, given the fact that a part of the income generated by SGBs is generally distributed among participants (individuals or teams) and/or organising committees, in accordance with the financial provisions of the event's statutes/regulations.

ii. eSports sector As creators of eSports titles, game developers 'own' their games. Whether professional or amateur, all users of computer games customarily adhere to an end-user licensing agreement, which clearly indicates that the game cannot be used by the end-users for commercial purposes and any copyright or similar

219 See, for example, article 67 §1 of the FIFA Statutes and article 48 §1 of the UEFA Statutes.
220 Article G.4.1 of the annex G of the UEFA Champions League Regulations.

right accruing to end-users is allocated to the game publisher. Accordingly, intellectual property rights of eSports titles, which include the right to broadcast sequences from the game, accrue to game developers.[221] Regarding the intellectual property rights of eSports tournaments, like in the sports sector, any image rights or similar rights vested in pro-gamers and teams are transferred to the game developer. It can, therefore, be concluded that game developers are the exclusive owners of eSports tournaments' broadcasting rights. As opposed to the sports sector, a sharing system does not exist in eSports. Game developers usually keep the majority of the broadcasting income, instead of allocating a meaningful portion of it to participant teams as it is frequently done in the sports sector.[222]

C. BROADCAST RIGHTS PACKAGES

Distinct sets of broadcast rights tend to be 'bundled' together for commercialisation purposes.[223] The 'bundled rights packages' allow the rights-holder to ensure the exclusivity of the rights granted to different commercial partners. The rights are generally grouped in accordance with: (i) broadcast medium (radio, television, the internet, mobile phones and fixed media); (ii) transmission type (duration and time window – live, delayed transmission, retransmission, highlights, clips, etc.); (iii) territory (regional, national, global); and (iv) language.[224] Territory and language being straightforward matters, only broadcast mediums and transmission types are examined in more detail.

i. Broadcast mediums The sports sector's revenue-generating broadcast mediums are radio, television, the internet, mobile phones and fixed media. Television constitutes the most lucrative sports broadcast instrument, since commercial channels and subscription-based platforms attribute a high value to sports programming for a number of reasons, such as building a broad subscriber pool and increasing their advertisement income by attracting a special target group of viewers that is particularly appealing to advertisers.[225] On the other hand, the

221 Both pro-gamers and regular gamers often stream their video gameplay on online platforms, such as Twitch.tv. Such conduct, usually tolerated by game developers for the sake of keeping a positive image in the eyes of the game's fans and increasing their game's popularity, raises fascinating copyright and taxation issues. However, since the content shared consists of an individual video created by the gamer and does not relate to eSports tournaments, this subject falls outside the scope of this book.

222 CHAO, p.7.

223 This practice is also referred to as 'collective selling'. A potential difficulty of bundling the rights is, once again, the violation of the applicable competition law. Competent authorities may force SGBs to 'unbundle' the broadcasting rights, in pursuance of increasing the possibility of acquisition of the rights by more broadcasters and, thereby, promoting the competition within the sports broadcasting market. This issue is not developed further in this book.

224 See also BENTATA, p.1225.

225 LEFEVER, p.9.

eSports broadcast industry is almost exclusively dominated by the sale of online-streaming rights, i.e. the internet.

The oldest technique of sports broadcasting is radio broadcasting. Radio stations usually enter into a contract with the rights-holder of a sports event in order to obtain the right to broadcast the event's live commentary, generally produced directly at the venue. Television channels obtain the right to transmit audio-visual feeds of sports events. In the last decade, television broadcasting has begun to be disrupted by online distribution mechanisms – particularly audio and video streaming, download technologies and social software such as video-sharing sites and social-networking sites.[226] This disturbance is a result of 'convergence', which means that all networks are able to deliver any kind of service to any kind of platform, without different services (such as voice, sound, data and pictures) being confined to their 'specialised' infrastructure.[227] Simply put, as a result of convergence, footage transmitted by television channels may also be broadcast on the internet or via mobile phones.

Despite its significant growth as a technology and its common use, the internet has not replaced television in sports broadcasting, i.e. it has not become a centre of substantial profit for sport.[228] Nonetheless, the value of the internet as a broadcasting tool should not be underestimated. Sports organisations, well aware of the internet's importance, have been using it as a broadcast medium for almost a decade. For instance, the IOC sold separate internet broadcasting rights for the 2008 Beijing Olympics.[229] Online-streaming constitutes the key broadcasting method in the eSports sector and it is quite lucrative. For example, BAMTech, a video-streaming company, signed a deal with Riot Games to obtain the exclusive right to stream the LoL tournaments, in exchange for a minimum of 300 million USD.[230]

The expansion of mobile phones as a broadcast medium mainly occurred after the invention of the 3G[231] technology, which allowed sending/receiving moving images from/to mobile phones. Mobile phone companies offer a variety of other services such as sports information by SMS or voice services, fixtures, sports branded ring tones and interactive games.[232] Football has a particularly suited content to this medium, as entertaining summary videos may be compiled from a combination of goals and best positions.[233] For this reason, commercialisation of

226 HUTCHINS/MIKOSZA, p.281.
227 LEFEVER, p.16.
228 BOLOTNY/BOURG, p.131.
229 HUTCHINS/MIKOSZA, p.280.
230 The deal was reportedly signed in 2016 and for a period of seven years, i.e. until 2023. The company would stream by means of an application (destined to be used in computers and smartphones) and distribute the content to other streaming platforms, such as Twitch.tv and YouTube. See MLB's BAMTech inks $300M exclusive deal with Riot Games by Darin Kwilinski, article on *ESPN* published on 17 December 2016, https://www.espn.com/esports/story/_/id/18292308/mlb-bamtech-streaming-platform-inks-300-million-exclusivity-deal-riot-games-league-legends (accessed on 01.08.2019).
231 Third generation of mobile telecommunications technology.
232 LEFEVER, pp.19–20; BOLOTNY/BOURG, p.131.
233 BOLOTNY/BOURG, p.131.

football events' mobile platform broadcasting rights is a common phenomenon. For example, Orange[234] reportedly invested between 60 million EUR and 80 million EUR for the mobile broadcasting rights of the 2001–2008 period of the French football leagues, Ligue 1 and Ligue 2.[235]

A sports event may also be shared with the public via the creation and sale of DVDs, CD-ROMs and other similar storage instruments. These tools are commonly referred to as fixed media.

ii. Transmission types For the purposes of this book, the distinction is made between three sorts of transmission: (i) live transmission; (ii) delayed transmission; and (iii) replay/retransmission.

Live transmission refers to a broadcast in real-time, i.e. as the event happens. Live broadcasts are usually transmitted with a delay buffer of seven seconds in order to allow removal of inappropriate material (the so-called 'seven-second delay'). Although, on a purely technical view of things, the transmission is 'delayed' for several seconds, there is no doubt that the broadcast safeguards its 'live' status.

Delayed transmission refers to broadcasts made after the finalisation of the event, but as a first transmission of the event on the broadcast medium concerned. For example, when a football match takes place between 4 pm and 6 pm and is broadcast on television, for the first time, between 8 pm and 10 pm, there is a delayed transmission of the match.

Replay, or retransmission, signifies transmission(s) of an event that has already been transmitted on the broadcast medium concerned. For instance, when a football match, taking place between 4 pm and 6 pm is transmitted live in that time frame and the same event is transmitted one more time between 8 pm and 10 pm, the second transmission is a replay or a retransmission. Replays may also be 'recurring', i.e. the same event is retransmitted several times.

D. PRODUCTION OF THE FEED

i. Generalities Prior to the analysis of different contractual relations that are likely to originate from the broadcast of a sports event, the production of the feed is briefly described in order to identify the relevant actors of the broadcasting sector. The production of the audio feed, i.e. radio transmission, is quite a simple process. Usually, each radio broadcaster produces its own feed live from the venue[236] and, thereby, the intervention of third parties is not required. On the other hand, production of an audio-visual feed is a rather complicated procedure, involving a number of different actors (see Figure 3.4).

234 A French telecommunications company.
235 BOLOTNY/BOURG, p.131.
236 BENTATA, p.1215.

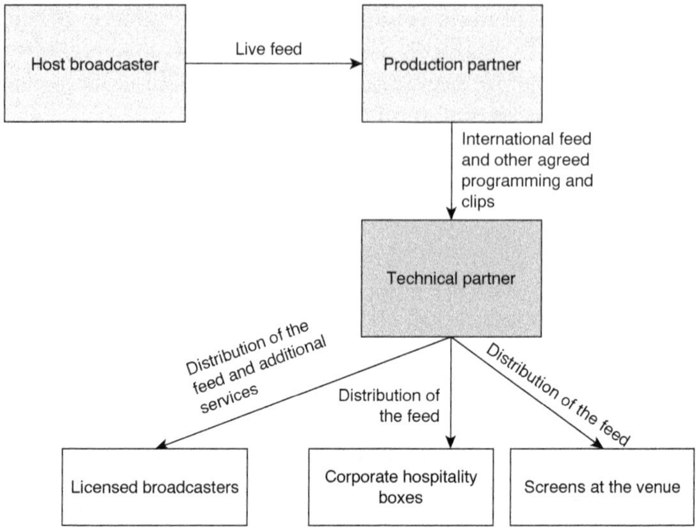

Figure 3.4

The 'host broadcaster' is the entity that records the main live coverage, i.e. the 'live feed' of the event.[237] Traditionally, the host broadcaster role is assumed by the broadcaster(s) licensed to broadcast the coverage of the event in the HS.[238] For some major sports events, the host broadcaster activities may be undertaken on an 'in-house' basis, i.e. the event owner may produce its own coverage either through a company it controls or by an organisation specifically established to produce the live coverage.[239] This is, for example, the case for the Olympic Games. Since 2009, OBS,[240] formed by the IOC, has served as the permanent host broadcast organisation for both the Summer and Winter Olympic Games.[241]

The feed is usually created with split audio tracks. One audio track is that of the event itself, meaning crowd noise and other sounds deriving directly from the venue, and the other one is the commentary track – usually in English – which is normally used as a 'guide track' to assist the production partner and licensed broadcasters in producing their own commentary.[242] As a general rule, the commentary track will be removed from the feed and be replaced by the production partner's or licensed broadcaster's own commentary.[243]

Once the live feed is recorded, the broadcast version of the feed needs to be prepared. To this end, the live feed is delivered to an access point by the host

237 Ibid.
238 Ibid.
239 Ibid.
240 Headquartered in Spain.
241 *Olympic Marketing Fact File*, p.26.
242 BENTATA, p.1217.
243 Ibid.

broadcaster, from where it is retrieved by the production partner.[244] The production partner is the entity in charge of preparing the international feed. To this effect, the production partner takes the 'clean live feed'[245] provided by the host broadcaster and proceeds to several modifications required by the event manager, such as including data and statistics and superimposing the branding of the rights-holder and its sponsors.[246] The production partner may also be required to produce certain programming or clips for the use of the rights-holder and its licensees, such as short trailers, highlights programmes and content destined to be used on the internet and/or smartphone broadcast.[247]

It is important to underline that the production of the international feed, along with the other related activities, may be undertaken either by a production partner or directly by the host broadcaster itself, i.e. without the intervention of a third party. It is also possible for the host broadcaster to produce the broadcast version of the feed exclusively for its own licensed territory and transmit the live feed to the production partner, which is in charge of preparing a generic international feed for all other broadcast licensees.[248]

Once the international feed is fully produced, it is relayed from the production facility back to the access point, from where the technical partner arranges for its distribution to each one of the licensed broadcasters.[249] For live transmissions, the distribution is made – either by satellite or by cable – via a signal, commonly referred to as ITVR signal. For delayed transmissions, the distribution may also be effectuated by means of tape delivery, electronic transfer or download from a server.[250] Delivery of the feed to the licensed broadcasters may take place at an agreed access point, in which case the broadcasters are responsible for the onward journey of the feed from that point, or by an up-linking service, i.e. the technical partner sends the feed to an agreed satellite transporter from where the broadcaster can downlink the feed to its play-out centre and broadcast the fully produced feed into its licensed territory.[251] The technical partner may also be required to provide additional services for the broadcast licensees, such as the provision of 'unilateral' facilities (e.g. commentary positions and unilateral positions for pre-/post-match interviews).[252] In addition to the distribution of the feed to licensed broadcasters, the technical partner is also usually in charge of delivering the feed to other relevant mediums and interested parties, such as corporate hospitality boxes and screens at the venue.[253]

244 Ibid, p.1218.
245 'Clean live feed' implies that the feed is devoid of all commercial influence as well as any kind of publicity.
246 BENTATA, p.1219.
247 Ibid.
248 Ibid, p.1216.
249 Ibid, p.1220.
250 Ibid.
251 Ibid.
252 Ibid.
253 Ibid.

It must be noted that the production partner and the technical partner are often the same entity.[254] It is also possible for the host broadcaster to be in charge of production and technical services in addition to the production of the live feed. In those cases, both the raw and the international feeds of the sports event are produced by the host broadcaster.

ii. Production of live transmission: example of the Olympic Games The Seven decision, rendered by the Federal Court of Australia, examines in great detail the production of the live broadcast of the Olympic Games, more specifically the 2004 Athens, the 2006 Torino and the 2008 Beijing Olympic Games (hereinafter – within this subparagraph – the relevant Olympic Games). A brief overview of the observations made by the Court is presented in this subparagraph to further clarify the technicalities of the broadcasting process.

For the purposes of the relevant Olympic Games, no recourse was made to a production or a technical partner. The host broadcaster produced the feed in its entirety. The footage was generated by the host broadcaster in the outside broadcast compounds situated at the competition venues of the Games.[255] It was also possible for other broadcasters to acquire some unilateral production facilities at the competition venue(s). For example, Seven had some isolated cameras and audio commentator spot at the outside broadcast compounds. However, these minor unilateral facilities were not sufficient to generate the feed of the entire event, which was produced and distributed by the host broadcaster.[256]

The footage generated by the host broadcaster was transmitted via ITVR signals. The host broadcaster transmitted each ITVR signal – over copper coaxial cable, fibre, microwave, satellite transmission or a combination of these methods[257] – to a telecommunications carrier, which received the signals from the outside broadcast compound and transmitted it to the IBC.[258] Within the IBC, the signals were received by the host broadcaster and then distributed, in a simultaneous manner, to Olympic broadcasters' spaces over copper coaxial cables.[259] The time between the occurring of an event at the Games and the delivery of the ITVR signal to broadcasters within the IBC was, in most cases, virtually instantaneous.[260] On rare occasions, there was a slight delay, which did not exceed 6/10th of a second.[261]

In their production facilities at the IBC, the Olympic broadcasters generally had their own storage devices.[262] Although recordings of the footage were also made by the host broadcaster at the IBC, they were not distributed to broadcasters,

254 Ibid, p.1219.
255 The Seven decision, §37.1.27.
256 Ibid.
257 Ibid, §37.1.39.
258 Ibid, §37.1.25.
259 Ibid, §37.1.28.
260 Ibid, §37.1.29.
261 Ibid.
262 Ibid, §37.1.31.

unless, for example, when a broadcaster missed recording an ITVR signal.[263] Those recordings constituted a 'protection copy' that was not transmitted as live signal to Olympic broadcasters.[264] In other words, the ITVR signals transmitted from the host broadcaster to Olympic broadcasters were live signals that were not stored or recorded by the host broadcaster prior to their transmission.[265]

The data sent by the ITVR signal was encoded by the host broadcaster. The broadcasters decoded and converted it into visual images and sounds by the use of appropriate equipment, i.e. a receiving device.[266] It must be underlined that although visual images and sounds may be produced from an ITVR signal with the use of a receiving device, nothing can be reproduced from a signal.[267] In other words, no picture, image or sound can be recorded or permanently stored in an ITVR signal. This is due to the fact that a signal is not tangible and does not give physical form to an image or sound.[268]

The ITVR signals received by the broadcasters were not suitable for broadcast in their 'raw' form.[269] In fact, Olympic broadcasters had access to multiple ITVR signals, one for each field of play, simultaneously.[270] Consequently, they had to process and organise the signals received before transmitting them to their home countries.[271] This process was conducted in the facilities they had at the IBC.[272] The preparation involved insertion of their own commentary, logos and graphics, unilateral camera feeds, clips of local interest as well as sequencing and synchronising of the transmission to their network schedule.[273] Once all arrangements were made, the signals were then transmitted to each broadcaster's home country, in Seven's case to Australia.

E. OWNERSHIP OF THE FEED

Whether the feeds are subject to copyright[274] or not – and if they are, at which stage of the production – determines the first owner of the feed. The modalities of the protection offered by copyrights vary from national law to national law. The purpose of this paragraph is to describe the most commonly applied method in practice and not to proceed to a detailed comparison of different national laws. Reference is made to Australian, English and Swiss laws for illustration purposes.

263 Ibid, §44.
264 Ibid.
265 Ibid, §40.
266 Ibid, §37.1.23.
267 Ibid, §37.1.9.
268 Ibid.
269 Ibid, §37.1.30.
270 Ibid, §37.1.10.
271 Ibid, §37.1.32.
272 Ibid.
273 Ibid.
274 '*Droit d'auteur*' in French. Although the two concepts are not exactly identical, they can be considered as equivalents.

When analysing the ownership of the feed, a distinction should be made between the feed/other contents produced by the host broadcaster (and the production partner, if any) and the feeds/similar contents generated by other broadcasters.

i. Ownership of the content produced by the host broadcaster The host broadcaster, as the originator, is the first owner of the copyright in the film, sound recordings and broadcasts of the event under the English law, as per the CDPA.[275] The originator of the footage ('*originärer Inhaber des Leistungsschutzrechtes*'), i.e. the host broadcaster, is also protected under Swiss law (CopA), not by a copyright but by the 'related rights'.[276] Article 37 of the CopA grants broadcasting organisations the following rights on an exclusive basis: (i) to retransmit their broadcasts; (ii) to make their broadcasts perceptible; (iii) to fix their broadcasts on blank media and reproduce such fixations; (iv) to offer, transfer or otherwise distribute copies of the fixations of their broadcasts; and (v) to make their broadcasts available through any kind of medium in such a way that persons may access them from a place and at a time individually chosen by them.[277] The fact that the host broadcaster only provides the raw-feed and some analogous content does not affect the protection offered by article 37.[278]

The ownership, or similar protection, of the host broadcaster would result in dependence of the SGB on the host broadcaster for accessing to and/or using the event's feed.[279] In order to avoid that outcome, host broadcaster agreements concluded between rights-holders and host broadcasters usually provide for a full assignment of relevant copyrights to rights-holders. Although the grant of rights is the most commonly used method, the host broadcaster and the SGB may also enter into an exclusive licence agreement (see Figure 3.5). Clearly, a similar clause is also found in the agreements signed between event owners (or, in some cases, host broadcasters) and production partners to the extent relevant.

SGBs become, thereby, the ultimate owners of the feeds. When the feed is protected by a copyright, the SGB becomes the owner of the copyright. When the feed is protected by a 'related right', the protection provided is passed on to the SGB, which becomes the '*derivative Inhaberin der Leistungsshutzrechte*'.[280]

ii. Ownership of the content produced by other broadcasters Other broadcasters create their own 'unilateral feeds' by making some alterations to the raw-feed provided by the host broadcaster, most commonly via inserting content such as their own commentary, logos and short clips of local interest. As a consequence,

275 BENTATA, p.1213.
276 Article 33ff of the CopA.
277 Article 37 lit.a-e of the CopA.
278 ARPAGAUS, p.95.
279 BARR-SMITH, p.555.
280 ARPAGAUS, p.95.

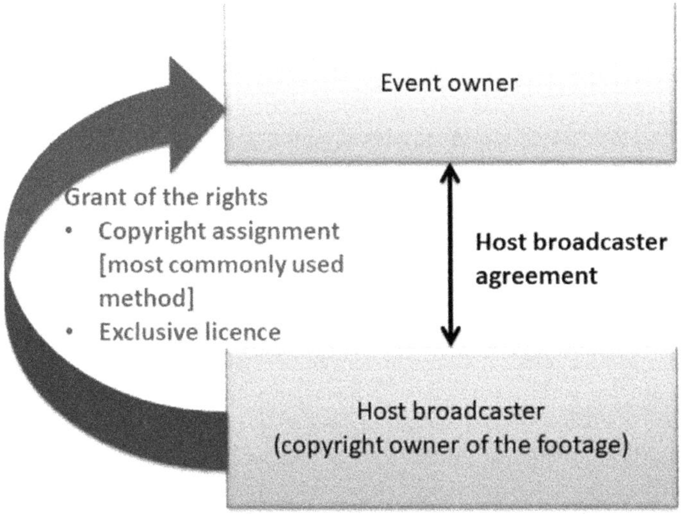

Figure 3.5

they are the originators, and thereby the copyright owners, of the 'unilateral' feed transmitted in their country along with other related content.

In order to safeguard their rights, SGBs usually insert in the contracts they conclude with broadcasters a clause regulating the copyright matters. Most typically, for the duration of the sports event, the copyright of the contents created belongs to the broadcaster that generated them within the country in which the broadcaster is allowed to transmit the event. Upon the completion of the event, the broadcaster is required to assign the relevant rights to the SGB. For example, article 5 of the Signal Utilisation Deed concluded between the Australian broadcaster Seven and the IOC on 30 September 2005 reads as follows:

> [d]uring the Games Period, Seven shall be the copyright owner in Australia of all depictions, transcriptions, recordings and television (visual broadcast) and audio broadcasts, or other dissemination by any means of the Games *produced from ITVR Signal* for the purposes of Australian Broadcasting, by or on behalf of, Seven in Australia ("Copyright"). At the end of the particular Games Period, Seven assigns to the IOC the Copyright.[281]

iii. Timing of the copyright's creation Timing of the copyright's creation is of the utmost importance, since it affects the legal categorisation of the income obtained by the SGB. For instance, while the sum of 6,108,913 AUD paid by Seven to the IOC in exchange for the ITVR signal for use in connection with delayed Australian broadcasting of the Olympic Games after the Games period was categorised as a

281 The Seven decision, §26 (emphasis already contained in the text of the decision).

royalty by the Federal Court of Australia, the amount of 97,742,609 AUD paid for the same signal but for use in connection with Australian broadcasting during the Games period was not.[282]

This difference of treatment was due to the 'embodiment requirement',[283] found in section 24 of the Australian Copyright Act.[284] 'Embodiment' implies giving to a creation a form in which it could be held for continued existence and use.[285] Embodiment should not necessarily be of a permanent nature.[286] It may also be transitory provided that the visual images and sounds are sufficiently permanent and stable to be identified and capable of being used to be shown as a moving picture.[287]

The amount of 97,742,609 AUD was paid for the distribution of the ITVR signal over copper coaxial cables to Seven. ITVR signals, which do not store visual images or sounds, are mere vehicles that let the data 'pass through'.[288] Moreover, the sounds and visual images can be produced from the ITVR signal only by the receiving device.[289] No reproduction is possible.[290] In other words, the ITVR signal is merely a medium of communication.[291] As a result, an 'embodiment' does not occur, at any stage, during the transmission of the ITVR signal from the host broadcaster to other broadcasters within the Olympic venue.[292] Accordingly, a copyright protected work under the Australian Copyright Act cannot be formed at this stage.[293] In accordance with section 91 of the Australian Copyright Act, the copyright is created when the broadcaster transmits the feed in Australia to the public.[294] Thus, the moment Seven transmitted its signal in Australia, the feed became subject to copyright. The owner of the copyright created was Seven, and not the IOC, which is in conformity with the deed concluded between the parties (until, of course, the rights were granted to the IOC in accordance with the deed signed between the parties).

The timing of the copyright's creation must be determined by means of a case-by-case basis analysis, since it may vary not only from country to country, but also according to the concrete circumstances of each specific case.

282 Fees paid by Seven to the IOC can be found in the Seven decision, §31.
283 'Embodiment' is similar to 'fixation' of the US Law (title 17 of the United States Code, §102).
284 Copyright Act 1968.
285 The Seven decision, §56.
286 Ibid, §70.
287 Ibid.
288 Ibid, §124.
289 Ibid.
290 Ibid.
291 Ibid, §127.
292 Ibid.
293 On this point, it is important to underline that the ITVR signal is protected under Swiss law in accordance with article 37 of the CopA.
294 The Seven decision, §147ff.

F. BROADCASTING CONTRACTS

Sports broadcasting gives rise to a rather complex network of contracts. In order to identify the main sources of income deriving from this web of contracts, this paragraph briefly describes the most commonly concluded contracts in practice, as shown in Figure 3.6. It must be underlined that not every contract examined in this paragraph needs to be concluded for the purposes of an ISE's broadcast. This will, for instance, be the case when one commercial partner assumes several roles, such as a host broadcaster that also acts as a technical service provider. In the same vein, the parties may enter into similar, but different, agreements than those developed in this book.

i. Host broadcaster contracts A host broadcaster agreement usually has three main components: (i) the obligation of the host broadcaster to originate the feed; (ii) the obligation of the host broadcaster to assign the copyright in the feed to the event owner; and (iii) the obligation of the event owner to grant to the host broadcaster the right to transmit the coverage (by one or a number of broadcast mediums) within the determined territory (generally the HS).

There does not exist an established remuneration model for host broadcasting agreements. The parties may agree upon one or a number of the following fees/ remuneration methods:

- The event owner may remunerate the host broadcaster for the production of the feed and other similar content.
- The host broadcaster usually pays a certain amount for acquiring the right to broadcast the event within the HS. Most typically, two separate amounts are

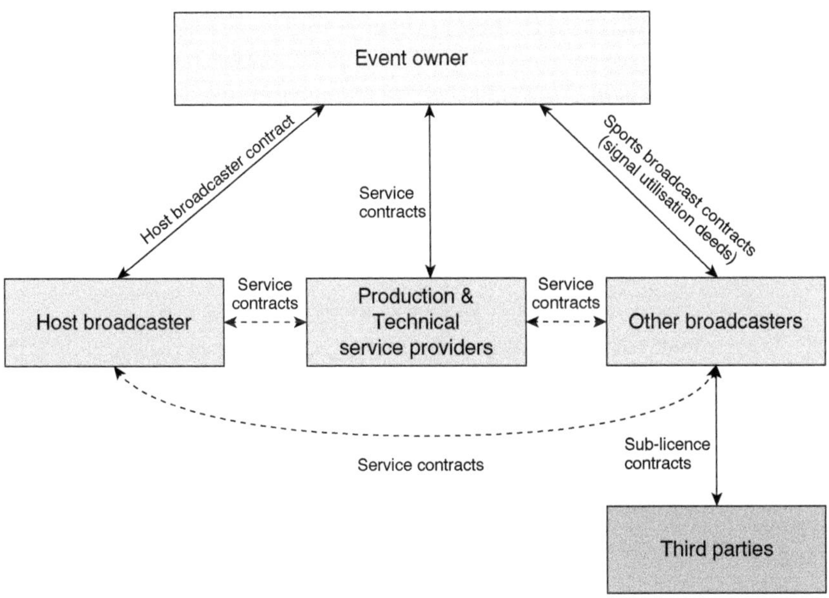

Figure 3.6

due: one for the transmission of the feed *during* the event and one for the transmission of the feed *after* the event. Generally, the fees paid for the former are much more significant than the amount paid for the latter due to the greater appeal of live coverage.

- In cases where the host broadcaster obtains the right to distribute the coverage via fixed-media, it may pay a separate fee to the rights-holder for these purposes. The fee may also correspond to a certain percentage of the sales.
- To the extent where the host broadcaster creates a logo incorporating the logo of the event or otherwise uses the logo and other protected insignia of the event – which is generally the case – it is liable to pay an additional amount to the rights-holder.

ii. Service agreements concluded between the host broadcaster and other licensed broadcasters The feed is provided to all licensed broadcasters by the host broadcaster. Moreover, in cases where the host broadcaster assumes the role of a technical partner, it may provide several other services – commonly referred to as technical services – to other broadcasters, such as delivery of the feed in different formats, provision of additional content – for instance 'discrete feeds'[295], provision of production spaces at the venue, provision of computers and other relevant equipment and relay of the broadcaster's signal to the nearest uplink or fibre terminal.[296]

The provision of the basic feed to licensed broadcasters may be regulated by the contract concluded between the licensed broadcaster and the event owner or between the former and the host broadcaster. This latter contract will also govern the services to be provided by the host broadcaster[297] to the licensed broadcaster. It may be stated that the agreement concluded between the host broadcaster and another licensed broadcaster predominantly constitutes a service agreement.

Although it is possible for the host broadcaster to charge other broadcasters with an 'access fee', as a general rule the basic feed is made available to them without any consideration.[298] In other words, the host broadcaster does usually not charge other broadcasters for any part of the actual production costs.[299] On the other hand, all other costs, i.e. technical costs, are generally charged in accordance with a previously published 'rate card', i.e. the standard price list for the provision of each of the required services.[300] Depending on the items selected from the host broadcaster's rate card, the costs incurred by broadcasters may be substantial.[301]

295 'Discreet feed' can be defined as a direct signal from a selected camera, such as the camera in the interview room, or from a specific venue at the event, for instance the figure-skating arena at the Winter Olympics (DENINGER, p.140).
296 Ibid, p.141.
297 In cases where it assumes the role of a technical partner.
298 HIGTON JON, Broadcasting: Rights and Issues in *Sports Law & Finance*, Volume 1, Issue 3, September/October 1993, p.26 cited by WISE/MEYER, p.1775, n.305.
299 Ibid.
300 Ibid.
301 DENINGER, p.141.

iii. Service agreements concluded between production and technical partners and the event owner The agreements concluded between the event owner or the host broadcaster and the production partner and/or the technical partner, are, in substance, service agreements. Accordingly, the production partner and the technical partner are remunerated by the event owner (or the host broadcaster) for the services they provide during the term of the contract.

iv. Service agreements concluded between technical partners and other broadcasters The technical partner usually enters into agreement with each of the licensed broadcasters. These contracts specify which feeds will be delivered to each broadcaster.[302] In addition to distribute the event's feed, a technical partner also provides other services. For example, it may be in charge of booking the unilateral facilities, such as commentary positions, presentation facilities and unilateral camera positions.[303]

The fees due by broadcasters, if any, will generally be set by the technical partner in accordance with its standard 'rate card'. As it is in the interest of the event owner to ensure that the technical partner is not charging the event's broadcasters with excessive fees, the contract concluded between the event owner and the technical partner may include a specific provision in this respect.[304]

v. Sports broadcast contracts/signal utilisation deeds The event owner enters into agreement with a number of broadcasters in order to transmit the sports event in different countries. These agreements may be referred to as sports broadcast agreements or signal utilisation deeds as they mostly consist of the use of the ITVR or the IR – depending on the broadcast medium concerned – signals.

The main obligation of the event owner is to grant the broadcaster the exclusive[305] right to transmit the event in a certain territory. The primary obligation of the broadcaster is to use the coverage in the most convenient way for the event owner. The event owner may, for instance, require the promotion of its other commercial partners, such as sponsors, during the transmission of the event via different methods such as incorporation of their logos in the feed and grant of advertisement spots.

In exchange for obtaining the right to transmit the sports event, broadcasters remunerate the event owner. Sports broadcast contracts usually contain a clause relating to the apportionment of the remuneration. Such clauses generally allocate the fees between four different privileges secured by broadcasters: (i) transmission during the event's time span; (ii) transmission after the event; (iii) access to some areas and facilities at the venue; and (iv) authorisation to use the event's and the

302 BENTATA, p.1220.
303 Ibid (the same services may also be provided by the host broadcaster when it assumes the role of a technical partner, as mentioned in subparagraph ii of this paragraph).
304 Ibid.
305 In most cases.

event owner's intellectual properties. Fees paid for the transmission during the event's time span, which notably includes the live transmission of the event, are normally higher than fees paid for other benefits. Owing both to the significance of the fees and to the fact that broadcasters usually enter into agreement with the event owner for several editions of the sports event, the payment is generally effectuated in instalments. For this reason, event owners generally require an interest at a rate determined in the contract.

Depending on the sports event, remuneration obtained by event owners for broadcasting rights may range from billions to nominal consideration.[306] The difference may be striking even within the sports events organised by the same SGB. For example, while the television broadcasting rights deriving from the 2014 Brazil FIFA World Cup amounted to 601 million USD, the fees generated by all of the other events organised by FIFA during the same year equalled to 29 million USD.[307] Consequently, modalities of payment vary to a great extent from sports event to sports event. Depending on the commercial opportunities available, the event owner may even agree to enter into a barter agreement with the broadcaster, in terms of which the former agrees to transmit the signal to the broadcaster free of charge and the parties equally split the advertising revenue.[308]

vi. Sub-licence contracts The licensed broadcasters may concede the rights that they obtained from the event owner to third parties. For example, a broadcaster that obtained the right to broadcast the event through television and fixed-media may enter into agreement with a third party regarding the production and the sale of DVDs. The sub-licensee may remunerate the broadcaster by means of a fixed sum or a percentage of the income generated by the exploitation of the rights concerned.

Sub-licensing is generally either prohibited or limited to a great extent by sports broadcast contracts. Consequently, sub-licence contracts are extremely rare in practice.

2. *Taxation of lawful broadcasting activities*

A. TAXATION OF THE RIGHTS-HOLDER

i. General observations Five main rights are transmitted by the rights-holder to host broadcaster(s) and broadcaster(s) in consideration of a fee, namely: (i) the right to transmit the footage live; (ii) the right to transmit the footage after the event; (iii) exploitation of the fixed-media rights; (iv) the right to use the name, the logo and other similar intellectual properties of the rights-holder; and (v) the rights to have access to and to make use of certain areas of the venue. These

306 BECKER, p.183.
307 *FIFA Financial Report 2013*, p.17.
308 BECKER, p.183.

different rights are grouped into three categories for the purposes of the income tax analysis and are examined as one category for VAT purposes.

As a preliminary remark, it must be stated that, for income tax purposes, if the rights-holder and the broadcaster concerned are residents of the same State, the taxation will occur in accordance with the domestic law of that State. The following analysis concerns the cases involving commercial partners that are residents of different States. The applicable DTT is the one concluded between the RS of the rights-holder and the RS of the broadcaster.

ii. Right to transmit the footage live If the applicable DTT's definition of royalty includes payments for transmissions by satellite, cable, fibre optic or similar technology, the payment effectuated in consideration of the right to transmit the event live will clearly fall within the scope of article 12. In all other cases, however, for a television transmission to be categorised as a royalty within article 12, it has to be considered as a 'copyright' by the domestic law of the State applying the DTT in view of taxation of the income concerned.[309] A DTT does not create the opportunity to tax the income in each country as a royalty simply because such income may be categorised as an intellectual property in either country. Each State must apply its own domestic law in this respect.[310]

The fact that the applicable DTT was concluded before live transmission became a frequently used method does not constitute an obstacle per se, as reference should be made to the domestic law in force when the tax is being imposed.[311] Subsequently, the evolution of the term over the years is generally taken into consideration.

The approach followed by countries is far from being unanimous on this point. While the US seems to protect live transmissions under its copyright law,[312] Australia[313] and India[314] take the opposite view. Consequently, depending on the CSs' domestic laws, the payment received in consideration of the right to transmit the footage live will be considered either as a royalty[315] or as business profits.[316]

If the income is categorised as royalties, the rights-holder will exclusively be submitted to tax in its RS in accordance with article 12(1).[317] Should the DTT follow the UN MC on this point and allow a source taxation of royalties,[318] the income earned by the rights-holder will be imposed in its RS as well as in the SS, i.e. the RS of the broadcaster.

309 It is rather obvious that a television transmission does not fall within the scope of other terms enumerated in article 12(2).
310 The Seven decision, §132.
311 *OECD Commentary* on article 3, §11. It is important to note that there are diverging opinions on this issue.
312 BOBBETT/JONES, p.27.
313 As analysed in the Seven decision.
314 As demonstrated by the High Court of Delhi's decision in the case of Commissioner of Income Tax v Delhi Race Club, [1940] Ltd (ITA No.6/2014).
315 Article 12(2).
316 Article 7(4).
317 The distributive rule uses the term 'shall be taxable only'.
318 Article 12(2) of the UN MC.

In cases where the income is not categorised as a royalty by the SS, it will be taxed as business profits. Consequently, it will be exclusively submitted to tax in the RS of the rights-holder, unless a PE is formed in the SS of the royalties.[319] A PE may be formed only in the RS of the host broadcaster, i.e. the HS, and not in the RSs of other broadcasters. The constitution of a PE of the rights-holder in the HS is examined in detail in subsection IV, B of this chapter.

iii. Right to transmit the footage after the event and exploitation of the fixed-media rights It seems to be undisputed that once the event is completed: (i) the footage becomes protectable under the copyright law; and (ii) the footage is owned by the rights-holder. In the light of these two conclusions, it is possible to state that the payment received in consideration of the right to transmit the footage after the event and/or to exploit the fixed-media rights will generally be considered as a royalty, within article 12(2), and taxed accordingly.

iv. Rights to use the name, the logo and other similar intellectual properties of the rights-holder and to have access to the venue The taxation of these rights is examined for hospitality purposes in paragraph V, E, 4, b of this chapter.

v. VAT modalities The rights granted by rights-holders to broadcasters constitute a B2B supply of service submitted to tax at the standard rate of VAT at the location where the broadcaster concerned has established its business.[320]

B. TAXATION OF THE HOST BROADCASTER(S)

The income generated by host broadcasters from an ISE can be divided into four categories: (i) income generated via the transmission of the event; (ii) remuneration obtained from the rights-holder; (iii) remuneration obtained from other broadcasters; and (iv) remuneration obtained from sub-licensees (if any).

i. Income generated via the transmission of the event Host broadcasters are generally entitled to broadcast the footage in the territory where the event takes place, i.e. the HS. Different types of revenue may be generated from this transmission, such as advertising fees and subscription fees. This first category of income is derived exclusively from domestic sources: the event is transmitted only in the territory of the HS, the advertisers and other broadcast sponsors are local companies[321] and subscribers are residents of the HS. Accordingly, the

319 Article 7(1).
320 In accordance with the general B2B services place-of-supply rule of the applicable legislation, such as article 44 of the VAT Directive.
321 Except for the official sponsors of the event, which do not remunerate the host broadcaster but the rights-holder.

income concerned shall be taxed in the RS of the host broadcaster, which is the HS, in accordance with its domestic law.

In the same vein, given the lack of any international component, all relevant transactions are subject to VAT in accordance with the domestic law of the HS. It is important to underline that broadcasting services provided to consumers may follow the same tax treatment as electronic services.[322] To the extent offered by public bodies, such services may also be VAT-exempt.[323]

The transmission may also be available outside the territory for which the broadcasting right has been granted to the host broadcaster by cause of 'overspill'.[324] Such availability cannot be considered as provision of services abroad, since overspill constitutes a problem that occurs due to the lack of a technology that would enable broadcasters to completely prevent it. Subsequently, no taxes shall be due in countries where the transmission is available by reason of overspill.

ii. Remuneration obtained from the rights-holder Host broadcasters are remunerated by the rights-holder for the preparation of the raw-feed and other similar content.

ii.a. Categorisation of the income for income tax purposes Often, at the end of the event, the rights held by the host broadcaster as the originator of the footage are fully assigned to the rights-holder, which becomes the ultimate owner of the rights concerned. Since the payment is effectuated for the transfer of the full ownership of the footage, and not for the mere 'use' or 'the right to use' of it, the consideration obtained by the host broadcaster cannot be categorised as royalties within article 12.[325] In some rare cases where the rights are not fully assigned to the rights-holder but are granted to it by means of an exclusive licence, the payment made by the rights-holder should be categorised as royalties, because what is being granted is the right to use the footage and not the full ownership.

Payments made for the transfer of an intellectual property's full ownership can be categorised either as 'business profits' within article 7 or as 'capital gains' within article 13.[326] In the case of the host broadcaster, the categorisation as business profits would be more appropriate, as the host broadcaster is remunerated not

322 See, for example, article 58 of the VAT Directive.
323 See, for instance, ibid, article 132(1)(q).
324 'Overspill' occurs when transmissions destined to be received in one country are accessible from other countries due to the technology (satellite) used. It is a common problem linked to the satellite's range. Although different technologies may be used to prevent overspill, like geo blocking, they are not effective enough to allow a complete eradication of the problem. Not only broadcasters but also other interested parties may attempt to benefit from overspill (see, e.g. Football Association Premier League Ltd and Others v QC Leisure and Others, Karen Murphy v Media Protection Services Ltd, Joined cases C-403/08 and C-429/08 [2011] ECR I-9083). When a broadcaster takes advantage of 'overspill' and broadcasts the feed in an unauthorised manner, its conduct amounts to 'piracy' (see sub-subsection 3 of this subsection).
325 *OECD Commentary* on article 12, §8.2.
326 Ibid.

only to alienate the property concerned, but also to produce it and to distribute it to other broadcasters and/or technical partners.[327]

Depending on the domestic law of the State applying the DTT, the income obtained by the host broadcaster may also be categorised as 'technical services fees'. For example, in Taiwan, transmitting broadcasting signals, signal uplinks and downlinks services are regarded as technical services,[328] which seem to include the activities of a host broadcaster. On the other hand, in India, the Authority for Advance Ruling delivered a ruling on 13 December 2013 stating that payments made to a non-resident for the production of programmes for broadcasting and telecasting purposes would not constitute 'fees for technical services' but 'business income' under the Indian Income Tax Act.[329] This ruling does not exclude the categorisation of a host broadcaster's activities as technical services in India. In fact, the services concerned by the ruling were not exactly broadcasting services but 'line production services'.[330] However, the reasoning followed by the Indian authorities can be interpreted as being applicable to the activities of host broadcasters as well.[331]

It is therefore possible to conclude that the income received by the host broadcaster from the rights-holder should be categorised as 'business profits' under the OECD MC and may be categorised as 'technical services fees'[332] under some DTTs.

ii.b. Income tax modalities of 'business profits' In cases where the host broadcaster is one of the major broadcast companies situated in the HS,[333] the remuneration it obtains from the rights-holder will be taxable only in the HS in accordance with article 7(1) of the DTT concluded between the HS and the RS of the rights-holder. That follows from the fact that the host broadcaster is an enterprise conducting its activities exclusively in its RS. Since the footage and other content are produced at the venue, a host broadcaster is usually not susceptible to have a fixed, or any other type of, PE in the RS of the rights-holder.[334]

In cases where the host broadcaster is not a resident of the HS, it must be determined whether its activities conducted in the territory of the HS are

327 It is also allowed to transmit it in a pre-determined territory.
328 Ruling of the Ministry of Finance, published on 11 April 2007 (*IBFD Tax News Service*, 25 April 2007).
329 The Authority for Advance Ruling's ruling of 13 December 2013 in the case of Endemol India Private Limited (Sanjay Sanghvi, *IBFD Tax News Service*, 16 January 2014).
330 'Line production services' consist of providing the necessary equipment and space as well as taking care of relevant administrative procedures, such as arranging local permits, for the shooting. Although it may include building sets and providing the necessary shooting equipment, it does not usually involve the act of preparing the footage itself.
331 This is a matter of Indian domestic law.
332 Article 12A of the UN MC.
333 The company concerned should be a resident of the HS within article 4.
334 Article 5(1).

constitutive of a PE under article 5(1) of the DTT concluded between the HS and the RS of the host broadcaster. The relevant parts of the sports venue and other structures that the host broadcaster has at its disposal form a PoB, through which the core business of the host broadcaster, i.e. creating and transmitting the footage, is carried on. The 'fixed' nature of the PoB will, however, heavily depend on the specific circumstances of the case at hand. The host broadcaster will usually have the venue at its disposal for a period of time shorter than six months. Consequently, the use of the venue should, in most cases, not constitute a PE per se. Nonetheless, the host broadcaster may have other installations situated in the HS at its disposal, such as an office. As a matter of fact, preparations of the broadcasting of a sports event usually begin several years in advance, especially for mega and large-scale sporting events. If the preparations are conducted through a 'fixed place' situated in the HS, a PE may be formed in that State in accordance with article 5(1). This being stated, it is possible to argue that the activities conducted up to the beginning of the sports event are merely of a preparatory nature.[335] If that argument is effectively retained by the HS, a PE will not be deemed to be formed in its territory.

The host broadcaster may also choose to operate via a subsidiary established in the HS for handling the broadcasting of the event. This was for example the case of the 2010 Vancouver Olympic Games, for the broadcasting of which OBS set up a subsidiary, Olympic Broadcasting Services Vancouver, situated in the HS.[336]A subsidiary constitutes a PE only to the extent where it is not independent from the parent company.[337] A subsidiary set up by a host broadcaster for the specific purpose of conducting the broadcasting activities related to the sports event concerned is likely to be dependent on its parent company and, thereby, to constitute a PE. Nevertheless, this categorisation will depend on a number of factors and can only be determined with certainty by means of a case-by-case analysis.

To conclude, it can be stated that in cases where a PE is formed in the HS, the profits attributable to it may be taxed by this State. In cases where a PE is not formed, the income of the host broadcaster will exclusively be taxed by its RS.

ii.c. Income tax modalities of 'technical services fees' Should the income be categorised as 'technical services fees', the relevant distributive rule of the DTT concluded between the RS of the rights-holder and the RS of the host broadcaster will generally grant to the former State the right to tax the income of the host broadcaster up to a certain percentage. The RS of the host broadcaster will usually credit the tax paid in the other State[338] in order to eliminate the residual double taxation.

335 Article 5(4)(e).
336 Televising the Olympics by Jeff Buckstein, article in the *Certified General Accountants-Canada Magazine*, January-February 2010 issue.
337 Article 5(7).
338 Article 23B.

ii.d. VAT analysis Production of the footage constitutes a B2B supply of service taxable at the place where the rights-holder established its business.[339]

iii. Remuneration obtained from other broadcasters Taxation of the remuneration obtained from other broadcasters in consideration of the services rendered does not differ from taxation of the remuneration obtained from the rights-holder. It is, however, important to point out that access fees collected by host broadcasters do not constitute royalties within article 12(2). Although the host broadcaster is the originator, and thereby the primary copyright owner of the feed, many jurisdictions consider that the signal itself is not protected by copyright or other similar intellectual property rights. Thereupon, in most cases, the host broadcaster will not be considered as granting the use of a material protected by the applicable intellectual property law.

iv. Remuneration obtained from sub-licensees In some cases, and to the extent authorised by the rights-holder, the host broadcaster may sub-license the use of the rights to a third party. This is typically the case when the host broadcaster enters into an agreement with a third party for the fixed-media exploitation of the rights.

To the extent where the sub-licensee and the host broadcaster are residents of different States, the income concerned will be taxed in accordance with the DTT concluded between the RS of the host broadcaster and the RS of the sub-licensee. The remuneration obtained by the host broadcaster from the sub-licensee should be categorised as royalties within article 12 and taxed accordingly, given the fact that the host broadcaster is granting the right to use a copyright – or a similar intellectual property right – protected material to a third party in exchange of a certain amount.

The grant of rights to the sub-licensee constitutes a B2B supply of service taxable at the place where the sub-licensee established its business.[340]

C. INCOME TAX MODALITIES REGARDING IN-HOUSE HOST BROADCASTERS

The host broadcaster role may be assumed by in-house companies established by the rights-holder to this end (see Figure 3.7). The fact that the host broadcasting services are rendered by an in-house company of the SGB does not alter the taxation modalities of the host broadcaster itself (under the RS2-HS DTT shown in Figure 3.7). Nonetheless, in cases where the in-house company and the SGB are established in different States,[341] the former may be considered as the PE of the latter and

339 In terms of the general B2B services place-of-supply rule of the applicable legislation, such as article 44 of the VAT Directive.

340 As per the general B2B services place-of-supply rule of the applicable legislation, such as article 44 of the VAT Directive.

341 This is for example the case of the IOC, situated in Switzerland, and the OBS, based in Spain.

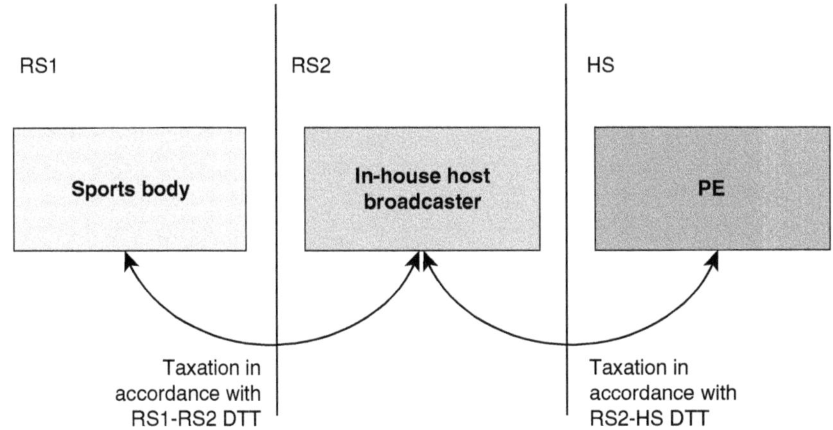

Figure 3.7

accordingly the SGB may be submitted to tax in the State where the in-house company is situated (in RS2, under the RS1-RS2 DTT as shown in Figure 3.7).

The in-house company constitutes a subsidiary of the SGB. While being separate legal entities subject to tax for the transactions they effectuate as a general rule, depending on the specificities of the relation between the subsidiary and its parent company, the former may be deemed to form a PE of the latter. Whether or not an in-house host broadcaster constitutes a PE of the SGB should be analysed on a case-by-case basis, in the light of all relevant circumstances.

D. TAXATION OF BROADCASTERS

Broadcasters derive income from two main sources: transmission of the event and sub-licensing contracts. Revenue generated by the transmission of the event (e.g. advertising and subscription fees) usually derives from commercial partners and clients residing in the same State as the broadcaster. Consequently, the earnings of the transmission of the event are generally taxed in the RS of the broadcaster in accordance with the applicable domestic law. The same holds true for the income obtained by the broadcaster from a sub-licensing contract to the extent where the sub-licensee is a resident of the same State as the broadcaster. In cases where the sub-licensee is a resident of a different State, the taxation will occur in accordance with article 12 of the DTT concluded between the RS of the broadcaster and the RS of the sub-licensee.

VAT modalities of these transactions are the same as the VAT modalities of the relevant host broadcasters' transactions examined in paragraph b.

E. Taxation of production and technical partners

Taxation modalities of production partners[342] should be determined in accordance with the DTTs concluded between the RS of the production partner and: (i) the HS;[343] as well as (ii) the RSs of different legal entities remunerating the production partner, i.e. the rights-holder, the host broadcaster(s) and/or other licensed broadcasters.[344]

Income received by production partners in exchange for the services they provide during an ISE may be categorised as 'business profits' under article 7 or 'technical services fees' under article 12A of the UN MC, depending on the applicable DTT and the domestic law of the relevant State. While taxation as technical services fees does not give rise to any specific problems, some observations need to be made with regards to taxation as business profits.

Business profits obtained by the production partner will usually be taxable exclusively in its RS in accordance with the DTT concluded between the RS of the production partner and the RS of its commercial partner. The production partner is not likely to have a PE in the RS of the rights-holder or in the RSs of other licensed broadcasters, since its activities are mainly conducted at the venue.

The production partner will, on the other hand, have at its disposal the relevant parts of the sports venue and other structures situated in the HS to the extent necessary. These installations may be considered as a PoB through which the core business of the production partner, i.e. contributing to the production of the feed, is carried on. Whether that PoB may be considered as being 'fixed' will heavily depend on the specific circumstances of the actual case, most importantly on the duration of the production partner's presence in the RS. Should this third criterion be met as well, a PE will be created in the HS within article 5(1), unless the activities conducted by the production partner are categorised as having a preparatory character.

For VAT purposes, the services rendered by production partners constitute B2B supply of services taxable at the place where the customer has established its business.[345]

3. *Taxation of unlawful broadcasting activities*

A. General considerations

Sport means audience. Large-scale and mega sporting events have the potential to reach billions of viewers across the world. For instance, the 2014 Brazil FIFA

342 For the sake of simplicity, reference is only made to 'production partners' throughout this paragraph, which should be understood as comprising technical partners.

343 The production partner may also be a resident of the HS. In that event, the DTTs concluded between the HS and other relevant States would apply.

344 Obviously, if the production partner is a resident of the RS of one – or more – of its commercial partners, the taxation regarding the domestic income will occur in accordance with the domestic law of the State concerned.

345 Under the general B2B services place-of-supply rule of the applicable legislation, such as article 44 of the VAT Directive.

World Cup had a global reach of 3.2 billion[346] and the 2012 London Olympic Games attained 3.6 billion viewers.[347] Given the exclusivity of broadcasting contracts and the price of acquiring broadcasting rights, a very limited number of broadcasters have the opportunity of obtaining the broadcasting rights of sports events. In order to attract audiences, a part of the remaining broadcasters, generally small-scale ones, may entertain risky commercial strategies, such as proceeding with an unauthorised broadcast[348] of the event. Legal remedies available for protecting the rightful owners of broadcasting rights do not seem to discourage some broadcasters from transmitting sports events in an unauthorised manner.

The most commonly used unauthorised broadcasting techniques are: unauthorised recording (b); off-tube coverage (c); and piracy (d). Overspill is a technical problem that cannot be considered as amounting to an unauthorised broadcasting of the event.

B. UNAUTHORISED RECORDING

i. General aspects Unauthorised recording signifies footage prepared and transmitted by a person other than the licensed broadcaster(s). Creating sports content in such an 'adventurous' manner constitutes a courageous, yet risky marketing strategy.[349] Given the circumstances under which the footage is prepared, unauthorised recording is highly unlikely to create an alternative sports media programme meeting the standards of professional quality.[350]

ii. Income tax analysis

ii.a. Relevant domestic law aspects Unauthorised recording does usually not violate the copyright law per se. In fact, copyright laws tend to protect the event feed prepared by the broadcaster and does not prevent others from preparing and broadcasting their own feed of the same event. This being stated, a violation of the applicable copyright law may exist in cases where the logo and other protected insignia of the rights-holder and/or the event are clearly visible on the footage or the law concerned contains a specific regulation on the issue.

Regardless of whether or not the relevant copyright law was violated, unauthorised broadcasting will not give rise to an obligation to repay, but to the payment of a compensation determined by the competent court. The amount paid as compensation should be taken into consideration not during the assessment of the taxable income but during the calculation of admissible deductions. Whether such a payment is an admissible deduction or not will depend on the modalities of the applicable national law.

346 http://www.fifa.com/worldcup/news/y=2015/m=12/news=2014-fifa-world-cuptm-reached-3-2-billion-viewers-one-billion-watched–2745519.html (accessed on 17.12.2015).
347 *London 2012 Olympic Games, Global Broadcast Report*, p.4.
348 In this context, 'unauthorised' means that the necessary authorisation of the sports organisation concerned has not been obtained, i.e. the use of the broadcasting rights has not been lawfully acquired.
349 ANDRIYCHUK, p.135.
350 Ibid.

ii.b. International tax law aspects A broadcaster that records and transmits an ISE in an unauthorised manner may be ordered to effectuate a compensation payment to the rights-holder[351] and/or to the broadcaster licensed to transmit the event in the territory concerned.[352]

The compensation payment made to the rights-holder aims to repair any reputational or similar damages caused and/or to indemnify the unauthorised use of the event's and/or the rights-holder's intellectual property. Such payment should be categorised as 'other income' within article 21, and submitted to tax exclusively in the RS of the rights-holder.[353]

The compensation payment made by the unauthorised broadcaster to the licensed broadcaster aims predominantly to repair the damage sustained by the latter broadcaster in terms of business profits. As a matter of fact, due to the unauthorised transmission of the event in the relevant territory, the licensed broadcaster is likely to suffer from a decrease of viewers/subscribers, which may in turn translate into a considerable profit loss. Thereupon, the payment made by the unauthorised broadcaster to the licensed broadcaster should be categorised as 'business profits' under article 7 and be submitted to tax exclusively in the RS of the licensed broadcaster.[354] It is important to underline that, in most cases, the unauthorised broadcaster and the licensed broadcaster will be residents of the same State. Accordingly, the taxation will occur under the relevant provisions of the domestic tax law of the State concerned.

iii. VAT analysis In cases where the payment is made to compensate a damage and/or a loss suffered by an entity, a supply for consideration cannot be deemed to exist. For this reason, in most jurisdictions, such payments fall outside the scope of VAT.

C. OFF-TUBE COVERAGE

i. Definition Off-tube coverage is an unauthorised radio broadcast that is effectuated by a commentator who watches someone else's transmission of a sports event and simultaneously produces and transmits their own unauthorised commentary.[355]

ii. Income tax analysis

ii.a. Relevant domestic law aspects Off-tube coverage does not necessarily constitute an unlawful activity. For instance, as per the TalkSport decision rendered in the UK, a broadcaster clarifying that their/its commentary is not 'live' from the event can produce an off-tube coverage without infringing any

351 The DTT concluded between the RS of the rights-holder and the RS of the broadcaster will apply to such payments.
352 The DTT concluded between the RS of the unauthorised broadcaster and the RS of the licensed broadcaster will apply to such payments.
353 Article 21(1).
354 Article 7(1).
355 BENTATA, p.1214.

rights. Following the TalkSport decision, which constitutes a milestone in this particular issue, off-tube coverage seems to have even become the industrial standard in the UK.[356] For example, Virgin Radio offered its listeners a 'complete unofficial' commentary of England's matches in the 2002 South Korea/Japan World Cup.[357]

Income deriving from an off-tube coverage that is considered to be lawful will be subject to corporate income tax in accordance with the domestic tax law of the country concerned. If the income generated from an off-tube coverage is considered to be unlawful, the producer of the coverage will usually not be under the obligation to repay the amount earned as a result of their/its activity. They/it may, however, be under the obligation to compensate the rights-holder in accordance with the modalities determined by the competent court.[358] The amount paid as compensation should be taken into consideration not during the assessment of the taxable income but during the calculation of admissible deductions. Whether such a payment is an admissible deduction or not will depend on the modalities of the applicable national law.

ii.b. International tax law aspects In cases where off-tube coverage is deemed to be a lawful activity, income deriving by it will be submitted to tax in accordance with the relevant domestic law provisions of the State where the conductor of the activity is domiciled. Since no payment is effectuated to the rights-holder in order to conduct an off-tube coverage of the event, an international tax law aspect does not exist in such cases.

To the extent where off-tube coverage is considered to be an unlawful activity, the conductor of the off-tube coverage may be under the obligation to effectuate a compensation payment to the rights-holder and/or the licensed broadcaster, as determined by the competent court. The taxation modalities of these compensation payments are identical to the ones already examined for the purposes of unauthorised recording.[359]

iii. VAT analysis Compensation payments usually fall outside the scope of VAT.

D. PIRACY

i. General aspects Piracy occurs when the footage prepared by the broadcaster is unlawfully accessed and streamed by unauthorised third parties, particularly online.[360] The unavailability of official content, for example due to blackout

356 BARR-SMITH, pp.146–147; BENTATA, p.1214.
357 BARR-SMITH, p.147.
358 For an obligation to compensate to arise, the rights-holder should submit an enforceable claim to the competent authorities.
359 In paragraph b of this sub-subsection.
360 BENTATA, p.1232.

rules,[361] tends to increase the attractiveness of piracy during the time frame concerned.[362]

ii. Income tax analysis

ii.a. Relevant domestic law aspects Piracy violates the copyright vested in the footage. Like other unauthorised broadcasting cases, the third party concerned will not usually be under the obligation to repay the amount earned as a result of their/its activity. They/it may, however, be under the obligation to compensate the owner of the footage – most likely another broadcaster – as determined by the competent court.[363] The amount paid as compensation should be taken into consideration not during the assessment of the taxable income but during the calculation of admissible deductions. Whether such a payment is an admissible deduction or not will depend on the modalities of the applicable national law.

ii.b. International tax law aspects Depending on the territory where the broadcaster 'pirating' the footage of the licensed broadcaster conducts its activities, the latter broadcaster may or may not suffer from a profit loss. If the 'pirated footage' is transmitted in the same territory as the rightful broadcaster has been granted the right to transmit the event, piracy is most likely to translate into a profit loss. On the other hand, to the extent where the unauthorised broadcaster transmits the footage outside the territory covered by the licence obtained by the authorised broadcaster, piracy does not result in a profit loss.

Accordingly, in the first case, the compensation payment effectuated by the unauthorised broadcaster to the licensed broadcaster should be considered as 'business profits' under article 7. In the second situation, the payment should be categorised as 'other income' within article 21.[364] Regardless of the categorisation, the income will be submitted to tax exclusively in the RS of the licensed broadcaster.[365]

Needless to state, if both broadcasters are residents of the same country, the taxation will occur in accordance with the relevant provisions of that country's domestic law.

iii. VAT analysis In principle, payments made to compensate a damage and/or a loss suffered by an entity fall outside the scope of VAT.

361 'Blackout period' refers to a time frame where the transmission of a given sports event is forbidden in a determined territory. Blackout rules aim for safeguarding the stadium attendance and encouraging the participation to amateur leagues. See, for example, Regulations governing the implementation of Article 48 of the UEFA Statutes.

362 BENTATA, pp.1232–1233.

363 For an obligation to compensate to arise, the broadcaster concerned should submit an enforceable claim to the competent authorities.

364 The applicable DTT is the one concluded between the RSs of the broadcasters concerned.

365 Articles 7(1) and 21(1).

I. Sponsoring

1. Concept of sports sponsorship

The ICC defines sponsorship as:

> any commercial agreement by which a sponsor, for the mutual benefit of the sponsor and sponsored party, contractually provides financing or other support in order to establish an association between the sponsor's image, brands or products and a sponsorship property in return for rights to promote this association and/or for the granting of certain agreed direct or indirect benefits.[366]

The idea behind sponsorship is to create, increase or maintain a brand awareness by means of transference or fusion of the goodwill and connotative values of the sponsored party to the sponsor's brand or branded objects.[367] This psychological transference is what convinces customers to select the sponsor's products/services over indistinguishable and comparably priced competitive products/services; or indeed, to pay a price premium.[368]

Sponsoring is, therefore, one marketing strategy among others and not a donation driven by altruistic motives where little or no recognition is given to the benefactor in exchange for their/its support. Quite the opposite, the recognition by the public of the financial support provided by the sponsor to the sponsored party is a *sine qua non* component of sponsorship. Sponsoring should also be distinguished from traditional advertisement. Sponsorship implies a long-term collaboration, during which a strong bond is created between the sponsor and the sponsored party. This special bond, which lacks in other advertising techniques, is what allows the delivery of a personalised message to the identified target group and makes sponsorship deals so unique and valuable.

Sports sponsorship constitutes an extremely significant ratio of sponsorship agreements. As per the European Sponsorship Association's Fact Sheet, the ratio of sports to non-sports sponsorships is 67:33.[369] This tendency can be explained to a great extent by the loyalty of sports fans to their chosen sport, to their teams and to particular events. This loyalty is what enables sports sponsorship to accurately target the desired customer group.[370] Also, sport, particularly sports events, has the advantage of delivering a large number of viewers and spectators.[371]

The sports sector offers a great number of commercial possibilities to interested companies. Depending on its marketing strategy, the sponsor may choose to

366 *ICC International Code on Sponsorship (2003)*, Document No 240/475rev3 Final, p.2.
367 WISE/MEYER, pp.1914–1917.
368 Ibid, p.1915.
369 *ESA Sponsorship Factsheet (2014)*, p.2.
370 MACLEAN/MOORHOUSE, p.1241.
371 BECKER, p.31.

sponsor one or several of the following: a venue, an event, an SGB, a confederation, a federation, a league, a club, a team, a sportsperson, the broadcast of an event. To initiate or to maintain a worldwide brand awareness campaign, a company would tend to sponsor an internationally significant event, an SGB or a sportsperson/team recognised worldwide. On the other hand, to promote its brand in a more geographically localised manner, a company would opt for concluding a sponsoring contract with a venue owner, a national league or a team competing mostly in national competitions. For example, Continental, which had been a FIFA World Cup sponsor since 2006, decided to end its sponsorship deal in 2015 in order to focus on regionalised sponsorship deals. In that vein, the company concluded contracts with UEFA, the Asian Football Confederation and Major League Soccer.[372]

Sports sponsorship deals frequently present an international character. First, it is commonplace for a company from one country to become a sponsor of an event, an athlete or a team from another country. Second, due to the internationalisation of sport in general, the sponsored 'local' event, athlete or team usually reaches beyond the borders of a given country and, thereby, takes the sponsorship contract to an international level or reinforces its international character.

While sponsoring contracts may be concluded by different actors active in the sports sector, all conflictual contractual arrangements are eliminated by means of rules and regulations put in place within the hierarchical sports pyramid.[373] This implies that entities ranking higher in the hierarchy may impose restrictions regarding the sponsorship deals concluded by the persons occupying the lower ranks. Thus, a person may derive a sponsoring income related to an ISE only if and to the extent where they/it is allowed to do so by the SGB and in accordance with the rules and regulations of the event concerned.

A great variety of entities may conclude sponsorship deals in relation to sport. This book examines only the taxation modalities of the sponsoring agreements concluded by a rights-holder and a sportsperson.

2. *Sponsorship agreements concluded by rights-holders*

A. GENERALITIES

A rights-holder may enter into sponsoring contracts forming a general bond with the commercial partner and itself or relating exclusively to one specific event.

The highest degree of partnership with a given sport occurs by means of SGB sponsorship, which constitutes, thereby, the most valuable sponsorship agreement in the sports sector. SGB sponsorship also includes, in most cases, the sponsorship of the ISEs organised by the SGB concerned. Customarily, the SGB keeps a

372 FIFA's reputation further in mire as three sponsors sever their ties by Oliver Kay, article in *The Times* published on 23 January 2015, http://www.thetimes.co.uk/tto/sport/football/international/ article4332103.ece (accessed on 28.01.2015).

373 For explanations about the hierarchical sports pyramid, see chapter 1, II, C, 8.

certain percentage of the income generated via the sponsorship deal and distributes the remaining amount to organising committees, participants and/or other relevant entities. The most notable example of SGB sponsoring agreements is the TOP Sponsorship Programme, which is administered by the IOC. TOP companies are granted exclusive worldwide marketing rights in their designated product category for a period of four years,[374] along with the sponsorship of the Olympic Games taking place during the partnership period. The Programme constitutes a significant source of income. For instance, during the Sochi and Rio Games (2013–2016) it generated 1.003 million USD.[375] The IOC retains 10 percent of the benefits obtained by the Programme and distributes the remaining amount to OCOGs (50 percent of the overall amount) and to NOCs (40 percent of the overall amount).[376]

In addition to the SGB, the LOC of the ISE may also enter into sponsorship agreements with the 'domestic sponsors' located in the HS to grant the marketing rights exclusively within the country concerned. For example, BMW was the official automotive partner of the 2012 London Olympics within the UK.[377] Given the lack of any international component for tax law purposes, taxation of such agreements occurs in accordance with the domestic law of the HS.

Event sponsorship constitutes a highly influential marketing instrument that has been long used by well-established companies, such as Coca-Cola. Events usually have several sponsors. For example, the FIFA World Cup has six to eight global sponsors[378] and up to 20 regional sponsors.[379, 380] The most valuable sponsorship deal that an event can offer is 'title sponsorship'. Becoming a 'title sponsor' allows a company to attach its name, or the name of its product, to the name of the sports event (such as the Rolex Tournament of Champions[381]). 'Title sponsorship' is, however, not a commercial opportunity provided by all sports events.

B. RIGHTS GRANTED TO SPONSORS

Sponsors are generally granted a 'sponsorship package', composed of different rights. The contents of the 'package' vary in accordance with the sponsor's marketing objectives and the budget it would like to allocate. The most typical rights that may be obtained by a sponsor can be summarised by means of the following categories: naming rights, use of designations/marks, official supplier rights, advertising and signage, hospitality and tickets, merchandising rights, presentation rights and on-field promotions, rights relating to teams/sportspersons and other rights.

374 GARDINER ET AL, p.307.
375 *Olympic Marketing Fact File*, p.15.
376 Ibid, p.8.
377 GARDINER ET AL, p.308.
378 In addition to six to eight FIFA Partners.
379 Possibility made available for the first time for the 2018 and 2022 FIFA World Cups.
380 http://www.fifa.com/aboutfifa/organisation/marketing/sponsorship/strategy.html (accessed on 29.01.2015).
381 A golf tournament.

- *Naming rights*: the sponsor may obtain the right to incorporate its name in the title of the event (the so-called 'title sponsorship'). In this case, the name of the sponsor will be mentioned, along with the title of the event, in all pre- and post-event publicity, such as posters, websites and television/radio advertising.[382] As a subtler alternative, the event owner may retain the original name of the event, but include the wording 'in association with' or 'presented by' the sponsor.[383]
- *Use of designations/marks*: sponsors will generally be granted certain designations, such as 'official sponsor' or 'main sponsor', representing their level of association with the sponsored party. A sponsor may also obtain the right to use the event's logo and/or create a composite logo, formed by a combination of the event's and the sponsor's logos. Respectively, event owners obtain the right to use their sponsors' logos. For example, the sponsor may use the logo of the event on its webpage and vice versa.
- *Official supplier rights*: official supplier rights give sponsors the right to furnish products or services to the sponsored party and/or to the audience during the event. These rights often provide for exclusivity in a given product/service category and the use of the designation 'official supplier'. For instance, The Championships, Wimbledon has six official suppliers in the beverage sector, namely, Robinsons (soft drink), Lanson (champagne), Stella Artois (beer), Evian (water), Lavazza (coffee) and Pimm's (spirits).[384]
- *Advertising and signage*: advertising and signage at the venue, or via other means, is a *sine qua non* component of sponsoring deals. The exposure of the sponsor's name and message is guaranteed by its 'branded presence'. Sponsors tend to use a combination of different advertisement opportunities made available by the event. A typical example is product placement. Sponsors may, for instance, place their products in locker rooms to imply that their products are 'preferred' by sports professionals.[385] A more direct advertisement method is product sampling. Sponsors may give away samples of their products and/or their services to the audience. Packaged goods, such as potato chips, are ideal for the purposes of sampling. Concerning the services, sponsors may hand out redeemable coupons, which may either be targeted to a specific group of fans or given away *en masse*.[386]
- *Hospitality and tickets*: sponsors are usually granted a number of tickets, giving access to the most desirable seats, and hospitality services. They also generally have access to sportspersons and/or other relevant personnel taking part in the sports event concerned. These privileges accord sponsors a unique opportunity to entertain their business associates. They can offer not only the

382 BECKER, p.35.
383 Ibid.
384 https://www.wimbledon.com/en_GB/atoz/official_suppliers.html (accessed on 01.08.2019).
385 WISE/MEYER, p.1923.
386 Ibid.

best seats and hospitality services but also 'chalk talks' by a coach or a sportsperson.[387]

- *Merchandising rights*: sponsors may intend to manufacture different premium items branded with both the event owner's and their own logos. Premium items can be defined as products that are given away or sold at substantially less than their retail-selling price in order to induce customers to buy the product concerned in the future.[388] Sponsors commonly use premium items in specific promotion windows in order to increase the sale of their products.[389]
- *Presentation rights and on-field promotions*: with the aim of increasing their exposure during the sports event by generating fan interest, sponsors may require to secure presentation rights or to organise on-field promotions. Regarding presentation rights, sponsors may obtain the right to present the event trophy as a part of an official ceremony.[390] In addition, sponsors may be granted the right to use the event trophy for specified periods, either before or after the sports event.[391] With respect to on-field promotions, sponsors may organise ceremonies, small-scale tournaments and/or other entertaining activities. For example, they frequently present awards based on performance, such as the performance of the year or the sportsperson of the tournament. For entertainment purposes, sponsors may arrange for dance shows, concerts or other similar performing acts. On-field promotions may also involve participation of fans, such as an athletic skills exhibition by a fan and races between fans.[392]
- *Rights relating to teams/sportspersons*: sponsors may obtain rights in relation to teams/sportspersons participating to the event. These rights include, in particular, promotional use of imagery and personal appearances.[393]
- *Other rights*: sponsors may negotiate to obtain other rights that they consider to be relevant, such as an access to the supporter lists or similar databases belonging to the event owner/manager (which is especially relevant for companies active in sports betting), a right to film or obtain film footage of the event, establish promotional outlets at various locations at the venue to sell their own merchandise[394] and the first right to acquire the sponsorship of the event concerned for the next cycle.

C. REMUNERATION AND INCOME TAX MODALITIES

For sponsors, the financial return of sponsorship resides in the increased recognition of their brands and the potential improvement of their sales. Accordingly, the value of a sponsorship deal depends on several factors such as the popularity of the

387 Ibid.
388 Ibid, p.1925.
389 Ibid.
390 BECKER, p.37.
391 MACLEAN/MOORHOUSE, p.1257.
392 WISE/MEYER, p.1923.
393 MACLEAN/MOORHOUSE, p.1258.
394 BECKER, p.40.

sponsored party, the package of rights granted to the sponsor and the degree of exposure the sponsor is able to get. The sponsorship payment may consist of a cash sum, merchandise or services up to the value of a fixed amount (value-in-kind) or a combination of both. Reflecting the different rights contained in a typical sponsoring package, the fee structure of sponsorship deals generally has three distinct components: a rights fee, a media fee and a royalty.[395]

The contract may specify the remuneration for each separate group of rights or may provide for an overall fee. In the latter case, an apportionment of the income may be necessary for taxation purposes.[396] The modalities of the apportionment will depend on the specificities of the contract at hand as well as on the practice and the domestic law(s) of the State(s) concerned.

In cases where the sponsor is a resident of the same State as the rights-holder, the taxation of the income deriving from the sponsorship contract will be effectuated in accordance with the domestic law of that State. The following analysis applies to cases where the sponsor and the rights-holder are residents of different States.[397]

i. Rights fee The rights fee is a sum paid in exchange for the promotional rights conferred to the sponsor, such as the use of footage related to the event and associational rights like the 'official sponsor' designation. The rights fee is generally a flat fee. In some cases, goods or services may be provided instead of or along with the flat fee. Taxation of these benefits-in-kind depends on the domestic law of the State where the income is taxable. Nonetheless, it is possible to state that such benefits are usually considered as taxable income. The estimated value of a benefit-in-kind may be calculated in accordance with the market value or deemed to be equal to the costs incurred by the entity granting it.

To the extent where they do not amount to royalties, the rights fee should be characterised as business profits under article 7, as they are not dealt with separately in other distributive rules,[398] and be submitted to tax exclusively in the RS of the rights-holder.[399]

ii. Media fee The media fee is a sum paid by the sponsor for signage and advertising purposes, such as the display of the sponsor's logo at the venue. Like

395 WISE/MEYER, p.1925.

396 Since the competent authorities are not bound by the apportionment specified by the contracting parties in their contract, an apportionment can also be made in cases where the parties have already agreed upon the pricing of each group of rights.

397 The applicable DTT is the one concluded between the RS of the rights-holder and the RS of the sponsor.

398 Article 7(4).

399 Article 7(1). Except in cases where a PE is considered to be formed in the HS, see subsection IV, B of this chapter on this point. For the purposes of the PE analysis, the applicable DTT is the one concluded between the RS of the rights-holder and the HS.

the rights fee, the media fee constitutes business profits and should be taxed exclusively in the RS of the rights-holder as per article 7(1).[400]

iii. Licence fee Sponsors generally obtain the right to use the logo and other similar intellectual properties of the event and/or the rights-holder. In some cases, it is also possible for the sponsor to manufacture premium items bearing the logo of the event. In consideration of granting the right to use its logo and other similar intellectual properties, the rights-holder receives a flat fee that may be combined with a percentage of the receipts procured by the sale of premium items.

As the licence fee is received in exchange for the right to use intellectual properties of the rights-holder, it should be categorised as a 'royalty' within article 12 and taxed accordingly.

3. Sponsorship agreements concluded by sportspersons

A. GENERALITIES

Sponsors may also opt for entering into agreement directly with a sportsperson. It is common grounds for sponsors to affix their logo[401] on the clothing items or equipment of the sponsored sportspersons. As a consideration, on top of a sponsoring fee, sponsors usually offer bonus payments and similar prizes to encourage the sponsored sportspersons in their sporting endeavours.

The rights that can be granted by an employed sportsperson to a sponsor are rather limited, given the fact that employment contracts concluded between sportspersons and sports teams generally contain considerable restrictions on sponsorship agreements that may be concluded by sportspersons in an individual manner. For this reason, sportspersons competing on an individual basis, such as tennis players and golfers, generally benefit from more lucrative sponsorship agreements. This being stated, such contracts may also suffer from limitations. In fact, the rights granted by independent sportspersons to sponsors are frequently subject to restrictions imposed by the rights-holders of sports events.

B. INCOME TAX MODALITIES

The OECD Commentary explicitly states that sponsorship income that has a close connection with the performance made in the HS falls within the scope of application of article 17.[402] Prior to the modification made in 2014, the Commentary used the terms 'directly or indirectly related' to the public performance instead of a 'close connection'.[403]

400 Except in cases where a PE is considered to be formed in the HS.
401 Not merely as a manufacturer, but for advertisement purposes.
402 *OECD Commentary* on article 17, §9.
403 *OECD Commentary* on article 17, version 2010, §9.

It is undisputed that bonus payments and similar prizes paid by a sponsor for outstanding sporting achievements have a close or direct connection, respectively, with the sports event concerned. Subsequently, such payments may be taxed by the HS in accordance with article 17.

Taxation of payments made by sponsors that are not linked to one specific sports event, for example, annual payments, is of a more ambiguous character. Until the modification of the OECD Commentary in 2014, it was not entirely clear which sponsorship payments should be considered as 'directly or indirectly linked' to a given event. Opinions brought forward by different authors also diverged to a great extent.[404] Stockmann indicated that the HS might tax the sponsorship income in accordance with article 17 even in cases where the contract concerned did not specifically relate to the event taking place in its territory.[405] On the other hand, Oberson recommended the sponsorship income to be covered by article 17 only to the extent where it had a direct link with a given event, which would be the case if the sponsorship contract specifically referred to the event concerned.[406] Oberson asserted this approach as a recommendation in the light of a decision rendered by the Swiss Federal Tribunal,[407] and not as an interpretation of the OECD Commentary. Lastly, Grossmann stated that sponsoring income linked to a performance[408] should be distinguished from sponsoring income linked to the personality[409] of the sportsperson. While the first type might be taxed by the HS under article 17, the second type falls within the scope of article 7 or article 15, respectively.[410]

Although the overall image and personality of the sportsperson clearly have an impact on sponsoring deals, the distinction suggested by Grossmann is extremely challenging to effectuate. Sporting activities form an important component of sponsoring contracts along with personality and vice versa. For example, when RadioShack ended its sponsoring contract with Lance Armstrong, it stated to be proud of having contributed more than 16 million USD for the fight against cancer.[411] While the sponsoring offered by RadioShack, which was the title sponsor of a professional road bicycle racing team led and co-owned by Lance Armstrong, seemed to relate to, *a priori*, the sporting activity of the cyclist, the comment made by the company at the end of the agreement referred exclusively to a personal trait ('cancer survivor') of Armstrong. As illustrated by this example, sponsoring contracts are usually inextricably linked to both the sporting success and the personal features of the sportsperson concerned. It is quite difficult to determine which aspect forms the predominant motive of a sponsor. It is even more challenging to apportion the overall amount paid by the sponsor between

404 The authors enumerated in this paragraph are for illustrative purposes only. The same or similar opinions have been invoked by a number of different authors.
405 STOCKMANN, §53.
406 OBERSON, §136.
407 The Cyclist decision.
408 '*Auftrittsbezogene Entgelte*'.
409 '*Personenbezogene Einkünfte*'.
410 GROSSMANN, p.117.
411 http://www.forbes.com/pictures/fhhh45eje/radioshack/ (accessed on 01.11.2015).

two distinct types of income, i.e. *Auftrittsbezogene Entgelte* and *Personenbezogene Einkünfte*. Accordingly, such a distinction, or similar distinctions, should be avoided for the sake of both practicability – from the HS' point of view, which will have to make the apportionment – and certainty – from the sportsperson's point of view, whose taxation will heavily depend on the apportionment made by different HSs.

The point of view expressed by Stockmann corresponds to the approach followed by the OECD. It is considered that there is a 'link' between an ISE and income derived from a sponsoring contract, even in cases where the latter does not specifically refer to the former. In other words, the fact that the sponsoring agreement is not concluded with respect to one particular sporting event does not destroy the link between the sponsoring income and the event concerned, as long as such event takes place during the term of the agreement.

The replacement of the words 'direct or indirect link' with 'close connection' does not seem to have altered this approach.[412] To illustrate the level of connection required, the OECD Commentary gives the example of payments made to a tennis player for wearing a sponsor's logo, trademark or trade name on their tennis shirt during a match,[413] i.e. typical obligations of a sportsperson under a sponsoring contract, which are commonly long-term contracts. A 'one-off' sponsoring contract is quite rare in practice.

Not distinguishing sponsorship contracts specifically related to an event from those that are not seems to be justified at first sight, since both contract types give rise to identical obligations. This being stated, in order to tax the sponsorship income that does not derive from one specific event, the HS must proceed to an apportionment of the income concerned. For sportspersons who participate to a number of ISEs during the same tax year, such an apportionment is effectuated by a number of States. The main problem is the absence of an internationally recognised allocation method. Each State may use a different method, such as days spent in its territory, the ratio of the amount earned by the sportsperson from that particular tournament to their overall yearly income and even the importance of the tournament concerned at an international level. This lack of uniformity is likely to cause a source-source conflict,[414] which results in a juridical double taxation that cannot be eliminated by any of the DTTs concluded between the States involved.

Limiting the scope of application of article 17 to sponsorship income that is 'directly related' to the event[415] (i.e. bonus payments and similar payments made by sponsors as a reward for the achievement of a certain sporting success) and to income derived by sponsorship contracts concluded exclusively with regard to the event concerned, would eliminate the need for an apportionment and thereby prevent double taxation to a great extent. However, this is not the approach that is being currently followed by the OECD and by a large number of States.

412 *OECD Commentary* on article 17, §9.
413 Ibid.
414 For more information on source-source conflicts, see n.52 and n.54.
415 As argued by the Swiss Federal Tribunal in the Cyclist decision and by OBERSON, §136.

Subsequently, taxation of sponsoring income constitutes a particularly problematic issue where uncertainty and a high risk of double taxation reign.

C. VAT MODALITIES

Sponsoring is generally considered as a B2B supply of service taxable at the standard rate at the PoE of the sponsor's business, regardless of whether the remuneration is effectuated by means of a certain sum or value-in-kind benefits.[416] It is important to underline that sportspersons acting in a self-employed manner in a given business transaction should also be considered as taxable persons for the purposes of VAT. Rent-a-star companies that may enter into contracts directly with the business partners of sportspersons constitute separate VAT subjects.

Even though sponsoring clearly goes beyond a simple commercial relation between the parties and generally the sponsor provides the sponsored party with a remuneration that exceeds what would otherwise be paid for the advertising services concerned, VAT legislations do not generally allow a splitting of the payment effectuated for the purposes of sponsoring into donation and advertising. In cases where such a split is allowed, the part of the payment that can be categorised as donation will not be submitted to tax, since donations are outside the scope of VAT due to lack of consideration.

J. Endorsement

1. Generalities and demarcation from sponsoring

Endorsement can be defined as the promotion of a company's ('endorsee') product by means of the personal recommendation of an individual ('endorser') who is sufficiently well-known and respected to influence the purchasing pattern of sections of the consumer public.[417] Simply put, endorsement can be defined as the 'sponsoring' of a product by the chosen individual.[418] The psychological basis behind endorsement is that the use of a specific product is the direct cause of a part of the personal and/or sporting success of a top sportsperson. Taleb designates this way of thinking as the 'swimmer's body illusion'. While one may believe that professional swimmers have perfect bodies due to their extensive training, and by extension to a variety of products they use, the truth is quite different: '[t]hose born with a natural tendency to develop a swimmer's body [simply] become better swimmers'.[419] Albeit being fallacious, this assumption certainly contributes to the popularity of endorsement agreements, which constitute a major source of

416 In terms of the general B2B services place-of-supply rule of the applicable legislation, such as article 44 of the VAT Directive.
417 BAGEHOT/NUTTALL, p.129.
418 Ibid.
419 TALEB NICHOLAS NASSIM, *The Black Swan: The Impact of the Highly Improbable*, 2nd edition, Random House, 2010, p.110.

income for sportspersons. In fact, endorsement income may even exceed sportspersons' salaries and other winnings related to sport. For example, Roger Federer earned a total amount of 7.4 million USD from his salary and winnings, while income derived from his endorsement agreements reached 86 million USD.[420] Products endorsed by sportspersons are not limited to sports equipment, but may include a great variety of products not related to sports, such as personal hygiene products, clothing items and beverages.

In the literature, endorsement is often defined as a sportsperson sponsorship.[421] Despite being highly similar and often combined, endorsement and sponsoring are different contracts. Sponsorship consists of a rather long-lasting relationship, the main purpose of which is to enhance a brand's or a product's recognition through 'association' of its own image with the image of its sponsored subject.[422] The pursuit of such a unique bond does not exist in endorsement contracts, which aim for a promotion of the merits of a particular product to its potential consumers.[423] Accordingly, whereas sponsorship constitutes a broad association with the sponsor's company as a whole (and not specifically with one service or product of the sponsor), endorsement is usually based on one specific product or service. Divergence in goals pursued by these two different marketing strategies also reflects on payment methods. While endorsement deals generally offer a remuneration calculated on the basis of the commercial success of the campaign, sponsorship deals' remunerations are more 'sport-oriented', often including bonus payments or other similar prizes for outstanding sports achievements. It can, therefore, be stated that endorsement constitutes a marketing strategy ranking between sponsoring and advertising, with a more pronounced similarity to the latter.

In practice, however, it may be difficult to differentiate an endorsement agreement from a sponsorship agreement. In fact, endorsement and sponsoring are often combined, not exclusively with each other but also with other commercial opportunities, such as merchandising. Contracts presenting a 'hybrid' character are therefore common. As contracts receive their *lex* from agreement,[424] categorisation as endorsement or sponsoring necessitates a detailed case-by-case basis analysis, in the light of the modalities of the contract concerned.

2. Main obligations and remuneration of sportspersons

Ordinarily, the endorsee requires two main services from the sportsperson: (i) using the product concerned in public; and (ii) recommending it to consumers. These ser-

420 *The 2019 Forbes List.*
421 See, for example, BLACKSHAW, *Sports Marketing Agreements*, p.124 and MACLEAN/MOORHOUSE, p.1245.
422 LIPSEY, p.71.
423 Ibid, p.79.
424 '*Contractus legem ex conventione accipiunt*', from The Digest, B.1, §6.

vices may be rendered in different ways, the most typical of which are as follows: the sportsperson uses the product in public, i.e. during a competition, at a press conference or in their daily life; the sportsperson's 'personal recommendation' is made available to public via commercials on television, radio and/or print media; and the sportsperson is required to make appearances at a variety of places, such as autograph sessions, interviews and other similar events.

In consideration of their services, the sportsperson is usually remunerated by means of a flat fee, a progressive payment, value-in-kind payments or a combination of these different methods. A flat fee can be described as the fixed fee granted to the sportsperson for 'attention getting'.[425] Occasionally, a progressive payment can be made on top of the flat fee, if the sportsperson has helped to increase sales of the product concerned above a pre-determined target.[426] Last but not least, merchandise and/or other non-monetary items are often given to the sportsperson as a part of the remuneration for their services (value-in-kind).[427]

3. *Taxation modalities*

A. INCOME TAX

Sponsorship and endorsement being highly similar contracts, their taxation modalities are comparable to a great extent as well. Although the OECD Commentary does not expressly refer to endorsement income, it is clear that such income is akin to 'sponsorship and advertising fees' specifically stated by the Commentary.[428]

Two main types of endorsement agreements should be distinguished for taxation purposes: 'off-court' and 'on-court'.[429] Off-court endorsement agreements do not require the use of products bearing a logo, trademark or similar designation of the endorsee during sports events. Conversely, on-court endorsement agreements contain an obligation for the sportsperson to use particular products designated by the endorsee during sports events in which the sportsperson participates. Since taxation modalities of these two distinct types of agreements differ to a certain extent, they need to be analysed separately.

i. Off-court endorsement agreements Clearly, off-court endorsement agreements cannot be considered as having a close connection – or any connection at all – with an ISE.[430] Accordingly, income obtained from such agreements should not be categorised as income derived from a public performance effectuated by a

425 WISE/MEYER, p.1948.
426 Ibid.
427 Ibid.
428 *OECD Commentary* on article 17, §9.
429 Reference may also be made to 'on-course' and 'off-course' endorsement agreements, especially in relation to golf players.
430 Clearly, such agreements cannot be considered as having a direct or an indirect link with sports events either.

sportsperson within the meaning of article 17. This implies that HSs of different ISEs in which the sportsperson takes part should not proceed with the taxation of the income concerned.

In cases where the endorsee and the sportsperson are residents of the same State, taxation of the off-court endorsement fee will occur in accordance with the domestic law of that State. In other cases, the dispositions of the DTT concluded between the RS of the sportsperson and the RS of the endorsee shall apply.

Fees deriving from off-court endorsement agreements are usually categorised as royalties, since they are effectuated in exchange for the right to use the sportsperson's image, likeness and other similar attributes. While endorsement agreements may also provide for a number of different obligations incumbent upon the sportsperson, such as participating in interviews and events organised by the endorsee, such obligations generally have a secondary character. For this reason, an apportionment of the endorsement fee between the grant of rights and the services provided will not usually be necessary. To the extent where the services provided by the sportsperson cannot be considered as ancillary to the grant of rights, an apportionment of the income may be made for taxation purposes in accordance with the domestic law of the endorsee's RS.

Accordingly, as a general rule, the endorsement fee will be considered as royalties and submitted to tax in accordance with the distributive rule provided in article 12, which grants the right to tax exclusively to the RS of the sportsperson.[431] Should the relevant article of the DTT be based on the UN MC, the RS of the endorsee will also be entitled to tax the endorsement income up to a certain percentage.[432]

This outcome will usually not change even if an apportionment is made. This is due to the fact that the part of the income relating to personal services will be categorised as business profits[433] or income deriving from independent personal services,[434] depending on the provisions of the applicable DTT, and be taxed accordingly. Since the sportsperson will usually not have a PE or a fixed base in the RS of the endorsee, the taxation will occur exclusively in their RS in accordance with both distributive rules.

ii. On-court endorsement agreements On-court endorsement agreements undisputedly have a close connection with ISEs to which the sportsperson participates during the term of the contract. This connection may derive from a one-off contract specifically related to one determined sports event ('direct link') or a general contract providing for a commercial relation during a certain, rather long, term ('indirect link'). In both cases, article 17 is applicable to the income obtained by the sportsperson.

431 Article 12(1).
432 Article 12(2) of the UN MC.
433 Article 7.
434 Article 14 of the UN MC.

Apportionment of the endorsement income between different HSs forms a significant problem. Each State determines the amount that needs to be allocated to the event taking place in its territory in accordance with the method provided in its domestic law and practice. The allocation may also be effectuated not on the basis of a clearly defined criterion, such as the working days spent in the HS, but in the light of the specific circumstances related to the sporting activity concerned. For instance, in the Goosen case, the US Tax Court decided to allocate 50 percent of the income deriving from the on-court endorsement agreements concerned to the US on the basis that the US formed the largest golf market in the world, and it is one of the largest markets for golf endorsements.[435]

Although the method applied or the reasoning followed, respectively, by an HS may be justified in itself, the probability of the occurrence of a source-source conflict[436] is extremely high in such cases. It suffices that the apportionment made by two HSs corresponds to 50 percent – each – of the income concerned. From then on, any allocation of the income made by an HS to its territory, whether a low or a high percentage, will give rise to a source-source conflict, which cannot be resolved by any of the DTTs concluded between the States involved. As a result, it is possible to state that the risk of double taxation is extremely high in the case of an income deriving from an on-court endorsement agreement.

The apportionment of the on-court endorsement income between different HSs constitutes the main but not the only issue. Once a certain amount has been attributed to the public performance(s) of the sportsperson effectuated in one of the HSs, the income concerned should be categorised for taxation purposes. As a matter of fact, endorsement agreements comprise both the use of the sportsperson's image rights and the personal services provided by the sportsperson, such as using the endorsee's products during sports competitions. Depending on the modalities of the endorsement contract concerned and the practice of the HS, the income may: (i) be considered as 'predominantly of a performing nature'[437] and taxed in its entirety in accordance with article 17; or (ii) be considered as a combination of the use of image rights, i.e. royalties within article 12, and personal services provided by the sportsperson, i.e. public performance under article 17. In this second scenario, an apportionment needs to be made.[438]

A clear international practice does not exist regarding such apportionments,[439] and local authorities usually seem to proceed on a case-by-case basis. As expressly

435 The Goosen decision, p.32.

436 For more information on source-source conflicts, see n.52 and n.54.

437 *OECD Commentary* on article 17, §4.

438 Ibid. As a matter of fact, in the majority of cases, it is not possible to argue that the performing element forms a negligible part of an endorsement agreement. Both obligations are important pieces of endorsement agreements, '[...] so if you pull one of those pieces out, like the house of cards kind of falls' (as stated by the chief marketing director of TaylorMade's with regard to the endorsement agreement concluded by the company with Sergio Garcia in the Garcia decision, p.21).

439 The *OECD Commentary* does not contain any guidelines on this specific point.

stated by the US Tax Court in its Goosen[440] and Garcia[441] decisions, '[...] precision in making such an allocation is unattainable' but local authorities 'do the best they can' in the light of the evidence presented in a given case.[442] After a detailed analysis of the endorsement agreements concluded by Goosen and by Garcia, respectively, the US Tax Court decided that the income obtained by Goosen should be apportioned 50–50 between royalties and income derived from public performance,[443] whereas the endorsement income of Garcia should be allocated as 65 percent royalties and 35 percent income derived from public performance.[444]

Such allocations add another layer of complexity to taxation of endorsement income. In an attempt to avoid this additional difficulty, an allocation clause may be inserted in the endorsement agreement itself. Nonetheless, HSs are not under an obligation to follow the allocation made by the parties if the allocation concerned is not considered to reflect the economic reality of the endorsement agreement. This was for example the case in the Garcia decision. The contracting parties adopted an 85 percent royalty and 15 percent income derived from public performance allocation in their contract. The US Tax Court, however, modified this allocation as 65 percent royalties and 35 percent income derived from public performance.

Once the allocation is made, royalties will be taxed in accordance with article 12 and income derived from public performance will be taxed under article 17. For the former income to be subject to tax in the HS, the State concerned should be the RS of the endorsee. In cases where the HS is a third State, it will not be entitled to tax the royalties paid to a non-resident sportsperson by a non-resident company.[445] Royalties will generally be submitted to tax exclusively in the RS of the sportsperson.[446] In cases where the applicable DTT provides for a source-taxation of royalties, the SS, i.e. the RS of the endorsee, may also levy a tax up to the percentage determined by the DTT concerned.[447] The part of the income that is considered to derive from (a) public performance(s) will be subject to tax in the HS in accordance with article 17.[448]

To conclude, it is possible to state that like sponsoring income, taxation of on-court endorsement income constitutes a particularly problematic issue where uncertainty and a considerable risk of double taxation reign.

440 The Goosen decision.
441 Ibid, p.21.
442 Ibid, p.26; the Garcia decision, p.28.
443 The Goosen decision, p.37.
444 Ibid.
445 In such cases it is unlikely that the HS will proceed to an allocation of the income. The income will usually be considered as falling within the scope of article 17 in its entirety.
446 In accordance with article 12(1). The applicable DTT is the one concluded between the RS of the sportsperson and the RS of the endorsee.
447 Article 12(2) of the UN MC.
448 The applicable DTT is the one concluded between the RS of the sportsperson and the HS.

B. VAT

Endorsement is generally considered as a B2B supply of service taxable at the standard rate at the PoE of the endorsee's business, regardless of whether the remuneration is effectuated by means of a certain sum or value-in-kind benefits.[449] As already indicated, sportspersons acting in a self-employed manner in a given business transaction should be considered as taxable persons for the purposes of VAT. Should the endorsement agreement be concluded by a rent-a-star company, the service provider would be the star company, which also constitutes a taxable person.

K. Advertisement

1. General observations on lawful advertisement activities

Advertisement can be defined as '[...] any form of marketing communications carried by the media, usually in return for payment or other valuable consideration'.[450] Albeit also forming an important component of sponsorship deals, advertising constitutes a distinct marketing method, which differs to a great extent from sponsorship. While sponsoring necessitates a long-lasting relation and a close association between the sponsor and the sponsored party, advertisement is a direct communication of the brand's message to the target audience via media channels. This reflects on the impact produced by the two methods. Sponsoring creates a durable effect on customers, whereas advertising has a rather short-term impact.

Sport is one of the sectors that provide advertisers with outstanding opportunities. The most lucrative advertising deals relating to the sports sector being the ones concluded with the rights-holders of sports events and sportspersons, this subsection concentrates on the advertising services provided by these two enterprises.

During sports events advertising is most typically effectuated by the following means: (i) billboards (fixed and static, electronic and/or in form of rotating panels) located at or around the venue; (ii) other areas of the venue such as scoreboards, video boards, pole wraps, goals nets, necessary equipment, seats and terrace boxes;[451] (iii) human billboards ('the ballboys');[452] (iv) product placement/sampling; (v) securing spots during commercial breaks and brand break-bumpers of the event's broadcast; and (vi) 'virtual advertising', a method frequently used by broadcasters, which consists of inserting advertising and other commercial messages on the broadcasting footage of an event,[453] such as a

449 In terms of the general B2B services place-of-supply rule of the applicable legislation, such as article 44 of the VAT Directive.

450 *ICC Advertising and Marketing Communications Code (2018)*, Document No. 240-46/745, p.8.

451 WISE/MEYER, pp.1920–1921; BECKER, p.36.

452 WISE/MEYER, p.1921.

453 BENTATA, p.1240.

temporary computerised branding of billboards during the competition for a limited period of time.[454]

From a sportsperson perspective, advertisement signifies the use of one or more attributes of the sportsperson, such as their likeness, voice and nickname, in order to promote a product or a service. Advertisement is primarily intended for visual effect and capturing the potential customers' attention.[455] Sportspersons, enjoying both a high degree of recognition and a positive reputation among key demographic groups, constitute useful 'vehicles' to capture the attention of the advertiser's target group.[456] Advertisement can be categorised as the 'lightest' form of use of a sportsperson's publicity rights. It implies neither the use of the product/service concerned by the sportsperson (as in endorsement deals) nor a close association and a long-lasting relationship between the company and the sportsperson (as in sponsorship deals).

Advertisers generally pay a flat fee to the rights-holder of the event or to the sportsperson, respectively. The payment can also be made, partly or wholly, with a value-in-kind consideration.

2. *Taxation of lawful advertisement activities*

A. INCOME TAX MODALITIES RELATING TO THE RIGHTS-HOLDER

The remuneration obtained by the rights-holder from the advertisers is akin to rights and media fees paid by sponsors, and thereby is submitted to tax in the same manner.[457]

B. INCOME TAX MODALITIES RELATING TO SPORTSPERSONS

Advertisement may be considered as being similar to off-court endorsement. In most cases, advertisement campaigns will have a connection with the sporting activity of the sportsperson as such but not with a specific sports event. For example, Michael Phelps was photographed with swimming goggles for the Louis Vuitton advertisement campaign, which was not linked to any specific sports event. A connection can be established only in cases where the advertisement is explicitly made in relation to a sports event and/or it contains the logo, a trademark or any similar distinctive image of the sports event concerned.[458] It is therefore possible to state

454 Some of these mediums, such as virtual advertising, may require the advertiser to enter into agreement directly with a broadcaster. Such contracts, and income derived from them, are outside the scope of this book.

455 WISE/MEYER, p.1944.

456 Ibid.

457 See subparagraphs I, 2, c, i and ii of this section.

458 The *OECD Commentary* gives the example of a payment made to a tennis player for the use of their picture on posters advertising the tournament in which they will participate (*OECD Commentary* on article 17, §9).

that advertisement fees will rarely be considered as income deriving from a public performance made by the sportsperson within article 17.

This being stated, the OECD Commentary explicitly indicates that the term 'entertainer' clearly includes a former sportsperson in a television commercial.[459] The OECD Commentary also states that article 17 can apply to a person who is not an actor but who gets a fee for a once-in-a-lifetime appearance in a television commercial.[460] Accordingly, although advertisement campaigns may not be linked to an ISE as such, the sportsperson may be considered as an entertainer and be subject to tax under article 17.

The main issue with regard to the taxation of an advertisement campaign under article 17 is the fulfilment of the requirement of a public performance. The term 'public performance' should be interpreted as comprising performances directly made in front of an audience, live transmissions and delayed transmissions. In other words, only the first transmission of a recording should be considered as a public performance effectuated through the media (indirect public performance).[461] Consequently, replays/retransmissions should not be interpreted as constituting a public performance within article 17.

An advertisement campaign is usually communicated to public through the media. The term 'media' does not exclusively refer to television commercials. It also includes other channels such as newspapers, billboards and radios. Even if 'acting' in a television commercial may be categorised as an activity performed by an 'entertainer' within article 17, appearing in photographs taken for the advertisement campaign is unlikely to be considered as a public performance. Accordingly, only the part of the advertisement fees that can be allocated to the first transmission of the television commercial in a given country may be considered as falling within the scope of article 17. Undoubtedly, if the sportsperson effectuates a public performance, such as a launching party, in a SS for the purposes of the advertisement campaign, the income attributable to such a performance may also be taxed by the SS under article 17.

It is, however, extremely difficult to determine the part of the income attributable to a first transmission of a television commercial or to a launching party unless the amount is expressly specified in the contract concluded between the parties. Should some of the SSs choose to proceed to such an allocation, the risk of double taxation increases to a great extent. Consequently, application of distributive rules other than article 17 seems to be a more viable option.

Non-application of article 17 would implicate that the HS of an ISE would not be entitled to tax advertisement fees in accordance with the dispositions of a DTT based on the OECD MC per se. Nonetheless, if the HS has another link to the income concerned, it may be granted a right to tax as per the other distributive rules of the applicable DTT. Such a link will typically exist in cases where the advertiser is a resident of the HS.[462]

459 *OECD Commentary* on article 17, §3.
460 Ibid, §9.1.
461 *The 1987 Report*, §§78 and 81; KREISL, p.149.
462 Consequently, the DTT concluded between the HS and the RS of the sportsperson will apply.

Since an advertisement campaign consists of using the sportsperson's image, in most countries the payments made in consideration of such campaign will be categorised as royalties.[463] Should the income not be characterised as royalties under the domestic law of the SS, it may be designated either as business profits[464] or as independent personal services.[465]

In cases where a part of the advertisement fee is considered to fall within the scope of article 17, the HS will be granted the right to tax the income at source.[466] In the event where the income is characterised as a royalty, the sportsperson will generally be taxable only in their RS.[467] Lastly, in the eventuality where the income is categorised as business profits or independent personal services, the sportsperson will, once again, usually be taxable exclusively in their RS as per article 7(1) of the OECD MC[468] and article 14(1) of the UN MC, respectively.[469, 470]

C. VAT MODALITIES

The advertising service provided by the rights-holder/sportsperson to advertisers is considered as a B2B supply of service taxable at the standard rate at the location where the advertiser has established its business.[471] The medium used to provide advertising services, such as billboards and newspapers, does generally not modify the applicable place-of-supply rule.

3. Ambush marketing

Ambush marketing, also known as 'parasite marketing', occurs when a company or a firm claims an association with a sports event, through advertising and/or consumer promotions, without having officially obtained the right to do so.[472] Ambush marketing harms, in some cases even renders void, the commercial

463 Article 12.
464 Article 7.
465 Article 14 of the UN MC.
466 In accordance with the DTT concluded between the HS and the RS of the sportsperson.
467 Article 12. If the applicable DTT (i.e. the DTT concluded between the RS of the sportsperson and the RS of the advertiser) follows the UN MC on this point, the SS may also tax the income up to a certain percentage as determined by the DTT.
468 The creation of a PE in the HS is quite unlikely in these situations.
469 The creation of a fixed base in the HS is quite unlikely in these situations.
470 In accordance with the dispositions of the DTT concluded between the RS of the sportsperson and the RS of the advertiser.
471 In terms of the general B2B services place-of-supply rule of the applicable legislation, such as article 44 of the VAT Directive.
472 BLACKSHAW, *Ambush Marketing*, p.6. Companies engaged in 'parallel marketing' should be distinguished from ambush marketers. Parallel marketing can be defined as a marketing strategy that relies on the increasing interest that a sports event generates, without violating the sports federation's right to goodwill, reputation or identity. Demarcation between 'parallel marketing' and 'ambush marketing' is beyond the scope of this book. For more information on this matter, see CORNELIUS, *Ambush marketing*.

campaigns conducted by the business partners of the rights-holder. For example, while the official airline sponsor of the 2000 Sydney Olympic Games was Ansett,[473] 60 percent of Australians were under the impression that the official airline sponsor of the Games was Qantas,[474] which conducted a remarkable advertisement campaign of 'Special Olympic Offers' and engaged well-known athletes to appear in these advertisements.[475]

Despite giving rise to fascinating civil law issues, ambush marketing does not constitute a subject of interest for taxation purposes. While ambush marketers are deriving some benefits (such as better recognition by the public and a 'pseudo-association' with sporting activities) from their unlawful activity, they do not obtain any taxable income as a direct result of, and do not take part in any taxable transactions in relation to, the activity concerned.

L. Sporting or gaming performance

1. General observations

This subsection analyses income deriving from sporting performance provided by sportspersons and from gaming performance effectuated by pro-gamers. 'Sporting/gaming performance' implies that the individual concerned is taking part in the sporting/gaming activity as a competitor, and not as, for instance, a member of the technical staff or a referee.

Sportspersons may participate to an ISE as a part of a team or on an individual basis. In the former case the sportsperson performs in accordance with the 'employment contract' (2) concluded with its team, while in the latter case a 'participation contract' (3) is to be concluded between the sportsperson and the organiser of the ISE. In the eSports sector, pro-gamers tend to compete as a member of a team, i.e. under an employment contract.

2. Employment contracts

A. GENERAL ASPECTS

Sportspersons competing as a part of a team – both at a national and an international level – enter into an employment contract with their team. Sportsperson employment contracts incorporate the rules of the relevant leagues and GBs in accordance with the organisational structure of sport. Some sportspersons simultaneously enter into contracts with two teams, i.e. one team of their choice as the main employer and the national team of the sport concerned. Employment contracts regulate the rather long-lasting contractual relationship between the parties,

473 Ansett Australia was a major Australian airline group, which ceased its activities in 2002.

474 An Australian airline company.

475 CORNELIUS, *Ambush marketing*, pp.12–13.

which also includes the relations between the sportsperson and their team with regard to ISEs.

This sub-subsection briefly mentions the main obligations of sportspersons as well as the principal obligations of sports clubs, and examines the relevant income tax modalities applicable to income derived by means of employment in the light of the most frequently used remuneration methods.

B. OBLIGATIONS OF SPORTSPERSONS

The main obligations of a sportsperson can be enumerated as follows:[476]

- participating in national competitions, including play-offs (national league championship and other similar tournaments);
- participating in international competitions (e.g. UEFA Champions League if the team has qualified);
- participating in friendly matches in which the team takes part, both at a national and an international level;
- participating in training camps and sessions at a time and place determined by the team;
- keeping themself in good physical condition at all times during the term of the contract;
- taking part in promotional activities as required by the club, the league and/ or the GB;
- complying with the contracts concluded between the club and its commercial partners, e.g. sponsors;
- allowing the club to use their image, i.e. likeness, name, signature and similar relevant attributes.

What needs to be understood by 'participation' is to make oneself available and ready to work. For example, a sportsperson may not refuse to travel with their team to an away-match by invoking that they are a substitute player. It is clear however that a sportsperson cannot be obliged to take part in matches or training sessions if they are suffering from an injury or a similar health problem.

With regard to the use of the sportsperson's image, a separate 'image rights contract'[477] may be concluded between the club and the sportsperson. This is especially the case for sportspersons who are well-known to the public.

C. OBLIGATIONS OF SPORTS CLUBS

The main obligation of a sports club is to remunerate the sportsperson for the services rendered. The extent of other obligations of a given club depends on the terms of the contract concluded with the sportsperson concerned.

476 The same list of obligations can be applied *mutatis mutandis* to pro-gamers.
477 See subsection M of this section.

Nonetheless, sports clubs have a general duty of offering the sportsperson an adequate environment for the expansion of their sporting skills (typically by means of adequate training areas and equipment, appropriate technical/medical staff and proper health care) as well as for the development of their career (by ensuring that the sportsperson has the opportunity to participate as much as possible in the official matches of the team, in correlation with their sporting performance).

D. REMUNERATION AND TAXATION MODALITIES

i. Main types of remuneration Sportsperson employment contracts may give rise to four main types of payment, namely base salary, bonuses, sign-on bonuses and transfer fees. Sportspersons, as well as pro-gamers, are typically remunerated with a combination of a base salary and bonus payments. Albeit being frequent in the sports sector, sign-on bonuses and transfer fees seem to be rare in the eSports sector, at least for the time being. While sign-on bonuses accrue to sportspersons, transfer fees accrue to sports clubs.

ii. Salaries paid by sports clubs Just like other employees, sportspersons are entitled to a number of other benefits on top of their base salaries, such as sickness allowances and holiday entitlement, as a part of their employment contract. A much-disputed component of sportspersons employment contracts is 'image rights'. The remuneration for the use of image rights may either be included in the overall salary (with no additional payment) or an additional fixed amount – composed of royalties and fees – may be provided on top of the base salary. In cases where, the sportsperson and the employing club have entered into a distinct image rights contract, the club will make the additional image rights payment in accordance with the terms of the contract concerned.[478]

Since salaries do not fall within the scope of VAT, this subparagraph exclusively concentrates on income tax. First, the general income tax modalities applicable to the employment income are examined. Then, the specific case of second-choice players is described in detail.

ii.a. General income tax modalities As explicitly stated in article 17(1), employed entertainers and sportspersons clearly fall within the scope of article 17. Accordingly, unless otherwise specified in the DTT concluded between the RS of the entertainer/sportsperson and the HS, entertainers'/sportspersons' salaries may be subject to tax in the HS. This being stated, some countries do not share this opinion and hold the view that entertainers'/sportspersons' salaries fall within the scope of application of article 15.

478 This aspect has been further developed in subsection M of this section.

For example, the Swiss Federal Tribunal held in its Cyclist decision that an income accruing to the sportsperson on a regular basis, regardless of whether he participates in a given sports event or not – and in the affirmative, to which one – and even during sickness periods has merely an indirect link with the sports events in which the sportsperson concerned takes part.[479] Thereupon, it should be considered that such income does not have its source in the country where the ISE takes place, i.e. the HS, but in the RS of the sportsperson's employer.[480] Accordingly, as per the Swiss Federal Tribunal's approach, even if the personal scope of article 17 covers both independent and employed sportspersons, only the income that is directly linked to a public performance, such as prize monies and bonuses, should be considered as falling into the material scope of application of this distributive rule.[481]

A similar decision has been rendered by the Court of Appeal of Amsterdam.[482] The Court of Appeal held that article 17 should not be applied to a remuneration that is not specifically related to a given performance or a certain sports event.[483] The Court then noted that since a sportsperson employed by a team is always entitled to a basic salary, no connection can be established between participation in a certain tournament and a basic salary.[484] This decision does not, however, reflect the common opinion in the Netherlands on the matter. In fact, two other decisions rendered by the Court of Appeal of 's-Hertogenbosch prior to the decision of the Court of Appeal of Amsterdam reached the exact opposite result.[485] Regarding a cyclist who had received a prize money with regard to a competition and who had a basic salary deriving from his employment contract with his team, the Court of Appeal of 's-Hertogenbosch[486] held that article 17 did not only relate to a remuneration directly paid to the sportsperson, but also to the salary paid by the employer.[487] The same Court rendered a similar decision[488] concerning a professional football player who had participated in a number of matches taking place outside the Netherlands.[489] All three decisions were subject to appeal.[490] In its conclusions,[491] the Advocate General held that the view of the Court of Appeal of 's-Hertogenbosch should prevail.[492] Consequently, basic

479 The Cyclist decision, §6.2.
480 Ibid.
481 Ibid, §§5.3. and 5.5.
482 Decision No 03/04112, The Court of Appeal of Amsterdam, 6 October 2004.
483 BETTEN, *Netherlands Ice Skater*, p.260.
484 Ibid.
485 Ibid, pp.261–262.
486 Decision No 01/03822, The Court of Appeal of 's-Hertogenbosch, 10 June 2003.
487 BETTEN, *Netherlands Ice Skater*, p.261.
488 Decision No 02/04607, The Court of Appeal of 's-Hertogenbosch, 5 November 2003.
489 BETTEN, *Netherlands Ice Skater*, p.261.
490 BETTEN, *Advocate General's Conclusion*, p.231.
491 Conclusions of 11 July 2005, Cases Nos 40465, 40604 and 41478.
492 BETTEN, *Advocate General's Conclusion*, p.235.

salaries seem to be considered as falling within the scope of article 17 in the Netherlands.[493]

Basic salaries are also considered as falling within the scope of article 17 in a number of other countries such as Germany, Belgium, Spain, the US and Italy.[494] In the light of the OECD Commentary,[495] it is possible to state that basic salaries are indeed covered by article 17. Should a State prefer excluding such income from the scope of article 17, it would be advisable to amend the wording of the distributive rule concerned accordingly. Should this option be effectively entertained, taxation of this category of income will occur in accordance with article 15. In most cases, income derived by pro-gamers taking part in a tournament and sportspersons participating to ISEs will fulfil all three conditions enumerated in article 15(2) and be submitted to tax in the RSs of the pro-gamers/sportspersons concerned and not in the HS.

In the absence of an amendment expressly excluding the employment income from article 17's material scope of application, such income should be submitted to tax in accordance with the distributive rule concerned. Given the fact that salaries are paid to pro-gamers/sportspersons in consideration of a number of obligations, including participation in ISEs (and eSports tournaments, respectively) in different countries – to the extent where the team is qualified – an HS is clearly not entitled to tax at source the salary of a pro-gamer/sportsperson in its entirety. Therefore, the HS must determine the part of the salary that should be allocated to the ISE/eSports tournament taking place in its territory.

The OECD Commentary suggests to allocate the salary on the basis of the working days spent in the HS, in the territory of which the pro-gamer/sportsperson has been required to perform under their employment contract.[496] Also included in the computation should be part of a day, the day of arrival and the day of departure.[497]

Working days should be interpreted as comprising not only the days where the public performance actually takes place, but also days devoted to training, travelling or simply being 'on-call'.[498] The following two conclusions may be reached on this point:

- The days that will be taken into account for the allocation of the salary include training days.[499]

493 It is important to underline that, since 2007, the Netherlands does not tax at source income derived by non-resident entertainers and sportspersons to the extent where the RS of the individuals concerned has entered into a DTT with the Netherlands.

494 OBERSON, §99.

495 Which even provides for an allocation method of salaries in its §9.2 (*OECD Commentary* on article 17, §9.2).

496 *OECD Commentary* on article 17, §9.2.

497 *OECD Commentary* on article 15, §5. Since the reference is expressly made to article 15 in §9.2. of the *OECD Commentary* on article 17, the explanations made regarding the computation of 'days of physical presence' may be applied where relevant.

498 Newman v Franchise Tax Bd., Court of Appeals of California, Second Appellate District, Division Four, [1989] 208 Cal.App.3d 972, 4a. See also STOCKMANN, §55.

499 On this point, see also *OECD Commentary* on article 17, §9.1.

- Even if substitute pro-gamers/sportspersons, i.e. gamers/players waiting on the bench for the eventuality where a substitution will be necessary during the competition, may not actually 'play' (take part in the 'gaming', respectively); the days they spend to travel to the HS, to train, and to be 'on-call' are taken into consideration for the purposes of their taxation in the HS.[500]

It can, therefore, be concluded that the HS may tax the part of the pro-gamer's/sportsperson's salary that may be allocated to the activities performed in its territory under article 17.[501]

ii.b. Specific case of second-choice players Second-choice players can be defined as players who are not included in the team for the event concerned. While the reference is exclusively made to 'sportspersons' for the sake of simplicity, the following observations apply *mutatis mutandis* to second-choice pro-gamers.

Taxation modalities depend on the purpose of the second-choice player's presence in the HS. Three different scenarios can be conceived: (i) the player does not take part in any activities whether involving their team, such as training, or not, like events organised for advertisement purposes, but only watches the match in the stadium as a fan; (ii) the player takes part in training sessions and other activities, like press conferences, with their team; and (iii) the player does not take part in any activities involving their team, but takes part in public performances organised by their own business partners, like a party thrown by one of their endorsees.

In the first scenario, it is not possible to consider that the player derives an income from an activity exercised in the HS. In fact, the sportsperson does not take part in a public performance. Even if the mere fact that the player is watching the match of their own team in the stadium may attract some media attention, this occurrence alone should not be considered as a public performance under article 17.[502] Moreover, the player does not exercise any activities involving their team in the HS. Subsequently, they may not be regarded as exercising an activity related to their employment within article 15 in the State concerned either. As a result, in this scenario, the second-choice player should not be subject to tax in the HS.

500 The main issue regarding the taxation of substitute players is to determine whether they are providing a 'public performance' or not. Substitute players who participate in the sports competition, even for a short duration, clearly do so. On the other hand, the situation of substitute players who do not effectively take part in the match is more difficult to determine (OBERSON, §71). This being stated, these players are on the field with the team during the match. Since article 17 does not differentiate between a direct and an indirect participation in the sporting activity, such an indirect participation should also be considered as falling within the scope of application of the distributive rule concerned (DANIS, p.107). Moreover, a different tax treatment among substitute players on the basis that they effectively participate in the match or not does not seem to be equitable.

501 In accordance with the DTT concluded between the HS and the RS of the sportsperson.

502 See also DANIS, pp.107–108.

In the second scenario, although the player does not take part in the sports event itself, they participates in training sessions and other similar activities with their team. As per the OECD Commentary, training sessions fall within the scope of article 17 regardless of whether or not they are related to a specific public performance taking place in the territory of the HS.[503] Accordingly, the part of the salary that may be allocated to the training activities may be taxed by the HS under article 17. The allocation should occur on the basis of the working days spent in the HS.[504] Other activities that may be exercised by the sportsperson in the HS will also be taken into consideration while computing the relevant days.

In the third scenario, the second-choice player does not take part in an activity involving their team but participates in another public performance. In such a case, their salary will not be subject to tax in the HS, since the player is not exercising any obligations deriving from their employment contract. Nonetheless, the income derived by the public performance concerned may be taxed by the HS under article 17.

Undoubtedly, the sportsperson may also participate in both team activities and personal activities taking place in the HS. In those cases, they may be taxed in the HS under articles 15 and 17, depending on the specific circumstances of the case and the dispositions of the applicable DTT.[505]

iii. Bonus payments Sports teams usually remunerate sportspersons with a combination of a base salary and bonus payments for the achievement of predefined goals, such as getting a certain ranking in a championship – ranking bonus – and reaching a certain stage of the competition. Bonuses may also be paid to sportspersons by national federations, associations or leagues. In the same vein, pro-gamers may benefit from bonus payments made by their team or game developers. Since employees do not constitute taxable persons for VAT purposes, bonus payments fall outside the scope of VAT. Accordingly, only income tax modalities are examined in relation to the payments concerned.

In most cases, bonus payments may straightforwardly be attributed to a specific public performance. Nonetheless, an allocation between different events may be necessary in cases where to move up to the next level of the competition the team must participate in a number of matches played in different States. For example, in cases where a home match and an away match need to be played to reach an upper stage of the competition, 50 percent of the bonus needs to be allocated to the RS of one team, for the home match, and the remaining 50 percent should be allocated to the RS of the other team, for the away match.[506] An allocation may also be necessary in cases where the team employing the sportsperson is competing in a multinational league. In that event, the allocation may be effectuated on the basis of different factors, such as number of matches played and working days

503 *OECD Commentary* on article 17, §9.1.
504 Ibid, §9.2.
505 The applicable DTT is the one concluded between the HS and the RS of the sportsperson.
506 BUCHSTEINER, p.267.

spent in the HS.[507] In order to avoid double taxation, however, allocation keys used by the States concerned should coincide.[508]

Bonus payments are subject to tax in the HS in accordance with article 17, regardless of who pays the income.[509] Subsequently, whether paid by a national federation or directly by a team, a bonus received by a sportsperson may be taxed by the HS under article 17.[510] The same reasoning applies *mutatis mutandis* to pro-gamers.

An interesting problem may arise in cases where the event organiser pays a certain amount not to the pro-gamer/sportsperson themself but to the participant teams. On this specific point, the OECD Commentary states that article 17 covers prizes and awards that a sportsperson or a team may receive in relation to a particular sports event.[511] Accordingly, article 17 seems to be applicable to bonuses paid to participant teams. This being stated, these bonuses are not intended for distribution to pro-gamers/sportspersons. As a matter of fact, eSports/sports teams do not usually allocate a percentage of each type of revenue they derive from the commercialisation of eSports/sports events and products to their employees. Television fees, sponsoring fees, gate receipts, merchandising income and other similar income are generally kept by the team for its own use. The pro-gamer/sportsperson receives a salary, bonus payments for their services and in some cases (mostly for sportspersons well-known to the public) an additional payment for their image rights.

Consequently, it is possible to state that payments made by event organisers to teams should be excluded from the scope of article 17, since they are not intended for distribution to pro-gamers/sportspersons. Should the event organiser allocate an income to participant teams specifically for being distributed to pro-gamers/sportspersons, such income must be subject to tax in accordance with article 17. A similar approach should also be followed in cases where the employment contract of the pro-gamer/sportsperson does not provide for a fixed-amount bonus payment but for the allocation to the pro-gamer/sportsperson of a certain percentage of the income derived by the team from the event(s) in which the pro-gamer/sportsperson takes part. Undoubtedly, only the percentage that is allocated to the pro-gamer/sportsperson should be considered as falling within the scope of article 17.

iv. Sign-on bonuses paid by sports clubs A sign-on bonus can be defined as an amount paid to a sportsperson upon the signature of the employment contract. Depending on the arrangement between the club and the sportsperson, the

507 See also ibid, p.268.
508 To adopt coherent allocation keys, the CSs may use the interpretative mutual agreement procedure provided in the first sentence of article 25(3).
509 *OECD Commentary* on article 17, §8.1.
510 The applicable DTT is the one concluded between the HS and the RS of the pro-gamer/sportsperson.
511 *OECD Commentary* on article 17, §8.1.

sign-on bonus may be paid upfront or in several instalments. Even in cases where the contract is ended prematurely, the sportsperson is entitled to keep the sign-on bonus in its entirety.

Since the sign-on bonus is paid upon the signature of an employment contract, i.e. to an employee of the team, it falls outside the scope of VAT. For this reason, the following analysis concentrates exclusively on income tax.

Sign-on bonuses are especially relevant in cases where the amount that the club can pay to the sportsperson is restricted due to a 'salary cap', i.e. a global limitation on the amount permitted to be paid to the playing staff of a team over a given time period – most commonly one season.[512] Since the amount paid to the sportsperson as a sign-on bonus is divided into the number of seasons for which the contract has been concluded and only the amount per one season is included in the salary cap calculations for each year,[513] sign-on bonuses allow sports clubs to pay more substantial amounts to sportspersons without being restricted due to salary caps, at least to a certain extent. Accordingly, sign-on bonuses are frequently paid in countries where salary capping constitutes a well-established practice, such as the US and Australia. However, such payments are also made in countries where no salary cap restrictions are imposed on clubs, as an incentive for the sportsperson to enter into contract with the team concerned. This being stated, in Europe, sign-on bonuses are generally included in transfer fees that accrue to teams and not to sportspersons. Consequently, taxation of sign-on bonuses will not occur at the hands of the sportspersons but at the hands of the teams receiving the transfer fees. Taxation modalities of transfer fees are examined in the following subparagraph (v).

Given the fact that sign-on bonuses are kept by sportspersons in their entirety even when the employment contract is cancelled before its term, this type of income should not be considered as being closely connected to sports events in which the sportsperson participates during the term of their employment contract. For this reason, sign-on bonuses do not seem to fall within the scope of application of article 17, and thereby they should not be taxed at source by HSs.[514] Nevertheless, some States may follow a different approach on this matter. For example, in a decision[515] rendered by the US Tax Court, it was held that the fact that a sign-on bonus is not in itself compensation for services did not preclude the Court from allocating a part of the income concerned to public performances taking place in the territory of the US.[516]

512 GOULDING PAUL QC/MULCAHY JANE, Individual's Contracts with Clubs, Teams and Event Organisers in LEWIS ADAM/TAYLOR JONATHAN (eds), *Sport: Law and Practice*, 2nd edition, Tottel Publishing, 2008, p.565.

513 For example, if the sign-on bonus is 500,000 USD and the employment contract has been concluded for five years, only 100,000 USD will be taken into account for each season during those five years.

514 See also OBERSON, §167.

515 Ken Linseman v Commissioner of Internal Revenue, United States Tax Court, 82 T. C. 514 [1984] Docket No 23315-81.

516 The team employing the sportsperson concerned took part in a multinational league (Canada-US).

Albeit the existence of different interpretations, sign-on bonuses will generally be submitted to tax in the RS of the sportsperson, considering that a sportsperson employed by a team will usually be a resident of the State where the team is situated. Should the sportsperson be a resident of another State, the bonus will usually be taxable in the RS of the team in accordance with article 15(1).[517, 518] In cases where the HS considers that a part of the sign-on bonus should be allocated to the public performance made in its territory, the allocation will be effectuated in accordance with the same rules applicable to taxation of salaries.

v. Transfer and player loan fees

v.a. General observations When a player is transferred from one team to another, a fee, commonly referred to as a 'transfer fee', becomes due. A 'player transfer' signifies the termination of a sportsperson's employment relationship with one club, followed by the creation of another such relationship with a different club.[519] Simultaneously, the sportsperson is de-registered from their old club and registered with their new club.[520] A transfer fee consists of a sum paid by the acquiring club to the selling club to secure the transfer of the player's registration.[521] It is mostly compensation for the early termination of the employment contract and ancillary release of the registration.[522]

In some cases, the club with which the sportsperson is registered may decide to send them to another club on a temporary basis (a 'player loan'). Player loans are frequently practiced for several reasons, such as the number of available sportspersons playing in the same position. When a player is loaned to another club, their registration must still be transferred – to the borrowing club. However, the registration reverts to the lending club following the termination or the expiry of the loan period of registration.[523] As the registration of the player is not permanently transferred, the player remains employed by the lending club and does not enter into an employment contract with the borrowing club.[524]

The financial arrangements of the loan are a matter of negotiation between the two clubs. Usually, the borrowing club will be required to pay a loan fee to the lending club and to contribute to the sportsperson's remuneration. The loan fee may be paid as a non-refundable upfront fee, in several instalments or as a monthly fee. The contribution to the player's salary may amount to a certain percentage of the overall amount or cover it in its entirety. Usually, the wages to which the player is entitled are paid to them by the borrowing club on behalf of the lending

517 The applicable DTT is the one concluded between the RS of the team and the RS of the sportsperson.
518 The conditions of the 183-day rule, provided in article 15(2), will ordinarily not be fulfilled in these cases.
519 SAMPSON ET AL, p.572.
520 Ibid.
521 Ibid.
522 Ibid.
523 Ibid, p.574.
524 Ibid.

club.[525] In addition, the sportsperson generally receives bonus payments, for example, a ranking bonus, from the borrowing club.

The loan agreement between the two clubs may also provide an option for the borrowing club to buy the player for a specified amount. If the borrowing club exercises the option, it pays the amount concerned, i.e. the transfer fee, to the lending club and obtains the definitive transfer of the player's registration.

v.b. Income tax modalities Transfer and player loan fees clearly constitute business profits of sports clubs. In cases where the two clubs are situated in the same State, taxation will occur in accordance with the domestic law of the State concerned, i.e. the amount will be subject to corporate income tax under domestic provisions. In the event where the two clubs are residents of different States,[526] the amount will be taxable only in the RS of the selling/lending club under article 7.[527]

In some cases, a part of the transfer fee may accrue to the sportsperson themself. The part concerned, passed on to the sportsperson by the selling club, constitutes a severance payment. Subsequently, it should be categorised as an income derived from employment. As the sportsperson will generally still be a resident of the same State as the selling sports club, the amount will usually be taxable in the State concerned in accordance with the applicable domestic law.

v.c. VAT modalities Transfers and loans of sportspersons constitute B2B supply of services (intangible rights) provided by one sports club (the selling/lending club) to another sports club (the acquiring/borrowing club). Such transactions are generally submitted to tax at the PoE of the acquiring/borrowing club's business under the standard rate.[528]

3. Participation contracts

A. GENERALITIES

Organisers of an ISE enter into participation contracts with all participating teams or sportspersons. Those contracts may take the form of an agreement signed by both contracting partners or, more commonly, of regulations, for example, the Olympic Charter and the UEFA Champions League Regulations. Participation contracts regulate diverse aspects of the ISE, such as the sporting rules of the event, dispute resolution mechanisms, participation fees, use of the sportspersons'

525 Ibid.
526 The applicable DTT is the one concluded between the RS of the selling/lending club and the RS of the acquiring/borrowing club.
527 Article 7(1). A PE will not be created under these circumstances.
528 Under the general B2B services place-of-supply rule of the applicable legislation, such as article 44 of the VAT Directive.

image rights for the purposes of the event's promotion (e.g. in photographs, videos and advertisements of the event) – generally without an extra fee, participants' obligation (if existent) to attend interviews, press conferences or other similar event-related occasions – without an additional payment – and sponsoring/advertising authorised during the event.

All observations made in this sub-subsection may also be applied to pro-gamers and eSports teams, as appropriate.

B. REMUNERATION AND TAXATION MODALITIES

Participation contracts contain a provision about the fees that will be paid to the participants by the event owner. Those fees may include, but are not limited to: (i) an appearance fee that may be progressive, i.e. increasing with each stage reached by the participant; (ii) prize monies; and (iii) a percentage of revenues linked to the event, such as income deriving from broadcasting and sponsorship – usually only in cases where the participants are teams.

i. Appearance fees and prize monies

i.a. Income tax modalities Appearance fees and prize monies[529] form typical examples of income sources that can be considered as being 'closely connected' to the performance provided by a sportsperson during an ISE, as they arise directly out of the sportsperson's participation in the event concerned.[530] Subsequently, it is possible to state that appearance fees and/or prize monies may be taxed in the HS under article 17(1).

The taxation of ranking bonuses is more problematic. In fact, the rank of a sportsperson in a given sports competition may be based on their performance in tournaments taking place in different countries. This is typically the case for golf and tennis tournaments. In those cases, it is obvious that the bonus obtained is linked to the performance provided by the sportsperson during all relevant tournaments, and therefore it may be taxed by all HSs.[531] How the bonus needs to be allocated between different HSs is, however, rather ambiguous.[532] Sandler enumerates three different allocation methods that may be applied by an HS: (i) based

529 Prize monies may also take the form of benefits-in-kind. While taxation of such benefits depends on the domestic law of the State where the income is taxable, it is possible to state that they are usually considered as taxable income.

530 The *OECD Commentary* expressly states prizes paid to winners of sports competitions taking place in the HS as an example of an element of income 'closely connected' to public performances provided by sportspersons (*OECD Commentary* on article 17, §9.2). Although reference is made only to winners in this example, it is clear that also covered are similar payments made to all sportspersons participating in ISEs.

531 In accordance with article 17(1).

532 Although a new paragraph dealing with allocation rules for activities performed in various countries was added to the *OECD Commentary* in 2014, the paragraph concerned contains only a clarification on the allocation of employment income (*OECD Commentary* on article 17, §9.2).

on 'points' earned with respect to a tournament in the particular HS compared to aggregate points earned in the year; (ii) based on tournament winnings compared to total winnings; and (iii) based on the number of days (or tournament days) that the individual spends on the public performance concerned in the HS.[533] The lack of an established – or recommended – international practice on the applicable allocation method not only causes a great level of uncertainty, which is highly undesirable, but also is prone to cause a source-source conflict.[534]

i.b. VAT modalities Appearance fees and prize monies attributed to self-employed (i.e. independent) sportspersons and sports teams may be deemed to constitute remuneration for a B2B supply of service. As a matter of fact, prize monies and appearance fees are paid by the rights-holder directly in return for the sporting performance provided by the sportsperson or the sports team, respectively. Accordingly, such fees should normally be subject to VAT at the place where the recipient of the service, i.e. the rights-holder, has established its business, unless a specific provision provides a taxation at the place where the event actually takes place. In cases where the provider of the service is established abroad and is not liable to register for VAT purposes in the country where the services are effectuated (which will typically be the case of a sportsperson/sports team participating to an ISE), the tax may be collected by means of reverse-charge mechanism.

Appearance fees and prize monies are submitted to tax at the standard rate to the extent where the applicable VAT legislation does not provide for a reduced rate. For instance, as per the European VAT Directive, supply of services by artists may be subject to a reduced rate, whereas supply of services provided by sportspersons cannot.[535] It is important to note that pro-gamers should not be characterised as 'artists' under the provision concerned.

Some countries may opt for exempting prize monies obtained by sportspersons/sports teams or may deem that they fall outside the scope of VAT.[536] In such cases, no VAT will be due on the transactions concerned.[537] For instance, under the European system, prize monies are considered to fall outside the scope of VAT, given the fact that the award of prize is subject to a specific level of sporting performance in comparison to other competitors and, thereby, to a certain degree of uncertainty.[538] Such uncertainty breaks the direct link that must exist between the supply and the consideration actually received by the taxable person for the transaction to be considered as a 'transaction for consideration' covered by the scope of VAT.[539]

533 SANDLER, *Artistes and Sportsmen*, p.228, n.31.
534 For more information on source-source conflicts, see n.52 and n.54.
535 Annex III(9) of the VAT Directive.
536 On the other hand, appearance fees do not generally benefit from an exemption and they are not considered to fall out of the VAT's scope.
537 Depending on the circumstances, this approach may result in non-deductibility of a part of the input VAT of certain taxable persons.
538 The Baštová decision, §37.
539 Ibid, §§28–29.

Prize monies granted to a sportsperson/sports team to honour their/its overall sporting performance (such as 'life-time achievement' awards) cannot be deemed to constitute a consideration for any specific sporting performance, and therefore fall outside the scope of VAT.[540]

ii. A percentage of the revenues linked to the event

ii.a. Income tax modalities The rights-holder may grant a share of the event's overall income to participant teams.[541] To the extent where the rights-holder and the sports club concerned are residents of the same State, taxation of these payments will occur in accordance with the domestic law of that State. In cases where they are residents of different States, which will usually be the case, such payments will generally be categorised as business profits within article 7[542] and be taxable only in the RS of the sports club concerned.[543]

The main issue regarding the taxation of these payments is to determine whether they may be considered as accruing to sportspersons employed by the team. Should that be the case, the income may be taxed at the hands of the sportspersons concerned in the HS under article 17.[544] Since most of these payments are intended for the participant clubs and not for the sportspersons, the application of article 17 should be reserved to cases where: (i) the rights-holder allocates an income to participant clubs specifically for distribution to sportspersons; or (ii) the employment contracts of the sportspersons concerned do not provide for fixed-amount bonus payments but for the allocation of a certain percentage of the income derived by the team from the event(s) to the sportspersons. In this latter case, only the percentage that is allocated to the sportspersons should be considered as falling within the scope of article 17. The rest of the amount should be taxed at the hands of the club in accordance with article 7.

ii.b. VAT modalities A percentage of the revenues linked to the event is attributed to the team in consideration of the sporting performance provided by this latter. Accordingly, the payment is effectuated in exchange of a B2B supply of service, which should normally be subject to VAT at the place where the recipient of the service, i.e. the rights-holder, has established its business, unless a specific provision provides a taxation at the place where the event actually takes place. Teams that are not residents of the HS may be liable to register in the State concerned for VAT purposes or the tax may be collected by means of reverse-charge mechanism. A reduced rate or an exemption may apply, depending on the provisions of the applicable VAT legislation.

540 See also SCHREMPF, pp.540–541.
541 See, for example, articles 58–61 of the UEFA Champions League Regulations.
542 The applicable DTT is the one concluded between the HS and the RS of the sports club.
543 A PE will usually not be formed in these cases.
544 The applicable DTT is the one concluded between the HS and the RS of the sportspersons concerned, which usually is the same State as the RS of the sports club.

M. Image rights

1. Concept of 'image rights'

Although commonly used in sports law, both in practice and in the literature, the term 'image rights' does not constitute an accurate legal categorisation. In fact, 'image rights' are designated by a variety of terms in different jurisdictions, including 'rights of personality' in Continental Europe, 'rights of privacy' in the UK and 'rights of publicity' in the US.[545] For the purposes of the term 'image rights', the expression 'image' should not be understood in its narrowest sense of 'likeness' but in its wider sense of 'persona' or, to use the marketing term, 'brand'.[546] Irrespective of the term used, image rights designate the legal right of sportspersons, as human beings, to control the commercial use of their identity.[547] Accordingly, it is possible to define image rights as rights intended to protect the use of a sportsperson's identity and personal attributes, such as their name, nickname, signature, image and likeness.

Even if the exact legal nature and the level of protection offered to 'image rights' may vary to a certain extent from country to country,[548] there is an increasing universal acknowledgement – especially via case law and commercial practice – of 'image rights' as a form of intellectual property rights.[549] Nonetheless, to the extent known, this recognition in practice has not yet been translated into the enactment of image rights as a specific form of intellectual property rights.[550] As a result, although commonly treated as intellectual property rights, image rights cannot be registered per se. In order to protect their image rights, a sportsperson must register their essential attributes as trademarks, which constitutes the most viable legal option, albeit falling short of providing the necessary level of protection.

Sportspersons may exploit their image rights by means of entering into agreement either with a third party or with their employing sports club.

2. Image rights contracts concluded with third parties

Sportspersons may conclude contracts relating to the exploitation of their image rights directly with the interested parties, such as an advertiser. This being stated, incorporation of intermediary image rights companies constitutes a frequent practice, especially among top-level sportspersons. Under such a scheme, the sportsperson contractually assigns – generally on a perpetual, exclusive and worldwide basis[551] –

545 BLACKSHAW, *Sports Marketing Agreements*, p.256; HIGGINS ET AL, p.1154.
546 Ibid.
547 BLACKSHAW, *Sports Marketing Agreements*, p.256.
548 For a comparative overview of the legal status of image rights see, for example, HIGGINS ET AL, p.1156ff.
549 DAY COLLAS/ROMER JASON/DOFFING BRANDON, Comparative survey on sports image rights: Guernsey in *Global Sports Law and Taxation Reports (GSLTR)*, November 2010, Volume 1, p.20.
550 Ibid.
551 See, for example, the rights assigned by Wayne Rooney to his image rights company, Stoneygate 48 Ltd in the Rooney decision, §187.

Figure 3.8

the right to use and exploit their image to a company incorporated to this end and solely owned by them. The image rights company then enters into agreements with commercial partners interested in obtaining the right to use the sportsperson's image. These agreements are commonly referred to as 'image rights contracts', to the extent that they do not specifically constitute another commercial agreement, namely advertisement, endorsement, sponsorship or merchandising (see Figure 3.8).

The employment of this structure may offer a number of benefits, such as the possibility to take advantage of certain tax breaks, shielding the sportsperson against unlimited liability (by using the company as a vehicle, the sportsperson will be able to limit potential losses to the value of the company's share capital) and allowing the sportsperson to focus on their sporting performance by letting directors who are commercially experienced and skilled in the relevant areas (such as endorsement and merchandising) to operate the image rights company.[552] It is common for sports agents to assume the role of a director of an image rights company or to be otherwise in charge of the exploitation of a sportsperson's image rights. Different arrangements between the image rights company and the sports agent can be made to this end. For example, the sports agent may be appointed as the sole and exclusive representative of the image rights company.

3. *Image rights contracts concluded with sports clubs*

It is common practice for sportspersons to contractually segregate their arrangements with their sports clubs. One contract is concluded for the provision of playing services, i.e. an employment contract, and another one is concluded for the provision of promotional services, i.e. an image rights contract.[553] This web of contractual arrangements, mainly put in place for tax planning purposes, is illustrated in Figure 3.9. Customarily, image rights contracts have the same duration as the relevant employment contract. When the sportsperson gets transferred to another club or their employment comes to an end for another reason, their image rights contract is also terminated.

Concluding a separate image rights contract is only justified when the identity of the sportsperson concerned has a significant commercial value. In cases where the sportsperson's image rights' monetary value is rather low, for example when the sportsperson is not very well-known to the public at large, only an employment

552 HARRINGTON/WHITE, p.336.
553 HIGGINS ET AL, p.1182.

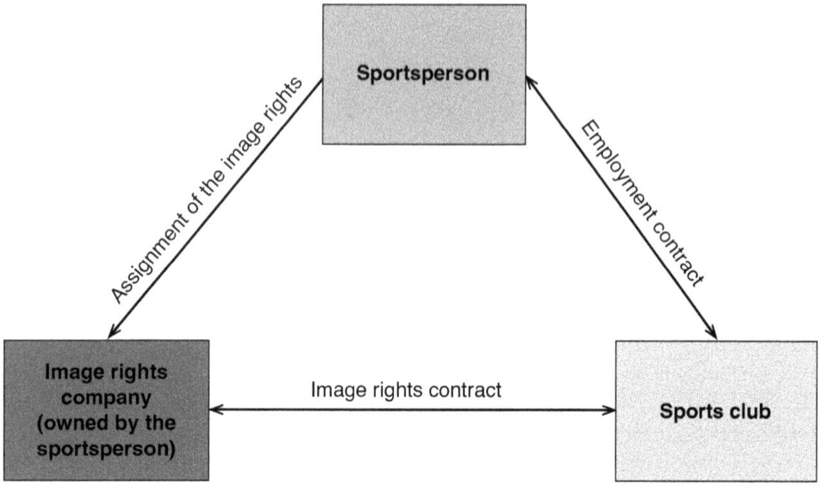

Figure 3.9

agreement is to be concluded. The relevant clauses granting the use of image rights and regulating the provision of other services are included in the employment contract. Standard player contracts,[554] generally drafted by leagues, may also contain such clauses, especially if the sport concerned is a popular one, such as football.

Image rights contracts, or such clauses included in employment contracts, allow the club to exploit its players' reputation for both its own and its commercial partners', such as sponsors and merchandisees, promotion. Such exploitation may be highly valuable for sports clubs. In fact, income deriving from the use of high-profile sportspersons' image rights may almost equal the benefit obtained from their playing services. Accordingly, the value of their image rights may nearly be equivalent to the worth of the playing services provided. The commercial impact of 'image rights' may be illustrated by the example of Real Madrid C.F., which is considered to be '[…] a money making machine thanks to the marketing of its players'.[555] For instance, shortly after the transfer of Cristiano Ronaldo, Real Madrid C.F. earned more than 80 million EUR from sales of T-shirts bearing Ronaldo's name and other similar memorabilia.[556] The figure of 80 million EUR was especially relevant in that particular case, as it was the signing fee paid by Real Madrid for Ronaldo's transfer from Manchester United F.C.

554 Standard player contracts are standard employment contracts.

555 Booming business thanks to Cristiano Ronaldo by J.I. García-Ochoa published on 3 September 2013, available online at the following link: https://www.marca.com/2013/03/09/en/football/real_madrid/1362823886.html (accessed on 26.06.2015).

556 Cristiano Ronaldo shirt sales 'have already paid off £80m' by Alistair Potter published on 15 April 2010, available online at the following link: http://metro.co.uk/2010/04/15/cristiano-ronaldo-shirt-sales-have-already-paid-off-80m-fee-to-manchester-united-real-madrid-claim-242129/ (accessed on 26.06.2015).

4. *Legal nature of image rights contracts*

Image rights contracts grant to third parties a bundle of rights that can be exploited in different forms with a variety of commercial partners during a fixed period of time rather than a specific right that can exclusively be used by the third party concerned in a pre-determined manner. For example, when a third party obtains the right to manufacture sports shoes displaying the sportsperson's signature, the agreement concerned constitutes a merchandising agreement. On the other hand, when a sports club obtains the rights to use the sportsperson's image in its advertisements, to affix their name on several products produced by the club and to exploit their identity in other relevant ways throughout their employment, the contract concluded between the parties forms an image rights contract. This grant of rights component constitutes a licence agreement, given the fact that the rights granted are considered as a form of intellectual property rights.

Image rights contracts also typically contain different obligations for the sportsperson, such as appearing in photographs taken for the promotion of the club/the commercial partner or for informational purposes, making public appearances, giving interviews, taking part in press conferences and other promotional or social awareness events. This second component of image rights agreements is akin to a service agreement.

Based on this, it seems plausible to categorise these contracts as mixed-contracts containing components of both licence and service agreements.

5. *Remuneration and taxation modalities*

A. IMAGE RIGHTS CONTRACTS CONCLUDED WITH THIRD PARTIES

i. General aspects The income received by the image rights company or – in the absence of such a company – the sportsperson should be categorised as a combination of royalties and fees for services. The payment can be made on a yearly-basis or as otherwise agreed by the parties. The contractual arrangement between the sportsperson and the image rights company also gives rise to a payment. The sportsperson may either opt for obtaining a periodical distribution of the company's benefits or for accumulating the earnings in the company and proceeding to its sale, or dissolution, at a later stage to obtain a lump-sum amount.

ii. Income tax modalities Income derived from commercial partners by means of grant of 'image rights' should be considered as royalties under article 12 and submitted to tax accordingly.[557] This categorisation holds valid even in cases where the sportsperson/the image rights company is under an obligation to

557 The applicable DTT is the one concluded between the RS of the commercial partner and the RS of the sportsperson/image rights company.

provide some services in addition to the grant of rights. In fact, as explicitly stated by the OECD Commentary, in the case of mixed-contracts if one component of the contract constitutes by far its principal purpose and the other components are only of an ancillary character, the whole amount of consideration should be submitted to the tax treatment applicable to the principal component.[558] In a typical image rights contract, the principal component is clearly the grant of the right to use the image rights belonging to the sportsperson or to the image rights company, respectively.

Distributions made by the image rights company to the sportsperson may take the form of dividends[559] – in the case of regular distributions – capital gains[560] – in the case of the alienation of the company – or other income[561] – in cases where the company is liquidated.[562] This being stated, image rights companies are generally incorporated in low-tax jurisdictions, which do not have a large network of DTTs. Accordingly, sportspersons will usually be submitted to tax in their RS in accordance with the applicable domestic law.

It is important to underline that employment of an image rights company is likely to be considered as being abusive under the domestic law of the sportsperson's RS. In these cases, anti-abuse rules provided in the domestic law of the State concerned will also apply.

iii. VAT modalities The grant of rights constitutes a B2B supply of service (intangible) taxable at the standard rate at the place where the commercial partner acquiring the use of rights concerned has established its business.[563] The taxpayer can be the sportsperson or the image rights company, in cases where a recourse is made to such a company. If the taxpayer is not registered for VAT purposes in the State where the VAT debt arises, the reverse-charge mechanism may be employed to collect the tax.

Distributions made from the image rights company to the sportsperson are likely to fall outside the scope of VAT.

B. IMAGE RIGHTS CONTRACTS CONCLUDED WITH SPORTS CLUBS

i. General aspects Sports clubs may have recourse to 'player pools' for the purposes of image rights remuneration. Player pools consist of accumulating the income deriving from the image rights exploitation of all team members – such as the appearance fees paid for media and other promotional work undertaken on behalf of the club – for a certain period of time and then distributing it to the entire team.[564]

558 *OECD Commentary* on article 12, §11.6.
559 Article 10.
560 Article 13.
561 Article 21.
562 The applicable DTT is the one concluded between the RS of the sportperson and the RS of the image rights company (if any).
563 As per the general B2B services place-of-supply rule of the applicable legislation, such as article 44 of the VAT Directive.
564 HIGGINS ET AL, p.1193.

In cases where an intermediary image rights company does not exist, the sportsperson is entitled to a combination of royalties and fees for services under the image rights contract concluded with their sports club. As already indicated, a separate image rights contract may not be deemed as necessary by the contracting parties. Under such circumstances, the employment contract concluded between the sportsperson and the club contains the relevant clauses for the exploitation of the image rights. Accordingly, the sportsperson receives their salary along with royalties and fees deriving from the exploitation of their image rights.

In the scenario where the image rights company owned by the sportsperson enters into an agreement with the employing sports club, the latter remunerates the sportsperson and the image rights company separately. The sportsperson receives their salary under the employment contract and the image rights company obtains a combination of service fees and royalties in accordance with the image rights contract. The image rights company may then remunerate the sportsperson by means of periodical benefit distribution (dividends). The sportsperson may also opt for accumulating the income and obtaining a lump-sum amount (capital gain) by the sale or the dissolution to the company (see Figure 3.10).[565]

ii. Income tax modalities Under normal circumstances, payment(s) made for the image rights of a sportsperson is/are not closely connected to an ISE, except in cases where a specific use of the sportsperson's image is made in relation to the event concerned.[566] Thereupon, remuneration obtained by a sportsperson under an image

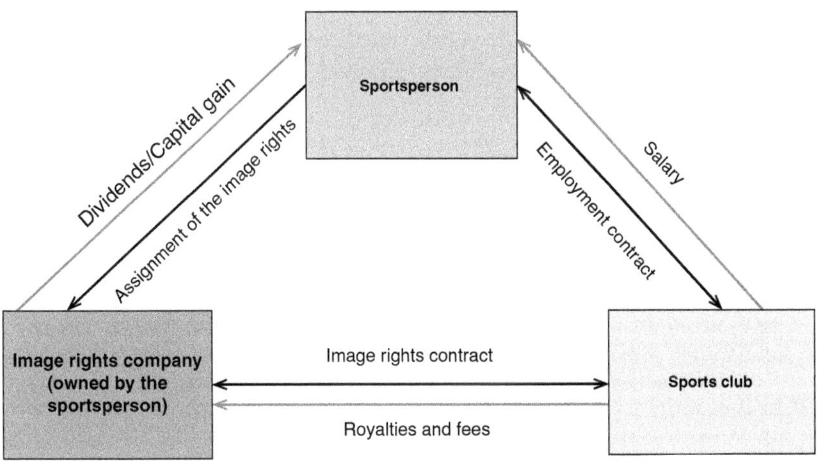

Figure 3.10

565 Taxation of the distributions made by the image rights company to the sportsperson is analysed in the previous paragraph (a).
566 *OECD Commentary* on article 17, §9.5.

rights contract will usually not be subject to tax under article 17.[567] As a result, such income will generally be submitted to tax in the RS of the sportsperson.[568]

Nonetheless, there are numerous examples where image rights contracts have been used as a 'disguise' for remunerations made for sporting services provided by sportspersons.[569] According to the OECD Commentary, in such cases, article 17 (1) or (2)[570] should be applied to the payment made for image rights, i.e. the income concerned should be submitted to tax in the HS.[571] This being stated, this rule is extremely difficult to implement for two main reasons: (i) the HS may not be aware of such payments; and (ii) it is rather complicated to determine whether a certain image rights agreement effectively constitutes a 'disguise' for remunerations made for sporting services or not.

First, to be able to tax the image rights payments made to a sportsperson by their team, the HS must be aware of such payments, which may not usually be the case. Despite the fact that well-advised sportspersons seem to not take a chance and report their income,[572] it is not possible to exclude altogether the possibility of an HS to be unable to detect, and thereby to submit to tax, image rights payments made to sportspersons.

Second, determining whether a payment made under an image rights agreement constitutes a 'disguise' for employment remuneration does not seem to be straightforward. As a matter of fact, the value of the image rights is inextricably linked to the reputation of the sportsperson concerned. An amount that may be considered as appropriate for one sportsperson may be either too high or too low for another. Moreover, domestic laws and practices seem to differ to a great extent on this point,[573] which is likely to increase dramatically the risk of double taxation.[574] For example, in their Sports Club decision,[575] the UK Special Commissioners decided that the separate image rights agreements concluded between two footballers[576] and their sports club[577] had an independent value and were not 'smokescreens' for the

567 Ibid.

568 To the extent where the income does not accrue to an image rights company. Since the payment is made by a resident of a State, i.e. the team, to another resident of the same State, i.e. the sportsperson, the taxation occurs in accordance with the domestic law of the State concerned.

569 Specific provisions may also be provided in domestic laws in order to prevent such abusive situations. See, for example, article 92 of the Spanish Income Tax Act (*Ley 35/2006, de 28 de noviembre, del Impuesto sobre la Renta de las Personas Físicas y de modificación parcial de las leyes de los Impuestos sobre Sociedades, sobre la Renta de no Residentes y sobre el Patrimonio*).

570 In cases where the payment is not made directly to the sportsperson but to an image rights company created to this end.

571 *OECD Commentary* on article 17, §9.5.

572 BETTEN, *Taxation*, p.380.

573 For a comparison of taxation modalities of income derived from image rights in a number of different countries, see BETTEN, *Taxation*, pp.378–379.

574 Due to source-source conflicts.

575 Sports Club plc v Inspector of Taxes [2000] STC (SCD) 443.

576 Namely, Dennis Bergkamp and David Platt.

577 Arsenal FC.

payment of an additional employment remuneration.[578] It is interesting to note that although image rights are not recognised as a distinct type of property in the UK, they have been considered to form a specific sort of property for fiscal purposes and treated as 'capital assets', which were tax-exempt, in the decision concerned.[579] On the other hand, the courts in Netherlands have decided on a number of occasions that income derived by sportspersons participating in team sports from the exploitation of their image rights in a way related to the their sporting activities should, for income tax purposes, be deemed as connected with their employment income and, thereby, be submitted to tax in the same way as a salary.[580]

The application of article 17 to income derived by image rights agreements may, therefore, be problematic and increase the risk of double taxation. For this reason, the most efficient way to counteract abusive image rights transactions seems to be the enactment of detailed domestic regulations to this end. This being stated, the OECD Commentary clearly indicates otherwise for the time being.[581]

iii. VAT modalities If the remuneration for image rights is included in the salary of the sportsperson, no VAT will arise, since employees are not considered as taxable persons for VAT purposes. In the rare eventuality where the sports club enters into a separate image rights agreement with the sportsperson themself, the transaction concerned may fall outside the scope of VAT, to the extent where the sportsperson is not registered (and is not under the obligation to register) for VAT purposes. In cases where the sportsperson concerned constitutes a taxable person or a sports club effectuates the payment for image rights to an image rights company set up by the sportsperson to this end, the sportsperson/company concerned should be deemed to provide a B2B supply of service (grant of intangible rights) to the sports club. The VAT will arise at the location where the sports club has established its business, in accordance with the destination principle. The standard rate will apply.

N. Provision of services by the workforce

1. General aspects

A number of individuals provide their services during an ISE either on an independent or on an employed basis. This subsection examines the taxation modalities of the general workforce, technical staff and referees. Despite the fact that they are not providing any specific services linked to an ISE, the taxation of employees obtaining value-in-kind benefits relating to a sports event (such as free tickets) is also examined.[582]

578 HARRINGTON/WHITE, p.317.
579 BLACKSHAW, *Sports Marketing Agreements*, pp.261 and 381.
580 BETTEN, *Taxation*, p.378.
581 *OECD Commentary* on article 17, §9.5.
582 Under 'general workforce'.

2. *General workforce*

A. GENERAL OBSERVATIONS

All sports events necessitate a workforce, the significance of which tends to grow in correlation with the magnitude of the event. While a small-scale sports event may be put in place by 10 to 25 staff members, a mega sporting event may necessitate thousands of workers. For example, during the 2008 Beijing Olympic Games, the number of workforce members reached 266,000.[583] A sports event's workforce generally comprises different categories of persons, namely: (i) volunteers; (ii) employees directly hired by the event manager (and/or the rights-holder);[584] and (iii) employees of different companies providing their services at the venue.

Major sports events benefit from a considerably high number of volunteers, without the efforts of whom such events could simply not be held.[585] In the 2008 Beijing Olympics example, the exact number of volunteers was 74,202.[586] Voluntary work can be defined as an unpaid activity that involves spending time doing something which aims to benefit someone – individual or groups – other than, or in addition to, close relatives.[587] Volunteers are not remunerated for the work they provide, but the event manager may cover their expenses.[588]

In addition to volunteers, the event manager usually needs to employ a number of 'paid staff'. The skills and the number of the employees that need to be directly hired by the event manager depend on the type of the event as well as on the venue hire contract. For example, if there is a need for event registration, check-in staff should be hired.[589] Employees in charge of waste management, custodial services, parking services and sports production[590] constitute other typical examples.[591]

Last but not least, different companies rendering their services during sports events, such as caterers, hospitality providers, on-venue results providers and media members deploy their personnel to the venue(s). In most cases, the employees concerned are remunerated by the company they work for, and not by the event manager.

583 PARENT/SMITH-SWAN, p.73.
584 For the sake of simplicity, a distinction is not drawn between the rights-holder and the event manager and the reference is made only to event manager in this subsection.
585 PARENT/SMITH-SWAN, p.80.
586 Ibid, p.73.
587 ANDREFF WLADIMIR, Voluntary work in sport in ANDREFF WLADIMIR/SZYMANSKI STEFAN (eds), *Handbook on the Economics of Sport*, Edward Elgar Publishing Limited, 2006, p.219.
588 Ibid.
589 GREENWELL ET AL, p.170.
590 Sports production signifies fan entertainment, before the competition, during pauses in the competition and after the competition. It includes the music, information provided on the jumbotrons and scoreboards as well as ceremonial aspects (PARENT/SMITH-SWAN, pp.154–155).
591 GREENWELL ET AL, pp.170–175; PARENT/SMITH-SWAN, pp.154–157.

It is important to mention that all the workforce, along with everyone who needs to access the venue and its surroundings without a ticket, need accreditation.[592] Being accredited simply signifies being security cleared.[593] There are several types of accreditation cards meeting different needs.[594] For example, some cards may give access to some parts of the venue only and some may be limited in time, i.e. not covering the entire duration of the event.[595]

B. INCOME TAX MODALITIES

Employees deriving an income related to an ISE can be grouped into two main categories: (i) employees providing services during the event; and (ii) employees obtaining hospitality packages and/or other similar benefits from their employers without providing services linked to the sports event concerned.

Employees are generally remunerated with a combination of a base salary and other benefits, including benefits-in-kind, which can be broadly defined as a benefit that is derived in a form other than in cash.[596] Although benefits-in-kind undeniably provoke an increase of the income of the person concerned – in the economic sense of the word[597] – whether or not they constitute a taxable income depends on the domestic law of the State where the employee is taxable. Nonetheless, it is possible to state that such benefits are usually considered as taxable income. Their estimated value may be calculated in accordance with the market value or be considered as equal to the costs incurred by the granting-entity.

Taxation of benefits-in-kind and other types of remuneration, i.e. monetary compensation, is generally regulated by the same set of rules. Subsequently, the developments set out in the following subparagraphs with regard to taxation of employees apply to all types of compensation obtained by an employee in consideration of the services provided by them.

i. Employees providing services during the event Employees providing their services during an ISE may either remain in their RS or be deployed to the HS from other countries. Taxation modalities of the former group of employees is exclusively determined by the domestic law of their RS, due to the lack of an international component. The tax treatment of the latter group should be analysed in the light of international tax law rules.

The taxation of employees travelling to the HS to render their services, such as employees of broadcasters, is to be determined in accordance with the DTT

592 PARENT/SMITH-SWAN, p.157.
593 Ibid.
594 Ibid.
595 Ibid, p.158.
596 HOLMES, *Concept of Income*, p.463.
597 For an explanation of the Schanz-Haig-Simons Model, see, for example, HOLMES, *Concept of Income*, p.67.

concluded between their RS and the HS.[598] As per the general rule contained in article 15(1), the income of an employee may be taxed in the State where the employment is exercised, i.e. the HS.[599] Nevertheless, the employees rendering their services during an ISE are likely to benefit from the 183-day rule[600] and be taxable only in their RS, given the facts that: (i) they usually stay in the HS during the ISE, and for a short period before and after the event, which does not exceed 183 days; (ii) they are usually remunerated by their employers, which often do not reside in the HS; and (iii) they are not usually remunerated by a PE that is situated in the HS.

In cases where an employee is 'physically present' in the HS for a period longer than 183 days, they may be taxed by the HS.[601] In the event that the employee remains in the HS for a period longer than 183 days but shorter than 12 months, an apportionment of their annual remuneration must be made for taxation purposes. To the extent identifiable, the parts of the income that are paid directly in respect of the activity exercised in one of the CSs have to be allocated to this State.[602] The parts of the income that cannot be attributed specifically to the activity exercised in one of the States, which will usually be the case for employees, should be allocated between the two States in accordance with the works day spent[603] in each State.[604]

ii. Employees obtaining benefits-in-kind without providing services linked to a sports event Companies acquiring hospitality packages or tickets to a sports event may distribute them to their employees as benefits-in-kind. This will usually be the case for the companies situated in the HS.

Generally, the employee is not the unique beneficiary of such a benefit-in-kind.[605] In other words, the employer who offers the benefit-in-kind commonly derives an actual or expected advantage from it as well.[606] It must, therefore, be underlined that the provision of tickets or access to hospitality areas to an employee should be considered as constituting a benefit-in-kind, even in cases where the employee is present at the event together with the clients of the company concerned[607] in order to 'reinforce' business relations.

598 The RS of the employer is not relevant, except in cases where the employment is exercised in that State.
599 Article 15(1) *in fine*.
600 Article 15(2).
601 Article 15(1).
602 AUMAYR, p.123.
603 The ratio used shall be calculated in the following manner: (i) the amount of agreed work days of the employee in one calendar year is identified; (ii) the amount of work days spent in the work State is identified; and (iii) the work days spent in the State concerned are divided by the total amount of work days in a calendar year. The days that are not work days, for example holidays, are not taken into account in the calculation of the ratio (AUMAYR, p.123).
604 AUMAYR, p.123.
605 HOLMES, *Concept of Income*, p.482.
606 Ibid.
607 Who are also provided with hospitality packages by the company.

Since the benefit-in-kind is not offered for services provided during the ISE, the employee will, in any case, be subject to tax in their RS for the income concerned. This follows from the fact that the company providing the benefit-in-kind and the employee are residents of the same State, and the latter does not provide any services in the HS. Subsequently, the taxation of the benefit-in-kind will be effectuated in conformity with the domestic law of the RS of the employee – and simultaneously of the employer.

C. VAT MODALITIES

Services provided by the employees to their employers are outside the scope of VAT. Benefits-in-kind offered to employees will generally give rise to VAT consequences, the modalities of which will be determined by the applicable national legislation. Employers may be under an obligation to calculate the fair market value of the benefits provided and be liable to pay VAT on them (as if they charged their employees for the services concerned).

3. *Technical staff*

A. GENERAL OBSERVATIONS

Sports teams and, in some cases, sportspersons competing on an individual basis employ a number of technical staff, such as technical directors (coaches), assistant technical directors, equipment managers, medical personnel and analysts.[608] Some of the technical staff members are present at the venue to assist the team/the sportsperson during sports competitions.

Technical personnel are usually remunerated with a salary and a number of other benefits that are typically linked to an employment contract, such as sickness allowance. Technical directors may also receive bonus payments in the case of the achievement of a pre-determined goal, for example, winning the championship. Although remuneration of most technical staff members is considerably modest when compared to sportspersons, technical directors may be entitled to substantial sums under their employment contracts. This can be exemplified by means of France Football's list of 'the top 5 best earning technical directors', which indicates that the earnings of the technical directors concerned vary between 23 million and 41 million EUR.[609]

B. INCOME TAX MODALITIES

i. Categorisation of the income It is commonly accepted that technical sports staff members do not fall within the scope of application of article 17. This is mostly due to

608 Analysts are regular members of eSports teams.
609 https://www.francefootball.fr/diaporama/Le-top-5-des-coaches-les-mieux-remuneres/7436/#5 (accessed on 07.08.2019).

the fact that they are not making a public performance. On this point, they may be compared to administrative or support staff mentioned by the OECD Commentary.[610] The Technical Explanation of the US MC has the merit of being more straightforward in this respect, since it explicitly states that 'others' involved in an athletic event, such as producers, directors, technicians, managers and coaches, are not covered by the personal scope of application of article 16 of the US MC.[611, 612]

Although some technical sports staff members clearly do not make a public performance – such as medical personnel – and thereby not fall within the personal scope of application of article 17, the status of some other staff members may be subject to discussion. For instance, Sandler gives the example of caddies for professional golfers performing their services in public during tournaments.[613] Another example would be technical directors of football teams, who often appear on television during the transmission of the matches. These individuals clearly do not constitute 'sportspersons' as they do not actively take part in the sporting activity itself. They should not be categorised as 'entertainers' either, since they are not the direct or indirect reason for which the audience attends or watches the performance – even if they may form an added value. Consequently, it is possible to state that income derived by technical staff members cannot be categorised as an income derived by an entertainer or a sportsperson under article 17.

Technical staff members generally enter into employment agreements with sports teams. They may also provide their services to individual sportspersons either under an employment agreement or on an independent basis. Income derived by technical staff members who are employed by a team or a sportsperson should be categorised as income from employment within article 15. Revenue generated by technical staff members who provide their services on an independent basis may be categorised as business profits under article 7, or independent personal services to the extent where the applicable DTT contains a distributive rule similar to article 14 of the UN MC.

ii. Taxation of the income Since the staff member will generally be a resident of the same State as the team or the sportsperson, the applicable DTT will be the one concluded between the RS of the staff member and the HS.

ii.a. Business profits Given the short-term duration of technical staff members' activities conducted in the HS during an ISE, neither a PE nor a fixed base is likely to be formed in that State. Accordingly, technical staff members rendering their

610 *OECD Commentary* on article 17, §3. The reference is mostly made to administrative and support staff of entertainers as it can be deducted from the examples given, such as cameramen for a film and film directors. This being stated, the reasoning clearly applies to support staff of sportspersons as well.
611 The equivalent of article 17 of the OECD MC.
612 *Technical Explanation of the US MC*, p.50.
613 SANDLER, *Artistes and Sportsmen*, p.224.

services in an independent manner will generally be taxable only in their RS as per article 7(1) of the OECD MC and article 14(1)(a) of the UN MC, respectively.

For the same reason, a technical staff member will usually not spend 183 days in the HS in a 12-month period. Consequently, they will not be subject to tax in the HS in accordance with article 14(1)(b) of the UN MC either.

ii.b. Income from employment It can safely be stated that technical staff members will usually be entitled to benefit from the 183-day rule provided in article 15 (2) and be submitted to tax exclusively in their RS. This holds true even in cases where the applicable DTT contains a limitation on the application of the rule to triangular situations, since technical staff members generally reside in the same State as their employer.[614]

C. VAT MODALITIES

No VAT arises in relation to technical staff members working as employees of sportspersons or sports clubs. Regarding technical staff members providing their services on an independent basis, a B2B supply of service will, in general, be deemed to exist. Depending on the applicable VAT legislation, the transaction may be submitted to tax at the location where the recipient has established its business or at the place where the sporting performance actually takes place. The European system entertains the second option in cases where the service supplied is a 'prerequisite' for the performance of the sporting activity,[615] which is clearly the case of the services provided by the technical staff members.

4. Referees

A. GENERAL OBSERVATIONS

Referees are recruited, trained and remunerated by GBs, both at a national (for domestic competitions) and at an international (for international competitions) level. They may be employed by sports organisations or offer their services in an independent, i.e. self-employed, manner.

Referees are appointed to matches or competitions by the relevant GB. They are mostly remunerated per match ('match fee'). The amount of the remuneration depends on the competition (premier league, second league, etc.) and on the rank of the referee concerned (referee, assistant referee, etc.). Referees employed by sports organisations are entitled to a basic annual salary in addition to match fees.

614 Article 15(2)(b).
615 See the Dudda decision, §27 and article 54 of the VAT Directive.

B. INCOME TAX MODALITIES

i. Categorisation of the income Revenue generated by referees from ISEs may potentially be categorised as one of the three following types of income: (i.a) income derived by a 'sportsperson' or an 'entertainer'; (i.b) business profits; and (i.c) income from employment.

i.a. Income derived by a 'sportsperson' or an 'entertainer' To categorise the income obtained by referees, it should first be determined whether this group of individuals falls within the personal scope of application of article 17. This problem has already been addressed by a number of scholars. In a nutshell, the common opinion seems to be that although referees must be physically fit and take part in sports events, they should not be considered as sportspersons under article 17, since they do not participate in the sporting activity as a competitor.[616]

A referee can be defined as '[a]n official who watches the game or match closely to ensure that the rules are adhered to and (in some sports) to arbitrate on matters arising from the play'.[617] It is undisputable that referees are *sine qua non* components of a sporting event. Without a referee, most sports competitions simply cannot take place. This being stated, referees are not 'playing the game' itself. They are merely observing it to ensure that the relevant rules are respected. Their participation in the 'game' is, thus, not active but passive. Moreover, although in some sports, such as football, referees need to make a significant physical effort, in most sports, such as tennis and boxing, they remain quite motionless.[618] Subsequently, it is possible to state that referees cannot be considered as 'sportspersons' under article 17.

Since the personal scope of application of article 17 does not exclusively cover sportspersons but includes 'entertainers' as well, it should also be examined whether referees can be considered as entertainers under the article concerned. It is undisputable that a referee makes a performance that is public – in most cases both directly before an audience and indirectly via the media. It is also evident that the performance in which a referee takes part, i.e. the sports event, has as its primary aim to provide the audience concerned with amusement or enjoyment.[619] However, the referee is not themself the direct or indirect reason for which the audience is watching the performance. Although, in some cases the referee themself may constitute an added value to the entertainment level provided by the sporting activity, for example Pierluigi Collina certainly did so, the audience watches the competition to see the sportspersons and the teams, respectively, perform. A

616 See SANDLER, *Artistes and Sportsmen*, pp.224–225; BLÁHA, p.132 and OBERSON, §73.
617 Definition given by *The Oxford Dictionary*, http://www.oxforddictionaries.com/definition/english/referee (accessed on 24.06.2014).
618 While a physical effort is not a *sine qua non* component of a sporting activity, in these examples, the activity itself, i.e. tennis and boxing, requires a physical effort, whereas the referee does not provide such an effort.
619 As stated in the Cheek decision, '[...] professional sports in itself is entertainment' (§21).

referee is generally not the reason why the audience attends the match, watches a sports event on television or listens to it on the radio. Consequently, referees cannot be considered as 'entertainers' within article 17.

It is therefore possible to conclude that referees do not fall within the personal scope of application of article 17. Accordingly, income they derive from an ISE cannot be categorised as an income derived by an entertainer or a sportsperson.

i.b. Business profits Referees are usually affiliated to a GB without being employed by it. They are remunerated on a per-match basis. This type of income should be categorised as business profits within article 7. In cases where the applicable DTT[620] contains a specific distributive rule on independent personal services, i.e. article 14 of the UN MC, this latter rule will override article 7 and the income concerned will be categorised as income deriving from independent personal services within article 14.

i.c. Income from employment Although it is a rare practice, referees may enter into employment agreements with GBs. In this case, the income obtained by a referee from an ISE should be categorised as income from employment under article 15.

ii. Determination of the applicable DTT

ii.a. Business profits Referees are remunerated by the GB. Accordingly, referees who reside in the same State as the GB to which they are affiliated will be subject to tax in that State in accordance with the applicable domestic law. Referees who are residents of another State will be taxed in accordance with the dispositions contained in the DTT concluded between their RS and the RS of the GB.

The DTT concluded between the HS and the RS of the referee will only apply in cases where: (i) the referee is considered to have a PE[621] in the HS; (ii) the referee is considered to have a fixed base[622] in the HS; and (iii) the referee spends at least 183 days in the HS in a 12-month period.[623]

ii.b. Income from employment Five possible situations may be distinguished with regard to employment income obtained by referees: (i) the referee and the GB are residents of the same State and the event is held in the State concerned; (ii) the referee and the GB are residents of the same State and the event is held in another State; (iii) the referee and the GB are residents of different States and the event is held in the RS of the GB; (iv) the referee and the GB are residents of different States and the event is held in the RS of the referee; and (v) the referee and the

620 The DTT concluded between the RS of the sports organisation and the RS of the referee.

621 Article 5.

622 Article 14(1)(a) of the UN MC.

623 Ibid, article 14(1)(b).

GB are residents of different States and the event is held in a third State (a so-called 'triangular case').

In the first case, the referee will be subject to tax in accordance with the domestic law of the State concerned. With regard to other scenarios, it must be borne in mind that the determinant DTT is the one concluded between the HS and the RS of the referee.[624] Accordingly:

- In the second situation, the DTT concluded between the RS of the GB/ referee and the HS will apply.
- In the third possibility, the DTT concluded between the RS of the referee and the RS of the GB will apply.
- In the fourth eventuality, the only international element is the fact that the employer is a resident of another State. Subsequently, the DTT concluded between the RS of the referee and the RS of the GB will apply.
- Lastly, in triangular situations, the determinant DTT will be the one concluded between the RS of the referee and the HS.

iii. Allocation of the taxing right

iii.a. Business profits Referees do not generally have at their disposal any specifically designated fixed workplaces in the HS (changing rooms made available to referees cannot be considered as PoBs). It can be argued that the situation is slightly different for 'video assistant referees' (VARs), who conduct their work by means of a 'video operation room', which is situated in the HS but not necessarily at the venue. This being stated, in any case, the short-term nature of referees' activities in the HS will prevent the formation of any PEs or fixed bases in the State concerned. Accordingly, referees rendering their services in an independent manner will generally be taxable only in their RSs as per articles 7(1) of the OECD MC and, respectively, 14(1)(a) of the UN MC. Also, since a referee will usually not spend 183 days in the HS in a 12-month period, they will not be subject to tax in the HS in accordance with article 14(1)(b) of the UN MC either.

iii.b. Income from employment

iii.b.i General considerations on article 15 Three cumulative conditions need to be satisfied to benefit from the 183-day rule: (i) the recipient must be present in the HS for a period or periods not exceeding in the aggregate 183 days in any 12-month period commencing or ending in the fiscal year concerned; (ii) the remuneration must be paid by, or on behalf of, an employer (i.e. the sports organisation) that is not a resident of the HS; and (iii) the remuneration must not be borne by a PE that the employer has in the HS.[625] Since the rights-holder does not usually have a PE in the HS, the last condition will be deemed to be fulfilled for the purposes of the analysis.

624 Article 15 refers to the State where the employment is exercised, which is, in case of a sports event, the HS.

625 Article 15(2).

Article 15 allocates the taxing right between the State where the employment is exercised and the RS of the employee. In other words, the RS of the employer is irrelevant for the purposes of the allocation.[626] Consequently, article 15 also applies in triangular cases. If, however, the CSs consider that it is inappropriate to extend the scope of the 183-day rule to cases where the employer is not a resident of the same State as the employee, they may formulate the second condition (ii) in the following manner: 'the remuneration is paid by, or on behalf of, an employer who is a resident of the first-mentioned State, and'.[627]

iii.b.ii General considerations on taxation of referees Given the short duration of the activities exercised by referees in the HS, these individuals may be entitled to benefit from the 183-day rule provided in article 15(2) and submitted to tax exclusively in their RS. Should a referee not qualify for the 183-day exception, they will be taxed in the State where the employment is exercised, i.e. the HS, under article 15(1).

iii.b.iii Examination of different scenarios that are likely to occur The different scenarios that are likely to occur have already been enumerated while examining the determination of the applicable DTT.[628] They are all briefly described one by one, except the first case where the taxation exclusively occurs in accordance with the provisions of the relevant domestic law.

iii.b.iii.a The referee and the GB are residents of the same State and the event is held in another State In cases where the referee spends fewer than 183 days in the HS, the taxation will occur in accordance with article 15(2). Consequently, the referee will be taxed exclusively in their RS. On the other hand, should the referee's presence in the HS exceed 183 days, they will be submitted to tax in the State concerned under article 15(1).

iii.b.iii.b The referee and the GB are residents of different States and the event is held in the GB's RS In this situation, the referee cannot benefit from the exception provided in article 15(2), since the second condition is not fulfilled. As a matter of fact, the employer paying the remuneration is a resident of the State where the employment is exercised, i.e. the HS. Thereupon, the taxation will occur in accordance with paragraph 1 of the distributive rule, which grants the right to tax to the HS.

iii.b.iii.c The referee and the GB are residents of different States and the event is held in the referee's RS In this eventuality, the referee exercises their employment

626 Unless, of course, the employment is exercised in the RS of the employer.
627 *OECD Commentary* on article 15, §6.
628 In the previous subparagraph (ii).

in their RS. Accordingly, the taxation will occur exclusively in the RS of the referee under article 15(1).

iii.b.iii.d The referee and the GB are residents of different States and the event is held in a third State This situation gives rise to a triangular case. To the extent where article 15 of the DTT concluded between the RS of the referee and the HS does not expressly exclude triangular cases from its scope of application, the referee may be submitted to tax exclusively in their RS in accordance with article 15(2). They must, of course, fulfil the first condition of the 183-day rule to this end, i.e. not being present in the HS for more than 183 days in any 12-month period.

In cases where the applicable DTT contains a limitation on triangular cases, article 15(2) will not apply, since the referee and the GB are not residents of the same State. As a consequence, the referee will be submitted to tax in the State where the employment is exercised, i.e. the HS, under article 15(1).

C. VAT MODALITIES

VAT modalities are the same as the ones laid out for the purposes of technical staff.[629]

O. Sports betting[630]

1. Definition

Sports betting can be defined as risking an item of value to take part in games of calculated chance that are connected with a competitive sporting event with the expectation of earning a prize of value (most commonly, a certain amount of money). It has traditionally been argued that sports betting is not a form of 'pure gambling' relying solely on chance but rather a 'calculated risk' allowing the bettors to employ their knowledge in the field of sport. In a typical sports betting agreement, the bookmaker[631] sells a betting slip (e.g. for 100 USD) that promises to pay the bearer a certain amount (e.g. 1,000 USD) if a named outcome occurs. In the eventuality where the outcome does not occur, the bearer is not entitled to any payments or refunds.

Sports betting constituted – almost exclusively – a national activity until the development of online sports betting, which enabled market operators to provide cross-border betting services and bettors to better evaluate their options. As a result of the rise of online sports betting, all forms of betting were enriched in an unprecedented manner, several forms of betting were born and new actors became active within the betting market.

629 Paragraph 3, c of this subsection.
630 Within this subsection, the term 'game' is not employed exclusively to refer to eSports activities; it also encompasses sporting competitions and games of chance.
631 A person who determines odds and receives bets on the outcome of events (GARNER BRYAN A. (ed), *Black's Law Dictionary*, 7th edition, West Group, 1999, p.177).

'Offline betting activities' mostly conducted on a national scale (between market operators and clients residing in the same country) are submitted to tax in accordance with the applicable domestic legislation. Such activities, which clearly lack any international component, are not examined further. This subsection focuses on the relevant specificities of online sports (and other similar fields) betting.

2. Different forms of online betting

This sub-subsection briefly describes: (a) sports betting; (b) fantasy sports betting; and (c) eSports betting. Reference is also made to betting exchanges (a) and 'skin gambling' (c).

A. SPORTS BETTING

Online sports betting services have empowered betting consumers, enabling them to search for the best odds and/or the most appealing products provided by bookmakers in different countries (either by themselves or by means of dedicated 'odds comparison services'). The emergence of such fierce competition among bookmakers gave rise to the innovation of new betting products. While in the past, one could only bet on the outcome of a match before the commencement of the game, and bookmakers, reluctant to accept wagers on single matches, tended to offer 'combination bets' across three or more games,[632] now it is possible to place bets during the game (the so-called 'in-play betting') on the final outcome of the match, on key events within the game (such as which team will score first) as well as on 'micro events' (i.e. particular discrete events in a match, such as the outcome of the next point in tennis).[633]

Increased online betting volumes even resulted in the creation of person-to-person betting, i.e. betting exchanges, thereby eliminating the recourse to bookmakers. A typical bet put in place by a betting exchange unfolds as follows: (i) the exchange sets up a market such as 'outcome X will occur'; (ii) the gamblers make offers to 'back' or to 'lay' the outcome X, indicating to what level of stake they are willing to trade and to what odds; (iii) the 'backing' and the 'laying' offers are then matched electronically; and (iv) the winner of the bet collects their prize and the exchange claims a commission from the successful party in each transaction.[634]

The recent forms of sports betting accentuate the element of chance rather than knowledge and intellectual skills in the field of sport. In fact, micro events, and even key events within a game, do not generally require an 'educated guess' but a simple 'taking a chance' on an event beyond the gambler's control.

632 FORREST, p.19.
633 RUSSELL ET AL, p.206.
634 FORREST, p.21.

B. FANTASY SPORTS BETTING

Proliferation of online sports betting also paved the way for the spread of 'fantasy sports' betting. Traditionally, the contestants of 'fantasy sports' create 'fantasy teams', i.e. their very own 'dream team' formed by means of virtually 'recruiting' real-life professional athletes. The 'team selection' process requires some skill, since the contestants cannot simply choose all the 'star-players', commonly deemed to be the best. The choice of sportspersons is effectuated on the basis of the salary values of each sportsperson and the maximum amount of salaries that can be paid by a fantasy sports team, both pre-determined by the fantasy league operator. The teams thus created 'compete' with each other, via a scoring system that takes into account the accumulated statistics of the real-life professional athletes chosen as a part of a fantasy team. The winning fantasy teams are entitled to a prize, either in the form of money or value-in-kind items.

'Traditional' fantasy sports, mimicking actual leagues, run from the first day of a professional sport's regular season until the conclusion of the season concerned. Such games effectively require a demonstration of skills and knowledge by their contestants. At the other end of the spectrum, the so-called 'Daily Fantasy Sports', i.e. games that last just for a single day on the basis of the statistics derived from a single match or 'event-based' games that offer prize money if a particular event occurs in the playing field, are akin to games of chance and are commonly referred to as 'fantasy sports betting'.[635]

C. ESPORTS BETTING AND SKIN GAMBLING

ESports constitutes a significant betting stream, which has succeeded in surpassing traditional mainstays such as golf and rugby in terms of popularity amongst the bettors.[636] Betting in eSports is highly comparable to traditional sports betting, i.e. bettors bet on the 'winning' team, but some specificities exist due to the inherent characteristics of the eSports titles, such as the need to determine the winner based on the completion of objectives rather than using an endgame score.[637]

The development of eSports has also given rise to the so-called 'skin gambling'. 'Skin gambling' does not entail a new type of gambling, but an unusual 'de facto currency', i.e. 'skin', used in traditional online betting (including, but not limited to, eSports betting). 'Skins' are virtual items, used in games such as CS:GO developed by Valve Corporation, which change the appearance of video game avatars and weapons. Aside from 'individualisation' by means of the modification of the aesthetic features of the components of a game, skins do not provide any advantage to gamers.[638] They are valuable since they may be

635 See also, TSAI, pp.397–398 and DAS MURALEE, International Regulation of Fantasy Sports: Comparative Legal Analysis of United States, Australian and Asian Laws in *UNLV Gaming Law Journal*, Number 8, Spring 2018, pp.93–96.

636 TSAI, p.402.

637 Ibid.

638 HASKELL, pp.140–141.

difficult to obtain. To collect a skin, a gamer typically needs to receive an in-game 'crate' that contains random skins or to make an in-game purchase. Some skins may be rather rare and require not only a significant gaming effort but also a great deal of chance to be collected. The value attached to skins by gamers caused these virtual 'decorations' to become a de facto currency used in lieu of traditional casino chips or money.

When a person places a bet using a skin, the skin concerned, which is typically stored in a software distribution platform created and operated by the game developer, is transferred to a third-party website's, i.e. a website or a system that is not operated by the game developer, 'bot' account. If the bettor wins, they are paid back the skin they used to place the original wager plus any additional winnings (other skins).[639] The bettor may then either use the skins in other bets or ask the third-party to return them to their personal inventory. Once the gamer receives the skins in their personal account, they can use them for their intended purpose (i.e. decorating in-game avatars and/or items), trade them with other gamers within the community, sell them on the game developer's software system for game credits or sell them for cash via a third-party website.

Skin gambling is not put in place by game developers but by third-party online gambling websites that allow skins to be used as a betting currency. Game developers that own all the intellectual property rights of their games, including the skins, can prevent skin gambling to a great extent. For instance, Valve's intervention into the CS:GO skin gambling market drastically reduced the market's size, which was projected to be worth approximately 7.4 billion USD in 2016 to 1 million USD in 2020.[640]

3. Potential sources of income and their taxation

A variety of different actors may derive income from online sports betting. This sub-subsection briefly summarises the main potential income sources accruing to the key actors of the sector, as well as the modalities of their taxation. For the purposes of tax analysis, it is assumed that an international component exists, which requires the application of international tax law rules.

Bookmakers derive their income from bettors, who invest money in bets. Their income should be categorised as profits deriving from their lawful business and submitted to tax in accordance with article 7. While betting services are akin to constitute B2C services for VAT purposes, they are generally exempt from VAT.[641] In fact, betting activities are usually covered by some specific taxes, such as a 'betting tax' or a 'tax on games of chance', the modalities of which depend on the applicable national law.

A 'winning' bettor is entitled to the prize money, either in the form of a certain sum or a value-in-kind item – such as a skin, promised by the bookmaker or put forward by

639 Ibid, pp.141–143.
640 Ibid, pp.144–145.
641 See, for example, article 135(1)(i) of the VAT Directive.

their competitor in the case of person-to-person betting. From an international tax law perspective, such income should be categorised as 'other income' under article 21 and be submitted to tax in the RS of the winner.[642] Regarding value-in-kind items, it can be argued that a taxable income comes into being only when the winner decides to cash-in the item, i.e. exchange it for real life money. As long as the item stays in the virtual world, it cannot be considered as being 'accrued' to the individual.[643] To the extent where the RS exempts lottery and similar games of chance winnings from income tax, a tax may not become due. This being stated, even in cases where such an exemption exists, countries tend to exempt the winnings from local games of chance organisers and submit to tax the winnings from foreign organisers.[644]

Betting exchanges are entitled to a commission from the successful party in each transaction. These commissions tend to be sufficiently low to render and keep exchanges more attractive than bookmakers.[645] Such commissions clearly constitute business profits under article 7. VAT or another tax may become due depending on the specificities of the applicable national law.

As is public knowledge, some bookmakers (commonly referred to as 'street bookies') make bets available in an unlawful manner. An industry, known as 'pay-per-head', has developed around such (most commonly small-scale) bookmakers. 'Pay-per-head' companies provide bookmakers with software for a state-of-the-art app through which their clients can bet. This app offers up-to-the-minute odds, a customer service call centre, instant accounting and, last but not least, 'in-play betting'. In exchange, the companies charge bookmakers a fixed amount (e.g. 10 USD) per week for every active 'head', i.e. bettor.[646]

Since bookmakers are only granted a right to use the software concerned within their own businesses, the income obtained by 'pay-per-head' companies in exchange of making the software available should be categorised, in most cases, as business profits under article 7.[647] To the extent where a 'street bookie' is deemed to be a taxable person for VAT purposes, the transaction between the bookie and the 'pay-per-head' company should be categorised as a B2B supply of service; in the negative, it will form a B2C service. In this latter case, it should be verified whether the applicable VAT legislation categorises

642 Article 21(1).

643 On this point, see CAMP BRYAN T., Play's the Thing: A Theory of Taxing Virtual Worlds in *The Hastings Law Journal*, Volume 59, 2007, p.1ff. For a rather diverging opinion on the matter, see LEDERMAN LEANDRA, 'Stranger than Fiction': Taxing Virtual Worlds in *New York University Law Review*, Volume 82, 2007, p.1620ff.

644 It is important to note that in the Lindman decision, the CJEU held that such a practice amounts to a violation of the freedom to provide services.

645 FORREST, p.21.

646 The big bet on sports betting by Ira Boudway and Eben Novy-Williams, article in *Bloomberg Businessweek*, 16 April 2018, p.65.

647 *OECD Commentary* on article 12, §14.2.

the transaction concerned as an electronic service and submits it to a specific place-of-supply rule.

In the specific case of skin gambling, online gambling operators act as bookmakers, and therefore derive profits from their business. 'Winners' obtain value-in-kind awards of skins. Game developers may be entitled to a certain commission not in relation to the gambling process but when skins are sold to third parties. For instance, when in-game items of Valve-developed games are sold, the company receives 15 percent of the transaction.[648]

The entitlement of game developers to such commissions is based on the intellectual property they hold in the items concerned. What is being granted to the purchasers of the skins, or other similar items, is a mere right to use the item within the virtual world created and operated by the game developer. Accordingly, it may be argued that such commissions should be categorised, in most cases, as business profits and be submitted to tax under article 7. From a VAT perspective, it should be deemed that a B2C supply of service exists, given the fact that the in-game items belong to the game developer and should not, in principle, be commercialised by third parties. The applicable place-of-supply rule will generally be the one covering electronic services and the transaction will be submitted to tax in the place where the consumer resides.

Sports organisations may also require, and obtain, a certain percentage of the bets placed, or profits made out of betting, in a given field of sport. For example, NBA assistant general counsel Dan Spillane has been trying to persuade legislators to make sports bookmakers pay leagues 1 percent of all wages placed on their sports, since 'betting is built on their games'.[649] In the States of Connecticut, Kansas and New York City a compromise fee of 0.25 percent is currently being paid to the sports leagues by the betting industry.[650] This income should be categorised as business profits of sports organisations and be submitted to tax in accordance with article 7. For VAT purposes, a B2B supply of service should be deemed to be provided from sports organisations to bookmakers. Such service would normally be subject to VAT at the standard rate at the place where the bookmaker has established its business.

Sports bookmakers seek to use players' names, likenesses, clubs' logos and other intellectual property belonging to sports organisations and sportspersons. In cases where the bookmaker is the official sponsor of the league or the club, which is rather frequent in practice, such a use is generally granted by the relevant party to the bookmaker by means of the sponsoring contract. In cases where there is no such (or no similar) contract, however, it is not clear whether sports betting companies may use the intellectual property belonging to sportspersons/clubs without being contractually entitled to do so and paying a

648 HASKELL, p.141.
649 The big bet on sports betting, op. cit. n.646, p.64.
650 Ibid.

fee. Should the domestic law of a country categorise such a use as allowed due to its newsworthy (public interest) nature, no payment would be necessary. On the contrary, should the domestic law of the country not allow such a use, royalties need to be paid to the rights owners to make use of their intellectual properties. Such royalties should be subject to income tax in accordance with article 12 and they constitute a consideration for a B2B supply of service rendered by a sports team, or alternatively by an independent sportsperson, to the bookmaker, for VAT purposes.

Sports bookmakers also need statistics of sporting performance in order to be able to set up their bets. Such statistics may be obtained either directly from sports organisations (on a free of charge or remunerated basis) or from professional companies compiling and selling such data. Sports organisations and professional companies are entitled to a fee in exchange for the data sold and services provided. Depending on the data and its compilation method, the fee concerned can be categorised as business profits under article 7, royalties under article 12 or fees for technical services under article 12A of the UN MC. From a VAT point of view, the sale of data constitutes a B2B supply of service, usually taxable at the standard rate at the location where the purchaser, i.e. bookmaker, established its business.

Last but not least, online sports betting has been extensively criticised for paving the way for match-fixing and spot-fixing.[651] In a typical match-fixing scheme, players and/or referee(s) conspire to make a team win or lose the match. In spot-fixing, a player, or a referee, stages or creates an ideal environment for a micro event. Spot-fixing is much easier to organise than match-fixing, since it tends to require only one single corrupt person and it is unlikely to impact the overall match performance of the team.[652] Clearly, match-fixing and spot-fixing may be used by criminal organisations to manipulate sports betting and to provide a cover for money laundering purposes. These aspects are, however, beyond the scope of this book and are not further developed.

P. Commercialisation of digital compendiums in relation to eSports tournaments

1. General aspects

Game developers may offer to their tournaments' audience (on-site and online) an 'entertainment package' in the form of a digital compendium. These entertainment packages include several benefits, such as information about the event and

651 For more information on this point, see, for example, TAK MINHYEOK/SAM MICHAEL P./ JACKSON STEVEN J., The problems and causes of match-fixing: Are legal sports betting regimes to blame? in *Journal of Criminological Research, Policy and Practice*, Volume 4, Number 1, 2018, p.73ff.

652 RUSSELL ET AL, p.220.

the teams, a right to sync with other gamers to play some rounds of the game against them, a chance of special in-game item drops and a right to vote for the tournament awards. In some cases, game developers may use a certain percentage of the income derived by compendiums to finance the prize pool of the competition.[653]

Sales of digital compendiums constitute typical sales contracts, whereby the seller (i.e. the game developer) provides a certain service and the buyer (i.e. the eSports fan) agrees to pay a certain amount to obtain it. In some tournaments, the purchase of a ticket to attend the tournament at the venue may include the right to have access to the entertainment package.

2. *Income tax modalities*

Digital compendiums mainly give access to data and additional game features that are put in place by the game developer specifically for the purposes of the tournament concerned. The main problem lies in determining whether the payment made for the right to use this software 'patch' prepared by the game developer can be characterised as royalties. This question has to be answered in the negative. As explicitly stated by the OECD Commentary, to the extent where the rights that are commercialised in relation to the copyright are limited to those necessary to enable the user to operate the program (as opposed to, for example, granting the right to reproduce and distribute to the public software incorporating the copyrighted program, or to modify and publicly display the program), the profits obtained by the entity commercialising the rights concerned should be categorised as business profits under article 7 and not as royalties under article 12.[654] From a computer game perspective, it is clear that the gamers obtain the right to operate the program and not any rights in the copyright as such. Hence, the categorisation that must be opted for is 'business profits'.

Business profits obtained from the sale of compendiums are submitted to tax in the RS of the rights-holder.[655] Even if formation of a PE in an SS cannot be excluded altogether, such an occurrence would be extremely rare given the fact that compendiums are commercialised by means of the game developer's website. In cases where the rights-holder already has a PE in the HS, the income deriving from the compendiums sold may be attributed to that PE.

3. *VAT modalities*

Compendiums being intangibles commercialised online, they are, as a general rule, submitted to tax in the country of residence of the consumer.[656] Should the compendium be provided as an ancillary service to admission to the event (i.e.

653 SCHOLZ, p.34.
654 *OECD Commentary* on article 12, §§13–14.
655 Article 7(1).
656 See, for example, article 58 of the VAT Directive.

ticket), the admission is likely to be considered as the principal supply and the entire consideration obtained for the overall service (including the portion of the price charged for the compendium) is likely to be submitted to tax at the place where the event is held (i.e. the HS).

Q. Sports agency

1. Definition and role of a sports agent

A sports agent may be defined as follows:

> [...] any natural or legal person occasionally or regularly engaging in one or more of the following activities in return for payment: [b]ringing together parties interested in concluding a contract relating to the performance of a sporting activity for remuneration; [n]egotiating and concluding different kinds of contracts on behalf of a professional sportsperson, such as image rights contracts, sponsoring contracts, advertising contracts, etc. [and][m] anaging the assets of a professional sportsperson.[657]

Despite the fact that when reference is made to a 'sports agent' a natural person comes to mind, as indicated in the definition, sports agency is practiced not exclusively by natural persons, but also by large-scale companies.

Sports agents may be hired by a sportsperson or by a sports club. It is quite frequent for a sports club to have recourse to the services of an agent, especially in order to spot and recruit new talents. Agents engaged by clubs represent the clubs' best interests in one or several of their negotiations with sportspersons and their agents, respectively.

Agents engaged by sportspersons provide a greater variety of services in order to allow sportspersons to concentrate on their sporting activities.[658] Sportsperson agents typically assume 'on-field duties' (i.e. brokering and negotiating player transfers and employment contracts, and participation contracts in the field of individual sports, respectively) as well as a number of 'off-field duties' depending on the specific needs of the sportsperson concerned (such as sourcing of endorsement deals, provision of legal advice, financial planning, image rights exploitation and tax advice).[659] The role of a sports agent can, in fact, be summarised as finding and fostering opportunities for their/its client[660] while providing a basis for this latter's long-term financial stability.[661]

The emerging internationalisation of the sports sector translated into internationalisation of activities conducted by sports agents as well, both in the field of

657 *Study on Sports Agents in the European Union*, p.25.
658 PARRISH, p.38.
659 DUTHIE ET AL, p.657.
660 REMICK/EISEN, p.57.
661 MASON, p.678.

individual sports and team sports. In individual sports, which are often tour-based, sports agents usually secure placements for the sportspersons they are representing in sports events taking place in different countries. In team sports, the international character of sports agents' activities derives from the transfer market. It is very frequent for sportspersons to be transferred from a club situated in one country to another club situated in another country, or simply to begin their careers in a foreign country. Consequently, sports agents, whose core duty is to broker and negotiate employment contracts and transfer agreements, often exercise an international activity. Lastly, the international dimension of sports agency may also derive from the contract itself, irrespective of the sportsperson's career. This will be the case when the sportsperson and their agent reside in different countries.[662]

2. *Legal nature and remuneration methods*

The contract concluded between the sports agent and the sportsperson/sports team may be categorised as an agency agreement, a mandate agreement or a mixed-agreement combining the elements of agency and mandate agreements.[663] The exact categorisation must be made on a case-by-case basis, depending on the precise extent of the services provided by the agent.

Sports agents are usually remunerated by commissions, which can be defined as a proportion of the contract amount negotiated on behalf of the player/team.[664] For instance, Proactive Sports Management Limited, the agent of Wayne Rooney, was entitled to 2.5 percent of the gross sum payable to Rooney under any contract of employment with any football club and 20 percent of the gross sum payable to the football player under any contracts or arrangements regarding promotion, endorsement and advertisement of any goods, products or services.[665] This being stated, agents may also be compensated in one of the three following options: (i) an hourly rate; (ii) a flat rate; and (iii) a combination of all payment methods, i.e. commission, hourly rate and flat rate.[666]

Reference must also be made to remunerations obtained by sports agents in an unlawful manner. In fact, corruption and use of unlawful methods have been a growing concern in the sports agent industry.[667] Numerous examples exist of agents charging unjustified fees, which may even amount to 50 percent of the fee earned by the sportsperson,[668] commingling their personal funds with those of their clients[669] and engaging in other unlawful practices in order to maximise their gains.

662 PINNA, p.338.
663 ZEN-RUFFINEN, pp.257–259.
664 MASON, p.679.
665 The Rooney decision, §57.
666 MASON, p.680.
667 This concern contributed to the development of specific rules governing sports agents both at a governmental and at an SGB level. On this point, see, for example, PARRISH, p.38ff; PINNA, p.339ff and DUTHIE ET AL, p.661ff.
668 See the example given by PARRISH, p.39.
669 PINNA, p.333; PARRISH, p.39.

For instance, in the US, it was revealed in Hilliard v Black that the sports agent William Black stole up to 14 million USD from the 35 professional football players that he was presenting at the time via two major financial scams.[670] Similarly, the agent of the NBA player Kareem Abdul-Jabbar commingled his personal funds with those of his client and secured his personal debts with his client's funds.[671]

A typical example of unlawful practice in the sector is 'bungs', i.e. payments made to sports agents by the interested parties, especially with an aim of securing the transfer of a certain sportsperson. Bungs may be categorised as 'secret commissions' that are defined by the OECD as follows: '[...] a form of bribery whereby an agent requests or accepts a payment to influence these [the relevant] contracts for the benefit of the payer, without the knowledge or consent of their principal. This may be to secure a contract, to gain favourable terms, or even to prevent a contract being entered into with a competitor'.[672] Since bungs constitute a typical unlawful practice in the sector, taxation of unlawful income that may be obtained by a sports agent will be analysed by means of this example.

3. *Taxation modalities*[673]

A. LAWFUL INCOME

i. Income tax modalities Sports agents who are residents of the same State as sportspersons they represent will be taxed in accordance with the domestic law of that State. This remains valid even in cases where the sportsperson enters into an agreement with a commercial partner situated abroad, unless the sports agent is directly remunerated by the commercial partner concerned. In these cases, as well as in cases where the sports agent and the sportsperson are residents of different States, the DTT concluded between the RS of the commercial partner or the RS of the sportsperson, respectively, and the RS of the sports agent will be applied.

The nature of the remuneration derived by the sportsperson as a result of the sports agent's efforts is not relevant for the categorisation of the sports agent's income. As a matter of fact, the sports agent is remunerated by the sportsperson, or by their commercial partner, for acting as an intermediary of the transaction concerned. In other words, the sports agent is entitled to a compensation for the personal services provided by them – if the sports agent is an individual – or for the services it provides – if the sports agent is a legal entity.

670 PARRISH, p.39.
671 PINNA, p.333.
672 *Bribery and Corruption Awareness Handbook*, p.11.
673 For the sake of simplicity, within this sub-subsection the reference is made to the commercial relations between a sports agent and a sportsperson. The reasoning followed may be applied *mutatis mutandis* to the commercial relations between sports agents and sports teams. Sports teams are only mentioned to the extent necessary for the purposes of the legal analysis.

Accordingly, under the current version of the OECD MC, the revenue generated by all sports agents, i.e. both individuals and legal entities, should be categorised as business profits within article 7.[674] Should the applicable DTT contain a separate distributive rule on income derived from independent personal services, i.e. article 14 of the UN MC, taxation of the sports agent who is an individual will occur in accordance with that specific rule. These distributive rules grant the right to tax the income derived by the sports agent exclusively to their/its RS,[675] unless they/it has a PE/fixed base in the RS of the sportsperson, or in another State.[676] Under the UN MC, the sports agent may also be subject to tax in the SS in cases where their stay therein is for a period or periods amounting to or exceeding 183 days in any 12-month period.[677]

ii. VAT modalities Services rendered by sports agents may be characterised as B2B or B2C supply of services, depending on whether the recipient of the service (i.e. sportsperson or sports team) can be categorised as a taxable person for VAT purposes. While the applicable place-of-supply rule will depend on this categorisation, it can be stated that the taxation is to occur in accordance with the destination principle. The service is expected to be submitted to tax at the standard rate.

B. BUNGS

i. Income tax modalities

i.a. Domestic tax law aspects In countries where the acceptance of bungs constitutes a criminal offence,[678] the income earned by the sports agent will most likely be forfeited – provided that the competent authorities can detect the unlawful payment and prosecute the sports agent. No taxable income arises in the event of forfeiture of assets.

In countries where the acceptance of bungs does not amount to a criminal offence, the sports agent may still be under the obligation to make a compensation payment to the sportsperson in accordance with the relevant dispositions of the domestic civil law – provided that the sportsperson submits an enforceable claim to the competent authorities. In that case, the unlawful payment will form a part of the taxable income of the sports agent and the compensation paid to the sportsperson may constitute a deductible expense in accordance with the applicable domestic tax law.

Lastly, in cases where the secret commission obtained by the sports agent remains undetected and does not give rise to a civil law or a criminal proceeding –

674 It is important to underline that income obtained by sports agents, impresarios and other similar persons is not covered by article 17, unless they receive it on behalf of the sportsperson concerned (*OECD Commentary* on article 17, §7).

675 Article 7(1).

676 If a PE is created in another State, the DTT concluded between the RS of the sports agent and that other State shall apply.

677 Article 14(1)(b) of the UN MC.

678 See, for example, article 158(2) of the SCrC – criminal mismanagement.

which would frequently be the case – it may be subject to income tax only to the extent where it is declared by the sports agent – most likely within the category of 'other income' – or detected by the tax authorities.

i.b. International tax law aspects To the extent where: (i) the payment of bungs is effectively detected and prosecuted; (ii) the amount concerned is not forfeited; and (iii) the sports agent is not a resident of the same State as the person making the payment, the income obtained by the sports agent should be categorised as 'other income' within article 21 and submitted to tax exclusively in their RS.[679]

In the eventuality where the sports agent is ordered to effectuate a compensation payment to the sportsperson in accordance with a decision rendered by the competent court and the sports agent and the sportsperson are not residents of the same State, the compensation payment received by the sportsperson may be categorised as 'business profits' within article 7, 'income from independent personal services' within article 14 of the UN MC, 'income from employment' within article 15, or 'other income' under article 21, depending on the circumstances of the specific case.[680]

From a purely academic view, it is possible to state that to the extent where the sports agent's unlawful activity resulted into a transfer fee or other sort of income lower than the fee that would have been obtained without the interference of that specific agent, the compensation payment should be categorised as business profits/income from independent personal services or income from employment, respectively. This being stated, determining whether the compensation payment was made to reimburse a profit loss – and if yes, to what extent – can be quite complicated in practice. Consequently, it can be argued that such payments should be categorised as 'other income' under article 21. In any case, all distributive rules grant the right to tax exclusively to the RS of the sportsperson.

ii. VAT modalities Bungs are secret commissions that are paid to sports agents without the knowledge of sportspersons they are representing. Since intermediation in view of conclusion of a contract between a sportsperson and a sports team/rights-holder is one of the main duties of a sports agent, it can be argued that the activity giving rise to the remuneration cannot be considered as being absolutely prohibited per se. Thereupon, this transaction should be treated in the same manner as its lawful counterpart, i.e. commissions obtained by sports agents, for VAT purposes.[681]

679 The applicable DTT is the one concluded between the RS of the sports agent and the RS of the person making the payment.
680 The applicable DTT is the one concluded between the RS of the sports agent and the RS of the sportsperson.
681 See the Lange decision, §§12 and 19; the Fischer decision, §§22 and 28; the Happy Family decision, §20.

4 Taxation of government funding

I. Introduction

Despite the significant development of the commercialisation of sport, and thereby the noteworthy increase of private funding, public funding still remains as one of the main income sources of the sports sector.[1] Government funding not only occurs via direct funding, i.e. providing financial assets, but it may also materialise through tax exemptions or reliefs, commonly referred to as 'the indirect subsidisation', which is available in most European countries.[2] In addition to direct financing and indirect subsidisation, governments may also take value-in-kind measures, such as providing the sports organisations with specialised technical managers who are directly paid by the government and ensuring security at sports events, notably by putting the police force at the disposal of the sports entities.[3] Governments usually provide funding for different purposes, such as the construction and maintenance of sports infrastructures, the development of elite sport, the sustenance of sports organisations and the fight against doping. Only government funding that has a close connection with ISEs is briefly analysed in this chapter.[4]

International sport provides a high-profile, low-cost and low-risk diplomatic resource that governments can use to improve or to maintain their relations with other countries.[5] For example, when the urgent need to establish better Sino-American relations emerged in 1971, China used its 'Ping-Pong diplomacy' to achieve that aim.[6] This political strategy was well received by the US and played a significant role in bringing the two nations together.[7] International sport also produces domestic political benefits ranging from generating a sense of social cohesion, national well-being and national pride,[8] the so-called 'feel good factor',

1 See, for example, CHAKER ANDRÉ-NOËL, *Good Governance in Sport, A European Survey*, Council of Europe Publishing, 2004, p.16.
2 Ibid, p.20.
3 Ibid.
4 The term 'close connection' is used in its everyday meaning in this sentence.
5 HOULIHAN, p.261.
6 HONG, p.42.
7 Ibid, p.43.
8 HOULIHAN, p.256.

to more concrete economic impacts, especially in relation to the hosting of mega and large-scale sporting events.[9]

Governments usually adjust their sports policy in order to benefit from these different advantages offered by international sport. Therefore, customarily, one of the main components of most governments' sports policy is to ensure the development of their country's image through hosting international competitions and developing national teams or sportspersons with a high level of competitiveness (elite sport development).[10] In order to reach these objectives, governments generally provide all three types of funding – i.e. direct funding, indirect subsidisation and value-in-kind funding – along with other relevant measures.

Examined in this chapter are taxation modalities[11] of government funding relating to elite sport development (II) and hosting of ISEs (III).

II. Elite sport development

A. Introduction

In order to be able to fully exploit the opportunities offered by international sport, governments must have assets in the form of recognised world-class elite athletes, who will generate publicity for the countries that they visit and the events in which they take part.[12] The majority of governments have recognised the importance of elite sport development and taken different measures to this effect.

While elite sport development policies followed by countries may vary to a great extent, from the '*juguo tizgi*'[13] of China to the non-interventionism of the US, most countries opt for providing a combination of direct funding, indirect subsidisation and value-in-kind funding.

B. Direct funding

Direct funding may be granted in two ways: (i) by funding sports organisations – especially national sports organisations; and (ii) by funding sportspersons. By funding sports organisations, governments aim to ensure that athletes have proficient support personnel and adequate training opportunities. By funding athletes, governments aspire to assist 'future talents' in reaching their full potential.

Different direct funding policies may be put in place. Usually, governments provide financial resources both to sports organisations and to sportspersons. This subsection concentrates on funding provided to athletes, which is generally composed of three main pillars: (1) funding provided to promote athletes' careers;

9 HOULIHAN/GREEN, p.15.
10 NYS, p.261.
11 All articles refer to the articles of the OECD MC unless otherwise specified.
12 HOULIHAN, p.256; HOULIHAN/GREEN, p.15.
13 'Whole country support for the elite sport system' (HONG, p.47).

(2) prize monies granted in case of sporting success; and (3) post-career funding. States may combine all three measures or opt for one or two of them.

1. Funding provided to promote sportspersons' careers

Governments may pay a certain amount (on an annual or a monthly basis) to sportspersons in order to promote their careers. The athletes who will benefit from this particular type of funding are designated by means of certain pre-established criteria. For example, in the UK, where the government allocated approximately 75 million GBP as direct financial support in the run up to the 2008 Beijing Olympic Games,[14] the priority was given to Olympic and Paralympic athletes, who fulfil several criteria such as being a British national or passport holder, not being in the course of serving a suspension or a period of ineligibility and not having an unspent conviction for a criminal offence.[15] The amount granted to sportspersons is generally determined in accordance with their sporting level. To this end, governments may establish several categories of sportspersons by means of objective criteria.

These annual and monthly salaries are not treated any differently than salaries paid by sports clubs from an international tax law perspective. Unless the applicable DTT[16] excludes sportspersons sponsored by public means from the scope of article 17, the HS may tax a part of this amount in accordance with this distributive rule. In cases where such an exclusion has been made, sportspersons will usually be taxable in their RS under articles 7, 14 (the UN MC) or 15 depending on the specificities of the case and the provisions of the applicable DTT. The RS, i. e. the State providing the funding, will generally exempt this income from income tax. From a VAT perspective, payments made by governments, and other government-approved entities, with the sole purpose of financially supporting the mental and the physical preparation of athletes are generally categorised as donations. Since donations cannot be considered as payments made as a 'consideration' of a certain supply, they fall outside the scope of VAT.

While being quite common, this type of funding is not provided in some countries, such as the US. To be able to finance the Olympic and Paralympic athletes, the United States Olympic Committee collects donations via the US Olympic and Paralympic Foundation (Team USA Fund).[17] The funds raised are then distributed to athletes and to NGBs.[18] However, most of the time the sums distributed fall short of covering the expenses of Olympic athletes. As a result, American sportspersons frequently have recourse to alternative funding

14 HOULIHAN/GREEN, p.14.
15 *UK Sport – Funding Eligibility Policy*, pp.2–5.
16 The DTT concluded between the HS and the RS of the sportsperson.
17 http://www.teamusa.org/us-olympic-and-paralympic-foundation/team-usa-fund (accessed on 17.08.2015).
18 SPARVERO EMILY/CHALIP LAURENCE/GREEN CHRISTINE B., United States in HOULIHAN BARRIE/ GREEN MICK (eds), *Comparative Elite Sport Development: Systems, structures and public policy*, Butterworth-Heinemann, 2008, pp.256–257.

options such as private donations and crowdfunding. Overall, taxation modalities of these alternative options are akin to those of government funding. The most notable divergence may be the income tax treatment under the applicable domestic law. While government funding is more likely to benefit from an exemption, such private donations may fall within the taxable income of individuals.

2. Prize monies

Most countries grant prize monies to their champions and medallists. Prize monies may be offered both to sportspersons competing on an individual basis and to sportspersons competing as team members.[19] The sums offered to athletes vary significantly from country to country. For example, during the 2012 London Olympic Games, the prize money for a gold medal amounted to 800,000 USD in Singapore, 182,000 USD in Italy, 65,000 USD in France and 25,000 USD in the US.[20] Governments may also grant value-in-kind prize monies along with cash payments. For instance, Chen Xiexia, the weight-lifting Olympic gold medallist of the 2008 Beijing Games, was rewarded with houses – for her and for her parents – and an Audi Q7 by her local government, on top of a 55,000 USD national prize money.[21]

As a general rule, prize monies (sums and value-in-kind[22]) paid by governments will not benefit from a tax treatment that is different than prize monies paid by other institutions. On this point, it is important to underline that governments generally pay prize monies to all sportspersons obtaining a certain success in some specific ISEs, as determined by their domestic law. In other words, a sportsperson does not necessarily need to be sponsored by public means in order to obtain a prize money from the government of their RS.

In cases where the sportsperson is sponsored by public means and article 17 of the applicable DTT[23] does not cover income accruing to such sportspersons, the HS will not be entitled to tax the prize money concerned; since article 17 will not apply and the distributive rules that may apply – article 7, 14 (the UN MC) or 15 – will generally grant the right to tax to the RS of the sportsperson. In all other cases, prize monies and other similar payments may be submitted to tax by the HS in accordance with article 17.

19 In case of team sports, the prize money is usually attributed to each team member personally and not to the team as a whole.

20 The Payoff From Winning an Olympic Medal by Victoria Black, article on *Bloomberg Business* published on 8 August 2012, http://www.bloomberg.com/bw/articles/2012-08-08/the-payoff-from-winning-an-olympic-medal (accessed on 18.08.2015).

21 Ibid.

22 As already mentioned, although taxation modalities of value-in-kind benefits depend on the domestic law of the State where the income is taxable, it is possible to state that such benefits are usually considered as taxable income.

23 The DTT concluded between the HS and the RS of the sportsperson.

3. Post-career funding

Post-career funding consists of providing athletes with wages and pensions either from the moment they retire from sports business or from the moment they attain a certain age. The financial support may continue to be provided after the death of the sportsperson to their surviving family members, most commonly spouse and/or children.

This type of funding, which usually takes the form of an annual or a monthly salary, will be taxed, or tax-exempt, in accordance with the domestic law of the State providing the funding. While participation in ISEs may be a criterion for the provision of post-career funding, this income type cannot be considered as deriving from an ISE as such, especially given the fact that the income concerned accrues to the individual when their career as a professional sportsperson has come to an end. Consequently, the risk of a source taxation in an HS is non-existent.

C. Indirect subsidisation and value-in-kind funding

Governments may also grant indirect subsidisations and value-in-kind benefits to sportspersons/national sports organisations as a part of their funding programme. The former is most commonly provided in the form of tax exemptions or reliefs, which may be specifically linked to a given sports event. For example, income earned only from World Championships of all types of sporting activity may be tax-exempt. The latter may take different forms. For example, in France, the aid granted comprises provision of technical advisers by the Ministry of Sports to sports federations[24] and in Norway a detailed nutrition programme is made available to sportspersons by their government.[25]

Regarding sports organisations, it seems rather straightforward that value-in-kind benefits do not give rise to any taxable income or transaction from an international tax law perspective.[26] Concerning sportspersons, given the fact that value-in-kind benefits are usually considered as taxable income and transactions under domestic laws, an HS may technically tax the benefits concerned under article 17. This being stated, it is extremely rare, if existent at all, for an HS to estimate the value of technical advisers, nutrition programmes or similar benefits-in-kind provided to the sportspersons by their RSs and tax it at source.

Should an HS proceed with such taxation, only the part of the amount that can be allocated to the event concerned should be subject to tax. Since the nature of the benefits-in-kind is akin to salaries – they are provided for a certain period of time to allow a higher performance at sports events taking place in that time frame – an allocation method similar to the one used for salaries needs to be used by the HS.

24 NYS, p.265.
25 AUGESTAD PÅL/BERGSGARD ASLE NILS, Norway in HOULIHAN BARRIE/ GREEN MICK (eds), *Comparative Elite Sport Development: Systems, structures and public policy*, Butterworth-Heinemann, 2008, pp.214–217.
26 Due to the lack of any international component, such taxation is, in most cases, exclusively a matter of domestic tax law of the country providing the subsidisation. It should be noted that value-in-kind benefits provided by governments are usually tax-exempt.

III. Hosting of ISEs

Governments of HSs must provide a significant support in order to host an ISE. This holds true especially with regard to mega and large-scale sporting events. Until the mid-1980s, the hosting of such events required substantial public funding with little expectation that the direct and indirect income deriving from the event would cover the costs.[27] Since the mid-1980s, while still necessitating significant public subsidy, mega and large-scale sporting events are mostly capable of generating considerable indirect benefits,[28] such as tourism promotion (the 2000 Sydney Olympics) and urban regeneration (the 1992 Barcelona Olympics and the 2012 London Olympics).[29] Governments usually combine all three types of funding in order to fulfil the obligations enumerated in their HCCs.

Direct funding is necessary to cover the costs of the organisation, which derive from different undertakings, such as construction of sports venues, sportspersons villages as well as other relevant structures and facilities, such as roads and parking lots. The most notable example is the 2014 Sochi Winter Olympics, for which the Russian Government constructed an entire 'Winter Olympic Park'[30] that cost approximately 34 billion GBP.[31]

Value-in-kind funding constitutes another cornerstone of the event hosting. When designating the HS, SGBs usually evaluate the candidates in the light of certain criteria, such as the country's commitment, the general country infrastructure, the available venues and the financial assets. Countries interested in bidding for ISEs either build the relevant infrastructure – such as hotels, medical centres, transportation facilities, etc. – beforehand or they proceed with the necessary changes after having become the HS in the light of the SGB's requirements. In either case, significant value-in-kind funding is required, along with direct funding. For instance, South Africa, the HS of the 2010 FIFA World Cup, was criticised for lack of security before the tournament took place.[32] The South African Police Service prepared a plan that included extra officers and deployment of specialist teams,[33] which must have constituted a substantial expenditure for the government, in other words a significant value-in-kind funding. South African funding may be considered as 'money well spent', since no major security problems arose during the 2010 World Cup.

27 HOULIHAN, p.256.
28 Ibid.
29 HOULIHAN/GREEN, p.15.
30 A list of different venues is available on the website of the Olympic Movement: http://www.olympic.org/news/all-about-the-sochi-2014-venues/219150 (accessed on 17.08.2015).
31 Russia spent £34 billion on Sochi, was it worth it? by Andrew Longmore, article on *The Sunday Times* published on 23 February 2014, http://www.thesundaytimes.co.uk/sto/sport/olympics/ article1378606.ece#commentsStart (accessed on 17.08.2015).
32 HOULIHAN/GREEN, p.14.
33 See notably, How dangerous is South Africa? by Finlo Rohrer, article on *BBC News Magazine* published on 17 May 2010, http://news.bbc.co.uk/2/hi/8668615.stm (accessed on 17.08.2015).

Direct funding and value-in-kind funding provided by a government in view of hosting an ISE are to be submitted to tax in accordance with the domestic law of the HS. It can, however, be stated that, in general, no taxable income or transaction will arise from such funding and even in the eventuality where a taxable income or transaction does arise, an exemption will apply.

Indirect subsidisation may exist either in the domestic law of the HS (sports organisations, including organising committees, are granted tax exemptions and/or tax reliefs under most national laws) or be expressly required by the HCC (notably, in relation to mega and large-scale sporting events). In the latter case, the HS is under the obligation to enact specific tax exemption regulations in relation to that particular ISE. While such regulations constitute a matter of domestic law, they have a significant relevance in international practice. For this reason, chapter 5 is dedicated to the examination of the regulations concerned.

5 Specific tax exemption regulations for mega sporting events

I. Introduction

As demonstrated by the detailed analysis made in chapters 3 and 4, the application of DTTs to different income sources derived from an ISE may not only be complex, but also result in residual double taxation cases and/or excessive taxation of some categories of taxpayers. Such outcomes are particularly due to provisions of the CSs' domestic laws as well as their interpretation of the rules contained in DTTs. To prevent the double, or excessive, taxation of their commercial partners and the participants (which constitutes a non-negligible obstacle), some SGBs may aim to ensure that the domestic law of the HS provides for tax exemptions. This tendency resulted in specific tax exemptions forming a quasi-classical component of bidding procedures.

Mega sporting events, namely the FIFA World Cup, the Olympic Games (both Summer and Winter) and the UEFA Champions League final, generally benefit from tax exemptions for all their editions. Large-scale sports events may also benefit from such exemptions, albeit not for each edition. The EURO seems to deviate from this rule, since it has given rise to the enactment of tax exemptions for most of its editions.[1] The Commonwealth Games, the ICC Cricket World Cup, the IRB Rugby World Cup and the America's Cup, which have obtained a special tax treatment for some of their editions, are more indicative of the overall trend in the area of large-scale events. At the other end of the spectrum, specific tax exemption regulations have never been enacted, at least to date,[2] for the purposes of hallmark sports events.

Specific tax exemption regulations are usually enacted in relation to one single event. Their scope may vary to a certain extent, depending on several factors, including the negotiating powers of the HS and the SGB and the domestic and/or international legal rules that the HS must observe. This chapter makes some general observations regarding the exemptions concerned (II); illustrates such exemptions by means of one specific regulation for each mega sporting event[3]

1 For an overview of the exemptions, see THIEDE/TRENCSIK, p.627.
2 December 2019.
3 Only exemptions relating to income tax and VAT are examined in detail. Customs duties are briefly mentioned where relevant, since they fall outside the scope of this book.

(III); lays out the rationale behind governments' acceptance to enact such exemptions (IV); and briefly describes the main points of concern that have been expressed by the tax law literature so far, along with the solutions that have been suggested (V). The author's opinion regarding the enactment of tax exemption regulations is expressed in chapter 6.

The analysis in this chapter mainly concentrates on tax exemption regulations enacted for mega sporting events, given the fact that there exists a more established practice in that particular area. Needless to state, the observations made apply *mutatis mutandis* to large-scale ISEs.

II. General observations on tax exemption regulations

Exemption regulations are mostly similar to a great extent. Nonetheless, as they are based on domestic laws of HSs, they have some discrepancies relating to both their form and their content. As per their form, it is possible to state that in most cases tax exemption measures are put in place by temporarily amending the relevant existing tax laws. No general conclusion may be drawn with regard to their content, since it varies in accordance with the relevant provisions of the HCC. As a matter of fact, when a country officially becomes the HS, it takes the necessary steps to fulfil the tax exemption requirement expressed during the bidding procedure and concretised by the HCC. The scope of the exemptions is thus determined by the HCC and the HS is not under an obligation to provide any further tax relief. For example, during the 2000 Sydney Olympic Games, the only guarantee given by Australia was to exempt the IOC from local taxes.[4] Therefore, even if the Australian tax levied on the Olympic athletes' earnings was criticised at the time, it remained entirely lawful. Undoubtedly, the HS may choose to extend the scope of tax exemptions beyond the requirements of the HCC. This being stated, such an extension would be rare in practice.

Income tax exemption offered to the SGB, its organisation committee and the national associations (along with their members) forms a constant of specific tax exemption regulations. While an income tax exemption may also be (and often is) offered to other entities, such as sportspersons and the commercial partners of the SGB, the existence and extent of such exemptions vary to a great extent from event to event. For instance, during the EURO 2000, which took place in Belgium and Netherlands, the latter State merely reduced its withholding tax rate from 20 percent to 18 percent with respect to non-resident football players to match the tax rate existent in Belgium in view of avoiding practical problems in levying and collecting the taxes due.[5] On the other hand, Russia completely gave up its right to tax income of sportspersons deriving from the 2014 Sochi

4 http://fulltext.ausport.gov.au/fulltext/2001/pmc/sydney_2000_games.asp#_Toc515091136, Taxation (accessed on 01.01.2012).

5 VAN HAAREN/CEULEMANS, p.441.

Olympics, irrespective of whether the income was paid in cash or by means of a value-in-kind benefit.[6]

Specific tax exemption regulations may also extend to other taxes – most frequently, customs duties and VAT. Most regulations provide for a customs duty exemption for the purposes of the sports material imported in relation to the ISE and re-exported in a certain time frame upon the finalisation of the event. Contrastingly, VAT exemptions remain rare. This rarity is due to several reasons. First, when the VAT can be offset against the input tax, an effective VAT burden does not arise, and therefore enaction of an exemption is not necessary. Second, the legislation of the HS may prevent the country from granting VAT exemptions. This is notably the case in the EU. For instance, while Ukraine granted a VAT exemption on ticket sales and related services for the purposes of the EURO 2012, its co-host, Poland, could not put in place a similar exemption due to the incompatibility of such an exemption with the EU VAT Directive.[7] Lastly, the HS may simply not agree upon (or the SGB may not request) a VAT exemption in relation to the event.[8]

The existence of specific tax exemptions does not automatically amount to the non-application of DTTs in place and/or to an overall dispensation from the 'regular' domestic laws of the CSs. First, exemptions may not extend to all income sources deriving from the sports event. The sources that are not covered by specific tax exemptions are subject to 'ordinary' taxation modalities, as described in chapters 3 and 4.[9] Second, specific tax exemption regulations provide for a tax exemption only in the HS and not a complete tax exemption. The income earned from the sports event remains taxable in the respective RSs of the persons concerned, in accordance with the relevant domestic law provisions. Clearly, under certain circumstances, an overall tax exemption may arise. This is typically the case when the DTT concluded between the relevant person's RS and the HS prevents the former from taxing the income by granting the exclusive taxing right to the latter, which exempts the income under the specific regulations.

III. Examples of tax exemption regulations

This section briefly describes one example of specific tax exemption regulations for each mega sporting event, namely Special Tax Measures Relating to the 2010 FIFA World Cup South Africa (A), the London Olympic Games and Paralympic Games Tax Regulations 2010 (B) and the amendments made to the FAs 2010 and 2012 for the 2011 and 2013 London UEFA Champions League finals (C).

6 THIEDE/TRENCSIK, p.617.
7 Ibid, p.625.
8 For an overview of exemptions enacted by different countries, see THIEDE/TRENCSIK, p.618 (Olympic Games) and p.622 (FIFA World Cup).
9 The taxation of income sources deriving from unlawful activities are obviously not covered by specific exemption regulations.

A. 2010 FIFA World Cup in South Africa

1. Generalities

Five African nations, namely Egypt, Morocco, South Africa and jointly Libya-Tunisia, placed a bid to host the 19th FIFA World Cup.[10] FIFA granted the right to hold the event to South Africa. The 19th FIFA World Cup took place in ten stadiums situated in nine host cities around the country from 11 June to 11 July 2010.[11]

During the bidding procedure, FIFA and SAFA signed the OAA 2010. The guarantees provided in this agreement were consolidated in the 2010 FIFA World Cup South Africa Special Measures Act that was assented on 1 September 2006. In addition, a Memorandum of Understanding dealing with tax matters was signed between the President of FIFA and the Minister of Finance of South Africa on 27 October 2006. This memorandum formed the basis of amendments made to Income Tax Act, Value Added Tax Act and Customs and Excise Act. The necessary modifications were made by the Amendment Act that was approved on 7 February 2007. Schedule 1 to the Amendment Act is entitled 'Special Tax Measures Relating to 2010 FIFA World Cup South Africa'. This schedule contains rules on income tax, VAT and some other duties and levies. Schedule 2 to the Amendment Act regulates customs and excise duties.

This subsection analyses the specific measures contained in schedule 1 to the Amendment Act. First, the entities exempt from all taxes are examined. Second, the specificities of tax exemptions granted to other entities are described. Lastly, the tax treatment of participating individuals is detailed.

2. Exemption of FIFA, FIFA's subsidiaries and all participating national associations

According to the OAA 2010, the HS and its authorities '[...] shall not directly or indirectly impose *any kind of taxes, duties or other levies* on FIFA, FIFA's subsidiaries, the FIFA Delegation and the Host Broadcaster [...]'.[12] This requirement was concretised in paragraphs 2 and 3 of schedule 1, which indicated that FIFA, FIFA's subsidiaries and all participating national associations other than SAFA were exempt from all taxes, duties and levies.[13] Confirming to these rules, any amount paid to the entities concerned by any person was tax-exempt in South Africa, irrespective of the regulations contained in the South African domestic tax law on the matter.

Another tax prerequisite made by the OAA 2010 was that FIFA and its subsidiaries '[...] [would] neither constitute a permanent establishment in the host

10 http://en.wikipedia.org/wiki/2010_FIFA_World_Cup#Host_selection (accessed on 07.01.2012).

11 Ibid.

12 Article 35.2.1(a) of the OAA 2010 (emphasis added by the author).

13 See notably, Amendment Act, schedule 1, §3(1)(a).

country, nor [...] they [would] in any other way [be] subject to taxation in the host country'.[14] Accordingly, FIFA, FIFA's subsidiaries and all participating national associations other than SAFA were deemed not to have a PE in South Africa, even if the activities exercised by these entities fulfilled the domestic law requirements of creation of a PE.[15] This exemption applied to the extent where the activities concerned were exclusively related to the Championship.[16] In cases where the activities conducted were not linked to the Championship, a PE might have been created in South Africa in accordance with the applicable domestic legislation.

Lastly, the HS was under the obligation not to levy any kind of withholding taxes or other similar taxes on payments to and from FIFA, FIFA's subsidiaries and/or the FIFA delegation.[17] This requirement was fulfilled by means of paragraph 3 of schedule 1, which exempted the entities concerned from withholding tax.[18] Subsequently, a person who was liable to make a payment to these entities was not required to withhold any amount from that payment in terms of the South African Income Tax Act. This exemption also covered royalties paid to such entities from the use of any patented processes or technical know-how and disposal of South African immovable property to the extent where the transaction was undertaken by these exempted bodies.[19]

The exemptions provided to the entities concerned did not apply to a number of taxes, such as VAT on the Championship tickets (including all matches and official events); accommodation and hospitality provided outside the designated sites; fuel taxes; excise duties; plastic bag levy; air passenger departure tax; provincial taxes (including gambling taxes) and local government taxes.[20]

3. *Tax treatment of certain other entities*

Paragraphs 6 to 8 of schedule 1 provided for tax exemptions granted to other entities, namely commercial affiliates, licensees, (the) host broadcaster(s)/ broadcasters or broadcast rights agencies, merchandising partners, FIFA designated service providers, concession operators, hospitality service providers and nominated FIFA flagship store operators.[21]

Income tax and VAT exemptions were granted to these entities by means of the creation of a 'tax-free bubble'. Profits on goods sold or services rendered within

14 Article 35.2.1(b) of the OAA 2010.
15 Amendment Act, schedule 1, §3(1)(b).
16 '"Championship" means all matches and ceremonies of the 2009 FIFA Confederations Cup and the 2010 FIFA World Cup and such other directly related official events, including draws, galas, conferences and cultural events, as may be agreed in good faith between FIFA and the Commissioner' (Amendment Act, schedule 1, §1).
17 Article 35.2.1(f) of the OAA 2010.
18 Amendment Act, schedule 1, §3(2).
19 WEST, p.178.
20 Amendment Act, schedule 1, §3(3).
21 Ibid, §6.

the 'bubble' (i.e. the designated sites) for the specified periods[22] were not subject to any form of income tax and the VAT was applied at zero rate.[23] Tax relief within the tax-free bubble applied both to residents and non-residents.[24] In order to qualify for these exemptions, goods sold should have been consumable and semi-durable.[25] Regarding the services rendered, they must have been: (i) intrinsic to the staging of the Championship; (ii) enjoyed or partially utilised at a site; and (iii) paid for by the individual members of the general public, FIFA or the LOC.[26] The Championship tickets (including all matches and official events), accommodation and hospitality provided outside the designated sites did not benefit from the VAT exemption.[27]

No allowance or deduction was allowed in respect of expenses or costs incurred to obtain the amounts that were not submitted to tax.[28] In cases where only a part of the income earned by the entity was tax-exempt, a reasonable allocation of expenses attributable to the exempt income was to be made.[29] With regard to refund of VAT input credits, as the goods and services were taxed at zero rate, the entities had the possibility to claim a refund.[30]

4. Tax treatment of certain individuals

According to paragraph 9 of schedule 1, income, which was derived from activities connected with the Championship, of the following non-resident individuals was tax-exempt: members of the FIFA delegation, Championship referees or assistant referees, officials of any participating national association, FIFA confederation officials, media representatives, staff members of commercial affiliates, staff members of merchandising partners, staff members of FIFA designated service providers and staff members of the host broadcaster/the broadcast rights agency/ broadcasters.[31] Explicitly excluded from this exemption's scope of application were: any officials of SAFA, any directors and staff members of the LOC and, last but not least, members of a team.[32] In order to determine the exact extent of the exemption, it was essential to define the ambit of the term 'members of a team'. Was it meant to include only sportspersons or did other team members such as medical staff and coaches fall within its range as well? Regrettably, the answer to this question was rather unclear.

22 Designated sites and specified periods depended upon the entity in question and were detailed in ibid, §7.
23 *Explanatory Memorandum on the 2006 Amendment Bill*, p.46.
24 Ibid.
25 Amendment Act, schedule 1, §7(1)(a).
26 Ibid, §7(1)(b).
27 Ibid, §4(2).
28 Ibid, §11(1).
29 Ibid, §11(2).
30 *Explanatory Memorandum on the 2006 Amendment Bill*, p.46.
31 Amendment Act, schedule 1, §9(1).
32 Ibid, §9(2).

As per article 47A of the South African Income Tax Act (as it read during the 2010 FIFA World Cup), the terms 'entertainer' and 'sportsperson' include any person who, for reward: (i) performs any activity as a theatre, motion picture, radio or television artiste or a musician; (ii) takes part in any type of sport; or (iii) takes part in any other activity which is usually regarded as of an entertainment character. Accordingly, technical sports staff such as bodyguards, coaches, doctors, personal trainers, physiotherapists and sport psychologists fall within this definition as they take part in a sporting activity.[33] Therefore, it is possible to state that under South African domestic law, both non-resident sportspersons and technical sports staff are subject to withholding tax.

On this point, Explanatory Memorandum of the World Cup Legislation made the following clarification: '[w]ithholding taxes are to be levied in respect of non-resident Team members in accordance with international practice'.[34] As previously examined, technical sports staff does not fall within the scope of application of article 17 of the OECD MC. This category of individuals is most likely to be covered by article 15 of the OECD MC. This being stated, definition of the term 'members of a team' remained rather ambiguous despite the explanation provided in the Explanatory Memorandum. As a matter of fact, it is not clear what should be understood by 'international practice'. It can be argued that the exact extent of the term depended essentially on DTTs concluded (if any) by South Africa with the RSs of the individuals concerned. In any case, non-resident sportspersons were not exempted by these regulations and were, thereby, subject to South African withholding tax.[35]

B. 2012 London Olympic and Paralympic Games

1. Generalities

Before the 2012 Games, London had already hosted the Olympic Games on two past occasions, namely the 1908 White City Games and the 1948 Wembley Games. The 2012 Olympics made London the first city to officially host the modern Olympic Games three times.[36] The final decision on the HC was made during the 117th IOC Session in Singapore on 6 July 2005. On the same day, the City of London and the British Olympic Association[37] signed the non-negotiable HCC prepared by the IOC.

One of the conditions for the 2012 Olympic and Paralympic Games being granted to London was the reduction of the tax burden of persons participating in the Games. The requirement of tax exemptions was concretised by articles 13 and 49 of the HCC. Article 13 of the HCC stated that all animals, equipment and

33 WEST, p.41.
34 *Explanatory Memorandum on the 2006 Amendment Bill*, p.51.
35 Article 17 of the OECD MC grants the right to tax non-resident sportspersons to the HS.
36 http://en.wikipedia.org/wiki/London_Olympics (accessed on 12.12.2011).
37 The UK's National Olympic Committee.

supplies necessary to the Olympic Games should enter the HS for this purpose, without any duties, customs, taxes or similar charges. Article 49 of the HCC provided for tax exemptions on payments to be received/made by the IOC or any third party owned and/or controlled by it, on any financial or other rewards received by the competitors as a result of their performance at the Games and on revenues of all other persons who temporarily carried out their Olympic-related business in the HS. Should the necessary exemptions not be put in place, the HC and/or the LOCOG would bear the tax burden.

In order to fulfil the UK's commitments on tax policy and to ensure that taxation had a minimal distortion effect on the Games, two major measures were taken. The first measure was the adoption of chapter 6 of the FA 2006. Sections 65 to 68 contained in this chapter regulated tax exemptions granted to the LOCOG, the IOC as well as competitors and staff members. Those provisions satisfied the requirements of article 49 of the HCC. The second important measure was the Temporary Admission Procedure[38] that allowed the relief of customs charges on goods temporarily imported to the UK for use there.[39] With this procedure, the requirements set out in article 13 of the HCC were implemented. It is to be noted that no specific VAT exemptions were enacted for the purposes of the Games. Therefore, the UK's domestic VAT legislation remained applicable without any modifications.

This subsection analyses the first measure, i.e. chapter 6 of the FA 2006. To this end, first, exemptions provided to the LOCOG (2) and the IOC (3) are briefly examined. Second, the taxation of athletes and other persons earning Games-related income is detailed (4). Third, the creation of a PE as a result of the activities conducted during the Games is described (5). Lastly, other relevant aspects, namely PAYE and National Insurance exemptions and the specific regulation on the tax avoidance, are briefly laid out (6).

2. Exemption of the LOCOG

The LOCOG was a private company limited by guarantee that was incorporated on 22 October 2004. As per section 65(2) of the FA 2006 it was exempt from corporation tax. By virtue of the same clause, withholding tax was not to be levied on royalties and other annual payments made to the LOCOG.

3. Exemption of the IOC

Article 49(a) and (b) of the HCC provided for a tax exemption of the IOC. The UK issued a specific tax rule in order to respect that requirement. As per section 67 of the FA 2006, the IOC and any non-UK resident person owned or

38 For more information on the Temporary Admission Procedure, see YAZICIOGLU, *London Olympics*, pp.57 and 60.

39 This procedure concerned especially non-EU countries, since, in general, goods brought into the UK from another EU MS do not need to be declared.

controlled by it: (i) would not become liable to UK tax because of their presence in the UK for the purpose of the London Olympic and Paralympic Games; and (ii) no withholding tax would be levied on interest, royalties and other annual payments made to them.[40]

4. Income and corporation tax exemptions of London 2012 competitors and staff members

Article 49(c) and (d) of the HCC provided for a tax exemption for the period of the Games to non-resident competitors and persons temporarily entering the UK to carry out Olympic-related business. Section 68 of the FA 2006 empowered the Treasury to make necessary regulations on this matter. Correspondingly, the 2010 Regulations, which provided exemptions of income and corporation income tax, were adopted. The Regulations came into force on 1 January 2011.

The 2010 Regulations provided for a temporary exemption. Their scope of application was not limited merely to London. It comprised the whole territory of the UK. The individuals entitled to an exemption were non-UK resident individuals carrying out activities that constituted 'Olympic-related' business.[41]

Thus, in order to benefit from an exemption, the person should not have been resident or ordinarily resident in the UK in the tax year during which the London 2012 activity was carried out. This signifies the 2012/2013 tax year or the 2011/2012 tax year for the exemptions that applied from April 2011. The scope of the term 'resident' under the UK domestic law is rather unclear. This did not constitute a problem for individuals residing in countries that had concluded a DTT with the UK as these agreements contain an article (article 4 of the OECD MC) dealing with residence matters. It might, however, have caused problems for persons coming from non-treaty countries, especially if they had spent significant time in the build-up to the Games training in the UK or making similar preparations.[42]

The exemptions were, as a general rule, limited to 'accredited individuals',[43] who were defined as persons who had one or more of the London 2012 functions and an accreditation card.[44] The London 2012 functions were the following: competitor, media worker, representative of an Official Body, service technician, team official and technical official.[45] Olympic/Paralympic Identity & Accreditation Cards were issued and validated by the LOCOG. Accreditation process, which was conducted by the Home Office and the LOCOG, consisted of background checks and issuance of a pass that enabled the individual to access the Olympic venues and to attend the Games in an official capacity.[46] Some

40 Section 67 of the FA 2006.
41 *Explanatory Memorandum to the 2010 Regulations*, §4.5.
42 See on this point, ANDERSON/GRAEME, p.27.
43 *Explanatory Memorandum to the 2010 Regulations*, §4.6.
44 Regulation 5 of the 2010 Regulations.
45 Ibid, regulation 5(2).
46 http://www.direct.gov.uk/en/Governmentcitizensandrights/LivingintheUK/DG_199478 (accessed on 11.12.2011).

individuals carrying out London 2012 functions did not receive accreditation cards, as they did not need an access to the site of the Games to accomplish their activities. These persons could still qualify for a tax exemption due to the nature of the services they provided.

The modalities of the tax-exemptions granted to competitors (a), other accredited individuals (b), ceremony performers (c), Rights Holding Broadcasters' and OBS' workers (d), and London 2012 Partners' workers (e) are examined separately.

A. COMPETITORS

The 2010 Regulations defined the term 'competitor' as an individual who had been entered by a National Olympic or Paralympic Committee to perform in a sporting event that formed part of London 2012.[47] The exemption applied to competitors performing in a sporting event or taking part in an activity primarily to support or promote London 2012, the Olympic and Paralympic Movements, respectively.[48] To benefit from the exemption, the contract of the competitor must have been concluded before 25 July 2012 (two days before the beginning of the Games). Income received on the basis of any contract entered or any amendments done to an existing contract after this date did not fall within the scope of the exemption.

The exemption encompassed any financial or other reward earned by the competitor between 30 March 2012 and 8 November 2012 'wholly and exclusively' as a result of one of the above-mentioned activities. Payments made to a third party instead of the competitor were also covered. The obligation on the payer to withhold the tax was lifted during the exemption period for payments falling within the scope of the exemption.

The extent of the exemption depended on the individual's contract. HMRC enumerated the following examples of income as being tax-exempt:

- Any payment or bonus, from an existing endorsement/sponsoring contract, that was specifically related to the Games. The exemption was put in place by excluding both the number of UK and worldwide performance days when calculating the ratio.
- Trackside interviews that did not cover any commercial issues. This also included the income received by an athlete who was eliminated from the competition and joined a media body as a commentator of the Games.
- Appearance in an advertisement or personal appearances in order to promote London 2012.[49]

Conversely, the following income types were not considered to be Games-related – and thereby not exempt: payments made to the competitor on the basis of an existing

47 Regulation 5(3) of the 2010 Regulations.
48 Regulation 4(2)(a) of the 2010 Regulations.
49 https://webarchive.nationalarchives.gov.uk/20140207001951/http://www.hmrc.gov.uk/2012games/tax-exemptions/competitors.htm (accessed on 05.09.2011).

endorsement/sponsoring contract that was not specifically related to the Games; income received for participation in a radio or television show, the content of which was not related to the Games; payments to endorse a commercial product as an Olympic and Paralympic Games winner and remuneration obtained in exchange for advertisement of products.[50]

B. OTHER ACCREDITED INDIVIDUALS

Accredited individuals other than competitors were the following: media workers (e.g. media managers, producers, radio/television workers and journalists), representatives of an Official Body, service technicians, team officials and technical officials.[51]

The income earned during the period of 30 March 2012 to 8 November 2012 by these categories of workers from carrying out the official function for which they had been accredited was tax-exempt. If an accredited person also exercised activities that were not covered by their official functions, the extent of the exemption was determined by the splitting method described below.[52]

C. CEREMONY PERFORMERS

A ceremony performer was defined as a person making a performance at, or at rehearsal of, an opening or closing ceremony of London 2012.[53] The exemption covered income earned from both public and closed rehearsals.[54] Like competitors, to benefit from the exemption, the activity of ceremony performers must have been 'wholly and exclusively' connected to London 2012.

D. RIGHTS HOLDING BROADCASTERS' AND OBS' WORKERS

Rights holding broadcasters (hereinafter RHB)[55] were organisations to which the IOC or the LOCOG had granted the exclusive television, internet or radio rights to broadcast the Games in a particular State.[56] OBS was defined in the 2010 Regulations as: '[…] the organisation responsible for producing international television and radio signals and providing broadcasters with the facilities and services necessary for broadcasting London 2012 […]'.[57]

50 Ibid.
51 Regulation 5(2) and (3) of the 2010 Regulations.
52 See paragraph d of this sub-subsection.
53 Regulation 6 of the 2010 Regulations.
54 https://webarchive.nationalarchives.gov.uk/20140206181002/http://www.hmrc.gov.uk/2012games/tax-exemptions/ceremony-performers.htm (accessed on 05.11.2011).
55 Only for the purposes of this subsection.
56 Regulation 7(4) of the 2010 Regulations; https://webarchive.nationalarchives.gov.uk/20140206180956/http://www.hmrc.gov.uk/2012games/tax-exemptions/uk-income-tax-exempt.htm (accessed on 12.12.2011).
57 Regulation 7(4) of the 2010 Regulations.

Individuals who were: (i) employed by an RHB or OBS; (ii) directly connected to an RHB or OBS as self-employed; or (iii) employed by a person or a business that was directly contracted to work for an RHB or OBS qualified for the tax exemption.[58] In order to benefit from the exemption, these individuals should have earned a 'wholly and exclusively' Game-related income between 6 April 2011 and 5 April 2013.

In cases where a person carried out both Games-related and non-Games related activities and received a payment that covered both, the tax exemption could only be claimed on the part of the payment that related to the part of the work necessary for the broadcast of the Games.[59] HMRC gave the following example on this point:

> Stefan receives one payment of £1500 for 80 hours work from his employer. Of those 80 hours, he spent 60 hours editing footage of the Games to be broadcast and 20 hours editing footage of news items that were unrelated to the Games. The payment must be divided as follows: £1500 x 60/80 = £1125 qualifies as exempt income.[60]

E. LONDON 2012 PARTNERS' WORKERS

A London 2012 Partner was a Commercial Delivery Partner or a person connected to a Commercial Delivery Partner.[61] A Commercial Delivery Partner was defined as a person who had been authorised to use the London Olympics Association Right[62] by the LOCOG and who provided services to the LOCOG in return.[63]

Fell within the scope of the exemption the individuals who: (i) were employed by a London 2012 Partner, or were holding an accreditation card or were providing timing, scoring or on-venue result services; and (ii) were directly contracted to work for a London 2012 Partner, or employed by a person that was directly contracted to work for a London 2012 Partner.[64]

The exemption was limited to income earned from activities exercised specifically for the purpose of the Games, i.e. activities undertaken by the London 2012 Partners in return for the right to market and advertise themselves or their products for commercial purposes by reference to their association with the Games.[65] To benefit from the exemption, activities must have been carried out during the period from 30 March 2012 to 8 November 2012. In cases where the

58 Ibid, regulation 7.
59 https://webarchive.nationalarchives.gov.uk/20140206180956/http://www.hmrc.gov.uk/2012games/tax-exemptions/uk-income-tax-exempt.htm (accessed on 13.12.2011).
60 Ibid.
61 Regulation 8(3) of the 2010 Regulations.
62 Exclusive right in relation to the use of any representation (of any kind) in a manner likely to suggest to the public that there was an association between the London Olympics and goods or services/a person providing goods or services (FA 2006, chapter 6, schedule 4).
63 Regulation 8(4) of the 2010 Regulations.
64 Ibid, regulation 8(2).
65 https://webarchive.nationalarchives.gov.uk/20140206181001/http://www.hmrc.gov.uk/2012games/tax-exemptions/partner-workers.htm (accessed on 13.12.2011).

person concerned carried out both exempt and non-exempt activities, the splitting method described above[66] was applied.

5. *Creation of a PE*

Activities performed by the accredited individuals, the RHBs'/OBS' workers and the London 2012 Partners' workers were not considered to create a PE of the employer of the individual(s) carrying out the relevant activity.[67] Companies were thus prevented from falling within the scope of the UK corporation tax as well as VAT. This exemption was put in place by simply ignoring the presence of the employees during the 'relevant period' (from 30 March 2012 to 8 November 2012). In other words, the days spent for the exercise of Olympic activities did not add up to other days spent in the UK for the calculation of the necessary time frame for the constitution of a PE, i.e. six months.[68]

The 'relevant period' applicable to the London 2012 Partners and their direct contractors that provided timing, scoring or on-venue result services[69] was longer than the one applied to other persons. It ran from 1 January 2011 to 31 December 2012. This exception was due to the fact that the necessary preparations that must have been effectuated prior to the Games required them to be present much longer than the other London 2012 Partners.

Once again, only the Games-related activities were ignored in view of determining whether a PE was created or not. In cases where a non-resident company carried on both Games-related and non-Games related activities at the same location, the PE exemption may not have been applicable. In that event, the income earned by that PE would be subject to corporation tax in its entirety.

6. *Other relevant aspects*

This sub-subsection develops two other important aspects of the 2012 London Olympic tax exemptions, namely: (a) PAYE and National Insurance exemptions; and (b) the specific regulation on tax avoidance.

A. PAYE AND NATIONAL INSURANCE EXEMPTIONS

PAYE is the system put in place in the UK to collect income tax and NICs from employees' pay. For the purposes of the 2012 London Olympics, employers who

66 See paragraph d of this sub-subsection.
67 Regulation 10 of the 2010 Regulations.
68 Most of the OECD countries consider that a PE exists in situations where a business had been carried on in a country through a fixed place that was maintained for a period of at least six months (*OECD Commentary* on article 5, §28). The UK follows the same approach.
69 Employees could be residents or ordinarily residents in the UK for the purpose of regulation 10.

did not have a PE in the UK did not need to deduct UK income tax and NICs from employees' earnings. In cases where a PE was created in the UK, the deduction was exclusively made with regard to non-exempt amounts paid to non-resident individuals. No deduction was made on income exempt by the application of the 2010 Regulations.

Employers that needed to make a deduction had the possibility to apply for a Short Term Business Visitor Arrangement, which allowed PAYE to be disregarded in circumstances where the individual concerned: (i) was a resident of a DTT country; (ii) came to work in the UK for a UK company or the UK branch of an overseas company; and (iii) was expected to stay in the UK for 183 days or less in any 12-month period. Moreover, it should have been proven that the UK company or branch would not ultimately bear the specified remuneration.

B. TAX AVOIDANCE

The 2010 Regulations contained a specific tax avoidance clause, which provided that the tax exemptions would not apply in cases where the arrangements had as their main purpose, or one of their main purposes, the obtaining of the exemption or benefit.[70]

C. 2011 and 2013 London UEFA Champions League finals

1. General observations regarding the tax exemptions granted to UEFA Champions League finals

Tax exemptions provided for UEFA Champions League finals are generally not as comprehensive as exemptions provided for the other two mega sporting events. This is due to the fact that the former sports event itself is not as voluminous as the latter ones. While the FIFA World Cup and the Olympic Games usually take place at several venues with the participation of sportspersons from a great number of countries for a time period varying between 15 days and a month, a Champions League final consists only of one football match between two teams. Subsequently, most of the tax related issues that may arise during the World Cup and the Olympic Games are not susceptible to emerge during a Champions League final, which thereby necessitates much less detailed tax exemption regulations.

It is also important to underline that UEFA may not benefit from specific tax exemptions for the purposes of a Champions League final. This 'lack' of exemption is not, however, likely to give rise to the taxation of UEFA in the HS. In fact, as a general rule, no PE can be formed by UEFA under articles 5 and 7 of the OECD MC during a Champions League final. In cases where no DTT was concluded between the HS and Switzerland (UEFA's RS) UEFA

70 Regulation 11 of the 2010 Regulations.

may still not be subject to tax in accordance with the domestic law of the HS, given the short duration of its activities.

2. General observations relating to the tax treatment of the 2011 and 2013 London UEFA Champions League finals

The UK lost the bid to host the 2010 UEFA Champions League final[71] due to its refusal to grant a tax exemption to non-resident sportspersons.[72] Following this 'incident', the UK authorities agreed on taking the necessary tax measures, which resulted in the grant of the right to host the 2011 UEFA Champions League final to Wembley Stadium situated in London.[73] Shortly after the final took place, the right to host the UEFA Champions League final was granted to Wembley Stadium one more time. This rather unusual choice was announced by UEFA as follows: '[n]ever before has a stadium been awarded Europe's premier club fixture twice in three years but hosting the 2013 UEFA Champions League final is Wembley's reward for the spectacular success of last month's event. It also marks the 150th anniversary of the foundation of the Football Association[74] [...]'.[75] Apparently, the hosting of the 2013 final was also considered as a 'spectacular success' by UEFA, since London has been elected the HC of the EURO 2020 final and semi-finals.[76]

Income derived by a Champions League final is allocated between the two finalist teams, the host association and UEFA in accordance with the financial distribution model determined by the Executive Committee before the final.[77] No tax exemption was granted to UEFA, since no income tax was due by UEFA in accordance with the UK domestic tax law to begin with. Furthermore, such a tax could not have been imposed even if it was due under the national law, since articles 5 and 7 of the DTT concluded between the UK

71 The 2010 Champions League Final was held in Santiago Bernabéu Stadium, Madrid, Spain.

72 See, on this point, Wembley's Champions League final off by Martin Smith, article on *The Telegraph* published on 29 March 2008, http://www.telegraph.co.uk/sport/football/2295712/Wembleys-Champions-League-final-off.html (accessed on 11.12.2014).

73 See, on this point, Tax break aids Wembley 2011 bid by John Sinnott, article on *BBC Sport* published on 13 May 2008, http://news.bbc.co.uk/sport2/hi/football/7397206.stm (accessed on 12.12.2014).

74 The UK Football Association, founded in 1863, celebrated its 150th anniversary in 2013. See the following link for more information on this matter: http://www.thefa.com/about-football-association/fa150 (accessed on 11.10.2015).

75 Champions League final returns to Wembley in 2013, article on the UEFA website published on 16 June 2011, http://www.uefa.com/uefachampionsleague/news/newsid=1643545.html (accessed on 12.12.2014).

76 At the time of writing (April 2020), the EURO 2020 has been postponed for 12 months. It is scheduled to be held from 11 June to 11 July 2021. Both semi-finals and the final are to be held at Wembley Stadium. See the following link for more information: https://www.uefa.com/uefaeuro-2020/news/0259-0e8ef42865e4-5c7f552e7662-1000–lowdown-euro-2020-final/ (accessed on 09.04.2020).

77 Article 61.02 of the UEFA Champions League Regulations.

and Switzerland[78] clearly attribute the exclusive right to tax the income concerned to Switzerland.[79]

Since the tax exemptions enacted for the 2011 final and the 2013 final are similar to a great extent, they are described together.

3. Exemptions granted to 'employees' and 'contractors' of 'overseas teams'

Were considered to be exempt from the UK income tax 'employees' or 'contractors'[80] of an 'overseas team'[81] competing in the final, who were not UK residents at the time of the final and who performed duties or services in the UK in connection with the final.[82]In other words, the exemptions covered the employment income, self-employment income and any endorsement income of the football players and the teams' officials relating to the Champions League final held in the UK, to the extent where the team was an overseas team and the players and the officials concerned were not residents of the UK.[83] Accordingly, in 2011 only employees and contractors of FC Barcelona benefited from the exemption, as the other competing team was Manchester United, which was not an overseas team. In 2013, players and officials of both teams, namely Borussia Dortmund[84] and Bayern Munich,[85] were entitled to benefit from the exemption put in place.

Excluded from the scope of the exemptions were: (i) income derived by the persons concerned as a result of a contract entered into after the final or any

78 Convention between the United Kingdom of Great Britain and Northern Ireland and the Swiss Confederation for the avoidance of double taxation with respect to taxes on income, signed at London on 8 December 1977.

79 As examined in chapter 3, UEFA is exempt from corporate income tax in Switzerland.

80 'Contractors' were defined as individuals who are not employees of the overseas team but who provide services for the team under the terms of a contract concluded with the team or under the terms of a contract concluded with a company that is a member of the same group of companies as the team (paragraph 6 of schedule 20 to the FA 2010 and section 13(6) of the FA 2012).

81 'Overseas team' signified a football club that is not a member of the Football Association, the Scottish Football Association, the Football Association of Wales or the Irish Football Association (paragraph 6 of schedule 20 to the FA 2010 and section 13 (6) of the FA 2012).

82 Paragraph 1(1) and (2) of schedule 20 to the FA 2010 and section 13(1) and (2) of the FA 2012.

83 HMRC, *Taxation of Non-Residents: Champions League Final 2013*, p.5, available online at the following link: https://assets.publishing.service.gov.uk/government/uploads/system/uploads/attachment_data/file/192098/champions_league_final.pdf (accessed on 11.10.2015).

84 A German sports club.

85 A German sports club.

amendment, after the final, of a contract entered into before the end of the final;[86] and (ii) income obtained through tax avoidance.[87, 88]

IV. Rationale behind the enactment of specific tax exemption regulations

From a government point of view, granting specific tax exemptions is especially justified by the need of securing the right to host an ISE, which translates into urban regeneration, creation of employments (albeit mostly temporary), a flood of tourists (that may be accompanied with a less significant loss of tourists who prefer not to visit such a crowded area at that particular time) and a great advertisement opportunity for the country. Given the fact that SGBs require such exemptions and most countries accept to grant them, the refusal of a country to enact tax exemptions is likely to cause a significant disadvantage for it during the bidding procedure. Nonetheless, this 'disadvantage' does not necessarily translate into the non-allocation of the right to host the event to the country concerned. For instance, the co-hosts of the EURO 2008, Austria and Switzerland, agreed on not granting a tax exemption for the income obtained by the football players during the event despite the request made by UEFA.[89]

A heavy tax burden may also discourage prominent sportspersons from participating in some sports events. The most well-known, and often mentioned, example is the refusal of Usain Bolt to compete in the 2010 Diamond League that took place at the Crystal Palace in the UK.[90] Such 'vetoes' tend to cause a strong public reaction. For instance, a journalist from The Telegraph expressed his deception over the absence of the Jamaican sprinter as follows: 'There is something deeply wrong about this turn of events. The joy of watching Bolt is one of the simplest, purest feelings available to mankind. It is the sheer thrill of seeing someone burst the bounds of what is humanly possible. So for the beige envelope brigade to be spoiling our fun – that is a tough one to swallow'.[91] These incidences, which may produce a negative effect on not only the country's potential to host ISEs but also

86 Paragraph 2 of schedule 20 to the FA 2010 and section 13(3)(a) of the FA 2012.

87 Tax avoidance was defined as an arrangement that has as its main purpose, or one of its main purposes, the obtaining of the exemption and that results in a person obtaining the exemption concerned (paragraph 3 of schedule 20 to the FA 2010 and section 13(3)(b) and (4) of the FA 2012).

88 Paragraph 3(4) of schedule 20 to the FA 2010 and section 13(3)(b) of the FA 2012.

89 See *Anfragebeantwortung*, No 293/AB XXIII.GP, Austrian Ministry of Finance, March 2007, available online at the following link: https://www.parlament.gv.at/PAKT/VHG/XXIII/AB/AB_00293/fname_075096.pdf (accessed on 30.08.2019).

90 See, for example, Usain Bolt turns down London and Britain's high taxes to run in Paris, article on *The Guardian* published on 12 July 2010, https://www.theguardian.com/sport/2010/jul/12/usain-bolt-london-taxes (accessed on 01.09.2019).

91 Diamond League 2010 Paris: Usain Bolt sees off Asafa Powell to win 100m in 9.84sec by Simon Briggs, article on *The Telegraph* published on 16 July 2010, https://www.telegraph.co.uk/sport/othersports/athletics/7895826/Diamond-League-2010-Paris-Usain-Bolt-sees-off-Asafa-Powell-to-win-100m-in-9.84sec.html (accessed on 01.09.2019).

on its overall image, constitute a significant pressure on the competent authorities of the countries to alleviate the tax burden for the purposes of mega and large-scale sporting events.

Tax exemptions may also be justified from a practical point of view. In cases where most non-resident participants and relevant entities will be exempt from (corporate) income tax (in the HS) under the provisions of the applicable DTTs (or the HS' domestic law, respectively) and/or no, or very insignificant, effective VAT burden will arise for them, the enactment of specific tax exemption regulations may allow administrative costs and efforts, which are not likely to be compensated by collecting the tax due, to be reduced considerably.

V. Criticism and suggestions made in the tax law literature

A. Main points of criticism

Specific tax exemption regulations are generally criticised for causing: (i) an unequal tax treatment of sports events, and thereby distorting the competition in the sports events sector; (ii) a risk of double non-taxation;[92] and (iii) the HSs to give up on a considerable tax income, which can be used to compensate the losses that are likely to be incurred as a result of hosting the event.

The author's opinion on the first two points is developed in chapter 6. Regarding the third point, it is important to stress, once again, that hosting an ISE is indeed extremely costly and likely to yield a non-negligible loss for the HS. This fact highlights even more the amounts that could have been collected but that were foregone due to tax exemptions. Nevertheless, it must be borne in mind that countries bidding to host an ISE are well-aware of these costs. They are voluntarily opting to host the event for a variety of reasons, which must, in their opinion, compensate the expenses that will be incurred. Also, it is clearly not possible for an SGB to coerce a country to enact such exemptions. The SGB may have better powers of negotiation in a given situation, but the country always safeguards its option to not to host that particular sporting event, and choose instead to become the HS of other sports events.

Albeit not a criticism per se, some authors have made the point that specific tax exemption regulations may not be entirely compatible with the European state aid provisions.[93] As per article 107(1) TFEU, for state aid to be incompatible with European legislation, four cumulative conditions need to be fulfilled: (i) the beneficiary of the measure must be an 'undertaking'; (ii) the aid must be granted through State resources and be imputable to the MS; (iii) the measure must translate into a selective advantage for the undertaking concerned; and (iv) the measure must distort the competition by favouring certain undertakings and affect trade between MSs.[94]

92 As stressed in section II of this chapter.
93 See, for instance, THIEDE/TRENCSIK, p.642 and JUÁREZ, p.322.
94 Article 107(1) TFEU.

'Undertaking' must be understood as an entity engaged in an economic activity, regardless of its legal status and its method of financing.[95] The EC underlines that since the legal status of the entity under the national law is not decisive, associations and sports clubs have to be regarded as 'undertakings'.[96] Also covered by the concept are non-profit entities, so long as they offer goods and services on a market.[97] In the light of these explanations, it seems clear that all entities deriving an income from an ISE, including SGBs, constitute 'undertakings' under article 107(1) TFEU.

In cases where the advantage is accorded to the undertaking by a public authority, the measure is, by definition, imputable to the MS.[98] A positive transfer of funds is not necessary for the aid to be considered as granted through State resources; foregoing State revenue, such as a 'shortfall' in tax income, is sufficient.[99] It is, thereupon, clear that tax exemptions enacted by public authorities are imputable to the MS and granted through State resources.

An advantage is any economic benefit, which an undertaking could not have obtained under normal market conditions, i.e. in the absence of State intervention.[100] An advantage is deemed to be present whenever the financial situation of the undertaking is improved as a result of State intervention, regardless of the intervention's cause and purpose.[101] The advantage may consist of not only a positive economic advantage, but also a relief from an economic burden.[102] To fall within the scope of article 107(1) TFEU, the advantage must be 'selective', which means that it must favour (a) certain undertaking(s) or certain economic sectors.[103] Measures of purely general application that do not produce a beneficial effect on only (a) certain undertaking(s) are not constitutive of a state aid incompatible with the EU law.[104] A specific and temporary tax exemption manifestly constitutes an advantage, since it relieves the undertaking from paying a certain amount of tax, which would be due under normal market conditions. When such an exemption is granted to only some ISEs, and not to all similar events, it becomes a 'selective advantage', rather than a general policy measure.

A measure is deemed to distort or threaten to distort competition when it is liable to improve the competitive position of the recipient compared to other undertakings with which it competes.[105] A tax exemption granted to certain ISEs, and not to others, on the basis of not pre-established (thus subjective) criteria, certainly has the effect of improving the competitive position of the events

95 *EC State Aid Notice*, §7.
96 Ibid, §8.
97 Ibid, §9.
98 Ibid, §39.
99 Ibid, §51.
100 Ibid, §66.
101 Ibid, §67.
102 Ibid, §68.
103 Ibid, §117.
104 Ibid, §118.
105 Ibid, §187.

concerned at the expense of other comparable events. Aside from the 'tax-free', and thereby more substantial, income made available only to some events; such a favourable treatment may produce other negative effects on the competition. For instance, some sports 'stars' may choose to compete in events that enjoy a tax exemption and refuse to participate in other events in the same category, which will in turn necessarily affect the event's popularity in a significant manner.

Lastly, the advantage under examination should have the potential to affect the trade between MSs. It is not necessary to establish that the measure has an actual effect on trade between MSs.[106] Demonstrating that the advantage is liable to affect such trade is sufficient.[107] While funding granted to local events that are unlikely to attract visitors and/or investment away from similar offers in other MSs is generally deemed not to constitute an unlawful state aid, economic advantages accorded to large and renowned events, which are widely promoted outside the host country, have the potential to affect the trade between the MSs.[108] ISEs (especially mega and large-scale), which are clearly akin to the latter category of events, have, thereby, the potential to affect the trade between the MSs.

Fulfilling all the conditions enumerated in article 107(1) TFEU, specific tax exemption regulations seem, indeed, to constitute an unlawful state aid; as long as the *de minimis* threshold[109] is also exceeded, which would be the case for the majority of the entities (with the notable exception of sportspersons – in most cases) deriving an income from the event. It would, thereupon, be advisable for a MS, which becomes the HS of an ISE and is under the obligation to grant specific tax exemptions to this end, to seek the approval of the EC on the exemptions concerned.[110] This being stated, to date, no investigations have been initiated by the EC regarding the tax exemptions enacted for the purposes of an ISE. Undoubtedly, should the EC effectively investigate and come to the conclusion that such exemptions are incompatible with EU law, European countries would (most probably) have a competitive disadvantage over non-European countries during bidding procedures.

B. Suggestions made in the literature

In her book published in 2014, Tetlak argued that a permanent HS should be designated for all 'major sports events'.[111, 112] This implies that each and every major ISE would be held in the same State for all its editions. The author also

106 Ibid, §190.
107 Ibid.
108 Ibid, §197(a) and (b).
109 On this point, see European Commission Regulation No 1407/2013 of 18 December 2013 on the application of Articles 107 and 108 of the Treaty on the Functioning of the European Union to *de minimis* aid (L 352/1).
110 Article 108(3) TFEU.
111 The term is used by Tetlak and should therefore be distinguished from the terms used in this book in relation to different categories of sports events (set out in chapter 1).
112 TETLAK, p.589.

designated the most suitable HS: '[...] because Dubai has no income tax, it seems to be an ideal candidate for the permanent hosting of major sports events'.[113]

Even if determining a permanent HS may indeed solve the current problems in a purely theoretical context, its implementation seems to be extremely unlikely in practice. Given the importance attributed by countries to the hosting of ISEs and SGBs' interest to organise their events in different countries, it is far from being clear why all countries and SGBs would agree that all such events would permanently be held in Dubai, or in another country. Also, in view of the financial and organisational burden it presents, hosting a considerable number of such events on a yearly basis seems to be quite gargantuan for the 'permanent HS'. Therefore, it is rather difficult to understand why a country would readily assume such a burden. Concerning the specific suggestion of Dubai, the weather conditions are not ideal for the hosting of ISEs throughout the year. A similar issue is likely to arise for any other 'permanent HS' for a myriad of different reasons.

In their article published in November 2017, Thiede and Trencsik suggested to eliminate the recourse to specific tax exemption regulations by means of public pressure, cooperation of all countries to refuse to grant such a beneficial treatment to certain SGBs or implementation of a unilateral tax exemption for all kinds of sports organisations in the national laws of all countries.[114] While public pressure constitutes a non-negligible driving force in solving most issues perceived as being problematic, it does not guarantee a fair and effective legal solution, as was also the understanding of the authors. Regarding the cooperation of countries, as long as such a cooperation remains voluntary, as suggested by Thiede and Trencsik, it would most probably not yield any concrete results. This point is, also, underlined by the authors themselves, who dubbed the problem as being akin to 'the prisoner's dilemma'. The 'cheating' countries would obtain an advantage in a bidding process over the countries not breaking the 'gentlemen's agreement'. Such cooperation may only work to the extent where its violation entails some legal repercussions.

The unilateral tax measure put forward by Thiede and Trencsik forms a very similar, while being much more restricted in scope, solution to the one that has been suggested by the author of this book in 2012[115] and 2016.[116] When the suggestion was made in 2012 and 2016, respectively, it constituted, and remained, the first solution[117] concentrating on domestic laws rather than international law. The suggestion made by the author of this book is developed in more detail in chapter 6. As can be observed, the solution put forward entailed considerably more extensive domestic law regulations, focusing on the tax treatment of not only 'sports organisations' but also other entities involved in ISEs. In the author's

113 Ibid, p.592.
114 THIEDE/TRENCSIK, p.640.
115 YAZICIOGLU, *London Olympics*, p.60.
116 YAZICIOGLU, *South African Draft Guide*, pp.17–19.
117 In accordance with the extensive research conducted by the author.

opinion, a unilateral measure exempting merely sports organisations does not constitute a sufficient remedy to the variety of tax related problems arising in this particular field. The adoption of an 'International Sports Events Tax Exemptions Act' and/or an 'International Sports Events Taxation Act' would be much more equitable and efficient.

6 Adoption of an 'International Sports Events Tax Exemptions Act' and/or an 'International Sports Events Taxation Act'

An effective solution

I. Introduction

This chapter describes the main problems caused by the current taxation system (II) and suggests a viable solution to eliminate them to a certain extent (III). Given the fact that the most controversial problems arise in the area of income tax, section II exclusively concentrates on this particular type of tax. The solution suggested in section III, however, is applicable to all types of taxes, most notably, income tax, VAT and customs duties.

II. Main problems of the current taxation system

As demonstrated by the previous chapters, tax rules and regulations applicable to ISEs are somewhat complex and depend heavily on several factors, such as the presence of an applicable DTT, enactment of specific tax exemption regulations, and the relevant aspects of the HS's domestic law.

Consequently, under the current system, similar categories of taxpayers may be subject to distinct tax treatments. The obvious legal question that arises from this situation is whether such a differentiation in the tax treatment may be characterised as 'discriminatory'. As examined in this chapter, in general, no discrimination exists, at least from a legal standpoint. This being stated, even if the dissimilarities in the tax treatment do not amount to a 'discrimination' per se, they most certainly constitute a 'tax obstacle', affecting the organisation of ISEs and the mobility of the taxpayers concerned.

Another adverse consequence of the current system is 'the chaos' formed by different layers of rules, regulations and their possible interpretations. Like in every chaos, a pattern does exist within this 'chaos of tax rules'. However, to discern that pattern, a number of tax law professionals are generally required.[1] One thing remains obvious: where there is chaos, there is no clarity. Such a situation may be

1 As a matter of fact, a tax lawyer practicing in the RS of the taxpayer will usually not be able to determine the potential tax treatment of their client in the HS, since the domestic law of this latter State plays a key role. On this point, the legal advice of a local practitioner will be necessary. Not to mention that in the case of enactment of specific tax exemption regulations, even local practitioners may encounter difficulties.

considered as highly intriguing in some fields, like physics; but not in law, one of the governing principles of which is '*[i]gnorantia iuris neminem excusat*'.[2]

This section analyses the two main problems caused by the current tax system: discrimination, alternatively a 'tax obstacle' (A) and lack of clarity (B).

A. Discrimination or a 'tax obstacle'?

As asserted by Nelson Mandela, sport has a unifying power that can potentially form a 'laugh in the face of all kinds of discrimination'. Regrettably, this 'unifying power' is yet to reach its true potential. The sports sector continues to be prone to different types of discrimination,[3] such as racism and sex discrimination.[4]

The tax treatment of persons taking part in ISEs seems to form yet another layer of discrimination. As demonstrated in chapters 3 and 5, several treatments that may be considered as 'discriminatory' occur in relation to taxation of ISEs. For instance, while sportspersons are taxed at source, other employees of the same team are not. Similarly, whereas persons taking part – as a participant, an employee or an enterprise rendering services – in mega and some large-scale sporting events can benefit from specific tax exemption regulations, persons taking part in other ISEs cannot. In the same vein, taxation of persons deriving income from the same ISE may vary to a great extent depending on whether or not their RS concluded a DTT with the HS.

This being stated, to the extent where the tax treatment remains lawful, i.e. it does not violate the domestic law of the HS[5] and any other applicable international law provisions, these differences should not be criticised from a legal standpoint. In fact, these variations derive directly from the tax policy of the State concerned. Some States[6] may consider that a source taxation of non-resident sportspersons is justified,[7] while some other States[8] may assume the opposite and prefer to exempt non-resident sportspersons and entertainers from income tax.

2 Can be translated as: '[i]gnorance of the law affords no excuse'.
3 The word 'discrimination' is used in its everyday meaning in this sentence.
4 For more information on sex discrimination in sport, see YAZICIOGLU ALARA E., Women in sport, a continuous battleground! (Part 1) and (Part 2) in *Global Sports Law and Taxation Reports (GSLTR)*, June 2017, Volume 8, Number 2, p.15ff and September 2017, Volume 8, Number 3, p.7ff.
5 The reference is not made merely to the tax law of the country, but to its overall domestic law. See, for example, NITIKMAN for an analysis of source taxation of entertainers and sportspersons under Canadian constitutional law.
6 Which is the case for a great number of countries, such as Switzerland, the UK and the US.
7 For example, SANDLER states that '[w]ithholding taxes levied in the source State (coupled with personal liability of those persons who fail to withhold tax) probably constitute the single most effective means of enforcing the payment of tax in the international community and any steps taken to limit the ability of countries to levy withholding taxes on these forms of income should be kept to a minimum and should be justified' (SANDLER, *Non-resident entertainers and athletes*, p.21).
8 Such as the Netherlands.

Likewise, some States may not be willing to grant specific tax exemptions to any sports events, whereas some others may agree to do so for some events.

It is not possible to state that one method results in a 'fairer' tax treatment than others. As a matter of fact, attaining fairness in taxation is predominantly a political question.[9] What is or is not considered to be fair depends entirely upon the position taken. The same tax treatment may be considered as fair by one group and as grossly unfair by another one.[10] This was also illustrated during Seminar E[11] of the 2010 IFA Congress[12] on taxation of entertainers and sportspersons. While one of the panellists[13] argued that article 17 of the OECD MC was discriminatory and should be abrogated, another panellist[14] claimed that article 17 was designed to protect the SS' right to tax and should therefore not only be retained but also be broadened. Both approaches are justified for a number of reasons. Which one is to be applied in a given State depends on that State's tax policy in its entirety.

Undoubtedly, governments are not entitled to discriminate a group of taxpayers under the guise of tax policy. Whether the differences in tax treatment effectively constitute discrimination in a given situation generally needs to be determined on a case-by-case basis. However, it is possible to make some general observations on that matter.

Defined very broadly, discrimination is the equal treatment of different cases or the unequal treatment of comparable cases.[15] In order to be acknowledged as 'comparable', the two (groups of) persons concerned should be in a quasi-identical situation in almost every relevant aspect. For example, a non-resident taxpayer, either employed or self-employed, who receives all or almost all of their income in the State in which their business activity is pursued (the so-called 'quasi-resident') is considered to be objectively in the same situation as a resident of that State who pursues comparable activities.[16] For discrimination to occur, the two comparable situations should be either differentiated on the basis of a factor that is regarded as illegitimate or treated disparately without a legally acceptable distinctness between the categories of persons concerned.[17]

To determine whether or not the current tax system results in discrimination, two separate analyses need to be made: (1) whether the distinct tax treatment of different categories of taxpayers can be considered as legitimate; and (2) whether the fact that some ISEs benefit from specific tax exemptions whereas others do not is justifiable.

9 HOLMES, *Concept of Income*, p.16.

10 ARNETT HAROLD E., The Concept of Fairness in *The Accounting Review*, 1967, April, p.292 cited by HOLMES, *Concept of Income*, p.16.

11 The seminar concerned was entitled '*Red Card 17*?'.

12 64th IFA Congress, Rome.

13 Aart Roelofsen, Ministry of Finance, the Netherlands.

14 Michael G. Pfeifer, Caplin & Drysdale, the US.

15 IBFD, *International Tax Glossary*, p.130.

16 The Ettwein decision, §47. On this point, see notably the Schumacker decision, the Wielockx decision and the Gschwind decision.

17 AIGNER, p.408.

1. Distinct tax treatment of different categories of taxpayers

As analysed in chapter 3, similar categories of taxpayers may be subject to different tax treatments for a number of reasons. Such a distinction typically occurs: (a) between residents of the HS and residents of other States (i.e. non-residents); (b) between non-residents domiciled in a State with which the HS has concluded a DTT and non-residents domiciled in a State with which the HS has not entered into such an agreement; and (c) between non-resident sportspersons and other non-resident individuals.

A. RESIDENTS VERSUS NON-RESIDENTS

Most countries distinguish between residents and non-residents for income tax purposes. It is therefore clear that individuals and legal entities deriving income from an ISE taking place in their RS will be subject to tax rules and regulations that diverge to a certain extent from the rules applicable to non-residents obtaining income from the same sports event.

This being stated, it is well-established that in relation to direct taxes the situations of residents and non-residents are, as a rule, not comparable.[18] As expressed by the CJEU in a number of its decisions,[19] this is mainly due to the following factors: (i) income received by a non-resident forms, in most cases, only a fraction of their/its total income, which is concentrated in their/its RS;[20] and (ii) a non-resident's ability to pay tax, which is determined by reference to their/its aggregate income and their/its personal/specific circumstances (for individuals, this includes the ones related to their families), is more easy to assess at the place where all their/its interests are centred (i.e. the RS).[21]

It is also important to underline that for the purposes of the OECD MC, the decisive criterion for discrimination is nationality, not residence.[22] In other words, insofar as article 24 of the OECD MC is concerned, States may distinguish between residents and non-residents while enacting their tax rules and regulations.[23]

It is therefore possible to conclude that the tax treatment differences between residents and non-residents do not amount to discrimination.

B. NON-RESIDENTS FROM A DTT COUNTRY VERSUS NON-RESIDENTS FROM A NON-DTT COUNTRY

Non-residents domiciled in a State that has concluded a DTT with the HS benefit from a more beneficial tax treatment than non-residents domiciled in a State that

18 The Schumacker decision, §31.
19 On this point, see notably the decisions cited in n.16.
20 The Schumacker decision, §32.
21 Ibid.
22 Article 24(1) of the OECD MC.
23 On this point, see also HOLMES, *International Tax Policy*, pp.420–424.

has not entered into such an agreement with the HS. As a matter of fact, in the first case scenario, the taxpayer may invoke the dispositions of the DTT to avoid or to alleviate to a certain extent, respectively, double taxation of their/its income. On the other hand, in the latter case, double taxation will only be alleviated in accordance with the unilateral measures adopted by the States concerned. Such measures are generally not as efficient as the rules contained in a DTT.

Although this inevitably results in a more beneficial treatment of some non-residents, a State is clearly under no obligation to enter into DTTs with all other States in order to ensure an equal treatment of persons all around the world who may derive an income in its territory. A problem in this regard may only arise in cases where there is/are another applicable international agreement or regulations providing rules that is/are binding on the HS, which is for example the case if both the HS and the RS are EU MSs. Since this aspect is clearly straightforward, it is not developed further.

C. NON-RESIDENT SPORTSPERSONS VERSUS OTHER NON-RESIDENT INDIVIDUALS

Whether or not the difference of tax treatment of non-resident sportspersons and other non-resident individuals, including 'celebrities',[24] results in a discriminatory practice is a controversial issue. It is possible to state that both categories of taxpayers are in a comparable situation as they derive an income in a relatively short period of time from an activity exercised in the State concerned without being residents thereof. Accordingly, the main problem resides in determining whether the rationale behind the differentiation may be regarded as illegitimate or legally inadmissible.

The OECD MC contains a number of distributive rules for a number of non-identical situations. For example, one rule provides the taxation regime for employees deployed to an SS, another one regulates the taxation of self-employed individuals and yet another one determines the taxation modalities of individuals making a public performance. The criterion of 'public performance' has been chosen for a number of reasons that may be briefly described by the following points: (i) the world of entertainment is considered to be characterised by an increasingly blurred distinction between dependent and independent services and business activities accompanied with sophisticated tax avoidance schemes;[25] (ii) public performers are seen as operating '[…] through complicated chains of limited companies, partnerships, joint-ventures and sole trading enterprises';[26] and (iii) entertainers and sportspersons frequently choose 'tax havens'[27] as their official RS.

24 In this context, the term 'celebrities' refers to individuals – other than 'sportspersons' and 'entertainers' – who are highly mobile and command substantial compensation for their services. The sector in which the individual is active is not relevant (See SANDLER, *Artistes and Sportsmen*, p.216).

25 *The 1987 Report*, §6.

26 Ibid, §8.

27 Although the term 'tax haven' does not have a precise technical meaning, it can be loosely described as '[…] countries which are able to finance their public services with no or nominal income taxes and that offer themselves as places to be used by

These concerns are often criticised for being 'disproportionate' and 'outdated'. Disproportionate, since entertainers and sportspersons who are being targeted, i.e. those who earn substantial amounts of money in a rather short period of time, form only a small fraction of the entertainment and sports sector.[28] Outdated, as evading taxes has become much more difficult in the last two decades due to the exceptional development of the exchange of information.[29]

Although these arguments are justified to a great extent, the existence of such tendencies among top earning public performers cannot be ignored. For example, in the last decade, HMRC conducted investigations regarding two loopholes in the domestic tax law that allowed Premier League football players to avoid paying substantial amounts of tax. First to be tackled were payments made by football clubs to image rights companies held by sportspersons, which allowed Premier League players to refrain from paying 100 million GBP in taxes per year.[30] Second were counteracted 'employer-financed retirement benefits' used by many leading Premier League clubs, including Manchester City and Chelsea, to reduce the tax liability of football players.[31] Similarly, in Spain, Lionel Messi stood trial, along with his father who is also his agent, for not having paid 3.1 million GBP in tax on his earnings between 2007 and 2009 through the creation of a web of shell companies in Belize and Uruguay.[32] Last but not least, the Pavarotti case is the milestone example of concerns relating to the problem of residence. The lawyer for the Italian tenor argued before the Tax Court of Modena that the world-traveller lifestyle of Pavarotti made it impossible to establish where his domicile was.[33] The Court clearly rejected this argument by stating that '[b]eing domiciled everywhere, and thus nowhere, he would not have any tax liability other than the one arising from his residence in a country where, as everybody knows, no individual income taxes are levied'.[34]

Given these examples and many others, the rationale put forward by the OECD for a different tax treatment of non-resident entertainers and sportspersons, which is shared by a significant number of countries imposing a withholding tax on

non-residents to escape tax in their country of residence' (IBFD, *International Tax Glossary*, p.425).

28 See especially MOLENAAR, *Discussion of Daniel Sandler's Paper*, p.249ff and chapter 1, section V of this book.

29 See, for example, WEST, p.151ff on this matter.

30 See Taxman chases football stars for £100m by Robert Watts, article on *The Sunday Times*, published on 21 February 2010, http://www.thesundaytimes.co.uk/sto/sport/football/Premiership/article198404.ece (accessed on 14.11.2015).

31 Premier League stars using loophole to save millions in tax by Sam Wallace, article on *The Independent* published on 28 October 2010, https://www.independent.co.uk/sport/football/premier-league/premier-league-stars-using-loophole-to-save-millions-in-tax-2118289.html (accessed on 21.11.2012).

32 Lionel Messi to stand trial for tax fraud after plea is dismissed, article on *The Times*, published on 9 October 2015, http://www.thetimes.co.uk/tto/sport/football/article4580112.ece (accessed on 15.11.2015).

33 The Pavarotti decision, p.81.

34 Ibid. Pavarotti argued he was a resident of Monaco, where he had a 90 sq metre flat on the 4th floor of a residential building.

income derived by them, cannot be considered as illegitimate or legally inadmissible. The purpose is to prevent tax avoidance and to allow an efficient fiscal supervision and collection of taxes. Although a general presumption of tax avoidance or fraud may not be sufficient to warrant a specific fiscal measure per se, fiscal supervision, to the extent where it is necessary and proportionate, may serve as a justification for a different tax treatment.[35] In fact, this purpose has been explicitly recognised as a viable justification by the CJEU in the Scorpio decision, as follows: '[t]he procedure of retention at source and the liability rules supporting it constitute a legitimate and appropriate means of ensuring the tax treatment of the income of a person established outside the State of taxation and ensuring that the income concerned does not escape of taxation in the State of residence and the State where the services are provided'.[36] The Court also added that the use of retention at source constituted a proportionate means of ensuring the recovery of the tax debts of the State of taxation.[37]

In the light of these explanations, it is possible to state that tax treatment of non-resident sportspersons cannot be considered as discriminatory per se.[38] Undoubtedly, enlarging, and at the same time limiting, the scope of application of article 17 of the OECD MC to all 'celebrities' earning more than 100,000 USD per year in a given SS[39] may respect the horizontal equity[40] better. Nevertheless, as already mentioned, this constitutes a matter of tax policy that is to be determined by countries.

2. *Distinct tax treatment of different categories of ISEs*

As demonstrated by chapters 3, 4 and 5, two types of ISEs may be distinguished for taxation purposes: (i) sports events benefitting from specific exemption regulations; and (ii) sports events that do not benefit from such exemptions. Although it may be argued that these two categories of sports events are comparable – and therefore need to be treated in an equal manner[41] – the divergence in their tax treatment is based on a straightforward and justifiable criterion: the public interest.

It is an established fact that some sports events attract much greater public interest than others. This fact alone is susceptible to legitimise the disparity of tax treatments between ISEs. A State may be willing to provide an overall tax exemption exclusively for the purposes of hosting mega sporting events, as such events are considered to be more prestigious. It is important to reiterate that the 'popularity of the event' also forms the basis of the list of events of major

35 VALIS, pp.432–433.
36 The Scorpio decision, §36. See also VALIS, p.433.
37 Ibid, §37.
38 On this point, see also the Gerritse decision, §44.
39 As suggested by SANDLER (*Artistes and Sportsmen*, pp.239–243).
40 Horizontal equity signifies like treatment of people in like circumstances (HOLMES, *Concept of Income*, p.19).
41 Both types of events are short-term ISEs organised in the territory of an SS.

importance for society mechanism, used by a number of EU MSs.[42] Accordingly, the fact that some sports events are entitled to benefit from specific tax exemptions, whereas some are not, should not, per se, be considered as amounting to a discrimination either.

3. Absence of discrimination, but presence of a 'tax obstacle'

In the light of the analysis made in this subsection, it is possible to conclude that the current regime of taxation of ISEs, including non-resident sportspersons, remains within the limits of legality. In other words, the current tax rules cannot be categorised as discriminatory. This does not mean, however, that the current system does not constitute an obstacle for the organisation of ISEs and the mobility of sportspersons.

The domestic tax law of a given State may have an important influence on the decision of rights-holders to grant the right to host an ISE to the State concerned. A 'favourable' tax system (consisting of clear tax rules and regulations, granting low withholding tax rates, providing for specific tax exemptions, etc.) may constitute an incentive for a rights-holder to appoint a State as an HS. Conversely, an 'unfavourable' tax system (involving highly burdensome procedures for non-resident taxpayers, opting for high withholding tax rates, not providing for specific tax exemption regulations, etc.) may dissuade a rights-holder from granting the HS status to the State in question. In the same vein, the domestic tax law of the HS may hinder the mobility of sportspersons, and other non-residents. It is not uncommon for sportspersons, or other individuals/entities, to opt for not engaging in a commercial activity in a given country due to the heavy tax burden.

B. Lack of clarity

The complex web of tax rules and regulations causes a significant lack of clarity, which inevitably translates into legal uncertainty, even in cases where specific tax exemption regulations are enacted. As a matter of fact, non-resident taxpayers deriving an income from ISEs cannot rely on clear and straightforward rules and regulations according to which they will be subject to tax. To make sure that they are compliant with the applicable law(s), they are under an obligation to systematically seek professional assistance.

The main reasons of this lack of certainty are examined separately for the two different categories of ISEs, i.e. ISEs that do not benefit from specific tax exemption regulations (1) and ISEs that benefit from such regulations (2).

1. ISEs that do not benefit from specific tax exemption regulations

In cases where no specific tax exemption regulations are enacted, the ordinary tax regime, as provided by the domestic law of the HS, applies. Participating

42 See article 14 of the AVMSD.

sportspersons and other persons deriving an income from the event, are under an obligation to either research the applicable tax law provisions themselves (which would be a rather difficult and risky strategy) or to hire local professionals to assist them. This obligation remains valid even in the presence of a DTT based on the OECD MC, as local requirements and interpretations generally play a key role in the tax practice.

For persons participating in a number of ISEs per year in different countries, this may be quite a burdensome procedure. Not only does consulting with several tax professionals inevitably give rise to a considerable financial burden, but also not being able to check the applicable tax legislation personally – when needed – constitutes a significant psychological concern.

2. *ISEs that benefit from specific tax exemption regulations*

The situation remains the same for this category of ISEs for two main reasons: (a) lack of international practice; and (b) lack of national practice.

A. LACK OF INTERNATIONAL PRACTICE

As specific tax exemptions heavily depend on the domestic law of the HS, they vary to a great extent from sports event to sports event. For example, while the scope of the exemptions enacted for the 2010 FIFA World Cup in South Africa was limited to a designated area, i.e. the so-called 'tax-free bubble', exemptions granted in the UK for the 2012 Olympic Games were valid in the entire territory of the country.[43]

Although tax exemption regulations may have some similar traits, there is not a generally recognised model or practice on that matter. Each State prepares specific tax exemption regulations exclusively for the event concerned. As a result, persons deriving income from ISEs cannot rely on a certain established international practice or similar rules. Each new event requires a new information gathering process on regulations that have never been applied before.[44]

B. LACK OF NATIONAL PRACTICE

Lack of national practice presents itself in regard to: (i) the very existence of exemption regulations; and (ii) the interpretation and modalities of exemption regulations.

First, it may not be certain whether an HS will effectively enact specific tax exemptions. Since the exemptions are a one-off, like the sports event itself, in some cases it may even be unclear whether or not the same sports event taking

43 As examined in chapter 5.

44 An exception to this general assumption can be seen in the regulations enacted for the 2011 and 2013 London UEFA Champions League finals (see chapter 5). However, as a general rule, mega sporting events do not take place twice in the same country in such a short time frame. Accordingly, this example should remain as a rare occurrence.

place in the same country a couple of years later will benefit from similar tax exemptions. This was for example the case for the 2013 UEFA Champions League final that took place at Wembley Stadium two years after another Champions League final[45] that was held at the same stadium and that benefited from tax exemptions. As the scope of application of the specific regulation enacted for the 2011 Champions League final was exclusively limited to that event, a new regulation had to be enacted by the UK for the 2013 final. Nonetheless, UEFA granted the right to host this latter event to London without a prior negotiation on tax exemptions. On this point, Gianni Infantino[46] stated that signalling the desire to appropriately celebrate the 150th anniversary of the Football Association was more important than the 'rest of the issues'.[47] When the question was raised, the UK Government announced that it was not officially approached about the exemptions concerned, the enactment of which might be considered if such a request was made by UEFA.[48] In other words, due to the lack of a tax exemption requirement made beforehand, the provision of such exemptions was left to the discretion of the HS, i.e. the UK, in its entirety. No specific problems arose in that particular case as the UK Government finally enacted a similar exemption to the one granted in 2011, even if it was not legally obliged to do so.

Comparable situations are likely to occur on a frequent basis as each specific tax regulation provides for one-off exemptions, the exact scope of which is determined on the basis of negotiations conducted with the SGB concerned. For instance, the same State may grant a tax exemption for non-resident sportspersons for one sports event and may not do so for another similar event held in its territory, simply because of the fact that such an obligation was not contained in the HCC signed for the latter event. Subsequently, persons envisaging to engage in professional activities related to ISEs cannot rely on established national practices on the very existence of tax exemptions.

Second, in cases where specific tax exemption regulations are effectively enacted, their exact scope cannot be precisely determined until the taxation occurs. Despite the fact that governments give guarantees to organising sports bodies and amend their domestic laws accordingly, the exact scope of the exemptions depends heavily on the local authorities' interpretation and the domestic law of the State concerned. Moreover, since the relevant regulations are specifically prepared for a particular event, it is, once again, impossible to rely on a developed national practice on the interpretation and the modalities of application of such regulations. For these reasons, the ambit of exemptions cannot generally be accurately known until the taxation takes place.

This uncertainty is mostly due to vague regulations. For example, China's tax exemption rule for athletes participating in the 2008 Beijing Olympics consisted of

45 The 2011 Champions League final.

46 The UEFA General Secretary at the time.

47 UEFA yet to get tax break for 2013 Wembley final by Rob Harris, article on *USA Today*, published on 21 June 2011, http://usatoday30.usatoday.com/sports/soccer/2011-06-21-751231331_x.htm (accessed on 16.12.2015).

48 Ibid.

one sentence: '[t]he income of reward in the 29th Olympic Games and other matches of athletes shall be exempt from individual income tax according to existing laws and regulations'.[49] Another ambiguous regulation example can be found in the regulations enacted for the purposes of the 2010 FIFA World Cup. As per the regulation concerned, income earned by 'members of a team' during the World Cup was not tax-exempt.[50] Although sportspersons clearly fell within the scope of this notion, the tax treatment of technical staff (such as coaches, medical staff, trainers, etc.) remained rather unclear.[51]

Even when the provisions of the applicable regulations are very detailed and unambiguous, problems may still arise, mostly due to other aspects of the relevant domestic law. For instance, although the regulations enacted for the 2012 London Olympics had the merit of being extremely clear, the domestic law definition of the term 'resident' was ambiguous and subject to litigation itself.[52] Subsequently, sportspersons who were residents of countries that had not concluded a DTT with the UK[53] had to be cautious about not becoming UK residents 'by mistake'.

Application of specific tax exemption regulations is also prone to practical complications. Such a problem materialised during the 2000 Sydney Olympic Games. SOCOG was tax-exempt in accordance with the regulations enacted. Nonetheless, due to a decision rendered by the High Court, which did not involve SOCOG, the Australian Taxation Office considered that the definition of 'public authority' was modified and decided to remove SOCOG's sales and income tax exemptions. To remedy this, the Australian Government decided to reimburse SOCOG for its potential taxation costs. However, this resulted in administrative difficulties and additional costs. Finally, a separate bill had to be adopted to restore SOCOG's tax-exempt status.[54]

III. From chaos to clarity

As demonstrated throughout this book, the current taxation system of ISEs can be described as 'chaotic', despite the existence of the OECD MC and the international efforts to harmonise rules applicable to taxation of foreign income to a certain extent.

This chaos can be turned into clarity by means of steps taken at a national level.[55] The enactment of an 'International Sports Events Tax Exemptions Act' (hereinafter, Exemption Act) and/or an 'International Sports Events Taxation

49 Circular of State Administration of Taxation and General Administration of Customs on Issues Relating to 29th Olympics Taxation Policy, CS [2003] No. 10, clause 2(3).
50 §9 (2) of schedule 1 to the Amendment Act.
51 For more information on this point, see WEST, p.41.
52 ANDERSON/GRAEME, p.27.
53 In cases where a DTT is concluded the residence is determined in accordance with article 4 of the OECD MC.
54 http://www.parliament.nsw.gov.au/prod/parlment/hansart.nsf/V3Key/LC19971119005 (accessed on 20.02.2012).
55 Instituting a solution at an *international* level, which is acceptable by all States that may potentially host an ISE in the future, may be extremely laborious. More importantly, the adoption of such a solution and its implementation in all relevant States

Act' (hereinafter, Taxation Act) and/or a 'General Explanatory Report on the relevant domestic tax law rules' (hereinafter, Explanatory Report) by a State relating to ISEs it will host, will allow the alleviation of the uncertainty to a great extent. These Acts and Explanatory Report are suggested for all types of taxes, including notably income tax, VAT and customs duties.

The Explanatory Report can be used as an effective instrument both in the absence and in the presence of an Exemption Act and/or a Taxation Act. In the former case, the Explanatory Report may provide guidance on the existent applicable domestic tax law rules with regard to the taxation of ISEs. By regrouping rules and regulations that are otherwise contained in separate acts and circulars, such a Report will restore a significant level of certainty for non-resident taxpayers. In the latter case, the Explanatory Report may contain guidelines on the application and interpretation of the Exemption Act and/or the Taxation Act with an aim of improving the clarity even further.

These legislative documents, either combined or adopted on a standalone basis, will have the merit of both establishing clear rules and building up, gradually, a national practice that can be relied upon by the taxpayers concerned. It is clear that the suggested Acts and Report will only regulate the taxation of the taxpayers concerned in the HS.

To be effective, all such Acts and Reports, as well as other similar documents, should be accessible and comprehensible by taxpayers. This implies that the documents concerned should be published in English and made available online. Also, a written language that is comprehensible by taxpayers must be used in their redaction. In other words, technical jargon needs to be avoided. Swiss law constitutes the perfect example on that matter. The laws are written in a way that can be easily understood by the general public.

While enacting an Exemption Act or a Taxation Act, it would be highly beneficial for the State concerned to attenuate heavy tax burdens as well as excessive administrative burdens[56] – if any – as much as possible. It is an established fact that both types of burden represent a serious obstacle for ISEs. Eliminating them to a certain extent will certainly render the State concerned more attractive for SGBs organising the events.

A similar approach was, in fact, followed by two countries, namely South Africa and New Zealand, in another important legal aspect of ISEs: protection of trademarks. As ambush marketing activities constitute a recurrent problem of sports competitions, an adequate protection of trademarks is vital. Even if some legal remedies exist in each country's domestic law, governments frequently adopt special legal provisions for ISEs that they are hosting, in order to provide more efficient protection and to fulfil their obligations deriving from HCCs. South Africa is

may take several decades (especially considering that there is currently no discussion at an international level on this point).

56 Extra administrative burdens incumbent upon non-residents constitute a frequent practice that is usually justified by States' need to exercise effective fiscal control over taxpayers (AIGNER, p.420).

the first country to have created special rights that can be invoked for any 'major sports event'.[57] New Zealand followed the example of South Africa and adopted the Major Events Management Act,[58] which entered into force on 28 August 2007.

Interestingly, South Africa is also the first (and only)[59] country to publish a Draft Guide that can be considered as an 'incomplete pilot project' of the Explanatory Report suggested by this book. The Draft Guide on the Taxation of Professional Sports Clubs and Players (South African Draft Guide), published by the South African Revenue Service in May 2016, mostly concerns taxation of the income derived by resident sports clubs and players and summarises taxation of non-resident sportspersons very briefly (more, specifically, one and a half pages out of 59). Despite its limited scope, the Guide, which is yet to be adopted,[60] may be considered as a very promising starting point.

The existence of an Exemption Act, a Taxation Act and/or an Explanatory Report will increase not only the clarity in this particular field of international tax law but also the appeal of the State concerned as an HS of an ISE. The importance of such legislation was emphasised by Alec Erwin (the South African Trade and Industry Minister at the time the Merchandise Marks Amendment Act was voted on[61]), who stated that the Act concerned was 'vital' to protect South Africa's small but growing position in the world sports and entertainment market.[62] The Amendment Act can, indeed, be seen as one of the factors that persuaded FIFA to award the 2010 FIFA World Cup to South Africa.[63]

A. Exemption Act

The suggested Exemption Act consists of an act quasi-identical to clear and detailed specific tax exemption regulations for mega sporting events. There is one main difference: the material scope of application of the Exemption Act is not limited to one ISE, it covers all ISEs that will be held on the territory of the State concerned.

The regulations enacted for the 2012 London Olympic and Paralympic Games constitute a great example of clear and detailed regulations, which may be converted into an Exemption Act. Needless to say, some of the modalities contained within the regulations have to be adapted to the national law of the State enacting such an Act.

A tax exemption that applies to a number of ISEs has already been enacted by France.[64] This exemption, however, does not amount to an Exemption Act that is being suggested in this book. As a matter of fact, the French exemption, codified

57 The rights were adopted with the Merchandise Marks Amendment Act 2002. KELHAM, p.1396.
58 Public Act 2007 No 35.
59 To the extent known by the author.
60 At the time of writing, in December 2019.
61 More specifically November 2002.
62 GARDINER ET AL, p.340.
63 KELHAM, p.1396.
64 The exemption was adopted by the article 51(V) of the Law No 2014-1655 of 29 December 2014.

in article 1655^{septies} of the General Code of Taxes,[65] has very limited temporal and personal scopes of application. The article covers ISEs that are officially attributed to France before 31 December 2017.[66] Its personal scope of application is limited to the bodies responsible for the organisation of an ISE in France and, where relevant, to the subsidiaries[67] of such bodies.[68]

Described in this subsection are: (1) the temporal scope of application; (2) the territorial scope of application; and (3) the material and the personal scopes of application of the suggested Exemption Act.

1. Temporal scope of application

The application of the Exemption Act should not be limited in time. Exemption Acts that are valid only during a short period of time, such as the French 'exemption-article', will not be adequate for establishing a national practice. Therefore, the level of clarity that is aimed for will not be reached.

2. Territorial scope of application

Since it is a national law adopted by the HS, the territorial scope of application of an Exemption Act is exclusively limited to the HS. This implies that the adoption of such an act will not result in an overall tax exemption of the income concerned per se. In fact, the taxpayers covered by the personal scope of application of an Exemption Act will still be subject to tax in their RS in accordance with the applicable domestic law of this latter State.

It must, however, be noted that an overall tax exemption may occur in cases where the income concerned is also tax-exempt in the RS, as per the applicable national law or the relevant rule of the applicable DTT (if any). Such an outcome is highly undesirable and may be prevented either by adoption of relevant provisions by RSs or a specific clause added in Exemption Acts of HSs, which provides for a source taxation in cases where the domestic law of the taxpayer's RS also exempts the income concerned.

3. Material and personal scopes of application

It is imperative to determine with great precision which events are entitled to benefit from tax exemptions. Undoubtedly, a State may opt for providing all ISEs

65 *Code général des impôts.*
66 Article 1655^{septies} (III) of the General Code of Taxes.
67 It must be noted that as per the French domestic law, in cases where at least the half of the capital of a company is owned by another company, the former company is considered as a subsidiary of the latter one (article L233-1 of the French Commercial Code (*Code de Commerce*)).
68 Article 1655^{septies} (III) of the General Code of Taxes. Persons falling within the scope of article 1655^{septies}, as well as their employees, are exempt from a number of taxes, including income tax and corporate income tax, enumerated in an exhaustive manner in section I of the article concerned (article 1655^{septies} (I) of the General Code of Taxes).

held in its territory with the same exemptions. This will have the merit of treating all events, and thereby all persons deriving income from such events, in an equal manner. However, in cases where such a general exemption is not deemed to be appropriate by the State concerned, the Exemption Act must elucidate which events fall within its scope of application.

To this end, the events concerned may be enumerated one by one in an exhaustive manner. It is also possible to fix a number of criteria along with the authority in charge of determining whether a certain event fulfils those criteria. The established criteria may be, for example, similar to the first three conditions of the 'events of major importance for society' of the AVMSD, which are the following: (i) the event and its outcome have a special general resonance in society, not only to those who ordinarily follow the sport or activity concerned; (ii) the event has a generally recognised, distinct cultural importance for the population and, in particular, contains elements of the cultural identity; and (iii) it involves the national team in the sport concerned in a major international tournament.[69] In addition to the criteria, a list of events[70] fulfilling the criteria may also be established, and updated from time to time, by the State concerned for the sake of further clarity.

For example, in the French exemption-article the following criteria were chosen to determine the ISEs that fall within its scope of application: (i) be awarded to France, via the decision of an international committee, upon the candidature of a public entity or a delegate national sports federation;[71] (ii) be at least equivalent to the level of a European Championship; (iii) be organised in the territory of France on an 'exceptional' basis;[72] and (iv) generate substantial economic benefits.[73] ISEs that fulfil these criteria have to be recognised by decree.[74] The ISEs recognised as such by the French authorities are the following: the EuroBasket 2015, the EURO 2016, the World Men's Handball Championship 2017, the Ice Hockey World Championship 2017, the Ryder Cup 2018, the Ryder Cup Junior 2018 and the FIFA Women's World Cup 2019.[75]

After determining the ISEs falling within its scope of application, the Exemption Act should enumerate all persons that are entitled to benefit from tax exemptions, such as SGBs and their subsidiaries, non-resident sportspersons and broadcasters. The extent of exemptions for each category of taxpayers must also be clearly laid out. For example, concerning sportspersons, whether or not their

69 *Explanatory Report to the ECTT*, European Treaty Series No. 132, 05.05.1989, §182.
70 Similar to the 'lists of major events' established by a number of EU MSs, which are available online at: https://ec.europa.eu/digital-single-market/en/avmsd-list-major-events (accessed on 24.12.2019).
71 Before 31 December 2017.
72 i.e. a sports event that is 'not tied to a place'.
73 Article 1655^{septies} (II) of the General Code of Taxes.
74 Ibid.
75 Article 1 of the Decree No 2015-910 of 23 July 2015 establishing the list of international sports events organised in France that are entitled to benefit from the tax regime provided in article 1655^{septies} of the General Code of Taxes.

sponsoring/endorsement income is subject to tax in the HS; if it is the ratio used in determining the income attributable to an event should be expressly stated. Further clarifications that are necessary, for example the definition of terms such as 'residence', should also be made.

B. Taxation Act and Explanatory Report

In cases where only some events are granted specific tax exemptions, it would be advisable to either enact a separate act regulating all relevant tax aspects of ISEs that do not benefit from an overall exemption or to publish a general explanatory report on the existing domestic tax law rules that are applicable. Needless to state, the same approach is also recommended in cases where the country concerned does not grant tax exemptions to any ISEs as a general policy.

Such an endeavour will allow all interested parties to be informed of the tax consequences of their professional activities linked to an ISE taking place in that particular State. Thereupon, the legal uncertainty currently reigning on that matter will be alleviated to a great extent.

It is clear that to fulfil that purpose, Taxation Acts and Explanatory Reports should cover all categories of taxpayers that may derive an income from an ISE, as enumerated, to a great extent, in chapter 3. They should also contain detailed rules/explanations comprising all relevant aspects of the national tax law. The level of precision required can be illustrated by means of the South African Draft Guide.

The South African Draft Guide is extremely thorough with regard to resident sports clubs and sportspersons.[76] Concerning sports clubs, it examines, by means of detailed explanations and illustrative examples, income tax and VAT implications of the following receipts and accruals: transfer fees, sign-on fees, sponsorships (including sponsorships in kind), prizes, ticket sales, sale of merchandise and other sundry items, insurance premiums (relating to, for example, sportspersons, training kits, equipment and facilities) paid by clubs, and fringe benefits that clubs may provide to their players (such as residential accommodation and use of a club-owned vehicle).

In relation to sportspersons, the South African Draft Guide analyses taxation modalities of the following receipts and accruals: player salaries and other remuneration, transfer fees, player signing-on fees, image rights payments, sponsorships, prizes (received either directly or indirectly[77]), indemnification payments, bonus payments, income derived from benefit matches, allowances, advances and

76 It must be underlined that the scope of the South African Draft Guide is limited to professional sports clubs and professional sportspersons. However, as already explained, professionalism is not relevant for the purposes of the issues examined in this book.

77 The South African Draft Guide distinguishes between two types of indirect accruals: (i) the prize is paid to the club for its benefit but is subsequently distributed to the player(s); and (ii) the prize is paid to the club for the benefit of the player(s) (*The South African Draft Guide*, p.33).

reimbursements (namely, travelling allowance, reimbursements and accommodation), fringe benefits (such as medical expenses, uniforms, transfer costs and personal use of business mobile phones and computers), pension fund contributions, retirement annuity fund contributions and other deductions for players (such as agents' commissions).

Should the same level of precision be reached in the Taxation Acts and Explanatory Reports suggested by this book, the lack of certainty will be overcome to a great extent.

Conclusion

A plea for clarity

This book demonstrates the *existent chaos* in the area of taxation of ISEs by means of a brief description of diverse commercial relations and the wide web of contracts that are commonly concluded in relation to ISEs (chapters 1 and 3) and an overview of the highly complex set of tax rules (chapters 2, 3, 4 and 5).

Chapter 6 argues that the current problems may be minimised to a great extent simply by *improving clarity*. Such an improvement can best be achieved at a national level, by means of the adoption of an Exemption Act, a Taxation Act and/or an Explanatory Report. In fact, although the academic debate almost exclusively concentrates on the advantages and disadvantages of international tax law rules, national practices and interpretations constitute the backbone of taxation. Clear national rules and regulations, which are accessible to all taxpayers, constitute a *sine qua non* condition of a 'fair' taxation, especially in cases where the international component of the activity exercised by the taxpayer in question is considerably accentuated, as it is the case of ISEs.

Assuredly, a significant effort will have to be made to achieve that level of clarity. Nevertheless, that effort is justified by the right of the taxpayers concerned to know their rights and obligations with regard to their taxation in different States. It should be remembered that this right constitutes one of the fundamentals of the rule of law. The chaos *must*, therefore, be turned into clarity.

Bibliography

Literature

ANDREFF, WLADIMIR, Globalization of the sports economy in *Rivista di Diritto ed Economia dello Sport*, Volume IV, Fasc. 3, 2008, p.13ff.

ANDERSON, DAVID/GRAEME, PERRY, London 2010-Olympic Income and Corporation Tax Exemptions in *Global Sports Law and Taxation Reports (GSLTR)*, Volume 2, Number 1, 2011, p.27ff.

ANDRIYCHUK, OLES, The Legal Nature of Premium Sports Events: 'IP or Not IP – That Is the Question' in BLACKSHAW, IAN/CORNELIUS, STEVE/SIEKMANN, ROBERT (eds), *TV Rights and Sport Legal Aspects*, T.M.C Asser Press, 2009, p.115ff.

AIGNER, MARTINA, Administrative Burdens for Non-Resident Artistes and Sportsmen in the light of Non-discrimination Clauses in LOUKOTA, WALTER/STEFANER, MARKUS (eds), *Taxation of Artistes and Sportsmen in International Tax Law*, Linde Verlag, 2007, p.405ff.

ARPAGAUS, RETO, Fragen im Zusammenhang mit den UEFA-Lizenzen für das Public Viewing bei der Fussball Europameisterschaft 2008 in *sic!*, 2008, p.87ff.

AULT, HUGH J./ARNOLD, BRIAN J., *Comparative Income Taxation, A Structural Analysis*, 3rd edition, Wolters Kluwer, 2010.

AUMAYR, ELKE, The 183-days rule in the OECD Model Convention in HOHENWARTER, DANIELA/METZLER, VANESSA (eds), *Taxation of Employment Income in International Tax Law*, Linde Verlag, 2009, p.109ff.

BAGEHOT, RICHARD/ NUTTALL, GRAEME, *Sponsorship, Endorsement & Merchandising, A Practical Guide*, Waterlow Publishers, 1990.

BARR-SMITH, ADRIAN, United Kingdom in BLACKSHAW, IAN/CORNELIUS, STEVE/SIEKMANN, ROBERT (eds), *TV Rights and Sport-Legal Aspects*, T.M.C. Asser Press, 2009, p.549ff.

BECKER, DAVID, *The Essential Legal Guide to Events*, Dynamic Publishing, 2006.

BELOFF, MICHAEL/KERR, TIM/DEMETRIOU, MARIE/BELOFF, RUPERT, *Sports Law*, 2nd edition, Hart Publishing, 2012 (cited as BELOFF ET AL.).

BENARD, MARC/BERDOZ, DENIS/BOURTOURAULT, PIERRE-YVES, Article 5 in DANON, ROBERT/ GUTMANN, DANIEL/OBERSON, XAVIER/PISTONE, PASQUALE (eds), *Modèle de Convention fiscale OCDE concernant le revenu et la fortune, Commentaire*, Helbing Lichtenhahn, Editions Francis Lefebvre, 2013, p.176ff (cited as BENARD ET AL.).

BENTATA, MORRIS, Broadcasting and New Media in LEWIS, ADAM/TAYLOR, JONATHAN (eds), *Sport: Law and Practice*, 2nd edition, Tottel Publishing, 2008, p.1205ff.

BETTEN, RIJKELE, Netherlands Ice Skater not Eligible for Relief for Foreign Training Days, Decision Number 03/04112 of the Court of Appeal of Amsterdam of 6 October 2004 in *European Taxation*, Volume 45, Issue 6, 2005, p.259ff (cited as BETTEN, *Netherlands Ice Skater*).

BETTEN, RIJKELE, Taxation in BLACKSHAW, IAN S./SIEKMANN, ROBERT C.R. (eds), *Sports Image Rights in Europe*, T.M.C. Asser Press, 2005, p.375ff (cited as BETTEN, *Taxation*).

BETTEN, RIJKELE, Annex to Advocate General's Conclusion on Whether or Not Art. 17 of the OECD Model Applies to the Basic Salaries of Sportsmen in *European Taxation*, Volume 46, Issue 5, 2006, p.231ff (cited as BETTEN, *Advocate General's Conclusion*).

BITTKER, BORIS IRVING, Taxing Income From Unlawful Activities, Yale Law School Faculty Scholarship Series, Paper 2289 in *Case Western Reserve Law Review*, Volume 25, 1974, p.130ff.

BLACKSHAW, IAN, Combatting 'Ambush Marketing', The 2010 South Africa FIFA World Cup Experience in *Global Sports Law and Taxation Reports (GSLTR)*, Volume 2, Number 1, 2011, p.5ff (cited as BLACKSHAW, *Ambush Marketing*).

BLACKSHAW, IAN, *Sports Marketing Agreements: Legal, Fiscal and Practical Aspects*, T.M.C. Asser Press, 2012 (cited as BLACKSHAW, *Sports Marketing Agreements*).

BLÁHA, JAROMÍR, Treatment of 'Training Activities' for Artistes and Sportsmen according to the OECD Model in LOUKOTA, WALTER/STEFANER, MARKUS (eds), *Taxation of Artistes and Sportsmen in International Tax Law*, Linde Verlag, 2007, p.115ff.

BLAIS, JEAN-PIERRE, The protection of exclusive television rights to sporting events held in public venues: an overview of the law in Australia and Canada in *Melbourne Law Review*, 1991–1992, p.503ff.

BOBBETT, CATHERINE/JONES, JOHN AVERY, The Treaty Definition of Royalties in *IBFD Bulletin-Tax Treaty Monitor*, January 2006, p.23ff.

BOLOTNY, FRÉDÉRIC/BOURG, JEAN-FRANÇOIS, The demand for media coverage in ANDREFF, WLADIMIR/SZYMANSKI, STEFAN (eds), *Handbook on the Economics of Sport*, Edward Elgar Publishing Limited, 2006, p.112ff.

BOURG, JEAN-FRANÇOIS/GOUGUET, JEAN-JACQUES, Sport and globalisation: sport as a global public good in ANDREFF, WLADIMIR/SZYMANSKI, STEFAN (eds), *Handbook on the Economics of Sport*, Edward Elgar Publishing Limited, 2006, p.748.

BRINKMANN, JÜRG P., De minimis Clause According to the US Model in LOUKOTA, WALTER/STEFANER, MARKUS (eds), *Taxation of Artistes and Sportsmen in International Tax Law*, Linde Verlag, 2007, p.349ff.

BUCHSTEINER, MARKUS, Employment income of Artistes and Sportsmen under Article 17 paragraph 1 OECD Model Tax Convention in HOHENWARTER, DANIELA/METZLER, VANESSA (eds), *Taxation of Employment Income in International Tax Law*, Linde Verlag, 2009, p.249ff.

BURAIMO, BABATUNDE, The demand for sports broadcasting in ANDREFF, WLADIMIR/SZYMANSKI, STEFAN (eds), *Handbook on the Economics of Sport*, Edward Elgar Publishing Limited, 2006, p.100ff.

CAILLAT, MICHEL, *Le Sport*, Le Cavalier Bleu Editions, 1st edition, 2002.

CHAO, LAURA L., 'You must construct additional pylons': building a better framework for eSports governance in *Fordham Law Review*, Volume 86, November, 2017, p.737ff.

COATES, DENNIS, Not-so-mega events in MAENNIG, WOLFGANG/ZIMBALIST, ANDREW (eds), *International Handbook on the Economics of Mega Sporting Events*, Edward Elgar Publishing Limited, 2012, p.401ff.

CORNELIUS, STEVE, Ambush Marketing in Sport in *Global Sports Law and Taxation Reports (GSLTR)*, 2011, Volume 2, Number 4, p.12ff (cited as CORNELIUS, *Ambush Marketing*).

CORNELIUS, STEVE, The legal nature of media rights in sport: part one [1] in *Global Sports Law and Taxation Reports (GSLTR)*, 2014, Volume 5, No 4, p.6ff (cited as CORNELIUS, *Media Rights*).

Coulombe, Gérard, Taxation of payment to non-residents for independent personal services, General Report in *IFA Cahiers*, 1982, Volume 67b, p.39ff.

Crompton, John L., Ticket pricing/sales in Bartlett, Roger/Gratton, Chris/Rolf, Christer G. (eds), *Encyclopedia of International Sports Studies*, Routledge, 2012.

Danis, Jozef, Treatment of Income from Inaction of Artistes and Sportsmen according to the OECD Model in Loukota, Walter/Stefaner, Markus (eds), *Taxation of Artistes and Sportsmen in International Tax Law*, Linde Verlag, 2007, p.91ff.

Deninger, Dennis, *Sports on Television, The How and Why Behind What You See*, Routledge, 2012.

Duthie, Max/Higgins, Iain/Lynam, Ian/Lewis, Adam, Players' Agents in Lewis, Adam/Taylor, Jonathan (eds), *Sport: Law and Practice*, 2nd edition, Tottel Publishing, 2008, p.656ff (cited as duthie et al.).

Faltin, Alexandre, Article 6 in Danon, Robert/Gutmann, Daniel/Oberson, Xavier/Pistone, Pasquale (eds), *Modèle de Convention fiscale OCDE concernant le revenu et la fortune, Commentaire*, Helbing Lichtenhahn, Editions Francis Lefebvre, 2013, p.225ff.

Forrest, David, Betting and the Integrity of Sport in Anderson, Paul M./Blackshaw, Ian S./Siekmann, Robert C.R./Soek, Janwillem (eds), *Sports Betting: Law and Policy*, T.M.C. Asser Press, 2012, p.14ff.

Fort, Rodney/Quirk, James, Cross-Subsidization, Incentives, and Outcomes in Professional Team Sports Leagues in *Journal of Economic Literature*, Volume 33, Number 3, 1995, p.1265ff.

Gardiner, Simon/O'Leary, John/Welch, Roger/Boyes, Simon/Naidoo, Urvasi, *Sports Law*, 4th edition, Routledge, 2012 (cited as gardiner et al.).

Getz, Donald/Svensson, Bo/Peterssen, Robert/Gunnervall, Anders, Hallmark Events: Definition, goals and planning process in *International Journal of Event Management Research*, Volume 7, Number 1/2, 2012, p.47ff (cited as getz et al.).

Goss, Ryan, *Criminal Fair Trial Rights, Article 6 of the European Convention on Human Rights*, Hart Publishing, 2014.

Gratton, Chris/Solberg, Harry Arne, *The Economics of Sports Broadcasting*, Routledge, 2007.

Greenwell, Christopher T./Danzey-Bussell, Leigh Ann/Shonk, David J., *Managing Sport Events*, Human Kinetics, 2014 (cited as greenwell et al.).

Groot, Loek, *Economics, Uncertainty and European Football, Trends in Competitive Balance*, Edward Elgar Publishing Limited, 2008.

Grossmann, Martin, *Die Besteuerung des Künstlers und Sportlers im internationalen Verhältnis*, Difo-Druck GmbH, 1992.

Gupta, Ranjana, Taxation of Illegal Activities in New Zealand and Australia in *Journal of the Australasian Tax Teachers Association*, Volume 3, Number 2, 2008, p.106ff.

Han, Keefe, The Mistaken Removal of Article 14 from the OECD Model Tax Convention in *Auckland University Law Review*, 2010, Volume 16, p.192ff.

Harrington, Dan/White, Nick, United Kingdom in Blackshaw, Ian S./Siekmann, Robert C.R. (eds), *Sports Image Rights in Europe*, T.M.C. Asser Press, 2005, p.315ff.

Haskell, Vrooman John, More than just skin(s) in the game: how one digital video game item is being used for unregulated gambling purposes online in *Journal of High Technology Law*, Volume 18, 2017, p.125ff.

Higgins, Iain/Boyd, Stephen/Hawkins, Richard, Image Rights in Lewis, Adam/Taylor, Jonathan (eds), *Sport: Law and Practice*, 2nd edition, Tottel Publishing, 2008, p.1153ff (cited as higgins et al.).

HONG, FAN, China in HOULIHAN, BARRIE/GREEN, MICK (eds), *Comparative Elite Sport Development: Systems, structures and public policy*, Butterworth-Heinemann, 2008, p.38ff.

HORNE, JOHN, The Four 'Knowns' of Sports Mega-Events in *Leisure Studies*, Volume 26, Number 1, 2007, p.81ff.

HOULIHAN, BARRIE, Government objectives and sport in ANDREFF, WLADIMIR/SZYMANSKI, STEFAN (eds), *Handbook on the Economics of Sport*, Edward Elgar Publishing Limited, 2006, p.254ff.

HOULIHAN, BARRIE/GREEN, MICK, Comparative elite sport development in HOULIHAN, BARRIE/GREEN, MICK (eds), *Comparative Elite Sport Development: Systems, structures and public policy*, Butterworth-Heinemann, 2008, p.13ff.

HUTCHINS, BRETT/MIKOSZA, JANINE, The Web 2.0 Olympics, Athlete Blogging, Social Networking and Policy Contradictions at the 2008 Beijing Games in *Convergence: The International Journal of Research into New Media Technologies*, Volume 16, Number 3, 2010, p.279ff.

HOLMES, KEVIN, *The Concept of Income, A multi-disciplinary analysis*, IBFD, 2001 (cited as HOLMES, *Concept of Income*).

HOLMES, KEVIN, *International Tax Policy and Double Tax Treaties, An Introduction to Principles and Application*, 2nd edition, IBFD, 2014 (cited as HOLMES, *International Tax Policy*).

HUSTON, JOHN, The case against 'fixed base' in *Intertax*, Volume 10, 1988, p.282ff.

JONES, PETER, *Eureka! Everything you ever wanted to know about the Ancient Greeks but were afraid to ask*, Atlantic Books, 2014.

JUÁREZ, ANGEL J., Spain, Special Tax Regime Applicable to the Participants in the XXXII America's Cup 2007: An Overview in *European Taxation*, 2004, p.316ff.

JUCH, D., Unilateral measures to prevent double taxation, General Report in *IFA Cahiers*, Volume 66b, 1981, p.15ff.

KELHAM, ALEX, Tackling Ambush Marketing of the Olympic Games and Paralympic Games – London 2012: A Case Study in LEWIS, ADAM/TAYLOR, JONATHAN (eds), *Sport: Law and Practice*, 2nd edition, Tottel Publishing, 2008, p.1388ff.

KERN, MICHAEL, Fixed and Permanent Establishments in VAT/GST and direct taxation in PFEIFFER, SEBASTIAN/URSPRUNG-STEINDL, MARLIES (eds), *Global Trends in VAT/GST and Direct Taxes*, Linde Verlag, 2015, p.217ff.

KREISL, RENE, Treatment of Artistic Income where there is no Public Performance according to the OECD Model in LOUKOTA, WALTER/STEFANER, MARKUS (eds), *Taxation of Artistes and Sportsmen in International Tax Law*, Linde Verlag, 2007, p.137ff.

LAWRENCE, CLIVE, Merchandising and Licensing in LEWIS, ADAM/TAYLOR, JONATHAN (eds), *Sport: Law and Practice*, 2nd edition, Tottel Publishing, 2008, p.1278ff.

LEFEVER, KATRIEN, *New Media and Sport, International Legal Aspects*, T.M.C. Asser Press, 2012.

LIPSEY, RICHARD A., *The Sporting Goods Industry: History, Practices and Products*, McFarland, 2006.

LOPEZ-GONZALEZ, HIBAI/GRIFFITHS, MARK D., Understanding the convergence of online sports betting markets in *International Review for the Sociology of Sport*, Volume 53, Issue 7, 2018, p.807ff (the online version used by the author did not contain the page numbers of the article).

MACLEAN, ALISTAIR/MOORHOUSE, KAREN, Sports Sponsorship in LEWIS, ADAM/TAYLOR, JONATHAN (eds), *Sport: Law and Practice*, 2nd edition, Tottel Publishing, 2008, p.1241ff.

MAENNIG, WOLFGANG/ZIMBALIST, ANDREW, What is a mega sporting event? in MAENNIG, WOLFGANG/ZIMBALIST, ANDREW (eds), *International Handbook on the Economics of Mega*

Sporting Events, Edward Elgar Publishing Limited, 2012, p.9ff (cited as MAENNIG/ ZIMBALIST, *Mega Sporting Event*).

MAENNIG, WOLFGANG/ZIMBALIST, ANDREW, Future challenges: maximizing the benefits and minimizing the costs in MAENNIG, WOLFGANG/ZIMBALIST, ANDREW (eds), *International Handbook on the Economics of Mega Sporting Events*, Edward Elgar Publishing Limited, 2012, p.547ff (cited as MAENNIG/ ZIMBALIST, *Future Challenges*).

MALHERBE, JACQUES/MARAIA, JEAN-FRÉDÉRIC/TRAVERSA, EDOARDO, Article 12 in DANON, ROBERT/GUTMANN, DANIEL/OBERSON, XAVIER/PISTONE, PASQUALE (eds), *Modèle de Convention fiscale OCDE concernant le revenu et la fortune, Commentaire*, Helbing Lichtenhahn, Editions Francis Lefebvre, 2013, p.471ff (cited as MALHERBE ET AL.).

MALLEN, CHERLY/ADAMS, LORNE J., *Sport, Recreation and Tourism Event Management, Theoretical and Practical Dimensions*, Butterworth-Heinemann, 2008.

MASON, DANIEL S., Player agents in ANDREFF, WLADIMIR/SZYMANSKI, STEFAN (eds), *Handbook on the Economics of Sport*, Edward Elgar Publishing Limited, 2006, p.677ff.

MCKEOWN, JAMES T., The economics of competitive balance: sport antitrust claims after American Needle in *Marquette Sports Law Review*, Volume 21, Number 2, 2011, p.517ff.

MOLENAAR, DICK, Discussion of Daniel Sandler's Paper on Article 17 OECD Model Convention in LANG, MICHAEL/PISTONE, PASQUALE/SCHUCH, JOSEF/STARINGER, CLAUS (eds), *Source versus Residence: Problems Arising from the Allocation of Taxing Rights in Tax Treaty Law and Possible Alternatives*, Wolters Kluwer, 2008, p.248ff (cited as MOLENAAR, *Discussion of Daniel Sandler's Paper*).

MOLENAAR, DICK, *Taxation of International Performing Artistes*, IBFD, 2005 (cited as MOLENAAR, *Taxation of Artistes*).

MOLENAAR, DICK/GRAMS, HARALD, Rent-A-Star – The purpose of Article 17(2) of the OECD Model in *Bulletin for International Fiscal Documentation*, Volume 56, Number 10, 2002, p.500ff (cited as MOLENAAR/GRAMS, *Rent-A-Star*).

MOLENAAR, DICK/GRAMS, HARALD, Scorpio and the Netherlands: Major Changes in Artiste and Sportsman Taxation in the European Union in *European Taxation*, Volume 47, Number 2, 2007, p.63ff (cited as MOLENAAR/GRAMS, *Scorpio*).

MOLENAAR, DICK/GRAMS, HARALD, Article 17(3) for Artistes and Sportsmen: Much More than an Exception in *Intertax*, Volume 40, Issue 4, 2012, p.270ff (cited as MOLENAAR/ GRAMS, *Article 17(3)*).

NITIKMAN, JOEL A., Article 17 of the OECD Model Treaty – An Anachronism? in *Intertax*, Volume 29, Issue 8/9, 2001, p.268ff.

NYS, JEAN-FRANÇOIS, Central government and sport in ANDREFF, WLADIMIR/SZYMANSKI, STEFAN (eds), *Handbook on the Economics of Sport*, Edward Elgar Publishing Limited, 2006, p.260ff.

OBERSON, XAVIER, Article 17 in DANON, ROBERT/GUTMANN, DANIEL/OBERSON, XAVIER/ PISTONE, PASQUALE (eds), *Modèle de Convention fiscale OCDE concernant le revenu et la fortune, Commentaire*, Helbing Lichtenhahn, Editions Francis Lefebvre, 2013, p.564ff.

O'DOWD, PAUL, Venues and Event Management in LEWIS, ADAM/TAYLOR, JONATHAN (eds), *Sport: Law and Practice*, 2nd edition, Tottel Publishing, 2008, p.1128ff.

PARENT, MILENA M./SMITH-SWAN, SHARON, *Managing Major Sports Events, Theory and Practice*, Routledge, 2013.

PARRISH, RICHARD, Regulating Players' Agents: A Global Perspective in *International Sports Law Journal (ISLJ)*, Number 1-2, 2007, p.38ff.

PERDELWITZ, ANDREAS, A Certain Degree of Permanence–Between Temporary and Everlasting Business Activities in GUTIÉRREZ, CARLOS/PERDELWITZ, ANDREAS (eds), *Taxation of Business Profits in the 21st Century, Selected Issues under Tax Treaties, Essays in Commemoration of IBFD's 75th Anniversary*, IBFD, 2013, p.27ff.

PHELOPS, WARREN, Hospitality in LEWIS, ADAM/TAYLOR, JONATHAN (eds), *Sport: Law and Practice*, 2nd edition, Tottel Publishing, 2008, p.1307ff.

PICKERING, ARIANE, Enterprise Services, General Report in *IFA Cahiers*, Volume 97a, 2012, p.17ff.

PINNA, ANDREA, La prestation internationale de service d'agent sportif, The international supply of sports agent services in *RDAI/IBLJ*, Number 3, 2005, p.333ff.

PINTO, DALE, *E-Commerce and Source-Based Income Taxation*, IBFD, 2002.

PISTONE, PASQUALE, General Report in LANG, MICHAEL/PISTONE, PASQUALE/SCHUCH, JOSEF/STARINGER, CLAUS (eds), *The Impact of the OECD and UN Model Conventions on Bilateral Tax Treaties*, Cambridge University Press, 2012, p.1ff.

PRACHT, LORENZ, Special Issues Due to the Way of Financing Artistes and Sportsmen in LOUKOTA, WALTER/STEFANER, MARKUS (eds), *Taxation of Artistes and Sportsmen in International Tax Law*, Linde Verlag, 2007, p.327ff.

RASMUSSEN, MOGENS, *International Double Taxation*, Wolters Kluwer Law & Business, 2011.

REIMER, EKKEHART, Income from Immovable Property (Article 6 OECD Model Convention) in LANG, MICHAEL/PISTONE, PASQUALE/SCHUCH, JOSEF/STARINGER, CLAUS (eds), *Source versus Residence: Problems Arising from the Allocation of Taxing Rights in Tax Treaty Law and Possible Alternatives*, Wolters Kluwer, 2008, p.1ff.

REMICK, LLYOD ZANE/EISEN, DAVID SPENCER, The Personal Manager in the Entertainment and Sports Industries in *Entertainment and Sports Law Journal*, Number 57, 1986, p.57ff.

ROCHA, SERGIO ANDRÉ, Enterprise Services, Brazil in *IFA Cahiers*, Volume 97a, 2012, p.155ff.

ROGERS-GLABUSH, JULIE (ed), *IBFD International Tax Glossary*, 6th edition, IBFD, 2009 (cited as IBFD, *International Tax Glossary*).

RUSSELL, ALEX M.T./HING, NERILEE/BROWNE, MATTHEW/LI, EN/VITARTAS, PETER, Who Bets on Micro Events (Microbets) in Sports? in *Journal of Gambling Studies*, Volume 35, 2019, p.205ff (cited as RUSSELL ET AL.).

SAMPSON, STEPHEN/OSBORNE, ANDREW/LIMBERT, PETER/LEWIS, ADAM, Player Transfers in LEWIS, ADAM/TAYLOR, JONATHAN (eds), *Sport: Law and Practice*, 2nd edition, Tottel Publishing, 2008, p.570ff (cited as SAMPSON ET AL.).

SANDLER, DANIEL, Non-resident entertainers and athletes – Taxing problems in *Taxation of Non-Resident Entertainers*, IFA, Kluwer, 1996, p.3ff (cited as SANDLER, *Non-resident entertainers and athletes*).

SANDLER, DANIEL, Artistes and Sportsmen (Article 17 OECD Model Convention) in LANG, MICHAEL/PISTONE, PASQUALE/SCHUCH, JOSEF/STARINGER, CLAUS (eds), *Source versus Residence: Problems Arising from the Allocation of Taxing Rights in Tax Treaty Law and Possible Alternatives*, Wolters Kluwer, 2008, p.215ff (cited as SANDLER, *Artistes and Sportsmen*).

SANDLER, DANIEL, Problems taxing Non-resident Artistes and Sportsmen in OBERSON, XAVIER (ed), *International Taxation of Artistes & Sportsmen*, Bruylant/Schulthess, 2009, p.191ff (cited as SANDLER, *Problems taxing sportsmen*).

SASSEVILLE, JACQUES/SKAAR, ARVID A., Is there a permanent establishment?, General Report in *IFA Cahiers*, Volume 94a, 2009, p.17ff.

SCANLON, THOMAS F., Sports and Media in the Ancient Mediterranean in RANEY, ARTHUR A./JENNINGS, BRYANT (eds), *Handbook of Sports and Media*, Routledge, 2009, p.3ff.

SCHOENY, ALAIN, L'importance de la mise en relation semi-contextuelle dans la consommation d'événements sportifs in BOUCHET, PATRICK/SOBRY, CLAUDE (eds), *Management et marketing du sport: du local au global*, Presses Universitaires du Septentrion, 2005, p.17ff.

SCHOLZ, TOBIAS M., *eSports is Business, Management in the World of Competitive Gaming*, Palgrave Macmillan, 2019.

SCHREMPF, BERNHARD, Entertainers and Sportspersons in Direct Taxation and VAT in PFEIFFER, SEBASTIAN/URSPRUNG-STEINDL, MARLIES (eds), *Global Trends in VAT/GST and Direct Taxes*, Linde Verlag, 2015, p.521ff.

SOBRY, CLAUDE, Essai d'approche théorique de la très inégale répartition des revenus des sportifs participant au sport spectacle in BOUCHET, PATRICK/SOBRY, CLAUDE (eds), *Management et marketing du sport: du local au global*, Presses Universitaires du Septentrion, 2005, p.35ff.

SPRAGUE, GARY D./BOYLE, MICHAEL P., Taxation of income derived from electronic commerce, General Report in *IFA Cahiers*, Volume 86a, 2001, p.21ff.

STOCKMANN, FRANCK, Article 17 in VOGEL, KLAUS/LEHNER, MORIS (eds), *Doppelbesteuerungsabkommen: DBA*, 5th edition, Münich, 2008.

TETLAK, KAROLINA, *Taxation of International Sportspersons*, IBFD, 2014.

TSIELEPIS, ALEXIS, The Devil Is in the Detail: An Analysis of the ECJ's Attributes to the Fixed Establishment Concept in *International VAT Monitor*, Volume 28, Number 3, 2017, published online.

THIEDE, JESKO/TRENCSIK, STEFAN, For the Good of the Game? A Comparison of the Taxation of Sportspersons and Sports Organizations outside of and during Major Sporting Events in *World Tax Journal*, 2017, p.599ff.

THURONYI, VICTOR/BROOKS, KIM/KOLOZS, BORBALA, *Comparative Tax Law*, Kluwer Law International, 2nd edition, 2016.

TIEDEMANN, CLAUS, '*Sport (and Culture of Human Motion) for Historians. An Approach to Precise the Central Term(s)*', lecture held at the IX International CESH-Congress, Italy, 25 September 2004.

TORKILDSEN, STURLA BLANCK, Norway: a free haven for international ticket touting? in *Global Sports Law and Taxation Reports (GSLTR)*, Volume 3, Number 4, 2012, p.18ff.

TRELLES, OSCAR M., Double Taxation/Fiscal Evasion and International Tax Treaties in *Indiana Law Review*, Volume 12, Number 2, 1979, p.341ff.

TSAI, MATTHEW R., Fantasy (e)Sports: The Future Prospect of Fantasy Sports Betting amongst Organized Multiplayer Video Game Competitions in *UNLV Gaming Law Journal*, Volume 6, 2016, p.393ff.

VALIS, JURAJ, Withholding Taxes for Non-resident Artistes and Sportsmen in the light of Non-discrimination Clauses in LOUKOTA, WALTER/STEFANER, MARKUS (eds), *Taxation of Artistes and Sportsmen in International Tax Law*, Linde Verlag, 2007, p.421ff.

VAN DER BRUGGEN, EDWIN, Source Taxation of Consideration for Technical Services and Know-How with Particular Reference to the Treaty Policy of China, India and Thailand in *Asia-Pacific Tax Bulletin*, Volume 7, Number 3, 2001, p.42ff.

VAN HAAREN, JOEP/CEULEMANS, YVEN, Euro 2000 Taxation in *European Taxation*, September 2000, p.440ff.

VEROW, RICHARD, Commercial Rights Sales Agency Agreements in LEWIS, ADAM/TAYLOR, JONATHAN (eds), *Sport: Law and Practice*, 2nd edition, Tottel Publishing, 2008, p.1328ff.

VOGEL, KLAUS, Double Tax Treaties and Their Interpretation in *Berkeley Journal of International Law*, Volume 4, Issue 1, 1986, p.1ff.

WAGNER, MICHAEL G., *On the Scientific Relevance of eSports*, Conference Proceedings of the 2006 International Conference on Internet Computing & Conference on Computer Games Development, US, 26–29 June 2006.

WEST, CRAIG, *The Taxation of International (non-resident) Sportspersons in South Africa*, University of Cape Town, 2009 (PhD Thesis).

WISE, AARON N./MEYER, BRUCE S., *International Sports Law and Business*, Volume 3, Kluwer Law International, 1997.

YAZICIOGLU, ALARA EFSUN, Specific Tax Exemption Regulations for Major Sports Events: Example of London Olympic and Paralympic Games in *The International Sports Law Journal (ISLJ)* , Number 1-2, 2012, p.53ff (cited as YAZICIOGLU, *London Olympics*).

YAZICIOGLU, ALARA EFSUN, South Africa: Draft Guide on the Taxation of Professional Sports Clubs and Players issued: a very promising starting point in the path of restoring clarity! in *Global Sports Law and Taxation Reports (GSLTR)*, Volume 7, Number 3, 2016, p.16ff (cited as YAZICIOGLU, *South African Draft Guide*).

ZEN-RUFFINEN, PIERMARCO, *Droit du sport*, Schulthess, 2002.

ZOUBEK, JIRI, Notion of Sportsmen in Art. 17 OECD Model in LOUKOTA, WALTER/STEFANER, MARKUS (eds), *Taxation of Artistes and Sportsmen in International Tax Law*, Linde Verlag, 2007, p.35ff.

OECD documents

Bribery and Corruption Awareness Handbook for Tax Examiners and Tax Auditors, OECD, 2013 (cited as *Bribery and Corruption Awareness Handbook*).

Commentaries on the Articles of the Model Tax Convention on Income and on Capital, OECD, 2017 edition (cited as *OECD Commentary*).

Discussion Draft on the Application of Article 17 (Artistes and Sportsmen) of the OECD Model Tax Convention, OECD, 23 April 2010.

Issues related to article 14 of the OECD Model Tax Convention, Number 7, OECD, 2000 (cited as OECD, *Issues related to article 14*).

International VAT/GST Guidelines, OECD, 2017 (cited as *International VAT/GST Guidelines*).

The Taxation of Income Derived from Entertainment, Artistic and Sporting Activities, adopted by the OECD Council on 27 March 1987, OECD (cited as *The 1987 Report*).

Other documents and studies

Commentaries on the Articles of the United Nations Model Double Taxation Convention Between Developed and Developing Countries, 2017 edition (cited as *UN Commentary*).

Explanatory Memorandum on the Revenue Laws Amendment Bill, 2006, Republic of South Africa (cited as *Explanatory Memorandum on the 2006 Amendment Bill*).

Explanatory Memorandum to the London Olympic Games and Paralympic Games Tax Regulations 2010, the United Kingdom (cited as *Explanatory Memorandum to the 2010 Tax Regulations*).

Explanatory notes on EU VAT place of supply rules on services connected with immovable property that enter into force in 2017 (Council Implementing Regulation (EU) No 1042/2013), European Commission, 2015 (cited as *Explanatory notes on immovable property*).

Explanatory Report relating to the draft legislation on tax treatment of financial sanctions [*'Rapport explicatif relatif au projet de loi fédérale sur le traitement fiscal des sanctions financières (mise en œuvre de la motion 14.3450 Luginbühl)'*], 18 December 2015, Swiss Federal Department of Finance (cited as *Explanatory report on financial sanctions*).

Explanatory Report to the European Convention on Transfrontier Television, Council of Europe, 5 May 1989.

Info TVA 24 concernant le secteur Sport, Swiss Federal Tax Administration, 2013 (cited as *Info TVA*).

London 2012 Olympic Games, Global Broadcast Report, Sponsorship Intelligence/IOC, December 2012.

Olympic Marketing Fact File, 2019 edition, IOC.

Statement of the Chairman of the Adjudicatory Chamber of the FIFA Ethics Committee on the Report on the Inquiry into the 2018/2022 FIFA World Cup™ Bidding Process prepared by the Investigatory Chamber of the FIFA Ethics Committee, 13 November 2014 (cited as *Statement on the Report on the Inquiry into the 2018/2022 FIFA World Cup Bidding Process*).

Study on Sports Agents in the European Union, commissioned by the European Commission (Directorate-General for Education and Culture), KEA European Affairs, Centre de Droit et d'Economie du Sport, European Observatoire of Sport and Employment, November 2009 (cited as *Study on Sports Agents in the European Union*).

United States Model Technical Explanation Accompanying the United States Model Income Tax Convention of November 15, 2006 (cited as *Technical Explanation of the US MC*).

Index

For Product Safety Concerns and Information please contact our EU
representative GPSR@taylorandfrancis.com
Taylor & Francis Verlag GmbH, Kaufingerstraße 24, 80331 München, Germany

www.ingramcontent.com/pod-product-compliance
Ingram Content Group UK Ltd.
Pitfield, Milton Keynes, MK11 3LW, UK
UKHW020152200926
475702UK00016B/2662
9780367521547